Variability in Grain Yields

This publication is the outcome of collaboration between the International Food Policy Research Institute and the Deutsche Stiftung für Internationale Entwicklung / Zentralstelle für Ernährung und Landwirtschaft (German Foundation for International Development / Food and Agriculture Development Center).

Variability in Grain Yields
Implications for Agricultural Research and Policy in Developing Countries

EDITED BY
JOCK R. ANDERSON AND PETER B. R. HAZELL

Published for the International Food Policy Research Institute

The Johns Hopkins University Press
Baltimore and London

© 1989 The International Food Policy Research Institute. Copyright does not include the separate content of chapter 14, which is a work of the U.S. government.
All rights reserved
Printed in the United States of America

The Johns Hopkins University Press, 701 West 40th Street, Baltimore, Maryland 21211
The Johns Hopkins Press Ltd., London

The paper used in this publication meets the minimum requirements of American National Standard for Information Sciences—Permanence of Paper for Printed Library Materials, ANSI Z39.48-1984.

LIBRARY OF CONGRESS CATALOGING-IN-PUBLICATION DATA

Variability in grain yields: implications for agricultural research and policy in developing countries/edited by Jock R. Anderson and Peter B. R. Hazell.
    p.   cm.
  Bibliography: p.
  Includes index.
  ISBN 0-8018-3793-6 (alk. paper)
    1. Wheat Trade—Developing countries—Seasonal variations. 2. Wheat trade—Government policy—Developing countries. 3. Wheat—Developing countries—Varieties—Research. I. Anderson, Jock R., 1941-   II. Hazell, P. B. R.
HD9049.W5D448   1989
338.1′7311′091724—dc19
                                               88-32079
                                                  CIP

Contents

List of Tables and Figures   ix

Foreword   xvii

Acknowledgments   xix

1   Introduction   1
    JOCK R. ANDERSON AND PETER B. R. HAZELL

PART I   Evidence on Patterns of Changing Yield Variability

2   Changing Patterns of Variability in World Cereal Production   13
    PETER B. R. HAZELL

3   Changing Patterns of Variability in Chinese Cereal Production   35
    BRUCE STONE AND TONG ZHONG

4   An Analysis of Variability in Soviet Grain Production   60
    JOHN R. TARRANT

5   Agricultural Planning Policy and Variability in Syrian Cereal Production   78
    HUNG NGUYEN

6   High-Yielding Varieties and Variability in Sorghum and Pearl Millet Production in India   91
    THOMAS S. WALKER

7   Variability in Wheat Yields in England: Analysis and Future Prospects   100
    ROGER B. AUSTIN AND MICHAEL H. ARNOLD

8   Variability in Wheat and Barley Production in Southeast England   107
    PAUL WEBSTER AND NIGEL T. WILLIAMS

9   Variability in Winter Wheat and Spring Barley Yields in Bavaria   118
    G. FISCHBECK

PART II Plant Breeding and Yield Variability

10 Plant Breeding and Yield Stability   127
    MICHAEL H. ARNOLD AND ROGER B. AUSTIN

11 Modern Rice Varieties as a Possible Factor in Production Variability   133
    W. RONNIE COFFMAN AND T. R. HARGROVE

12 Possible Genetic Causes of Increased Variability in U.S. Maize Yields   147
    DONALD N. DUVICK

13 Yield Stability in Bread Wheat   157
    W. H. PFEIFFER AND H. J. BRAUN

14 Genetic Improvement and the Variability in Wheat Yields in the Great Plains   175
    C. JAMES PETERSON, V. A. JOHNSON, J. W. SCHMIDT, AND ROBERT F. MUMM

15 Yield Stability of CIMMYT Maize Germplasm in International and On-Farm Trials   185
    H. N. PHAM, S. R. WADDINGTON, AND J. CROSSA

16 Variability in the Yield of Pearl Millet Varieties and Hybrids in India and Pakistan   206
    JOHN R. WITCOMBE

PART III Input Management and Yield Variability

17 Fertilizer and Crop Yield Variability: A Review   223
    JAMES A. ROUMASSET, MARK W. ROSEGRANT, UJJAYANT N. CHAKRAVORTY, AND JOCK R. ANDERSON

18 Irrigation and Crop Yield Variability: A Review   234
    SUSHIL PANDEY

19 Pest-Resistant Varieties, Pesticides, and Crop Yield Variability: A Review   242
    GERALD A. CARLSON

20 Yield Stability and Modern Rice Technology   251
    JOHN C. FLINN AND DENNIS P. GARRITY

21 Influence of Nitrogen Fertilizer and Fungicide on Yield and Yield Variability in Wheat and Barley   265
    H. HANUS AND P. SCHOOP

22 Influence of Technology and Weather on the Variability in U.S. Maize and Wheat Yields   270
    JAMES B. FRENCH AND J. C. HEADLEY

Contents vii

PART IV   Impacts of Yield Variability and Implications for Policy

23 Can Yield Variability Be Offset by Improved Information? The Case of Rice in India   287
    VISHVA BINDLISH, RANDOLPH BARKER, AND TIMOTHY D. MOUNT

24 Are Modern Cultivars More Risky? A Question of Stochastic Efficiency   301
    JOCK R. ANDERSON, CARLY J. FINDLAY, AND G. H. WAN

25 Yield and Household Income Variability in India's Semi-Arid Tropics   309
    THOMAS S. WALKER

26 The Implications of Variability in Food Production for National and Household Food Security   320
    DAVID E. SAHN AND JOACHIM VON BRAUN

27 Synthesis and Needs in Agricultural Research and Policy   339
    JOCK R. ANDERSON AND PETER B. R. HAZELL

References   357

Contributors   381

Index   385

Tables and Figures

Tables

2.1 Variability of world cereal production around linear trend: 1960/61-1982/83   15

2.2 Changes in the mean and variability of world cereal production: 1960/61-1970/71 to 1971/72-1982/83   16

2.3 Changes in the mean and variability of total cereal production by major countries: 1960/61-1970/71 to 1971/72-1982/83   18

2.4 Mean yields and coefficients of variation by crop and country: 1960/61-1970/71 and 1971/72-1982/83   20

2.5 Summary of trends in coefficients of variation between periods reported in Table 2.4   26

2.6 Components of change in production covariances   27

2.7 Disaggregation of the components of change in the average of world cereal production: 1960/61-1970/71 to 1971/72-1982/83   28

2.8 Disaggregation of the components of change in the variance of world cereal production: 1960/61-1970/71 to 1971/72-1982/83   30

3.1 Changes in the mean and variability of national foodcrop production, area, and yield in the People's Republic of China   44

3.2 Analysis of the components of change in mean foodgrain production in China, 1952-1957 to 1979-1983   46

3.3 Analysis of the components of change in the variance of total grain production in China, 1952-1957 to 1979-1983   48

3.4 Analysis of the components of change in the variance of rice production by province in China, 1952-1957 to 1979-1983   50

3.5 Analysis of the components of change in the variance of wheat production by province in China, 1952-1957 to 1979-1983   52

3.6 Analysis of the components of change in the variance of other crop production by province in China, 1952-1957 to 1979-1983   54

x *Tables and Figures*

3.7 Provinces exhibiting variance changes between 1952–1957 and 1979–1983 56

3.8 Wheat yield correlation coefficients among five major producing provinces, 1979–1983 57

4.1 Spatial variability in cereal production within Soviet regions 66

4.2 Annual variability in Soviet cereal production through time 66

4.3 Cereal production trends in Soviet regions 69

5.1 The mean and coefficient of variation of areas, yield, and production of cereals in Syria during the nonreform, land-reform, and post-land-reform periods 80

5.2 Changes in the mean and variability of barley and wheat areas in Syria 82

5.3 Changes in the mean and variability of barley and wheat yields in Syria 83

5.4 Changes in the mean and variability of barley and wheat production in Syria 84

5.5 Components of change in the average production of barley and wheat in Syria: 1950–57 and 1962–64 to 1971–81 85

5.6 Disaggregation of the components of change in the variance of total barley and wheat production in Syria: 1950–57 and 1962–64 to 1971–81 86

5.7 Yield correlations between provinces for barley and wheat in Syria 87

5.8 Yield correlations between barley and wheat in Syria 87

5.9 Percentage of wheat areas planted to high-yielding varieties in Syria 88

6.1 Contribution of different sources to increased interregional covariance in sorghum and pearl millet production in India, 1956/57–1967/68 to 1968/69–1979/80 93

6.2 Means and ranges of the data used to explain the increase in interregional yield covariance in sorghum and pearl millet production in India 97

6.3 Estimated regression coefficients of the determinants of changes in interregional yield covariance in sorghum and pearl millet production 98

7.1 Historical trends in English wheat yields 101

7.2 Interannual variation in English wheat yields 101

7.3 Interannual variation in wheat yields at individual sites in the United Kingdom 104

7.4 Variation in wheat yields from field to field in the United Kingdom 105

8.1 Changes in the mean and variability of wheat and barley production on two groups of farms in Southeast England: 1964–1974 to 1975–1984 109

8.2 Components of change in wheat production variance on 16 farms in Southeast England: 1964–1974 to 1975–1984 110

8.3 Interfarm yield correlations of wheat and barley significantly different from zero on selected farms in Southeast England 112

9.1 Coefficients of regression and standard deviation for kernel yield of winter wheat and spring barley in Bavaria in 10-year periods, 1950–1984 119

9.2 Changes in the mean and variability of winter wheat and spring barley yields in Bavaria, 1950–1966, 1956–1975, and 1967–1984 123

9.3 Mean and variability of kernel yield of old cultivars (O) or landraces and modern cultivars (M) of winter wheat and spring barley in different crop management systems in Bavaria 124

10.1 Coefficients of variation of yield computed for hypothetical cases 130

10.2 Components of variance in 174 winter wheat trials during 1967–1978 131

13.1 Proportion of genotypes in international spring wheat yield nurseries from 1964–1965 to 1978–1979 162

13.2 Correlations between parameters from one year to the next for a common set of genotypes and environments 173

14.1 List of locations in the southern and northern regional performance nurseries from which yield data were used for calculation of trends in yield and variance in productivity 177

15.1 Grain yield and stability parameters of maize varieties in consecutive cycles of selection tested in 1979–1984 191

15.2 Summary comparison of improved maize varieties with farmers' local varieties in on-farm variety trials, where inputs and management are at the farmer level 196

15.3 Grain yield and stability parameters for six variety × N fertilizer combinations at seven sites on the Cayes Plain, Haiti, 1983 202

15.4 Yield, slope, and economic data for three packages of inputs at 418 sites in Ghana, 1982–1983 204

16.1 Summary of international pearl millet adaptation trials 207

16.2 Characteristics of the two highest yielding entries in the mean and lowest yielding environments 214

16.3 Yield and stability characteristics of highest yielding entries averaged over all environments and in the lowest yielding environment   215

16.4 Mean yields, s_d^2 values, and regression coefficients for hybrids and varieties   216

16.5 Sources of genetic variation relative to environmental variation standardized to one hundred   217

16.6 Entries selected on basis of complex criteria of yield and stability   217

17.1 Elasticity of mean and variance of yield with respect to nitrogen fertilizer and optimal nitrogen use with risk-neutral and risk-averse decision preference   228

19.1 Sources of risk, utility formulation, and evidence on marginal risk effects of pest control inputs   246

19.2 Export price ratios of pesticides for rice and wheat   249

20.1 First-period coefficients of variation and their changes in production, area, and yield of rice in eight major rice-growing countries for periods before and during modern variety rice adoption   252

20.2 Adaptability and stability of rice cultivars tested in the international rice-testing program   255

20.3 Mean rice yields and yield distributions on farmers' fields in irrigated and upland rainfed sites in the Philippines   261

22.1 Crop-reporting districts with statistically different variance measures between low- and high-technology periods   277

22.2 Crop-reporting districts with no statistical difference in error variance but with statistical difference in normalized weather variance between low- and high-technology periods   277

22.3 Percentage of statistically significant crop-reporting district yield correlations for maize in the United States   281

22.4 Percentage of statistically significant differences between crop-reporting district yield correlations for periods 1931–1946 and 1967–1981 for maize in the United States   282

23.1 Slope estimates for the structural model, the model of farmers' expectations, and the model of the government's trend-based expectations   292

23.2 Slope estimates for the model of the government's adaptive expectations   296

23.3 Estimated variance of aggregate rice yield with and without the high-yielding varieties   297

23.4 Sums of district variances and interdistrict covariances with and without the high-yielding varieties   298

24.1 Wheat yields over time with changing cultivars   302

25.1 Agroclimatic and technological features for three villages in India's semi-arid tropics from 1975/76 to 1983/84   310

25.2 Descriptive information on the common crops sown in the study villages in India from 1975/76 to 1983/84   312

25.3 Simulated risk benefits from perfect crop yield stabilization   314

26.1 World cereal production, trade, and price of wheat during the "food crises," 1970–1976   323

26.2 Coefficient of variation for per capita cereal production, cereal consumption, and total food consumption   324

26.3 Correlation coefficients for cereal production, cereal consumption, total food consumption, and noncereal consumption, 1966–1980   327

26.4 Regressions of the coefficient of variation of daily calorie consumption on gross national product and the coefficient of variation of food production, and resulting elasticities   328

Figures

2.1 World cereal production, 1960/61–1982/83   14

3.1a Coefficients of variation for sown area of foodgrains in China, 1954–1982   36

3.1b Coefficients of variation for yields of foodgrains in China, 1954–1982   37

3.1c Coefficients of variation for production of foodgrains in China, 1954–1982   37

3.2 Fertilizer nutrient application per sown hectare in China, 1983   42

4.1 Cereal production in the Soviet Union and net cereal imports   61

4.2 Spatial variability in Soviet cereal production   64

4.3 Annual variability in Soviet cereal production   67

4.4 Diverging trends in Soviet regional cereal production   68

4.5 Spatial contrasts in Soviet production   70

4.6 Climatic factors in variability of Soviet cereal production, 1965   72

4.7 Climatic factors in the variability of Soviet cereal production, 1975   73

4.8 Regional compensation effects in the Soviet Union   74

6.1 Adoption of pearl millet hybrids in Bhir (Maharashtra) and South Arcot (Tamil Nadu), 1966-1980   95
7.1 U.K. wheat yields, 1948-1984   103
8.1 Number of sample farms showing change in variability of wheat and barley yields in Southeast England, 1964-1974 to 1975-1984   111
8.2 Nitrogen application per hectare, England and Wales, 1974-1984   114
8.3 Fungicide application on cereals, England and Wales, 1970-1984   115
8.4 Fungicide use and the change to winter-sown barley, England and Wales, 1969-1984   116
9.1 Changes in yield increase and yield variation of winter wheat and spring barley in Bavaria, 1950-1984   120
9.2 Mean yield of winter wheat and spring barley in Bavaria, 1960-1978   122
11.1 Twenty landraces, or traditional rice varieties, from eight nations in the genetic ancestry of IR64, released in May 1985   136
11.2 Maternal derivation of IR varieties   138
11.3 Comparison of breeding objectives, 1984 and 1975   141
12.1 Annual average grain yield of U.S. maize, 1930-1985   148
13.1 Response of four hypothetical varieties to higher productivity levels   160
13.2 Distribution of mean yields, coefficients of regression, and yield stability parameters for four groups of genotypes across International Spring Wheat Yield Nurseries 1 through 15   163
13.3 Yield of Veery "S" in the 73 environments of the 15th International Spring Wheat Yield Nursery   165
13.4 Relative yield performance of the respective highest yielding genotype (variety) in the Asian and tropical highlands regions   167
13.5 Relative grain yield of the CIMMYT variety Veery "S," the best locally developed variety (LDV), and the longtime check variety Siete Cerros in eight different environmental groupings for the 15th International Spring Wheat Yield Nursery   169
13.6 Input efficiency of old and new varieties under differing production conditions   171
13.7 Nitrogen response curves of Veery "S" and two old cultivars   172
14.1 Mean squares associated with the interaction of genotype and environment effects on yield of cultivars in the Southern Regional Performance Nursery, 1958-1984   179

14.2 Mean squares associated with the interaction of genotype and environment effects on yield of cultivars in the Northern Regional Performance Nursery, 1958-1984   180

14.3 Coefficients (b values) from regression of check cultivar yields on nursery mean yields at locations in the Southern Regional Performance Nursery, 1959-1984   181

14.4 Coefficients (b values) from regression of check cultivar yields on nursery mean yields at locations in the Northern Regional Performance Nursery, 1959-1984   182

15.1 Steps in population improvement and experimental variety development, evaluation, and use   188

15.2 Linear regressions of variety yield on the mean grain yield at a site for three improved maize varieties and the local variety in eastern Paraguay, 1984   197

15.3 Linear regressions of variety yield on the mean grain yield at a site for seven improved maize varieties and the local variety at 18 sites in Ghana, 1983   198

15.4 Linear regressions of variety yield on the mean grain yield at a site for V455 and the local variety at 14 sites in Guerrero, Mexico, 1984 and 1985   200

15.5 Linear regressions of variety/input treatment yields on the mean grain yield at a site for four variety/input treatments at 26 sites in Veracruz state, Mexico, 1973-1980   201

15.6 Linear regressions of input "package" yield on the mean grain yield at a site for four input packages at 25 sites in Thailand during 1984   203

16.1 to 16.5 Relationship of regression coefficients, yield, and s_d^2 values, International Pearl Millet Adaptation Trials, 1979-1983   208

16.6 Mean yield and standard deviation of the entries in the International Pearl Millet Adaptation Trial, 1983   218

16.7 Cumulative probability and predicted yield in the lowest yielding environment in the International Pearl Millet Adaptation Trials, 1979, 1980, 1981, and 1983   219

21.1 Yields and standard deviations of winter barley with increasing nitrogen levels with and without fungicide treatments based on averages over the different application systems   267

21.2 Yields and standard deviations of winter wheat with increasing nitrogen levels with and without fungicide treatments based on averages over the different application systems   268

24.1 Cumulative distribution functions for two cultivars and two crop histories   303

24.2 Example of cumulative distribution functions with second-period wheat yield that is first stochastic dominant over first-period yield, as found in seven local government areas   305

24.3 Example of cumulative distribution functions with second-period wheat yield that is first stochastic dominant over first-period yield, as found in 14 local government areas   306

24.4 Example of cumulative distribution functions with second-period wheat yield that is second stochastic dominant over first-period yield, as found in 24 local government areas   307

26.1 Production, price formation, and consumption: tracing market-level effects of instability for consumption   322

Foreword

Variability in foodgrain yields and production has entered into the food policy agenda in the wake of the green revolution, but debate and decision making have been stifled for lack of a systematically gathered body of cogent evidence.

Research by the International Food Policy Research Institute (IFPRI) on countries and crops shows that, in most cases, increases in yield variability and, more important, a loss in offsetting patterns of variation (increased correlations) in crop yields between regions are the predominant sources of the increase in production variability. There has been a tendency by some researchers to attribute this increased yield variability to improved seed- and fertilizer-based technologies. Some researchers have also argued that plant breeders should focus less on maximizing average yields and more on reducing yield sensitivity to environmental stress. Such recommendations may prove costly for future growth in foodgrain production, and they cannot be warranted before more thorough and quantitative studies of the sources of increased variability have been undertaken.

In view of the importance of this issue to national breeding programs and to the international agricultural research centers, the Deutsche Stiftung für Internationale Entwicklung (DSE) and IFPRI convened an interdisciplinary workshop for an intensive four-day discussion of a broad range of issues associated with increasing yield variability. There were about 60 participants, including biologists, social scientists, and policymakers, with particularly strong representation from the centers of the Consultative Group on International Agricultural Research (CGIAR).

Workshop participants discussed the relationship between changes in yield variability and yield correlations and such causal factors as changes in agricultural technology, weather, irrigation, input availability, and related variables. They also discussed the consequences of increasing yield variability, including its effect on different types of farmers and on poor urban and rural consumers. Participants were asked to make specific recommendations for agricultural research policy in the fields of plant breeding, farming systems, and management of irrigation, fertilizers, and pesticides, and to address the need for changes in national and international agricultural policies. (*Summary Proceedings of a Workshop on Cereal Yield Variability,* edited by Peter B. R. Hazell, was published by IFPRI and DSE in 1986.)

Selected papers from the workshop plus papers commissioned to fill gaps in coverage of issues constitute this volume. It is our hope that this collection of papers will stimulate debate and further research on the important topic of yield variability and that it will lead to improved policies and agricultural research priorities for coping with yield risks in the future.

JOHN W. MELLOR
ERHARD KRÜSKEN

Acknowledgments

The publication of this book completes a collaborative effort extending over more than four years. We are most grateful to the many people who planned and participated in the 1985 Feldafing Workshop and to those who have assisted subsequently in preparing papers to provide a more complete coverage of the subject.

The International Food Policy Research Institute and the Deutsche Stiftung für Internationale Entwicklung generously provided financial and institutional support. Lloyd T. Evans, through his exceptional synthesizing skill exercised at the workshop, provided important parts of the perspectives described in the concluding chapter. Robert E. Evenson reviewed the entire manuscript and contributed many helpful suggestions. Elizabeth A. Anderson helped to edit and rework the papers into the more cohesive forms herein.

JOCK R. ANDERSON
PETER B. R. HAZELL

1 Introduction

JOCK R. ANDERSON AND PETER B. R. HAZELL

Many countries have achieved impressive rates of growth in national foodgrain production in recent years. Much of this growth can be attributed to new technologies, especially improved varieties, and the increased use of irrigation, fertilizers, and pesticides. These increases in production have provided a lifeline for many developing countries and prevented the mass starvation predicted by some observers in the mid-1960s.

As agricultural output has grown, however, so has its variability, and this presents other problems and concerns that need to be addressed by the agricultural research and policymaking community. Prominent among these concerns are:

a. increased income risk, which may make new technologies less attractive to farmers and hence slow agricultural growth in developing countries;
b. increased instability in national and world food supplies, which may act to destabilize domestic prices, national income, and the food consumption of the poor, especially in poor agrarian countries;
c. increased variability in domestic production, which may add to the difficulties and cost of price support and stabilization schemes in many industrial countries.

There has been a tendency by some researchers to attribute this increased variability to the improved crop varieties underlying the new technologies (e.g., Mehra 1981, Barker et al. 1981, and Griffin 1988). Some researchers have also argued that plant breeders should focus less on maximizing average yields and more on reducing yield sensitivity to environmental stress. Such recommendations may prove costly for future growth in foodgrain production, and they cannot be warranted before more thorough and quantitative studies have been undertaken of the sources of increased variability or of alternative ways of redressing the problem.

In view of the importance of these issues to policymakers, to national breeding programs, and to the international agricultural research centers, this book attempts to bring together a significant body of empirical evidence on production variability, drawing on work in several disciplines, including plant breeding, agronomy, and economics. Chapters review available evidence on patterns of variability in cereal production and how these patterns have changed in recent years. The biological, climatic, and economic factors underlying these changes are discussed and implications sought for both agricultural research and policy.

To make the task more manageable, the scope of the material has been limited in two ways: First, there is a focus on yield risks. These are the most important source of increase in the variability of world food production (see ch. 2). Yield risks also lead to much of the variability in domestic prices in many countries, and they are often the predominant source of risk in rainfed agriculture. Second, attention is confined to cereals. These are the predominant foodcrops for most of the world's poor. They are also the crops that are most directly linked to recent advances in high-yielding varieties.

Structure of the Book

The book has four parts. The first examines patterns of yield variability for the world and for selected countries and how these patterns have changed in recent decades. While the chapters in this section are largely descriptive, they do suggest some important hypotheses about causal factors behind changing patterns of variability. Part II explores the relationship between plant breeding and yield variability. It includes empirical evaluations of the stability of many modern cereal varieties in comparison with their more traditional counterparts. Part III reviews the relationships between cultural practices, particularly the use of key inputs, and yield variability. The final part discusses the conditions under which increasing yield variability may be a problem for farmers, poor consumers, and governments; the consequences for these interest groups; and reviews the implications for agricultural policy and agricultural research priorities.

Part I. Evidence on Patterns of Changing Yield Variability

In chapter 2, Hazell introduces a variance decomposition procedure and examines the evidence for changing patterns of variability in cereal production for the world (excluding China because of data difficulties) and for the 34 most important cereal-producing countries. While the results vary by crop and country, it seems clear that there has been a general pattern of increase in the variability of total cereal production since the early 1970s. Hazell finds that this increase is predominantly due to increases in the variances and covariances of yield. This finding justifies the focus of this book on yield variability in that it is the major variable of interest in comprehending production variability. Perhaps the most important contribution of chapter 2 is the identification of yield covariances, and particularly increases in yield correlations between countries and crops, as a major source of increase in the variability of world cereal production. It is, therefore, as important to understand the causal factors underlying these increases in correlation as it is to understand those underlying changes in yield variances within crops and countries.

Additional insights into changing patterns of yield variability can be obtained by examining individual countries in more depth. This has the added advantage of allowing the analysis to be carried out at a more disaggregated regional level. Chapters 3 and 4 are devoted to analysis of changing patterns of variability in cereal production in the People's Republic of China and the Soviet Union. These countries were chosen because of their great importance in world cereal production, and because results for the other two major cereal-producing countries, that is, India and the United States, have been presented elsewhere (Hazell 1982, 1984). A similar analysis is undertaken for Syria in chapter 5. Syria is one of the riskiest cereal-producing countries in the world and is also one where public policy may be a most important factor underlying recent changes in variability.

In chapter 6, Walker reports an analysis of changing patterns of variability in sorghum and pearl millet production in the semi-arid tropical areas of India where these grains are major staple foods. His analysis at a district level provides additional evidence for the importance of increasing interregional yield correlations. Chapters 7 and 8 are devoted to changing patterns of variability in cereal production in the United Kingdom. Austin and Arnold (chapter 7) examine data on wheat yields for several centuries, whereas Webster and Williams (chapter 8) analyze variability in wheat and barley yields at the individual farm level over 21 recent years. Finally, in chapter 9, Fischbeck examines yield data for winter wheat and spring barley in Bavaria since 1950. During this period average yields more than doubled, and there is an excellent data base for examining the associated changes in variability.

In several of these chapters the authors use time-series data and variance decomposition methods to attempt to identify changing patterns in cereal yield variability. While the authors are able to identify the important components of change in yield variability and suggest some important hypotheses about why these changes may be occurring, they are unable to identify cause and effect relationships. This is an important deficiency because, without such an understanding, it is difficult to establish what kinds of interventions will be most appropriate and effective. The task of identifying causal relationships is taken up in parts II and III. However, before overviewing these, it is useful to introduce a conceptual scheme of sources of crop yield variability and in this way indicate how the chapters in these parts can be related.

A Conceptual Scheme of Sources of Crop Yield Variability

The variability observed in cereal yield results from the interaction of many factors—some emerging from the physical environment, such as those related to climate; some from the economic and political environment, such as prices and access to inputs; some from the intervention of farm decision makers themselves, such as choice of levels of factors of production (e.g., fertilizers, pesticides) and of other aspects of technique (e.g., varieties, mechanization). While any simple conceptualization surely cannot do justice to the complexity of such matters, an attempt is made here to sketch a framework into which much of the material in this book can be integrated. The treatment follows that of Byerlee and Anderson (1969) and Anderson, Dillon and Hardaker (1977, p. 174).

For brevity, symbols are introduced for prices (P), per hectare measure of yield (Y), fertilizer (F), irrigation (I), variety or cultivar (V), soil nutrients (S), rainfall (R), other stochastic climate variables (C), mechanization (M), and other controlled inputs such as pesticides (Z). In an industrial economy, some factors can reasonably be regarded as totally controllable (V, F, M, Z, and possibly I) and not, in themselves, as sources of risk or unpredictable variability. Over time, however, especially in response to changing P, decision makers may choose different levels of such controllable inputs so that consequent yields will vary and will show up as time-series variability that, in fact, is not risk per se to the extent that it is predictable and controlled.

The defined variables can be combined in a functional relationship in which the productive factors can be ordered from the most to the least predictable/controllable. This speculative exercise is attempted for the context of many developing countries where access to fertilizer is often unpredictable from season to season, desired quantities frequently cannot be acquired, and irrigation water supplies are highly unreliable, either from storage or via discontinuous supplies of electricity or fuel for pumps:

$$Y = f(V, M, F, Z, I \mid S, P, C, R). \tag{1.1}$$

The first five variables are technological variables more or less under the control of farmers, and the next four variables are environmental and essentially uncontrollable from the farmer's point of view. Part II of the book deals primarily with the first variable, V, while part III deals primarily with F, Z, and I.

There are important interactions among most of the explanatory variables so that much important complexity is assumed away if any of them are examined singly, as is done at several points in this volume. The difficulty is that attempts to grapple with several or all factors simultaneously falter on impracticalities and cognitive dissonance, if not contemporary analytical impossibility. Either exceptionally rich data sets that may admit detailed econometric investigation using methods that have been suggested by Just and Pope (1978) and Antle (1983c), or exceptionally detailed bioeconomic simulation models (Dent and Anderson 1971, Dent and Blackie 1979), would be required for such an ambitious task.

It is plausible that multifactorial investigation of some of the factors may provide greater insight than presently is readily available to some of the interactive effects of several variables. There is mounting evidence on the pervasive interactions between V (Simmonds 1962, 1981) and other factors such as fertilizer (F) (Roumasset et al., ch. 17), pesticides (Z) (Carlson, ch. 19; Hanus and Schoop, ch. 21), irrigation (I) (Pandey, ch. 18), soil nutrients (S) (Hanus and Schoop, ch. 21), stochastic climatic variables (C) (Coffman and Hargrove, ch. 11; Pfeiffer and Braun, ch. 13), and rainfall (R) (e.g., Thompson, 1975; Parry and Carter 1985; Walker, ch. 6; Duvick, ch. 12; Pham et al., ch. 15; Witcombe, ch. 16; French and Headley, ch. 22). In the considerable relevant literature, and especially in part II, such effects are described as genotype–environment (GE) interactions.

Part II. Plant Breeding and Yield Variability

While plant breeders are primarily interested in maximizing yield responsiveness to environment, they have for some years also been concerned with the stability of the genotypes that they select. In chapter 10, Arnold and Austin provide an overview of the methods that plant breeders use in selecting stable and adaptable varieties. They also discuss the limitations of commonly used methods and make some suggestions for improvements in the future.

There are numerous characteristics of a plant that determine its stability properties. These aspects are examined in detail by Coffman and Hargrove in chapter 11 for the case of rice. Studies of this kind are useful in identifying those agronomic features of plants that need to be emphasized by breeders if stability is to be enhanced. The fact that some characteristics that are favorable for yield responsiveness are also unfavorable for stability suggests that there may be real trade-offs between breeding for higher average yield and breeding for stability.

One issue raised by Coffman and Hargrove is that the widespread adoption of a few rice varieties throughout much of Asia has narrowed the genetic diversity of cultivated varieties. Most popular semidwarf rice varieties have similar cytoplasm, and virtually all have the same dwarfing genes. The common ancestry of many modern rice varieties does not necessarily imply that they increase production variability, but their common susceptibility to the same kinds of pest and weather stresses may mean that yields will tend to be more covariate across regions. Duvick addresses this same issue in chapter 12 for maize yields in the U.S. Corn Belt. He concludes though that observed increases in interregional maize yields in the United States are probably due more to changing weather patterns and more homogenous cultural practices than they are to narrowing of the genetic base.

Experimental data from varietal trials in numerous (mainly developing) countries are analyzed in chapters 13 through 16 to test the stability of modern cereal varieties. These chapters illustrate the common methods used by breeders for screening for stability and the superiority of modern varieties of wheat (chapters 13 and 14), maize (chapter 15), and pearl millet (chapter 16). The results demonstrate that high-yielding varieties typically have at least the same yield stability/adaptability as local varieties, but on a higher yield plateau. They are also more responsive to favorable environments and higher levels of inputs. There is also evidence that the modern varieties yield at least as well as traditional varieties in poor environments, although the range of environments tested may not be sufficiently wide to encompass the farming conditions of some of the most marginal farmers in the world.

Part III. Input Management and Yield Variability

The management of other factors of production can be at least as important as genotype in determining the variability of yields in farmers' fields, particularly when the potentially large interactions between genotype and environment, or in this case the farmer-manipulated environment, are allowed for. Chapters 17 through 19 provide reviews of the literature on the relationship between yield variability and the use of fertilizer (chapter 17), irrigation (chapter 18), and pesticides (chapter 19). These reviews suggest that the proper management of these inputs can have a stabilizing effect on yield, and particularly so for modern varieties.

The remaining chapters in part III address some of the joint effects of input management and shed some light on some of the interaction effects. In chapter 20, Flinn and Garrity discuss the relationships between nitrogen use, pesticide use, and agronomic practice in contributing to yield stability for rice in East Asia. Hanus and Schoop describe the relationship between fertilizer and fungicide use on barley in West Germany in chapter 21. In chapter 22, French and Headley use regression analysis to analyze causal factors behind changing yield variability and interregional yield correlations for maize in the United States. They are able to separate the effects of weather variables and technology factors and in this way challenge some of Hazell's (1984a) conclusions about change in correlation effects.

Part IV. Impacts of Yield Variability and Implications for Policy

Parts I, II, and III are largely concerned with whether yield variability and yield correlations are increasing and, if so, why. In the remaining part the question of whether increasing yield variability is important for decision makers, particularly for farmers and poor consumers, is addressed.

Measured from the farmers' point of view, high or increasing levels of yield variability need not be a problem. There are several reasons for this. First, if farmers were able successfully to anticipate yield outcomes each year, and thereby make appropriate adjustments to their resource allocation decisions in order to maximize returns each year, yield variability would not necessarily involve any economic cost. It is only when yield changes cannot be perfectly anticipated at the time of making resource allocative decisions that the possibility of resource misallocation and economic loss arises. This begs the question of how accurately farmers and others can forecast yield variations from year to year. This subject is taken up in chapter 23 by Bindlish, Barker, and Mount. Using district-level data from India, they explicitly model the expectations behavior of rice farmers and then calculate production risks over time as the difference between actual yield outcome and expected yield each year.

Second, from a decision-making point of view, measures of yield dispersion in themselves do not indicate much about riskiness except under rather extreme probability distributional assumptions, such as normality. For more general risk analysis it is necessary to employ more general concepts of stochastic efficiency, preferably using the economic returns from the crop rather than simply yield. Such an analysis is developed and illustrated in chapter 24 by Anderson, Findlay, and Wan for an Australian wheat farm.

Third, yield variability may not be important for farmers because yield risks are only some of many faced by farmers. For example, even for a single crop, yield variations could be compensated by price variations, providing the latter move in the opposite direction. Further, total household income usually comprises the returns from several crops and livestock activities, most of which are not perfectly correlated, as well as nonfarm sources of income, such as off-farm earnings. In chapter 25, Walker examines conditions for Indian farmers in the semi-arid tropics under which reduced yield risk for a major cereal crop might have a stabilizing effect on total family income.

Significant yield risk could have an important bearing on farmers' decision to adopt new technology. To the extent that they also destabilize national food supplies and prices, yield risks may also be detrimental to poor consumers. High production years for major cereals should, in principle, be good for poor consumers. They should gain from more plentiful food supplies, from lower prices, and perhaps from increased agricultural employment. The opposite might be expected in low production years. However, since consumers typically purchase a number of different foodstuffs, shortages or high prices for one may be offset by substituting other foods of which supplies are more plentiful or prices are lower. There is a surprising lack of evidence on the relationship between the variability of individual food supplies and the variability of the income and nutritional intake of the poor. Sahn and von Braun (chapter 26) muster much of the evidence available on this issue.

The book concludes with a synthesis of the issues in chapter 27, in which the editors attempt to summarize the main findings and draw implications for changes in agricultural research priorities and for agricultural policy. A particularly important consideration is the cost-effectiveness of different approaches. Should, for example, plant breeders be encouraged to give greater emphasis to crop stability rather than increased yield responsiveness if this would lead to a significant loss in the growth of yield over time? It may be more cost-effective to pursue alternative approaches to the problem, such as improved agronomic practices, or policy interventions that mitigate the consequences of yield variability.

Measures of Yield Variability

In interdisciplinary studies of this kind, difficulties can easily arise when different concepts and approaches are encountered in addressing a common problem. This problem is particularly acute when confronted by the very different concepts of yield variability held by plant breeders and economists. These differences do not invalidate the approach of either discipline, but rather they reflect differences in the clientele that breeders and economists seek to assist, and differences in the sources of variability that exist in yield data measured at different levels of aggregation.

Plant breeders are primarily concerned with developing higher yielding varieties that also provide acceptable levels of risk to farmers. As such, they tend to focus on reducing "downside" yield risks and on selecting varieties that will perform well for farmers under diverse conditions. Their analyses are based on yield data from experimental plots or farmer fields, and, because most stability tests on specific genotypes are typically carried out for only two or three years, there is a strong presumption that stability across different locations (or more correctly, "adaptability") is a good proxy for "stability" over time at specific locations. The evidence for this is mixed; whereas supportive evidence is offered in chapters 16 and 20, contrary evidence is to be found in Watson and Anderson (1977), and Evenson et al. (1979).

Economists tend to be more concerned with national food problems and, at this level of analysis, both high and low yields can present problems. Low national yields may result in food shortages, high food prices (especially for the poor), and balance of payments problems, whereas high yields may result in unacceptably low prices for farmers and excessive food stocks, perhaps publicly owned. Both upside and downside risks can, therefore, seem significant to economists. In addition, they often work with regional or national yield data that embody more diverse sources in their variability. The latter include covariance relations between more microlevel units of observation (e.g., fields or farms) which are usually ignored by plant breeders (ch. 2). A major limitation of using aggregate yield data is that it is much more difficult to isolate the impact of improved technologies (especially improved varieties) on yield variability.

There are usually differences in the types of yield distributions observed at the farm and national levels. For example, experimental plot and farm yields are often skewed (Day 1965, Anderson 1973), whereas national yields tend to be more symmetric or even normal. This is to be expected since the latter are a weighted sum of many individual farm yields, and many of these are only weakly correlated.

When yield distributions are symmetric, measures of variability that focus only on downside risks often give results similar to those based on general measures of dispersion. The variance and the coefficient of variation (cv) of yields are then satisfactory measures of variability for a wide range of purposes. If yield distributions are skewed, however, other measures of variability, such as the semi-variance or, indeed, part or all of the cumulative distribution function itself may be more relevant.

Several measures of variability are used in this volume, reflecting the purpose and preferences of individual authors. All authors choose to represent central tendency by the arithmetic mean (m). Dispersion is usually measured by the variance (var) or the standard deviation (sd), in most cases after trends have been removed. Procedures for decomposing variances of aggregate production into their component parts are introduced in chapter 2. Many authors work with the standardized (or dimensionless) coefficient of variation (cv) defined as cv = sd/m.

The sampling distribution for the cv is complex but tests are made in this volume by appeal to normality in the parent population and estimation of its variance (Kendall and Stewart 1977) as

$$\text{var}(cv) = c^2(1 + 2c^2)/(2n),$$

where c is the coefficient of variation in the parent population and n is the sample size.

Presuming that some attempt at testing for statistical significance is better than none, given the potentially controversial interpretation of changing variability, the editors have intruded significance tests (usually "two tailed" at the conventional, albeit arbitrary, 5 percent level) for many of the variances and cvs reported by several authors. Tests for changes in variances involve standard two-tailed F ratio tests. Tests for cvs involve a comparison of a cv for one period, cv_1 based on n_1 observations, with that for a second, cv_2 and n_2. The ad hoc procedure is adopted of assuming (a) that the "parent" population cv is approximated by cv_1, and (b) that the estimates of the cvs are statistically independent, so that a standard error of the difference between cvs is given by

$$D = c\{[(1 + 2c^2)/2](1/n_1 + 1/n_2)\}^{0.5},$$

and the approximately standard normal test statistic by

$$z = (cv_2 - cv_1)/D.$$

PART I

Evidence on Patterns of Changing Yield Variability

2 Changing Patterns of Variability in World Cereal Production

PETER B. R. HAZELL

Total cereal production for the world (excluding China for data reasons) grew at an average yearly rate of 2.7 percent between 1960/61 and 1982/83. The average yield during this period grew by 2.0 percent per year, and the total gross cropped area allocated to cereals by 0.7 percent per year.

As figure 2.1 shows, this growth in aggregate production has been accompanied by a seemingly widening band of variability with annual downswings of more than 50 Mt. (The unit here is for million metric tons, 10^6t; t is used throughout this volume to designate metric tons.) An encouraging feature is that successive trough low points in production are monotonically increasing over time.

The calculation of 10-year moving averages for the mean and, after linear detrending, the standard deviation and coefficient of variation (cv) of production resulted in the data shown in table 2.1.

Absolute variability around trend has increased substantially and significantly. In fact, it has increased faster than average production as shown by the increase in the cv which, although seemingly substantial, is not significant in a statistical sense (comparing successive decades). Note that cv measured in this way peaked in the decade ending in the early 1980s, with some recent gain in stability after the turbulent 1970s.

An increasing cv means that the probability of a major shortfall, say 5 percent, below trend changes in a similar manner (table 2.1).[1] This is moderated by a change (again not statistically significant) from negative to

---

1. Let detrended production in year t be denoted by $\hat{Q}_t = \bar{Q} + e_t$, where $\bar{Q}$ is the period mean and e_t is the deviation from the mean that year. Then the probability of a shortfall of 5 percent or more below trend is derived from $Pr\{\bar{Q} + e_t \leq 0.95\,\bar{Q}\} = Pr\{e_t/\sigma_e \leq -0.05\,\bar{Q}/\sigma_e\}$ where σ_e is the standard deviation of e_t. Assuming e_t is approximately normally distributed, the desired probability can be obtained from tables of the cumulative standard normal distribution.

FIGURE 2.1 World cereal production, 1960/61-1982/83

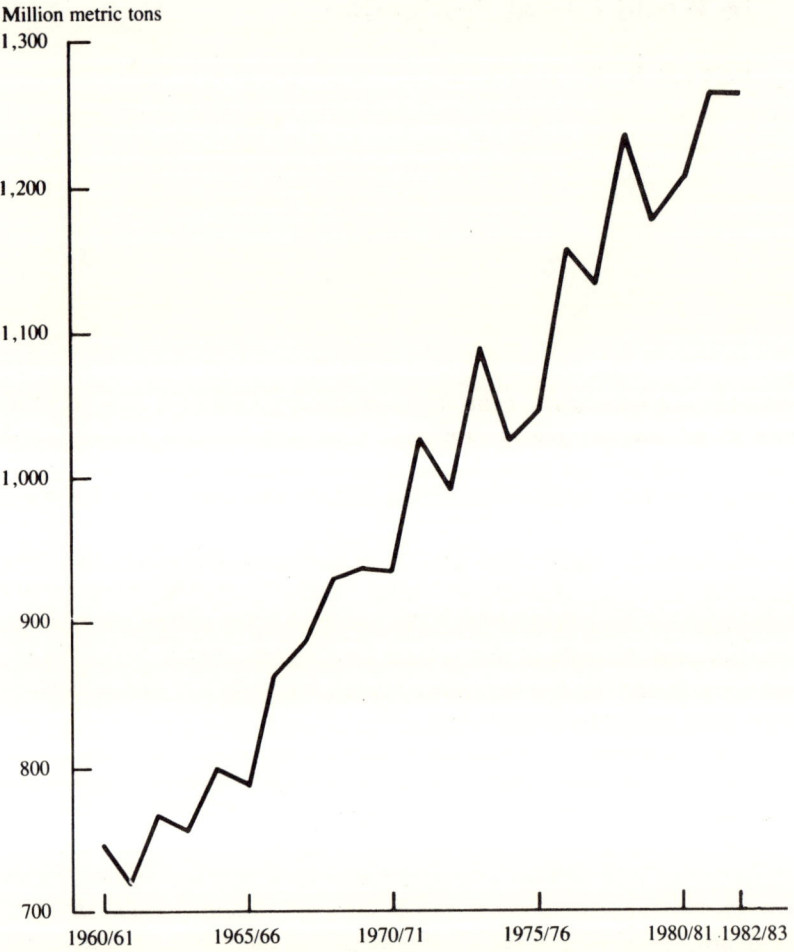

positive skewness (table 2.1). This shift implies that there is now less risk of extreme catastrophe at the global level, but more frequent falling below trend production.

Changes in World Cereal Production

To examine these changes more fully it is instructive to compare variability for important producing countries in two periods. U.S. Department of Agriculture (USDA) data by country and crop (area and yield) were as-

TABLE 2.1 Variability of world cereal production around linear trend: 1960/61–1982/83

Period	Average Production (million metric tons)	Standard Deviation (million metric tons)	Coefficient of Variation	Skewness	Probability of a 5 Percent Shortfall below Trend
Decade Beginning					
1960/61	819	24.3	0.030	−0.31	4.65
1961/62	837	20.7	0.025	−0.39	2.17
1962/63	867	22.4	0.026	−0.64	2.62
1963/64	890	24.1	0.027	−0.21	3.22
1964/65	923	26.8	0.030	−0.32	4.18
1965/66	946	31.2	0.034	−0.32	6.55
1966/67	972	32.5	0.034	−0.39	6.68
1967/68	1,001	34.3	0.035	−0.47	7.21
1968/69	1,026	34.4	0.035	−0.27	6.81
1969/70	1,057	40.0	0.037	0.05	9.01
1970/71	1,081	40.0	0.037	0.34	8.85
1971/72	1,108	40.1	0.036	0.37	8.38
1972/73	1,132	39.5	0.035	0.46	7.64
1973/74	1,159	38.5	0.033	0.37	6.68

Note: Does not include China.

sembled for years 1960/61 to 1982/83 and split into two periods: 1960/61 to 1970/71 and 1971/72 to 1982/83. This split

a. corresponds to speculated changes in yield variability that are possibly associated with the green revolution, usually regarded as occurring around 1970 in many developing countries;
b. corresponds broadly with the dramatic increase in price variability in the early 1970s;
c. more pragmatically, gives roughly equal sample sizes.

Data for each of the 34 more important cereal-producing countries were processed individually, and all other countries (excluding China) were pooled into a "rest of the world" category. The area and yield of each crop in each country were detrended separately, and production derived as the product of detrended area and detrended yield. Quadratic trends were used together with a generalized least squares estimating technique (Hazell 1984).

Table 2.2 summarizes the results by crop at the global level. Average production of total cereals increased by 37 percent between periods, and the cv increased by 21 percent—from 0.028 to 0.034. This increase is not significant at the 5 percent significance level.

TABLE 2.2 Changes in the mean and variability of world cereal production: 1960/61–1970/71 to 1971/72–1982/83

	Average Production			Coefficient of Variation of Production			F Ratios		
Crop	First Period (million metric tons)	Second Period	Change (percent)	First Period	Second Period	Change (percent)	Production	Area Sown	Yield
Wheat	253	353	39.3	0.054	0.048	−11.5	1.52	0.34	1.64
Maize	210	317	51.0	0.033	0.044	34.0	4.08*	1.65	4.17*
Rice	120	155	29.2	0.039	0.038	−4.3	1.52	2.45	0.88
Barley	95	150	58.5	0.048	0.075	55.9	6.18*	3.13	3.28
Millets	20	21	8.2	0.079	0.077	−3.2	1.10	2.17	0.67
Sorghums	40	53	32.7	0.052	0.057	9.2	2.10	0.78	2.32
Oats	49	48	−2.9	0.113	0.054	−52.6	0.21*	0.07*	4.42*
Other cereals	41	35	−14.9	0.046	0.093	103.7*	2.94	0.36	3.61*
Total cereals	829	1,134	36.7	0.028	0.034	21.2	2.75	2.18	2.73

Note: Does not include China.
*An asterisk denotes that the cv/variance in the second period is significantly different from that of the first period at the 5 percent level (two-tailed test).

Table 2.2 also shows important differences by crop. The cv for wheat and rice has diminished, notwithstanding these crops being the flag bearers of the green revolution. But the cv for coarse grains (maize, barley, and sorghum) has increased. The F ratios indicate the importance of increased yield variability rather than of variability in sown area.

Table 2.3 shows results for total cereals by major countries. The cv of production has increased in 14 and diminished in 20 countries. The results by crop within countries are also diverse but often feature high absolute levels of variability (Hazell 1985a). There is little observable relationship between a country's performance in increasing cereal production and the changes in production variability. The correlation across countries between the percentage change in average production and the change in the coefficient of variation is -0.15, which is not significantly different from zero at the 5 percent level.

Table 2.4 summarizes the changes in the mean and cv of yields of major cereals by country. In the following counts of trends in pairs of cvs in table 2.4, "total cereals" is regarded as another "crop," but the "rest of the world" is not regarded as another country. Inspection of the pairs reveals no clear pattern within crops, there being about equal numbers of increases and decreases in cv for each (except wheat and maize, if significance is ignored), or within countries (except the United States where all crops are more variable and Pakistan where all are less variable)—table 2.5. The situation seems similarly unclear with respect to such variables as size of country, the importance of a country as a producer of the particular cereal, and the rate of technological progress.

A Decomposition of the Components of Change

Method of Analysis

To analyze the components of change in the mean and variance of world cereal production, a variance decomposition procedure is used (Hazell 1982). Let Q denote production, A the area sown, and Y yields. Also, letting subscripts i and j denote crops, and h and k denote countries, total cereal production for the world is $Q = \Sigma_h \Sigma_j A_{hj} Y_{hj}$. Average production is

$$E(Q) = \sum_h \sum_j E(A_{hj} Y_{hj}), \tag{2.1}$$

and the variance of production is

$$V(Q) = \sum_h \sum_k \sum_i \sum_j \text{cov}(A_{hi} Y_{hi}, A_{kj} Y_{kj}). \tag{2.2}$$

TABLE 2.3 Changes in the mean and variability of total cereal production by major countries: 1960/61–1970/71 to 1971/72–1982/83

Country	Average Production			Coefficient of Variation of Production			F Ratios		
	First Period (million metric tons)	Second Period	Change (percent)	First Period	Second Period	Change (percent)	Production	Area Sown	Yield
United States	182.0	265.0	45.6	0.068	0.066	−2.8	1.97	1.24	8.23*
U.S.S.R.	138.4	181.0	30.7	0.122	0.143	17.3	2.35	1.28	1.69
India	74.8	104.0	39.1	0.077	0.054	−29.2	0.97	0.65	0.92
France	27.5	41.0	49.6	0.060	0.092	52.9	5.26*	1.58	4.30*
Canada	30.0	40.0	33.5	0.170	0.107	−37.6	0.69	0.22*	0.44
Brazil	16.5	26.1	58.5	0.051	0.089	70.9*	7.25*	4.30*	2.47
Argentina	17.2	23.8	38.3	0.118	0.140	19.0	2.72	1.04	2.12
Germany, F.R.	16.0	22.2	38.6	0.091	0.060	−34.7	0.82	3.24	0.59
Indonesia	13.5	20.3	51.1	0.061	0.052	−15.4	1.62	0.74	2.89
Turkey	12.9	18.4	42.0	0.071	0.097	37.5	3.80*	3.98*	3.45
Australia	12.6	17.4	38.2	0.195	0.232	18.5	2.66	1.65	1.67
Romania	11.6	17.4	49.6	0.109	0.099	−9.2	1.83	0.80	2.17
United Kingdom	12.4	16.8	34.7	0.087	0.083	−4.5	1.66	0.33	1.77
Italy	14.2	16.7	17.3	0.034	0.057	65.1*	3.72*	5.50*	0.66
Mexico	10.5	15.6	48.5	0.070	0.111	57.9*	5.58*	3.99*	3.40
Yugoslavia	11.4	15.0	32.2	0.100	0.052	−48.1	0.47	0.74	0.57
Spain	9.3	13.7	47.2	0.081	0.137	71.3*	6.37*	0.68	7.73*

Thailand	8.6	13.3	54.9	0.078	0.084	7.4	2.76	3.00	2.01
Pakistan	7.7	13.2	71.9	0.102	0.032	−69.2	0.28	0.44	0.27*
Poland	8.4	13.1	56.9	0.092	0.093	1.0	2.52	0.12*	4.00*
Bangladesh	10.5	12.9	22.0	0.072	0.050	−30.2	0.72	0.20*	1.05
Hungary	7.3	12.1	65.0	0.101	0.061	−40.0	0.98	0.35	1.39
South Africa	7.5	12.0	60.0	0.204	0.197	−3.3	2.40	2.63	1.99
Japan	14.6	11.3	−21.8	0.060	0.093	54.9	1.45	4.27*	1.58
Czechoslovakia	6.1	9.7	56.5	0.117	0.075	−35.7	1.01	0.07*	1.62
Nigeria	7.8	8.5	9.0	0.117	0.051	−56.7	0.22*	0.16*	0.14*
Bulgaria	5.4	7.7	41.9	0.103	0.075	−27.3	1.05	3.55*	0.72
Vietnam	6.0	7.3	21.9	0.089	0.056	−37.8	0.58	1.26	0.41
German D.R.	4.6	7.1	55.2	0.113	0.064	−43.3	0.78	1.18	0.65
Philippines	4.3	7.0	63.1	0.055	0.054	−1.5	2.56	6.87*	0.77
Iran	5.0	6.5	31.3	0.083	0.092	11.4	2.15	1.00	3.88*
Burma	4.9	6.5	32.6	0.099	0.077	−22.3	1.06	0.45	1.77
South Korea	5.3	6.2	18.3	0.060	0.108	80.4*	4.62*	0.96	7.76*
Egypt	5.7	7.1	22.8	0.050	0.027	−46.1	0.44	0.23*	0.37
Rest of world (excluding China)	98.5	117.7	19.6	0.032	0.028	−12.2	1.10	0.47	0.75
Total world (excluding China)	829.2	1133.9	36.7	0.028	0.034	21.2	2.75	2.18	2.73

*An asterisk denotes that the cv/variance in the second period is significantly different from that of the first period at the 5 percent level (two-tailed test).

TABLE 2.4 Mean yields and coefficients of variation by crop and country: 1960/61-1970/71 and 1971/72-1982/83

	Wheat		Maize		Rice	
Country	Mean (t/ha)	cv	Mean (t/ha)	cv	Mean (t/ha)	cv
United States						
First period	1.80	0.048	4.44	0.066	3.32	0.031
Second period	2.16	0.067	5.96	0.096	3.68	0.064*
U.S.S.R.						
First period	1.14	0.162	2.45	0.109	1.81	0.041
Second period	1.52	0.137	3.00	0.113	2.54	0.038
India						
First period	0.92	0.106	1.02	0.084	1.01	0.080
Second period	1.42	0.059	1.05	0.078	1.19	0.079
Canada						
First period	1.50	0.178	4.81	0.078	—	—
Second period	1.84	0.097	5.33	0.077	—	—
France						
First period	3.11	0.079	3.84	0.193	2.61	0.117
Second period	4.52	0.086	5.00	0.105	2.21	0.191*
Indonesia						
First period	—	—	0.96	0.050	1.43	0.025
Second period	—	—	1.25	0.042	1.95	0.028
Brazil						
First period	0.77	0.168	1.33	0.047	1.02	0.069
Second period	0.86	0.252	1.56	0.084*	0.96	0.052
Argentina						
First period	1.34	0.185	1.99	0.090	2.38	0.050
Second period	1.55	0.087	2.89	0.149*	2.26	0.074
Mexico						
First period	2.23	0.074	1.01	0.082	1.60	0.066
Second period	3.32	0.105	1.17	0.113	1.97	0.075
Turkey						
First period	0.96	0.074	1.42	0.086	2.44	0.097
Second period	1.39	0.103	2.03	0.067	2.81	0.065
Australia						
First period	1.23	0.158	2.16	0.099	4.80	0.102
Second period	1.24	0.216	2.82	0.087	4.27	0.109
Thailand						
First period	—	—	2.11	0.110	1.09	0.072
Second period	—	—	2.05	0.174	1.18	0.067
Germany, F.R.						
First period	3.59	0.091	4.01	0.077	—	—
Second period	4.70	0.057	5.58	0.088	—	—
Bangladesh						
First period	0.73	0.152	—	—	1.12	0.042
Second period	1.49	0.086	—	—	1.23	0.040

Barley		Millet		Sorghum		Total Cereals	
Mean (t/ha)	cv	Mean (t/ha)	cv	Mean (t/ha)	cv	Mean (t/ha)	cv
2.06	0.050	—	—	3.01	0.065	2.91	0.040
2.51	0.086*	—	—	3.45	0.120*	3.81	0.088*
1.30	0.147	0.80	0.189	—	—	1.20	0.132
1.54	0.177	0.79	0.341*	—	—	1.52	0.134
0.89	0.089	0.43	0.137	0.50	0.083	0.78	0.062
1.07	0.090	0.51	0.108	0.63	0.104	1.02	0.046
1.82	0.121	—	—	—	—	1.69	0.141
2.32	0.072	—	—	—	—	2.14	0.073
2.94	0.086	1.32	—	2.82	0.131	3.04	0.056
3.78	0.085	2.08	—	4.14	0.107	4.28	0.082
—	—	—	—	—	—	1.30	0.021
—	—	—	—	—	—	1.79	0.025
0.86	0.134	—	—	—	—	1.20	0.046
1.14	0.190	—	—	2.14	0.108	1.30	0.067
1.15	0.165	1.13	0.094	1.95	0.148	1.56	0.086
1.32	0.128	1.19	0.109	2.79	0.124	2.09	0.094
0.86	0.058	—	—	2.31	0.097	1.19	0.055
1.29	0.197*	—	—	2.60	0.155*	1.50	0.081
1.22	0.090	1.28	0.059	—	—	1.06	0.069
1.71	0.098	1.39	0.127*	—	—	1.50	0.091
1.15	0.156	0.97	0.170	1.58	0.192	1.20	0.152
1.19	0.198	0.94	0.161	1.92	0.124	1.27	0.185
—	—	—	—	1.53	—	1.17	0.064
—	—	—	—	1.41	0.373	1.29	0.081
3.24	0.106	—	—	—	—	3.23	0.088
4.13	0.042*	—	—	—	—	4.19	0.052
0.56	0.094	0.73	0.060	—	—	1.11	0.043
0.61	0.058	0.77	0.071	—	—	1.24	0.039

TABLE 2.4 Continued

	Wheat		Maize		Rice	
Country	Mean (t/ha)	cv	Mean (t/ha)	cv	Mean (t/ha)	cv
Poland						
First period	2.10	0.051	2.50	0.206	—	—
Second period	2.88	0.091*	3.75	0.186	—	—
Romania						
First period	1.54	0.169	1.96	0.091	1.78	0.156
Second period	2.49	0.105	3.08	0.098	1.53	0.177
United Kingdom						
First period	3.95	0.078	—	—	—	—
Second period	4.96	0.075	2.17	—	—	—
Italy						
First period	2.09	0.065	3.66	0.085	3.44	0.098
Second period	2.58	0.051	6.19	0.028*	3.62	0.127
Pakistan						
First period	0.90	0.098	1.06	0.082	1.08	0.119
Second period	1.39	0.041	1.23	0.031*	1.57	0.039*
South Africa						
First period	0.65	0.176	1.38	0.241	—	—
Second period	1.01	0.119	2.09	0.219	—	—
Yugoslavia						
First period	2.04	0.118	2.62	0.111	2.39	0.107
Second period	3.10	0.091	3.87	0.058	2.62	0.114
Burma						
First period	0.49	0.249	0.49	0.325	1.03	0.066
Second period	0.76	0.083*	0.83	0.100*	1.32	0.075
Japan						
First period	2.47	0.196	2.62	0.063	3.69	0.040
Second period	2.84	0.105	2.75	0.057	4.12	0.057
Vietnam						
First period	—	—	1.10	—	1.26	0.080
Second period	—	—	1.14	0.065	1.33	0.056
Hungary						
First period	2.09	0.125	2.89	0.084	1.20	—
Second period	3.76	0.106	4.76	0.067	1.25	—
Spain						
First period	1.11	0.106	2.68	0.189	3.95	0.043
Second period	1.57	0.150	4.26	0.062*	4.22	0.038
Philippines						
First period	—	—	0.70	0.043	0.88	0.078
Second period	—	—	0.88	0.035	1.22	0.048
Nigeria						
First period	—	—	0.90	0.148	1.20	0.085
Second period	—	—	0.85	0.035*	1.26	0.040
Czechoslovakia						
First period	2.62	0.077	2.91	0.146	—	—
Second period	3.87	0.091	3.91	0.192	—	—

Variability in World Cereal Production 23

Barley		Millet		Sorghum		Total Cereals	
Mean (t/ha)	cv	Mean (t/ha)	cv	Mean (t/ha)	cv	Mean (t/ha)	cv
2.09	0.085	0.96	0.064	—	—	1.97	0.062
2.81	0.074	0.91	0.146*	—	—	2.68	0.092
1.81	0.100	—	—	—	—	1.74	0.087
2.73	0.103	—	—	1.41	—	2.79	0.080
3.52	0.059	—	—	—	—	3.55	0.061
4.10	0.061	—	—	—	—	4.39	0.066
1.44	0.067	—	—	3.39	—	2.33	0.039
2.54	0.071	—	—	4.37	0.096	3.25	0.023
0.61	0.076	0.45	0.059	0.52	0.070	0.87	0.086
0.69	0.036	0.49	0.048	0.59	0.054	1.31	0.030*
0.57	0.248	—	—	0.89	0.229	1.08	0.198
0.89	0.228	—	—	1.86	0.269	1.66	0.182
1.54	0.107	—	—	2.59	0.081	2.23	0.094
2.13	0.092	—	—	2.28	0.105	3.34	0.047
—	—	0.71	0.349	—	—	1.00	0.064
—	—	0.53	0.475	—	—	1.28	0.066
2.69	0.177	1.63	0.091	—	—	3.42	0.054
2.99	0.084	0.95	—	—	—	4.01	0.058
—	—	—	—	—	—	1.26	0.082
—	—	—	—	—	—	1.32	0.050
1.99	0.110	—	—	—	—	2.31	0.072
3.10	0.110	—	—	—	—	4.04	0.048
1.48	0.102	—	—	2.30	0.222	1.29	0.069
1.88	0.168*	—	—	4.39	0.114	1.87	0.132*
—	—	—	—	—	—	0.81	0.059
—	—	—	—	—	—	1.05	0.040
—	—	0.61	0.175	0.75	0.087	0.71	0.093
—	—	0.60	0.059*	0.62	0.043	0.66	0.038*
2.53	0.121	—	—	—	—	2.45	0.084
3.52	0.076	—	—	—	—	3.60	0.073

TABLE 2.4 Continued

	Wheat		Maize		Rice	
Country	Mean (t/ha)	cv	Mean (t/ha)	cv	Mean (t/ha)	cv
German D.R.						
First period	3.39	0.095	2.03	—	—	—
Second period	4.19	0.060	3.19	—	—	—
Iran						
First period	0.84	0.055	1.09	0.090	2.22	0.099
Second period	0.99	0.054	1.33	0.146*	2.46	0.092
Bulgaria						
First period	2.25	0.152	3.04	0.135	2.16	0.151
Second period	3.67	0.064	4.05	0.111	2.39	0.148
South Korea						
First period	2.11	0.080	0.97	0.121	3.03	0.080
Second period	2.53	0.156*	2.87	0.175	3.95	0.126
Egypt						
First period	2.58	0.102	3.14	0.140	3.46	0.058
Second period	3.30	0.043	3.77	0.035*	3.64	0.038
Rest of world (excluding China)						
First period	1.09	0.063	1.15	0.042	1.22	0.032
Second period	1.32	0.048	1.34	0.034	1.47	0.010
Total world (excluding China)						
First period	1.35	0.050	2.27	0.030	1.25	0.033
Second period	1.78	0.049	3.02	0.046	1.46	0.026

Note: The first period is from 1960/61 to 1970/71; the second period is from 1971/72 to 1982/83.
*An asterisk denotes that the cv in the second period is significantly different from that of the first period at the 5 percent level (two-tailed test).

The variance can be expanded as

$$V(Q) = \sum_h \sum_j V(A_{hj}Y_{hj}) + \sum_h \sum_{i \neq j} \sum_j \text{cov}(A_{hi}Y_{hi}, A_{hj}Y_{hj}) \quad (2.3)$$

(sum of individual crop variances within countries)   (sum of intercrop covariances within countries)

$$+ \sum_j \sum_{h \neq k} \sum_k \text{cov}(A_{hj}Y_{hj}, A_{kj}Y_{kj}) + \sum_{h \neq k} \sum_k \sum_{i \neq j} \sum_j \text{cov}(A_{hi}Y_{hi}, A_{kj}Y_{kj}).$$

(sum of intercountry covariances within crops)   (sum of covariances between different crops in different countries).

| Barley | | Millet | | Sorghum | | Total Cereals | |
Mean (t/ha)	cv	Mean (t/ha)	cv	Mean (t/ha)	cv	Mean (t/ha)	cv
3.05	0.150	—	—	—	—	3.03	0.105
3.88	0.078	—	—	—	—	3.92	0.065
0.70	0.044	—	—	—	—	0.87	0.036
0.74	0.131*	—	—	—	—	1.01	0.061*
2.23	0.121	0.95	—	—	—	2.37	0.103
3.19	0.075	1.00	—	—	—	3.60	0.057
1.84	0.142	0.81	0.121	—	—	2.43	0.056
2.32	0.158	1.18	0.132	—	—	3.42	0.110*
2.40	0.206	—	—	3.76	0.018	3.07	0.045
2.80	0.053*	—	—	3.89	0.046*	3.60	0.023
1.44	0.045	0.60	0.044	0.75	0.034	1.20	0.032
1.78	0.068	0.56	0.062	0.82	0.032	1.36	0.025
1.63	0.043	0.53	0.073	1.01	0.040	1.45	0.026
1.97	0.064	0.56	0.058	1.27	0.046	1.85	0.034

Each of the component terms can be expanded as follows:

$$E(A_{hj}Y_{hj}) = \bar{A}_{hj}\bar{Y}_{hj} + \text{cov}(A_{hj}Y_{hj}), \tag{2.4}$$

and, following Bohrnstedt and Goldberger (1969),

$$\text{cov}(A_{hi}Y_{hi}, A_{kj}Y_{kj}) = \bar{A}_{hi}\bar{A}_{kj}\text{cov}(Y_{hi}, Y_{kj}) + \bar{A}_{hi}\bar{Y}_{kj}\text{cov}(Y_{hi}, A_{kj}) \tag{2.5}$$
$$+ \bar{Y}_{hi}\bar{A}_{kj}\text{cov}(A_{hi}, Y_{kj}) + \bar{Y}_{hi}\bar{Y}_{kj}\text{cov}(A_{hi}, A_{kj})$$
$$- \text{cov}(A_{hi}, Y_{hi})\text{cov}(A_{kj}, Y_{kj}) + R,$$

where $\bar{A}$ and $\bar{Y}$ denote mean area and yield, and R is a residual term consisting of higher order cross moments.

TABLE 2.5 Summary of trends in coefficients of variation between periods reported in Table 2.4

	Increases		Decreases	
Crop	Number Measured	Number Significant[a]	Number Measured	Number Significant[a]
Wheat	9	2	20	1
Maize	11	3	19	6
Rice	12	2	14	1
Barley	13	4	13	2
Millet	6	3	4	1
Sorghum	6	3	7	0
Total cereals	17	4	17	2

[a] A significant change at the 5 percent level using the procedure described in chapter 1.

The decomposition analysis partitions the changes in $V(Q)$ and $E(Q)$ between the first and second periods into constituent parts. This involves decomposing the changes in each of the terms in equations (2.1) and (2.3) with the aid of equations (2.4) and (2.5), and then summing the changes in different components over countries and crops. For a full exposition of this method, see Hazell (1982).

Using equation (2.4), but dropping crop and country subscripts for simplicity, average production in the second period is

$$E(Q_2) = \bar{A}_2 \bar{Y}_2 + \text{cov}(A_2, Y_2). \qquad (2.6)$$

Each variable in the second period can be expressed as its counterpart in the first plus the change in the variable between the two. Equation (2.6), therefore, can be written as

$$E(Q_2) = (\bar{A}_1 + \Delta \bar{A})(\bar{Y}_1 + \Delta \bar{Y}) + \text{cov}(A_1, Y_1) + \Delta \text{cov}(A, Y). \qquad (2.7)$$

The change in average production is then obtained from

$$\Delta E(Q) = E(Q_2) - E(Q_1) = \bar{A}_1 \Delta \bar{Y} + \bar{Y}_1 \Delta \bar{A} + \Delta \bar{A} \Delta \bar{Y} + \Delta \text{cov}(A, Y). \qquad (2.8)$$

There are four sources of change in $\Delta E(Q)$. Two parts, $\bar{A}_1 \Delta \bar{Y}$ and $\bar{Y}_1 \Delta \bar{A}$, arise from changes in the mean yield and the mean area. These "pure" effects arise even in the absence of other sources of change. The term $\Delta \bar{A} \Delta \bar{Y}$ is an "interaction" effect, and $\Delta \text{cov}(A, Y)$ arises from changes in the covariability of areas and yields.

The change in the variance of production can be decomposed in an analogous way. Using equation (2.5), the change in each of the production variance and covariance terms can be decomposed as in table 2.6. The first

TABLE 2.6 Components of change in production covariances

Source of Change	Components of Change
Change in mean yields	$\bar{A}_{1i}\Delta\bar{Y}_j \text{Cov}(Y_{1i}, A_{1j}) + \bar{A}_{1j}\Delta\bar{Y}_i \text{Cov}(A_{1i}, Y_{1j}) + [\bar{Y}_{1i}\Delta\bar{Y}_j + \bar{Y}_{1j}\Delta\bar{Y}_i + \Delta\bar{Y}_i\Delta\bar{Y}_j]\text{Cov}(A_{1i}, A_{1j})$
Change in mean areas	$\bar{Y}_{1i}\Delta\bar{A}_j \text{Cov}(A_{1i}, Y_{1j}) + \bar{Y}_{1j}\Delta\bar{A}_i \text{Cov}(Y_{1i}, A_{1j}) + [\bar{A}_{1i}\Delta\bar{A}_j + \bar{A}_{1j}\Delta\bar{A}_i + \Delta\bar{A}_i\Delta\bar{A}_j]\text{Cov}(Y_{1i}, Y_{1j})$
Change in yield variances and covariances	$\bar{A}_{1i}\bar{A}_{1j}\Delta\text{Cov}(Y_i, Y_j)$
Change in area variances and covariances	$\bar{Y}_{1i}\bar{Y}_{1j}\Delta\text{Cov}(A_i, A_j)$
Change in area-yield covariances	$\bar{A}_{1i}\bar{Y}_{1j}\Delta\text{Cov}(Y_i, A_j) + \bar{Y}_{1i}\bar{A}_{1j}\Delta\text{Cov}(A_i, Y_j) - [\text{Cov}(A_{1i}, Y_{1i}) + \Delta\text{Cov}(A_i, Y_i)]\Delta\text{Cov}(A_j, Y_j) - \text{Cov}(A_{1j}, Y_{1j})\Delta\text{Cov}(A_i, Y_i)$
Interaction between changes in mean yields and mean areas	$\Delta\bar{A}_i\Delta\bar{Y}_j \text{Cov}(Y_{1i}, A_{1j}) + \Delta\bar{Y}_i\Delta\bar{A}_j \text{Cov}(A_{1i}, Y_{1j})$
Interaction between changes in mean areas and yield variances	$[\bar{A}_{1i}\Delta\bar{A}_j + \bar{A}_{1j}\Delta\bar{A}_i + \Delta\bar{A}_i\Delta\bar{A}_j]\Delta\text{Cov}(Y_i, Y_j)$
Interaction between changes in mean yields and area variances	$[\bar{Y}_{1i}\Delta\bar{Y}_j + \bar{Y}_{1j}\Delta\bar{Y}_i + \Delta\bar{Y}_i\Delta\bar{Y}_j]\Delta\text{Cov}(A_i, A_j)$
Interactions between changes in mean areas and yields and changes in area-yield covariances	$[\bar{Y}_{1j}\Delta\bar{A}_i + \bar{A}_{1i}\Delta\bar{Y}_j + \Delta\bar{A}_i\Delta\bar{Y}_j]\Delta\text{Cov}(Y_i, A_j) + [\bar{Y}_{1i}\Delta\bar{A}_j + \bar{A}_{1j}\Delta\bar{Y}_i + \Delta\bar{Y}_i\Delta\bar{A}_j]\Delta\text{Cov}(A_i, Y_j)$
Change in residual	$\Delta\text{Cov}(A_i Y_i, A_j Y_j)$ − sum of the other components

five sources of change are "pure" effects, the next four are interaction effects that occur because of simultaneous changes in all the constituent parts, and the final term is a higher order term that is typically small, is of little importance, and has no ready interpretation.

Components of Change in World Cereal Production

Table 2.7 shows the results from decomposing the changes in average cereal production for the world. Increases in mean yields account for about 70 percent of the increase in total cereal production, and area expansion accounts for about 20 percent. Yield improvements are even more important in expanding the production of wheat. They are also more important than area expansion in increasing the production of maize, rice, and mil-

TABLE 2.7 Disaggregation of the components of change in the average of world cereal production: 1960/61–1970/71 to 1971/72–1982/83 (percent)

Components of Change	Wheat	Maize	Rice	Barley	Millet	Sorghum	Oats	Other Cereals	Total Cereals
Change in mean yields	80.93	64.21	60.62	39.52	63.64	45.63	−528.08	−179.99	72.40
Change in mean areas	14.94	28.61	33.64	49.11	44.76	44.42	534.84	220.53	22.36
Change in area-yield covariances	0.19	0.09	−0.02	0.45	2.96	0.20	15.21	−1.08	0.14
Change in interaction term	3.95	7.08	5.77	10.93	−11.36	9.76	78.05	60.54	5.10
Contribution of crop to change in mean production of total cereals	32.65	35.18	11.50	18.28	0.55	4.34	−0.47	−2.03	100.00

Note: Does not include China.

lets. Area increases, however, are more important in expanding barley production.

Table 2.8 shows the results from the decomposition of the change in the variance of world cereal production. The rows in these tables correspond to the four groups of production variances and covariances delineated in equation (2.3). The columns correspond to the 10 sources of change defined (table 2.6) for a production variance and covariance, though the four types of interaction terms have been added together. All entries in the table are expressed as a percentage of the change in the variance of total cereal production, hence both the rows and the columns sum to 100 percent.

The row sums in table 2.8 show that 35 percent of the increase in the variance of world cereal production is attributable to increases in the production variances of individual crops within countries. Wheat, maize, and barley account for nearly all of this 35 percent increase. The remaining 65 percent of the increase in the variance of world cereal production is due to increases in production covariances. Of these, the important ones are between different crops within and between countries. Changes in intercountry covariances within crops turn out to be a relatively minor component of the total variance increase (only 5 percent).

The column sums in table 2.8 show that 96 percent of the increase in the variance of world cereal production is directly attributable to changes in the variances and covariances of crop yields. Changes in yield variances within countries account for one-quarter of this increase, and most of this is attributable to increased yield variances for wheat and maize.

For most of the individual crops, increased yield variances account for the lion's share of the contribution to the variance of total cereal production. For example, when summed over countries, the increased production variances for wheat account for 7.61 percent of the increase in the variance of total cereal production. Of this, $100(5.27/7.61) = 69$ percent is due to increased yield variances. Similarly, the yield variance shares for other crops are: maize 124 percent, rice 36 percent, millets 57 percent, sorghum 77 percent, and total cereals 77 percent.

Changes in yield covariances seem to be more important than changes in yield variances for the variability of world cereal production. However, part of the increase in the yield covariances is itself a direct consequence of increased yield variances. Part of it may also be due to changing correlations between crops and countries. To separate these effects, it is useful to pursue the decomposition one step further.

Using the same kind of decomposition procedure, the change in a yield covariance between two periods can be decomposed into three terms (Hazell 1982). These are, respectively, the changes in the yield variances

TABLE 2.8 Disaggregation of the components of change in the variance of world cereal production: 1960/61–1970/71 to 1971/72–1982/83 (percent)

Variance Component	Source of Change						
	Change in Mean Yields	Change in Mean Areas	Change in Yield Variances and Covariances	Change in Area Variances and Covariances	Change in Area-Yield Covariances	Change in Interaction Terms	Change in Residual	Row Sums
Crop variances								
Wheat	2.06	−2.38	5.27	−0.57	3.57	−0.49	0.15	7.61
Maize	6.67	1.94	17.16	−6.15	−5.01	−1.54	0.73	13.80
Rice	0.11	0.25	0.45	0.12	0.16	0.13	0.05	1.26
Barley	0.43	2.30	1.87	0.86	1.37	4.67	0.96	12.46
Millet	0.01	−0.01	0.04	0.01	0.06	−0.02	0.00	0.07
Sorghum	0.19	0.07	0.57	−0.23	0.12	0.07	−0.05	0.74
Oats	0.83	0.27	0.11	−1.25	−0.54	−1.06	−0.19	−1.85
Other	0.14	−0.15	0.93	−0.14	0.29	−0.77	0.06	0.36
Sum crop variances within countries	10.44	2.28	26.40	−7.36	0.01	0.99	1.70	34.45
Intercrop covariances within countries	0.97	4.48	36.68	−0.94	−9.38	1.89	1.65	35.35
Intercountry covariances within crops	0.09	1.61	11.49	−3.61	−4.40	−0.98	0.49	4.70
Covariances between different crops in different countries	2.75	0.85	21.36	19.13	−28.51	6.43	3.55	25.50
Column sums	14.24	9.22	95.93	7.22	−42.28	8.33	7.40	100.00

Note: Does not include China.

alone, autonomous changes in the yield correlations, and the interaction between these two terms.

Application of this decomposition procedure shows that, for the world as defined, only 4 percent of the 69.5 percent increase in the variance of total cereal production arising from changes in yield covariances is directly attributable to changes in yield variances. Some 56 percent of the increase is attributable to changes in yield correlations alone, and the remaining 40 percent is due to interaction effects. Of the correlation increases, the predominant ones are between the yields of the same or different crops in different countries. Increases in the intercrop yield covariances within countries are nearly all attributable to increased yield variances.

Other results in table 2.8 show that changes in area-yield covariances had an important stabilizing effect on world cereal production; they reduced the variance of total cereal production by 42 percent. A further decomposition of these covariance terms showed that virtually all of this reduction can be attributed to a decline in area-yield correlations. Of the various area-yield correlations, the most important declines are between the crop yields in one country and the sown areas of the same or different crops in other countries.

Discussion

Three major components of the change in the variability of world cereal production since the 1960s have been identified. These are increased yield variances; an increase in correlations between the yields of different crops and countries; and a decline in area-yield correlations, particularly between the crop yields in one country and the sown areas of the same or different crops in other countries. Why have these changes occurred? Additional insights are to be found elsewhere in this book, but a number of hypotheses can be offered here.

Some researchers (e.g., Mehra 1981) have argued that the high-yielding varieties (HYVs) associated with the green revolution are more risky, hence their introduction since the late 1960s is an important source of increasing variability in farm and national yields. Several authors in this volume suggest, however, that, while high-yielding varieties (HYVs) typically lead to higher yield variances, their cvs are not generally larger than those of alternative varieties when grown under trial conditions; in many cases, HYVs have smaller cvs.

HYVs are selected to be more responsive to good growing conditions—indeed, this is largely how yield increases are obtained. This implies, however, that yields will fluctuate more if the use of inputs varies. Input variation may have increased with increases in price variability since the early 1970s, and with the difficulties of reliably supplying inputs in developing countries to meet the growing demands of the green revolution

(Jain, Dagg, and Taylor 1986). Input variation thus leads to behaviorally induced variability in yields, and the phenomenon is perhaps an inevitable consequence of the modernization of agriculture.

Weather patterns may have become more variable since the 1960s, although there is little evidence for this (Carter and Parry 1986). If anything, weather in some areas may have become more stable, at least in the U.S. Corn Belt (French and Headley, ch. 22). National yields may also have become more variable because increases in the areas cropped have pushed some cereals into more marginal land (e.g., barley in Syria, Nguyen, ch. 5). Other sources of increased variability include changes in policy and land reform (e.g., Tarrant, ch. 4; Nguyen, ch. 5).

Yields have become more correlated across regions within some countries (e.g., Hazell 1984; Anderson et al. 1988; Walker, ch. 6) and this may have contributed to increasing the variability of national yields. Possible causes of this phenomenon, as well as of the increase in yield correlations between countries, are still speculative but include:

a. the potentially narrowing genetic base—or is it the "too few" varieties problem? Whatever, there does seem to be more susceptibility to the same weather and pest stresses (Coffman and Hargrove, ch. 11);
b. varieties that are screened for stability across sites are likely to be more highly correlated across sites too;
c. more homogeneous cultural practices (Duvick, ch. 12);
d. yield variability induced by input variations is also likely to be more covariate (e.g., fertilizer application is adjusted similarly by farmers facing the same price movements). This problem is compounded by the green revolution, which has resulted in more farmers becoming more dependent on fertilizers, and other modern inputs.
e. irregularities in input supplies are likely to have covariate effects on yields, for example, electricity blackouts in India worsened just when more farmers had become dependent on electric pumps for irrigation (Hazell 1982);
f. an increase in irrigated area. Although irrigation may be effective in reducing yield variability within fields, it may, by reducing some dispersed climatic influences on yields, lead to more synchronized patterns of variability across locations (Pandey, ch. 18);
g. more covariate patterns of rainfall and climatic variation (Walker, ch. 6; French and Headley, ch. 22).

The tendency for correlations between crop yields to increase may well be a price-related phenomenon. This is suggested by examining the change in correlations among world prices since the early 1970s after detrending (Hazell 1985a).

		Maize	Wheat
Wheat	1961–71	0.30	
	1974–81	0.89	
Rice	1961–71	−0.62	−0.13
	1974–81	0.78	0.82

The dramatically increased correlations presumably reflect the progressive development of international markets in terms of numbers of traders, growth in net transfers from the industrial to the developing world, the increasing role of China in foodgrain arbitrage, and perhaps the greater substitutability of grains as greater quantities of foodgrains become feedgrains, to mention just a few possibilities. Whatever the true explanation, to the extent that producers of cereals are price responsive in yields (Guise 1969, Houck and Gallagher 1976), more correlated prices for grains will predispose more correlated crop yields.

Conclusions

World cereal production (excluding China) grew at an average yearly rate of 2.7 percent between 1960/61 and 1982/83, largely as a result of improved yields. This growth has been accompanied by a more than proportional increase in the standard deviation of production. The coefficient of variation of production around trend was 0.028 during the period 1960/61 to 1970/71. It increased to 0.034 over 1971/72 to 1982/83.

Increases in yield variances and a simultaneous loss in offsetting patterns of variation in yields between crops and countries are the overwhelming sources of the increase in production variability. Although more research is required before firm conclusions can be drawn about the cause of these changes, the increased use of improved varieties and fertilizer-intensive technologies since the 1960s may have been an important factor. However, this is less likely to be because of any higher sensitivity of new technologies to environmental stress, than because these technologies use purchased inputs and hence lead to more variable and synchronized patterns of input use across crops and regions in response to changing prices. This effect has been amplified by the sharp increase in the variability of world cereal prices since the early 1970s, and particularly by the increase in price correlations between crops.

Continued high levels of variability in world cereal prices seem likely. The United States is unlikely to return to its stockpiling policies of earlier years, and cereal imports by the Soviet Union remain unpredictable. World prices will also be affected by the levels of production variability now established. These factors, together with a continuing trend towards more input-intensive technologies, suggest that world cereal production is also likely to remain quite variable in the years ahead.

3 Changing Patterns of Variability in Chinese Cereal Production

BRUCE STONE AND TONG ZHONG

In 1984 the People's Republic of China produced 20 percent of the world's cereal and 42 percent of the developing countries' cereal output. It was the world's largest producer of both wheat and rice; the second largest producer of maize, sorghum, and millet; and a major producer of other cereals (State Statistical Bureau [SSB] 1985b, p. II; He Gang et al. 1984, pp. 85-90; FAO 1985, pp. 107-22). China is also becoming an important, though variable, trading nation in world cereal markets. The People's Republic was a net exporter of more than 2 million metric tons (Mt) of cereals in 1985 (General Administration of Customs of the PRC 1986, pp. 20, 28), following net imports averaging more than 10 million metric tons during the 1977-84 period. While the major trend shifts in China's cereal production and international trade performance have been more or less predictable (e.g., Eckstein 1966, Stone 1980, Stone 1985, 1986b), changes in typical year-to-year variations are much less so. Both are inevitably important for the rest of the world because the absolute magnitudes are so large. The more fundamental of these changes, production variability, is the focus of this paper.

Figure 3.1 plots coefficients of variation (cvs) of production, area, and yield for wheat, rice, maize, and total foodgrains for consecutive five-year periods against the midpoints of these periods. Two general conclusions can be drawn about these trends in cvs: (a) the coefficients for area have, if anything, been falling during the 28-year period analyzed, although slightly rising cvs during the past decade cannot be ruled out; (b) there is little evidence of single 28-year trends for the production and yield cvs, although the late 1950s and early 1960s were considerably less stable than recent periods for all crops, as well as for total foodgrains.

In seeking to understand the sources of variability in Chinese cereal production, it may be most useful to generate hypotheses regarding the relatively anomalous periods of higher cvs for particular crops, and then look at the structure of variability changes to the extent that the quality of

FIGURE 3.1a Coefficients of variation for sown area of foodgrains in China, 1954–1982

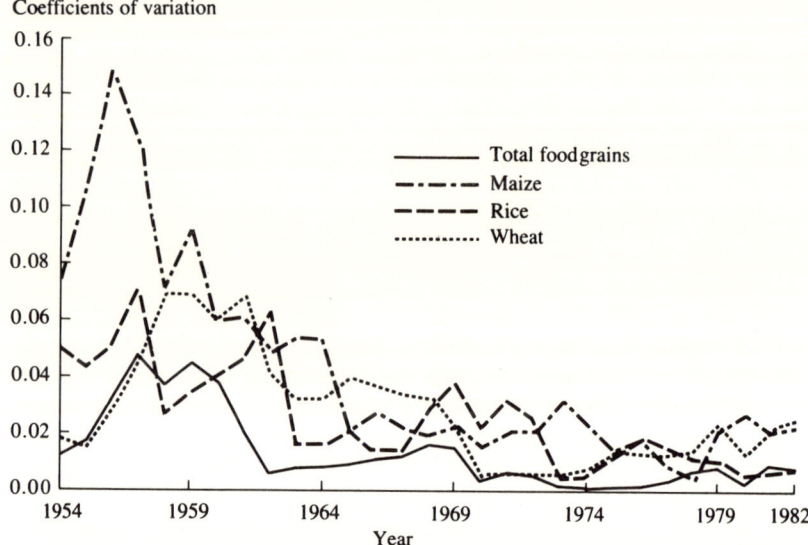

NOTE: Each data point represents a coefficient of variation, expressed as a proportion, of a five-year data period, plotted against the midpoint of that data period. Paddy rice, wheat, and corn comprised a 53–72 percent rising share of "total foodgrain" sown area during the 1952–82 period and a 63–83 percent rising share of production of "total foodgrains," which also include sorghum, millet, root and tuber crops (at one-fifth fresh weight), soybeans, and pulses.

disaggregated Chinese data may justify attempting a variance decomposition exercise.

Hypotheses Regarding Abnormally High Coefficients of Variation for Particular Crops and Periods

The outstanding subperiod to explain is undoubtedly the late 1950s and early 1960s. At the time, Chinese reports blamed the poor and erratic performance on consecutive years of catastrophic weather. But the period of greater sown area variability appears to predate those for production and yield, and Western observers have emphasized the dislocating policies of the Great Leap Forward period. Recent Chinese analysts have also emphasized policy-induced disaster (Kueh 1984, p. 80), as have Lardy (1983) and Walker (1984).

During this period, the State Statistical Bureau was disbanded and reporting units came under considerable pressure to report policy suc-

Variability in Chinese Cereal Production 37

FIGURE 3.1b Coefficients of variation for yields of foodgrains in China, 1954–1982

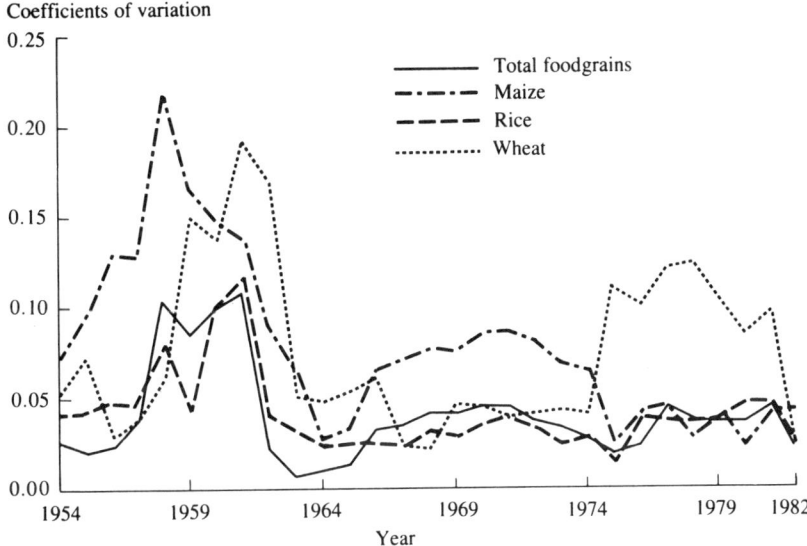

FIGURE 3.1c Coefficients of variation for production of foodgrains in China, 1954–1982

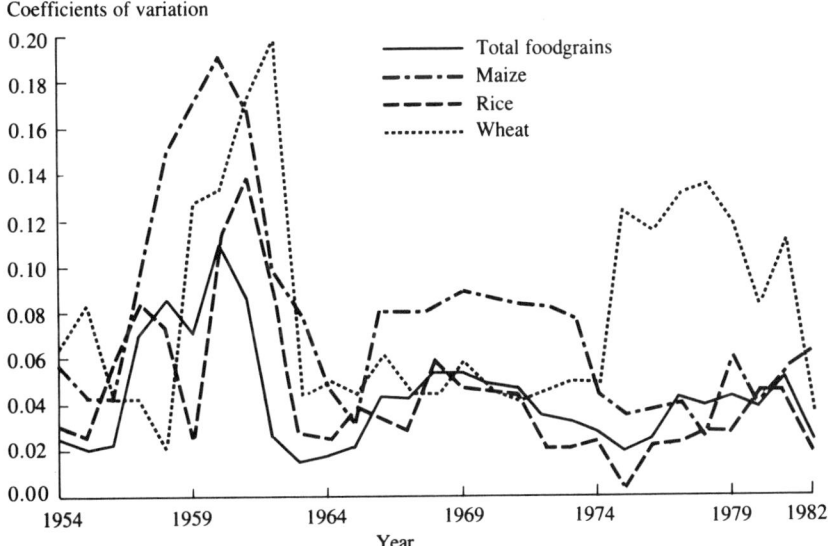

cesses. One of the destabilizing results of this development was that, with grossly exaggerated reports of grain production growth in 1958, the area sown with nongrain crops in 1959 was increased at the expense of grain. By the time the true grain production level was understood in April 1959, it was too late (Li 1962, Chao 1970, Walker 1984). To make matters worse, 1959 yields were low, due to poor weather. Catastrophic weather in 1960 and the political and administrative chaos precipitated by famine had devastating effects on subsequent production.

In contrast to the period from the late 1950s to the early 1960s for which major increases in cv were common to production, area, and yield for each crop, major cv increases since the mid-1960s were confined to production and yield. The declining trend in the cvs for areas sown to grain, as well as for each grain crop individually, may be ascribed to increasing administrative control over sown area in China.

The area cvs tended to increase after the mid-1970s, with increasing decentralization of production decisions to individual farm families. Yet the relative weakness of this increase is a testament to the inertia present in areas operating through agricultural administration and perhaps embedded in farmers' own decision-making processes. Though the decontrol is genuine in principle, substantial sown area planning efforts continue in many regions.

Significant cv increases in production and area since the mid-1960s are confined to particular crops, unlike the initial period of instability. The marked increase in maize yield cvs during the 1960s and early 1970s is difficult to investigate due to lack of data. The pattern is not easily explainable by weather or rapid expansion into risk-prone farm areas. Most Chinese maize is subject to damage from frost, drought, heat, and waterlogging, and planting is concentrated in particularly risky regions (e.g., North and Northeast China). But wheat has also been grown in very risk-prone areas, and irrigation of wheat did not accelerate until the 1970s, when its rising cv path paradoxically crossed the declining path for maize. Given the scanty data available, the following hypothesis may explain maize yields and yield cvs.

Maize yield cvs increased rapidly in the 1950s, due to rapid growth in sown area concentrated in the Northeast provinces of Liaoning, Jilin, and Heilongjiang, and the adjacent north China provinces of Hebei and Shandong. Maize areas in these regions are highly risk-prone (Stone et al. 1985), and weather patterns are highly correlated, further accentuating the increase in cvs.

The anomaly then becomes not the higher maize cvs of the late 1960s, but the sharp decline in cvs during the 1962–64 period to values below those of the 1950s. There is some statistical evidence that maize area was cut back sharply in 1962 (Zhongguo Kexueyuan 1980) in response to a maize disease epidemic in 1961 (Wiens 1978, p. 677). While maize area recovered somewhat in 1963, it remained quite constant during 1963-65, well below the aggregate levels of the middle and late 1950s (Zhongguo Guojia Tongjiju 1984b). Weather, according to Kueh's (1984, 1986) analyses, remained relatively favorable throughout this period and featured similar and low aggregate estimates of gross crop damage. Subsequently, as maize area recovered in the Northeast, yield variability increased. The year 1966, in particular, was reported as one of especially widespread maize disease (Wiens 1978), while throughout the late 1960s the increased weather variability and highly correlated weather patterns of the expansion region would contribute to higher cvs.

Disease-resistant hybrids covered 40 percent of maize area by 1973 (Wiens 1978, p. 677) and 60 percent by 1978 (Stone 1980, p. 158). With their success, maize area surpassed the 1950s peak years for the first time in 1974 and exceeded wheat area in a few years at the turn of the decade. Although irrigation of maize is increasing, most maize remains rainfed and the drop in cvs cannot be primarily ascribed to irrigation. It may be associated with the lower disease susceptibility of the single-cross hybrids and rapid expansion into regions for which weather patterns are not correlated with those of the Northeast and the northeastern North China Plain.

Rapid dissemination of semidwarf wheat varieties and rapid area expansion in highly correlated areas may also explain the increase in wheat cvs in the mid-1970s and early 1980s. The principal growth region in the 1960s was North China, characterized by highly correlated internal weather patterns and increased irrigation of winter wheat. In fact, irrigation provision was often a requisite condition for winter wheat introduction in the North.

More irrigated wheat, however, did not necessarily provide greater stability against drought, the predominant yield risk in the region. Irrigation facilities may have proved unreliable, in some years providing much higher yields and in others no change from the "unirrigated" state. This could be particularly destabilizing in the aggregate if unreliabilities and weather patterns were highly correlated. For surface irrigation there is considerable evidence that this is so. When winter wheat in North China requires irrigation, no rain usually means no river flow (Stone 1983 and Chinese papers in the same collection). The Yellow River remains the major exception, but its water has been difficult to use due to its high silt content. The years 1976, 1977, and 1978 all had poor weather with the principal disaster areas being within North China, and the principal disaster being drought.

Since a large portion of North China irrigation development has been tubewell construction during the late 1960s and 1970s, correlated yield failures may be due to a major administrative failure to deliver key requisite inputs. This could indeed have happened during the chaotic period associated with the Gang of Four successional struggle. For example, there is some evidence that agricultural users were among those most heavily penalized during the 1978 electrical shortage within the North and Northeast power grids (Stone 1980), but the availability of detailed information is low.

Why have foodgrain production cvs not fallen during the past four decades? If the data midpoints in figure 3.1 corresponding to the Great Leap Forward (1958–59) policies and the catastrophic weather (1960–61) are taken as an exceptional period of instability, then study must focus on the periods represented by the midpoints of 1954–56 and 1964–83, which, in turn, provide no clear evidence of long-term decline in cvs. Yet China's reduction of weather-related agricultural risk for thousands of localities is well known. Irrigated area increased from 16 to 45 million hectares (ha) (around 45 percent of cultivated area) and its reliability vastly improved. Flood control efforts have achieved considerable success. Modern varieties combining improved maximum yields with locality-specific weather and disease tolerances have been developed, along with considerable breeding for earlier maturing varieties. The resulting aggregate multiple cropping index increased from 1.2 to 1.5, thereby reducing the annual aggregate production risk associated with very bad weather in any one season.

Consequently "high and stable yield" areas now comprise one-third of cultivated area, around one-half of sown area, and account for not less than three-quarters of national grain production. Why then have production cvs not declined since the 1950s? The succeeding sections will try to answer this question and to clarify the issues relating to the increases in wheat production cvs since the early 1970s.

The Variance Decomposition Exercise:
The Data, Implications of Selected Data Periods, and Detrending

To better examine structural change in production variance across different periods for China, the variance decomposition method of chapter 2 has been employed. To identify the important components of the change in aggregate production variance, however, the selection of data period has been severely constrained by the availability and quality of provincial and crop data.

From original source material compiled in provincial statistical collections, including Chen (1967), Social Science Research Council (1969), CIA (1969), and Wiens (1980), an analysis of additional disaggregated provincial data by Walker (1984) and IFPRI has culminated in disaggregated series for 1952–57 of quality sufficient to attempt an initial variance decomposition study. Data reported by PRC provincial authorities prior to

1952 and for 1958-61 are unreliable, while full reliability and completeness of data even for 1962-78 present problems (Wiens 1980, Stone 1983, 1984a).

The data for the study are, therefore, constrained yet were the only disaggregated data available of sufficient quality and continuity for a variance decomposition during the People's Republic period, 1952-57 and 1979-83. Even within these temporal limitations, data for a number of crops and provinces had to be excluded due to insufficiently independent estimates for consecutive years or other problems of reliability. The final data cover only wheat (for 21 of 26 provinces), rice (for 18 provinces) and "other foodcrops" as a group (consisting of all other cereals, plus soybeans, other miscellaneous leguminous crops, and sweet and white potatoes). It was possible to include, however, almost all the important wheat- and rice-producing provinces.

While chosen solely on the basis of data availability, continuity, and reliability, the two periods are fully appropriate for a comparison of pre- and post-green revolution patterns. Seed selection and strain improvement along with organic fertilization had been traditional in Chinese agriculture. However, manufactured fertilizer application was not widespread in China until the late 1960s (Dalrymple 1978, p. 41; Stone 1980, pp. 122, 155-71; Stone 1986a,b).

Semidwarf rice varieties were first developed in Chinese research institutions during 1956-59 (Wiens 1978, p. 676; Dalrymple 1978, p. 78; IRRI/CAAS 1980, p. 9) and high-yielding hybrid rice, a fully Chinese technical innovation, was first grown by farmers in 1975 (Wiens 1978, p. 679; IRRI/CAAS 1980, p. 10). Semidwarf wheat varieties from Chinese-Mexican crosses were initially planted on farmers' fields in 1973 (Dalrymple 1978, p. 41; Stavis 1978, pp. 638, 645; Wiens 1978, p. 677), although imported fertilizer-responsive varieties were used on farms as early as 1957, and Chinese research institutions and breeding stations were releasing their own varieties by 1960 (Stone et al. 1985). Double-cross hybrid maize was released around 1958-59 and occupied a large share of maize area in the mid-1960s but proved susceptible to disease over large areas in 1961 and 1966 (Wiens 1978, p. 677). New single-cross maize hybrids were developed and released in the late 1960s and recovered to 40 percent of maize area by 1973 (Wiens 1978, p. 677) and 60 per cent by 1978 (Stone 1980, p. 158).

By 1977, high-yielding dwarf rice varieties were sown on around 80 percent of China's rice area (Wiens 1978, p. 677) and in 1985 the proportion was around 95 percent (Dalrymple 1986a). On-farm use of hybrid rice expanded quickly from its introduction in 1975 to 20.4 percent of rice area in 1983 (Stone 1984b, table 1). If semidwarf wheat can be construed to include all varieties under 105 cm at maturity, semidwarfs exceed 70 per-

FIGURE 3.2 Fertilizer nutrient application per sown hectare in China, 1983

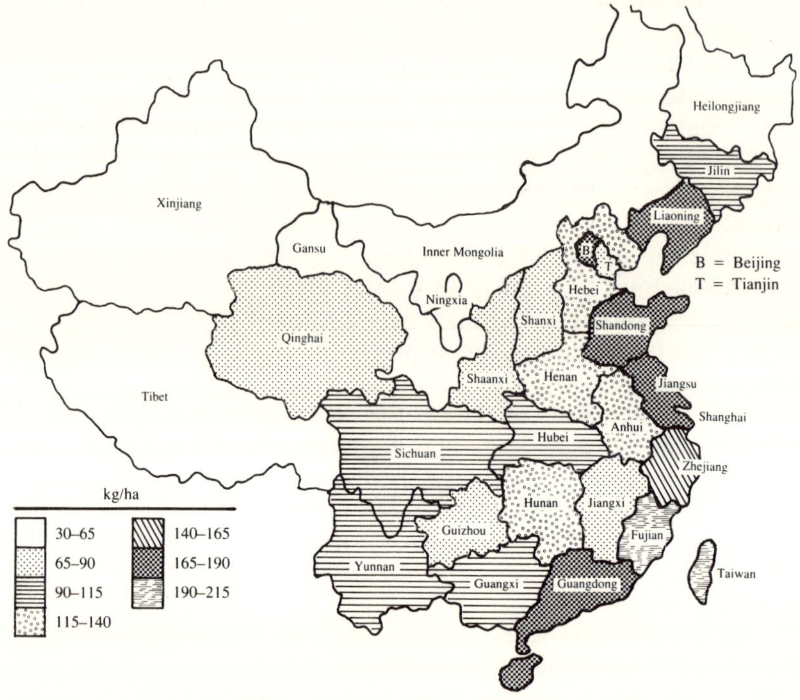

SOURCE: Stone (1986a, 460).

cent of Chinese wheat area. If the standard is 100 cm, the proportion is around 55 percent. If a standard of 85 cm is employed, the proportion is much smaller, but grew rapidly from 10 percent in 1980 to more than 30 percent in 1983 (Stone et al. 1985, Dalrymple 1986b).

Application of manufactured fertilizers averaged 0.6 kg/ha in 1952 and 2.4 kg/ha in 1957. From 1979 through 1983, average application grew from 73 to 115 kg/ha to exceed average rates in most other nations (Stone 1986a; Zhongguo Guojia Tongjiju 1984b, p. 137; FAO 1984, pp. 44-55). Such fertilizer is the principal purchased input in most Chinese provinces (figure 3.2). All in all it is clear that the period 1952-57 predates the green revolution in China and that, by 1979-83, the technical transformation of Chinese agriculture was already considerably advanced. The second period also falls within the peculiar years of higher wheat production cvs, while the first period considerably precedes them.

The data period ends prior to the formation throughout most of China of the people's communes and the radical policy initiatives of the Great Leap Forward (1958-59), as well as the unusually severe natural disasters which caused or seriously accentuated the famine of 1960-61. However, this first period spans the formation of agricultural cooperatives (1952-56), the establishment of a state grain market (1953), and the imposition of fixed quotas of grain to be delivered from each unit of farmland (1955) (Chao 1970, pp. 44-68; Stone 1980, pp. 147-8). It also spans a period of some instability in purchase prices for cereals, although the cash costs for inputs were consistently minor throughout the 1950s (Stone 1980, 1984c).

The second period postdates major rural organizational reforms, a three-tiered structure for grain prices including free-market cereals prices, and significant procurement pricing changes after the Cultural Revolution (Stone 1980, pp. 147-53). And while farm price and market structures remained reasonably constant during 1979-83, rapid growth in yields because of greater fertilizer availability allowed average and especially marginal prices that many farmers faced, as well as the degree with which they interacted with private versus public markets, to change considerably during the period. Thus while 1952-57 and 1979-83 (or even 1979-84) are periods of greater internal consistency than surrounding periods, such continuity is imperfect in both cases.

Detrending required to complete the variability comparisons and the variance decomposition exercise posed a problem, because of the lengthy period separating the two internally contiguous data sets. Due to major structural changes in Chinese agriculture during the 1960s and 1970s (Stone 1980), the factors governing trend increase in yields during the two data periods were thoroughly dissimilar. Yet the periods are so short that separate linear trends could jeopardize the results through loss of the extra degree of freedom. A single quadratic trend was, therefore, estimated for total foodcrops and for each crop (production, area, and yield) for the entire 1952-83 period.

Changes in Means and Variability

Table 3.1 summarizes the changes in Chinese foodgrain production between the two periods in the included provinces. Average foodgrain production increased from 166 to 317 million metric tons, or by 90 percent. This accords quite well with the increase for all provinces between the two periods: from an average of 173 (1952-57) to 344 million metric tons (1979-83) or by 98 percent (Stone 1984a, p. 605; Zhongguo Guojia Tongjiju 1984c, p. 145). Paddy rice production for the group of included provinces increased from 67 to 131 million metric tons, or 96 percent between periods (from 76 to 152 Mt, or 99 percent for all provinces). Wheat pro-

TABLE 3.1 Changes in the mean and variability of national foodcrop production, area, and yield in the People's Republic of China

Crop	Means			Coefficient of Variation				No. of Provinces
	I	II	Change (percent)	I	II	Change (percent)	F Ratio	
Production	(Mt)							
Total grains	166	317	90.5	0.022	0.085*	286.4	56.35*	8/11/21
Rice	67	131	95.6	0.050	0.063	26.0	6.12	6/7/18
Wheat	21	63	199.3	0.062	0.137*	121.0	44.02*	7/12/21
Other crops	79	123	56.6	0.022	0.063*	186.4	19.51*	4/6/21
Area	(million ha)							
Total grains	123	109	−11.6	0.007	0.031	342.9	16.01*	2/5/21
Rice	27	30	9.7	0.050	0.005*	−90.0	0.01*	2/2/18
Wheat	26	28	7.8	0.024	0.020	−16.7	0.79	3/3/21
Other crops	71	52	−26.6	0.011	0.041*	272.7	8.13	1/4/21
Yield	(t/ha)							
Total grains	1.35	2.91	115.6	0.020	0.056*	180.0	35.17*	6/15/21
Rice	2.52	4.49	78.2	0.026	0.061*	134.6	17.14*	5/5/18
Wheat	0.82	2.27	176.8	0.050	0.120*	140.0	45.35*	11/17/21
Other crops	1.11	2.37	113.7	0.025	0.037	48.0	10.46*	3/7/21

Note: I = First Period: 1952–57, II = Second Period: 1979–83. Asterisks on the F ratios indicate statistically significant homogeneity of variance tests and asterisks on the second period cvs denote that the cv in the second period is significantly different from that of the first, both at least at the 5 percent level. Although these are described as "national" results, they are based on sums of data for only the provinces included in the study (see text). The three numbers in the final column on the right indicate the number of provinces for which the F tests for homogeneity of variance over the two periods indicated apparently significant differences between the two periods at the 1 and 5 percent levels, and the total number of included provinces, respectively.

duction for included provinces increased 199 percent, from an average of 21 to 63 million metric tons (from 22 to 65 Mt, or by 200 percent, for all provinces).

Among remaining cereal crops, the outstanding contributor to foodgrain production growth was maize, which increased throughout China from a mean of 19 million metric tons in the first period to 62 million metric tons in the second period, or by 223 percent (Zhongguo Guojia Tongjiju 1984c, p. 145). Maize represented a rapidly increasing proportion of "other foodcrops" in China (23 percent in the first period and 49 percent in the second period). Together, rice, wheat, and maize increased their share of total Chinese food crop production (Chinese definition) from 68 to 81 percent. Production of "other foodcrops" (including maize) among included provinces increased from 79 to 123 million metric tons.

All of the increase in national foodgrain production is attributable to changes in average yields, which increased 116 percent to 2.9 tons per hectare among included provinces, while area declined by 12 percent. But this increase in average total grain yields was partly due to a shift in composition of grain sown area, with wheat and rice area among included provinces rising by 8 and 10 percent, respectively, while those of other foodcrops declined by 27 percent. Among other foodcrops, however, area sown with maize, the most widely planted "other" crop, increased throughout China by 36 percent, implying a very sharp decline in area sown with millet, sorghum, barley, soybeans, potato crops, and other minor grains and bean crops (Zhongguo Guojia Tongjiju 1984b, p. 138). Among these latter crop categories, only white potatoes increased in area (Stone 1984a, p. 628).

Although part of the total grain production growth was attributable to changes in crop composition, it was dominated by increasing yields. Among included provinces, average yields increased from 0.8 to 2.3 tons per hectare (177 percent) for wheat, from 2.5 to 4.5 tons per hectare for paddy (78 percent) and from 1.1 to 2.4 tons per hectare (114 percent) for other foodcrops. Among other foodcrops, final average yields and their rates of growth differed considerably, although all registered gains. For all of China the leaders in growth between the two periods were maize, sorghum, and potato crops, for which yields increased by 139, 129, and 84 percent to second period averages of 3.2, 2.6, and (at $1/4$ weight) 3.5 tons per hectare, respectively. In contrast, millet and soybean yields increased by 48 and 42 percent to 1.6 and 1.1 tons per hectare. Yields for barley and other minor grains and bean crops also grew slowly from very low base levels (Stone 1984a, p. 608, 1984b; Zhongguo Guojia Tongjiju 1984b, p. 47).

The coefficient of variation of total grain production increased 286 percent among included provinces, which was statistically significant at

TABLE 3.2 Analysis of the components of change in mean foodgrain production in China, 1952-1957 to 1979-1983 (percent)

Crop	"Pure" Changes in Yields	"Pure" Changes in Area	Changes in Area-Yield Covariances	Interaction between Mean Yields and Mean Areas
Rice	81	10.3	0.08	9
Wheat	95	6.5	−0.05	−1
Other crops	205	−45.0	0.53	−61
Total foodcrops	122	−7.1	0.18	−15

the 5 percent level or better. This significance result was echoed individually for wheat and "other crops" (for which the cvs increased by 121 and 186 percent, respectively) but not for rice. The cv for total grain area grew 343 percent, with the increase again significant but from a very small cv to another small cv. Wheat and rice actually registered nominal declines in area variability. The cv for yield increased by 135 percent for rice, 140 percent for wheat, 48 percent for "other crops" and 180 percent for total foodgrains, each (except for "other crops") proving to be a statistically significant increase.

Results from the Mean and Variance Decomposition Procedures

Applying Hazell's decomposition method to the change in average foodgrain production between the 1952-57 and 1979-83 periods, changes in yields are confirmed to be the most important component (table 3.2). For total foodcrops, changes in yields accounted for 122 percent of the mean production change between periods, while loss of area reduced the production impact of increasing yields by 7 percent, and interaction between mean yields and mean areas, by 15 percent. This last figure indicates that, where area increased (decreased), average yields decreased (increased). Reduction of foodcrop-sown area primarily involves low-yielding lands, despite well-publicized administrative complaints that considerable areas of high-yielding land have been lost to irrigation structures, roads, and buildings. Hence, where area increased (especially in the major reclamation provinces of Heilongjiang and Inner Mongolia) average yield tended to decline due to low productivity on the newly reclaimed land.

The area-yield interaction effect was very weakly negative for wheat (1 percent) and actually positive for rice (9 percent). In provinces where rice yields were rising, a particular effort was probably made to increase rice area, an influence related to the primacy of the fine-grains procurement issue in central policy and planning (Stone 1984c, Walker 1984). Wheat's weakly negative area-yield interactive effect could be considered a balance between a similar (positively correlated) effort for wheat and the (negatively correlated) expansion of wheat onto relatively unsuitable lands. "Pure" yield changes accounted for 81 percent of the change in the mean aggregate rice production level between periods (and 95 percent for wheat), while ("pure") increased rice area accounted for 10 percent of the aggregate rice production level change (and less than 7 percent for wheat).

Table 3.3 itemizes the contribution of various components of the increase in the variance of total foodgrain production between the two periods. Increases in interprovincial covariances account for 91.4 percent of the production variance increase for total foodcrops (table 3.3), 87.8 percent for rice (table 3.4), 84.6 percent for wheat (table 3.5) and 72.6 percent for "other foodcrops" (table 3.6). This is consistent with results obtained for India (Hazell 1982, 1984), the United States (Hazell 1984), the U.S.S.R. (Nguyen 1985, table 4), Syria (Nguyen, ch. 5), and Australia (Anderson et al. 1988), though the effect appears strongest for China.

Unlike the United States and India, but like the Soviet Union, the Chinese cross covariance contribution (between different crops in different provinces) exceeds the within-crop covariance effect among provinces. This may represent a characteristic feature of central planning where state-supplied inputs are allocated for specific crops in provinces where authorities aspire to purchase marketable surpluses. The state may also contribute to this peculiar pattern of interprovincial correlation through fixed quotas for specific grains in each province to facilitate exports, through pricing policies which have provided much higher marginal returns to grain deliveries above assigned quotas, and by allocating fertilizers in exchange for desired commodities (Stone 1980, 1984b, 1986b).

The changes in provincial crop production variances account for only 6.1 percent of the change in the variance of total foodgrain production (1.5 percent from rice, 2.4 percent from wheat, and 2.2 percent from other crops). This is a particularly small proportion compared with that found in other country studies. Also striking is the especially small contribution of intercrop covariances within provinces (2.5 percent), perhaps because intercrop covariances were already high in the first period.

The interaction effect between mean area levels and yield variances and covariances, and the interaction effect between mean yield levels and area variances and covariances are offsetting and particularly important for rice (see table 3.4). The positive value for the first of these interaction terms is not surprising. As area increases (onto less suitable and more poorly serviced lands) the variability of yields tends to increase. This interaction effect is particularly strong but negative for "other crops" (table

TABLE 3.3 Analysis of the components of change in the variance of total grain production in China, 1952-1957 to 1979-1983 (percent)

Crop Variance	Changes in Mean Yields	Changes in Mean Areas	Changes in Yield Variances and Covariances	Changes in Area Variances and Covariances	Changes in Area-Yield Covariances
Rice	1.4	0.2	1.6	−0.8	0.2
Wheat	0.5	−0.0	1.9	−0.0	0.0
Other	0.8	−0.4	3.5	−0.1	0.5
Total variances within provinces	2.6	−0.2	7.0	−0.9	0.8
Intercrop covariances within provinces	0.6	−0.0	1.1	−0.2	0.4
Interprovince covariances within crops	5.8	0.3	23.8	−1.8	1.9
Covariances between different crops in different provinces	5.9	−0.4	33.8	−1.1	9.8
Column sums	14.9	−0.3	65.7	−4.1	12.9

3.6). This may indicate that land going out of "other crop" production was relatively good land which left the remaining production of "other crops" in a more unstable state on average.

The interaction term between mean yields and area variances and covariances is negative for the aggregated provinces in each crop category and may also reflect central planning effects. The impact is especially strong for rice. In provinces exhibiting rising yields, successful efforts were made to stabilize area to help guarantee procurement despite relatively low prices for rice (Stone 1984b). Conversely, in areas where effective control was achieved, state authorities focused current inputs and infrastructural investments, thereby raising yields. In any event, several items in the decomposition suggest relative success in crop area stabilization between the 1950s and 1979-84.

The most important result of the variance decomposition is the particular dominance of the interregional covariances, especially among yields. This is very likely the reason that the cvs for yield and production of total foodgrains, as well as of the individual grains, do not appear to have de-

| | Change in Interaction Terms between | | | | Total |
Mean Yields and Mean Areas	Mean Areas and Yield Variances and Covariances	Mean Yields and Area Variances and Covariances	Mean Yields, Mean Areas, and Area-Yield Covariances	Changes in Residual	Contribution to Change in Variance of Production in China
0.0	0.1	−1.4	0.2	0.1	1.5
−0.0	0.1	−0.1	0.0	0.0	2.4
0.2	−1.8	−1.0	0.3	0.1	2.2
0.2	−1.6	−2.5	0.5	0.3	6.1
−0.0	0.3	−0.0	0.4	0.0	2.5
0.1	0.5	−4.3	2.9	0.8	30.0
−0.3	1.7	−2.2	12.2	2.0	61.4
−0.0	0.9	−9.0	15.9	3.0	100.0

clined during more than three decades (figure 3.1). The most plausible explanation for this increase in interprovincial covariances is that Chinese farmers are now much more responsive to central policy and to national market influences in general.

Issues relating to the genetic base for high-yielding crop varieties constitute an input hypothesis related to the central policy theme. It has been suggested for the United States and for the U.S.S.R. (Hazell 1984, Nguyen 1985) that many regionally adapted varieties of a crop were replaced by a very few higher yielding varieties sown broadly across regions, and that this development may have contributed to increased interregional correlations in yield and hence to increased aggregate variance. Comparing the 1960s in China (a period of particular national production variability but poor provincial data) with the 1950s, the proportions of wheat, rice, and maize area planted with just a few closely related varieties increased dramatically. Since the 1960s, however, more regionally adapted high-yielding varieties have proliferated, somewhat reducing the area sown with any single variety. Difficulties associated with central authorities promoting overly

TABLE 3.4 Analysis of the components of change in the variance of rice production by province in China, 1952-1957 to 1979-1983 (percent)

Province	Changes in Mean Yields	Changes in Mean Areas	Changes in Yield Variances and Covariances	Changes in Area Variances and Covariances	Changes in Area-Yield Covariances
Hebei, Beijing Tianjin	270.7	0.7	−47.4	−126.8	173.9
Nei Monggol	−101.7	−4.6	19.1	164.1	−70.3
Liaoning	−333.3	−90.9	15.6	36.8	37.5
Jilin	−212.6	−33.1	9.5	67.0	31.4
Heilongjiang	14.8	3.8	40.4	38.3	−29.7
Jiangsu and Shanghai	4.6	5.3	48.0	−5.3	10.7
Anhui	529.9	1.3	318.5	−265.4	6.4
Jiangxi	20.1	11.2	71.7	−8.8	−1.5
Shandong	6.1	8.6	0.3	19.4	−8.5
Henan	8.9	−0.1	43.7	2.7	21.5
Hubei	45.8	38.2	64.9	−14.2	−37.8
Hunan	26.7	22.2	17.2	−19.2	38.6
Guangxi	156.0	4.6	78.1	−61.5	37.4
Guangdong	3.8	−0.2	114.4	−0.8	9.6
Sichuan	−1,443.6	18.1	−878.0	1,040.1	−275.4
Guizhou	17.0	−0.8	145.8	−20.6	−5.7
Yunnan	0.2	0.1	29.7	9.5	35.7
Shaanxi	0.9	0.7	86.5	−0.1	−11.8
Interprovince covariances	41.8	3.0	83.6	−18.3	9.3
All provinces	47.7	4.1	86.9	−22.3	10.1

rapid and intensive adoption of specific high-yielding varieties have been documented for maize in the 1960s (Wiens 1978, p. 677; Stone 1980, pp. 157-8), and for hybrid rice in the late 1970s and early 1980s (Stone 1984c). But it may be more valuable to focus attention on wheat, for which the yield and production cvs increased most notably between 1952-57 and 1975-84.

During the late 1970s and early 1980s, nine varieties accounted for 14.5 million hectares (one-half of national wheat sown area) in a few of the major wheat-growing zones; and a number of these varieties have closely related genealogies (Stone et al. 1985). But although the numbers of varieties were considerably fewer than during the 1950s, they had been bred with greater experience and attention to disaster risks than those of the 1960s.

Mean Yields and Mean Areas	Change in Interaction Terms between			Changes in Residual	Total Contribution to Change in Variance of Production in China
	Mean Areas and Yield Variances and Covariances	Mean Yields and Area Variances and Covariances	Mean Yields, Mean Areas, and Area-Yield Covariances		
−99.7	−80.8	−396.8	384.9	21.4	0.0
−4.0	−6.3	1,213.8	−5.6	−14.4	0.0
−65.5	43.8	263.1	175.4	17.6	−0.1
−13.5	10.3	181.1	56.8	3.1	−0.1
−2.2	16.6	19.0	−13.1	12.2	0.0
−3.3	35.7	−12.5	15.3	1.4	3.5
−0.2	4.2	−558.5	4.9	58.9	0.5
−0.2	29.2	−20.7	−1.7	0.7	0.4
2.5	17.2	186.5	−135.2	3.2	0.0
0.5	−11.3	11.5	20.8	1.7	0.2
7.3	54.4	−22.8	−45.0	9.2	2.0
−5.1	10.3	−43.4	49.6	3.1	1.7
−6.7	29.8	−192.1	51.9	2.5	0.5
0.2	−31.7	−2.9	7.8	−0.2	2.9
−22.4	216.0	1,608.9	−106.1	−57.7	−0.4
−0.1	−18.1	−14.8	−1.3	−1.4	0.2
−0.0	4.6	6.6	14.3	−0.8	0.7
0.1	27.8	0.0	−5.0	0.8	0.0
0.2	16.1	−41.4	3.6	2.6	87.8
0.2	15.1	−48.0	4.1	3.0	100.0

Examining table 3.7, it is immediately clear that a much greater number of provincial yield (and even production) variances tested as nonhomogenous between the periods in the case of wheat than for rice and for "other crops." Of those testing nonhomogenous, only two recorded declines in variance (neither significant at the 1 percent level): for yields, only Anhui and Jiangsu; for production, only Anhui and Yunnan. Contrasting sharply with the results for rice and for "other crops," all of the largest five wheat producers exhibited significant increases in production variability.

Among the next nine provinces of intermediate importance for wheat (each with 1.2 to 7.3 percent of national production), production variability increases were not significant at the 5 percent level only for Xinjiang, Shanxi and Anhui. Some 81.5 percent of Xinjiang's farmland and virtually all Xinjiang wheat are irrigated, by far the highest proportion in China

TABLE 3.5 Analysis of the components of change in the variance of wheat production by province in China, 1952-1957 to 1979-1983 (percent)

Province	Changes in Mean Yields	Changes in Mean Areas	Changes in Yield Variances and Covariances	Changes in Area Variances and Covariances	Changes in Area-Yield Covariances
Hebei, Beijing Tianjin	6.0	0.8	49.5	−0.7	3.1
Shanxi	41.5	−9.8	161.5	−5.1	−0.5
Nei Monggol	2.7	17.7	34.7	−0.0	−12.5
Liaoning	−2,843.2	−4.7	−342.8	152.0	−29.2
Jilin	5.5	9.5	−6.7	16.8	−2.6
Heilongjiang	11.0	5.5	14.7	4.4	−1.5
Jiangsu and Shanghai	30.8	−1.5	60.9	5.9	−23.9
Anhui	63.0	−12.0	186.6	−2.4	1.3
Jiangxi	10.8	−4.2	156.0	−4.3	−12.9
Shandong	2.8	−0.8	94.5	0.1	8.0
Henan	78.2	−3.4	142.3	−5.2	−2.9
Hubei	22.6	1.5	48.7	−4.0	7.6
Hunan	107.3	−1.8	74.2	−16.2	11.9
Guangxi	−727.2	−31.6	−41.0	167.6	−51.7
Guangdong	101.6	−4.0	276.7	39.8	−185.9
Sichuan	0.1	1.4	28.0	0.2	0.1
Guizhou	2.5	262.4	−101.7	49.2	118.6
Yunnan	8.1	22.6	70.5	122.8	−161.3
Shaanxi	−1.5	0.2	75.2	0.8	12.0
Gansu	9.0	1.7	74.3	−1.5	1.3
Xinjiang	−1.2	283.9	84.3	139.6	−276.9
Interprovince covariances	4.8	0.5	68.1	−0.2	2.7
All provinces	7.0	0.4	69.8	−0.2	2.4

(Stone et al. 1985). The performance of Shanxi and Anhui may be related to the unusually high cv in the first period for both provinces (25 percent), coupled with relatively large wheat area reductions (21 and 26 percent), augmented by irrigation expansion.

But from table 3.5 it is clear that it is not the individual provincial changes in production variance, but the increased interprovincial covariances that account for most (85 percent) of the increased aggregate wheat production variance.

Mean Yields and Mean Areas	Change in Interaction Terms between			Changes in Residual	Total Contribution to Change in Variance of Production in China
	Mean Areas and Yield Variances and Covariances	Mean Yields and Area Variances and Covariances	Mean Yields, Mean Areas, and Area-Yield Covariances		
−0.4	34.9	−4.9	8.3	3.5	4.3
−3.0	−61.5	−26.0	−0.5	3.5	0.3
1.1	75.2	−0.1	−19.3	0.4	0.1
−52.5	312.8	2,915.6	−9.6	1.7	0.0
0.1	−8.7	85.7	−7.1	7.4	0.0
−0.6	65.2	15.3	−5.8	−8.3	0.7
1.4	−19.3	106.8	−61.5	0.4	1.2
−3.0	−84.5	−49.6	3.1	−2.4	0.5
−0.6	−37.5	−5.5	−4.1	2.4	0.0
0.0	−22.6	0.7	14.3	3.1	3.7
−2.7	−41.4	−59.9	−5.9	0.9	2.1
−2.4	31.9	−19.9	16.2	−2.2	0.2
0.3	−16.2	−65.7	11.8	−5.5	0.0
−63.5	39.3	774.2	25.9	8.0	0.0
0.1	−70.0	142.2	−145.2	−55.4	0.0
−0.8	71.5	0.9	0.3	−1.7	1.2
−43.7	−422.6	29.3	211.1	−5.1	0.0
−0.1	253.8	145.2	−339.8	−21.8	0.0
−0.0	1.1	1.9	10.3	0.1	0.9
0.5	16.1	−3.7	1.4	1.1	0.4
−5.6	274.1	90.2	−453.0	−35.6	0.0
0.5	10.0	−3.5	17.5	−0.4	84.6
0.3	8.9	−3.3	15.0	−0.2	100.0

Hypotheses Explaining Increased Interprovincial Correlations and Yield Variability

In table 3.8, detrended pairwise yield correlations for the 1979–83 period have been calculated for only those provinces contributing more than 1 percent to the increase in the variance of national wheat production. These provinces also happen to be the five largest wheat producers and five provinces within which wheat production increased most between the two

TABLE 3.6 Analysis of the components of change in the variance of other crop production by province in China, 1952-1957 to 1979-1983 (percent)

Province	Changes in Mean Yields	Changes in Mean Areas	Changes in Yield Variances and Covariances	Changes in Area Variances and Covariances	Changes in Area-Yield Covariances
Hebei, Beijing Tianjin	−43.0	85.2	71.4	18.0	−40.4
Shanxi	54.2	−5.3	172.0	−15.0	9.8
Nei Monggol	−36.8	68.1	15.3	10.8	7.0
Liaoning	−0.2	−1.9	122.5	1.2	16.8
Jilin	0.2	−1.1	122.4	0.1	11.4
Heilongjiang	6.6	−1.4	102.1	−5.0	4.7
Jiangsu and Shanghai	36,841.2	366.0	16,885.2	−4,178.4	2,758.7
Anhui	13.1	−53.6	102.7	10.7	50.0
Jiangxi	−167.5	76.2	170.8	99.8	−107.4
Shandong	142.2	202.2	−247.4	14.3	−108.1
Henan	1.4	−3.4	185.0	3.2	4.4
Hubei	−101.0	66.2	−4.2	34.7	7.8
Hunan	−6.1	−40.1	−83.6	34.8	16.6
Guangxi	−255.1	36.9	−88.7	115.2	−11.4
Guangdong	8.1	−6.2	3.6	35.0	21.2
Sichuan	−164.1	9.8	99.8	69.3	−65.3
Guizhou	537.7	−0.6	227.1	−205.8	33.9
Yunnan	68.7	17.7	31.6	−101.1	117.3
Shaanxi	23.0	−1.5	103.8	−16.3	35.2
Gansu	14.6	−96.0	186.5	14.6	97.8
Xinjiang	59.0	83.7	502.7	769.9	−1,215.4
Interprovince covariances	11.5	−1.7	98.0	3.1	9.8
All provinces	18.6	−6.3	115.9	0.4	13.6

periods. Although there was a decrease in wheat yield cv between the two periods for Jiangsu (and increases for each of the other provinces), the actual yields among all these provinces are highly correlated in the 1979-83 period. This includes some of the most distant pairs of provinces such as Jiangsu and Sichuan, and Hebei and Sichuan, for which reliability of the correlation appears quite high. In fact, the least correlated and least reliable correlation is for the adjacent provinces of Jiangsu and Shandong. Although some of these provinces have highly correlated weather patterns, this relationship does not include all of those with highly correlated yields during the period. Two important conclusions may be drawn from exami-

	Change in Interaction Terms between				Total Contribution to Change in Variance of Production in China
Mean Yields and Mean Areas	Mean Areas and Yield Variances and Covariances	Mean Yields and Area Variances and Covariances	Mean Yields, Mean Areas, and Area-Yield Covariances	Changes in Residual	
−11.0	−27.5	86.2	−35.8	−3.0	−1.1
3.1	−59.5	−70.2	9.1	1.9	0.6
4.0	−6.0	16.7	1.7	19.4	−0.4
0.2	−62.6	6.0	12.2	5.8	4.9
0.3	−48.2	0.4	8.6	5.8	10.7
0.0	−4.7	−5.5	2.0	1.0	3.5
6,253.7	−12,274.5	−48,564.7	2,346.7	−333.7	0.0
−1.7	−73.4	33.1	4.0	15.1	1.7
−42.3	−120.3	258.2	−3.1	−64.3	−0.1
−96.8	164.5	84.3	−56.0	0.7	−0.7
1.3	−116.2	14.6	1.9	7.8	8.2
7.8	2.9	79.9	0.2	5.7	−0.6
8.2	43.5	111.4	6.9	8.4	0.3
−0.8	33.3	255.5	−4.8	19.9	−0.1
−0.4	−2.3	44.7	−2.2	−1.3	0.4
−6.2	−14.0	226.4	−59.7	4.0	−0.9
0.0	−3.1	−531.1	29.8	12.0	0.0
−9.1	10.6	−126.3	85.9	4.6	0.1
4.0	−21.5	−56.8	31.1	−0.8	0.8
1.0	−123.8	9.9	−24.4	19.8	0.2
−44.4	460.4	601.3	−1,014.3	−103.0	0.0
0.5	−45.1	11.7	2.7	9.4	72.6
2.6	−55.4	−3.7	5.8	8.6	100.0

nation of tables 3.5 and 3.8: (a) Those provinces that are individually contributing the most to increased wheat production variance are not only China's largest wheat producers, but exhibit highly correlated wheat yields in the second period, and so are apt to be major contributors to the increased interprovincial yield correlations that are the predominant factor associated with increased wheat production variability; (b) While correlated weather patterns and the similar response of similar varieties may explain some of the yield correlation among these major wheat-growing provinces in the 1979–83 period, these factors certainly do not explain all of the yield correlation, nor is there convincing evidence to suggest that

TABLE 3.7 Provinces exhibiting variance changes between 1952–1957 and 1979–1983

Province	Production				Area				Yield			
	Total Grains	Rice	Wheat	Other	Total Grains	Rice	Wheat	Other	Total Grains	Rice	Wheat	Other
National	**	*	**	**	**			*	**	**	**	**
Hebei, Beijing, Tianjin		*	**								**	
Shanxi		n.a.		*	*	n.a.		*	*	n.a.	*	*
Nei Monggol		*										
Liaoning	**		**	**				**	**		**	**
Jilin	**		**	**	**		**		**			**
Heilongjiang	*											
Jiangsu, Shanghai	**	**	**						**		**	
Anhui	*								*		*	
Jiangxi											**	
Shandong	**	**	**		**	**			**	**	**	**
Henan	**	*	*	**	*				*		**	
Hubei			**		*						*	
Hunan	*											
Guangxi									*			
Guangdong	**	**		*				*	**	**	**	
Sichuan			**						*		**	*
Guizhou	**								**	**	**	
Yunnan	**	**	*			**	**		*	**	**	**
Shanxi		**	*	**					*	**	*	
Gansu		n.a.	*			n.a.			*	n.a.	**	
Xinjiang	**	n.a.				n.a.			*	n.a.		

Note: **, * indicate statistically significant F ratios (one-tailed tests) at 1 and 5 percent confidence levels, respectively. n.a. = not available.

TABLE 3.8 Wheat yield correlation coefficients among five major producing provinces, 1979-1983

Province	Jiangsu	Shandong	Henan	Sichuan
Hebei (plus Beijing and Tianjin)	0.71	0.96	0.92	0.80
	0.11	0.00	0.00	0.05
Jiangsu (plus Shanghai)		0.48	0.65	0.79
		0.33	0.16	0.06
Shandong			0.88	0.66
			0.02	0.15
Henan				0.61
				0.19

Note: The upper number represents the correlation; the lower number the percent level of "significance."

they would explain most of the increased correlation between the two periods.

What, then, could be the cause of increased wheat yield correlation among major wheat growing provinces, to the extent that it is not due to weather and similarity among the varieties sown over broad areas? Among the input-related hypotheses, the high correlation among distant provinces such as Sichuan and Hebei would argue against linked irrigation or regional power grid allocation being the dominant cause, although these again cannot be ruled out within the North China provinces. Little is known about difficulties with the seed distribution system, but some documentation related to manufactured fertilizer use is available.

The particularly rapid rate of growth of fertilizer use has elsewhere been established as a principal contributory factor to increased foodgrain yields since the 1960s and especially since the mid-1970s. Among foodgrains, wheat has been a high priority crop upon which yield-increasing attention has been focused (Stone 1984b, 1986a). Wheat yields grew most rapidly in these major wheat producing provinces but failed to reach the 1979 level in 1980 and 1981, resuming rapid growth in 1982 and 1984. While 1980 was a poor weather year for China's main wheat producers, 1981 was not (Kueh 1984). When the state budget collapsed between 1980 and 1981 under the weight of unmanageable food subsidies and overexpansion of capital construction (Stone 1984b, 1985), one of several adjustment measures (also aimed at alleviating foreign exchange difficulties) was curtailment of imports, including fertilizers. Thus, imports of fertilizers, though growing rapidly over the period, fell in 1981.

This decline began in late 1980, in time to affect the winter wheat crop. Between October 1980 and January 1981, monthly procurement and sales of manufactured fertilizer (both imported and domestically produced) by the central marketing organization were consistently 4 to 19 percent below corresponding data for the previous year (Zhongguo Guojia Tongjiju 1984a, pp. 312-13). Imports constituted 14-19 percent of total Chinese application during the period, but considerably more for these intensive user provinces (figure 3.2), and applications of imported fertilizers were concentrated on cotton and wheat. The variability in wheat yields of the major producing provinces and the high correlations among their yields since 1979 may indeed be at least partly related to irregularities in the institutional behavior affecting fertilizer supply and purchase. Whether such difficulties were also contributory to the high cvs for the remainder of the 1974-83 period (1974-78) is difficult to verify, but 1974-76 was a foreign exchange conservation period when imports were reduced somewhat, while 1977 and 1978 were the worst weather years in wheat-growing regions since 1960-61.

Conclusions

Although the coefficient of variation for sown area of wheat, rice, maize, "other crops," and total foodgrains showed some trend decline over the entire three and one-half decade period due to increasing administrative planning and control over sown area, the coefficients of variation for yield and production showed considerable variability and no long-term dominant trend, despite the measured increase between the 1952-57 and 1979-83 terminal periods. Between these two periods there were three main subperiods of higher variability: the late 1950s and early 1960s for all crops, 1966-73 for maize, and 1974-82 for wheat. Policy and administration seem to have been important causes of variability. Weather was highly contributory in the first period and partially so in others. But aggressive state-conducted area expansion efforts for wheat and maize in risk-prone areas for which weather patterns were highly correlated must be considered as both weather and policy related. The proliferation of disease-susceptible maize hybrids may also have been contributory, but any major problem appears to have been resolved before the mid-1970s. For wheat, there may have been a similar phenomenon related to the rapid proliferation of semidwarf wheat varieties beginning around 1973, but increasing concentration of production in areas with correlated patterns of weather and irrigation water availability and variability associated with centralized control of inputs, especially fertilizers, appear more important.

All in all, the lack of trend decline in production and yield cvs (despite area stabilization, multiple cropping increases, and substantial risk-reducing capital construction efforts and technology adoption) is predominantly related to increased yield correlations among provinces. Between the two terminal periods for which variance decomposition exercises were conducted, the proportions of increased foodgrain production variance explained by increase in interprovincial covariances were high: 88 percent for rice, 85 percent for wheat, 73 percent for other food crops, and 91 percent for all food crops taken together. Hypotheses for explaining this phenomenon include increased provincial responsiveness to central policy, increased market involvement, and especially the interaction of centralized policy with supply of the agricultural inputs now critical to yield levels, particularly manufactured fertilizers.

4 An Analysis of Variability in Soviet Grain Production

JOHN R. TARRANT

One of the most dramatic changes in the grain markets since 1970 has been the rise in importance of the U.S.S.R. as one of the world's largest importers (Tarrant 1984b). Apart from a brief period in the mid-1960s, the U.S.S.R. was a net exporter of grain until 1972 when a fundamental policy switch led to rapidly rising imports. This policy change was linked to other policies to increase consumer expenditure. Incomes, especially of urban Russians, had been rising (Laird 1982), but Soviet production of consumer goods had not been able to meet the rising demand. One important area where production had not kept pace with demand was in meat and other livestock products. The policy reaction to poor grain harvests had been to use livestock herds as a grain buffer by slaughtering in times of feed shortage and building up herds when grain was available. Following the introduction of the Five Year Plan in 1971 (Barbakov 1972) livestock numbers were planned to increase at a much faster rate than had previously proved possible. If livestock herds were not to be slaughtered in times of poor harvest, the only alternative was substantial grain imports. Protecting and building up livestock numbers meant that, although the grain harvest in 1972 was not far below trend, imports were necessary, and they have continued to rise (figure 4.1).

Total grain imports reached about 55 million metric tons (Mt) in 1984/85. This is estimated to be at or even above the port handling capacity of the U.S.S.R. without serious disruption to other forms of trade (Tarrant 1981). Although this capacity is expected to increase, the future level of Soviet imports is far from clear. One might expect them to remain at or close to the recent maximum until production of domestic grain (and other

---

The author gratefully acknowledges generous financial assistance for the research leading to this paper from the Economic and Social Science Research Council of the U.K. and from the International Food Policy Research Institute, Washington, D.C. Comments from the editors and others have been most helpful, but the responsibility for the opinions expressed remains with the author.

FIGURE 4.1 Cereal production in the Soviet Union and net cereal imports

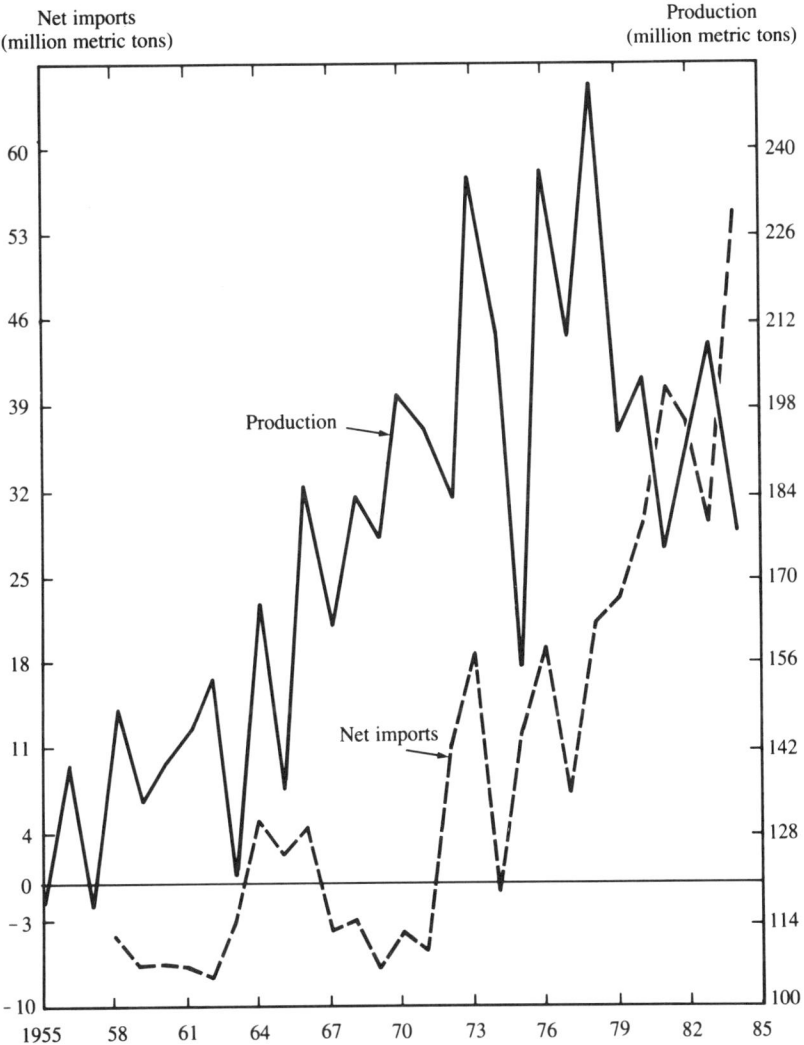

SOURCES: FAO trade yearbooks and compiled from various U.S.S.R. sources by the Foreign Agriculture Service of USDA.

fodder crops) increases sufficiently to ensure that large livestock herds can be fed from domestic resources. If, however, domestic feed production does increase, there will be a falloff in import demand. Current world prices for grains are low despite the record level of Soviet demand. The price effects of removing a substantial part of this demand would be considerable. It is, therefore, vital to understand the factors in Soviet agriculture that might bring about such a change.

Soviet grain production is characterized by great variability—a fact that has been noted by many authors (Laird 1982, Kogan 1983). Variability is also increasing in both space and time. The five years until 1985/86 were characterized by poor harvests and this has encouraged the buildup of imports. If the pattern of increasing variability continues, the market might well expect substantial falls in Soviet import demand associated with those years when harvests are good. The magnitude of the variability is much greater than imports (figure 4.1), hence a relatively small upturn in Soviet production, especially if it continued for more than one year, could more or less eliminate the need for imports.

This level of production variability is closely and linearly associated with variability in yields and has little to do with the area planted, which has been falling marginally since the expansion in the 1950s into the "newlands" of Kazakhstan and western Siberia (Nguyen 1985, Tarrant 1984a).[1] This chapter will concentrate on production rather than yield because there are generally more data on production, and it is grain production which determines food consumption and trade. Aggregated cereal production will be used due to the availability of data, rather than the production of separate cereal crops. The study will be mostly confined to the Russian Soviet Federated Socialist Republic (RSFSR), Belorussia, Moldavia, Ukraine, and Kazakhstan. These regions account for approximately 90 percent of Soviet cereal production.

There are many problems with using such Soviet data. The time series are short and there are gaps in the data runs—gaps which are not consistent throughout the U.S.S.R. Very little agricultural information is available after 1975 at an aggregate or local level. The data which are published have to be interpreted with caution. The crop area recorded is that planted not that harvested. In severe conditions the crop planted may be ploughed in and another planted—this is especially true in those areas where winter wheat may not survive the winter dormancy period and may be replaced by spring wheat. Yields have been recorded in many different ways in the U.S.S.R. In the early years biological yields were used (Hedlund 1984). Samples were taken of the growing crop and yield estimates were made on this basis. These produced considerable overestimates of true yields, especially in years of poor harvesting weather conditions. Currently the Soviets use "bunker yields"—that is, yields taken into the combines (Severin

---

1. A linear regression of production (Q), measured in millions of metric tons, against yield (Y), measured in metric tons per hectare, gives

$$Q = -2.85 + 126.5\,Y$$

with a coefficient of determination (R^2) of 0.977.

1984). Excessive moisture and often a severe shortage of vehicles to deliver the grain to elevators mean that the use of bunker yields probably overestimates yields and production by at least 10 percent over methods used in the United States and Europe (Hedlund 1984). Despite the difficulties, Soviet data do show a high degree of internal consistency, and it seems unlikely that the variations in overall production figures are seriously unreliable.

The production variability in the U.S.S.R. has both spatial and temporal elements interlinked. A marked feature is a two-year cycle where good harvests are almost invariably followed by poorer ones (Kogan 1981a). Good production in one year tends to deplete soil nutrients and moisture so that production is reduced the following year. This situation is aggravated where production is close to the dry margin for grain cultivation and where supplies of fertilizer are not reliable. Both these examples relate to the majority of Soviet grain lands and thus a marked two-year cycle is not unexpected. One of the most striking features over the past five years has been that the two-year cycle has been replaced by a run of poor harvests.

Another notable feature of Soviet production is that it is spread over at least three contrasting production regions. Most cereals are produced in the chernozem soil belt which can be divided into the dry east and the moist west. Increasingly important is the nonchernozem production area to the northwest of the country. There is little doubt that the bulk of the annual variability in production, superimposed on the two-year cycle, results from climatic conditions (Tarrant 1984a, Meshcherskaya 1983, Kogan 1981a,b) and that climatic conditions will often not be the same over these different production regions. A poor harvest in one area may be compensated by a good one elsewhere. This will be referred to here as the regional compensation effect (RCE). Once established, such regional contrasts will tend to be perpetuated in most years by the two-year production cycle. Exceptionally poor (or good) national harvests will be produced when all the major producing regions (and different cereal crops) move synchronously and there are no regional compensation effects.

Spatial Variability

If increased production is accompanied by no other significant changes, absolute spatial variability of production will rise through time—with fluctuations about a trend line (figure 4.2a)—as it will be directly dependent on production levels. Relative spatial variability will, therefore, be constant through time. There is an extensive literature in ecology concerning the relationship between mean population size and variability (Taylor, Woiwod and Perry 1978, Anderson, Turner and Taylor 1979, Taylor and

FIGURE 4.2 Spatial variability in Soviet cereal production

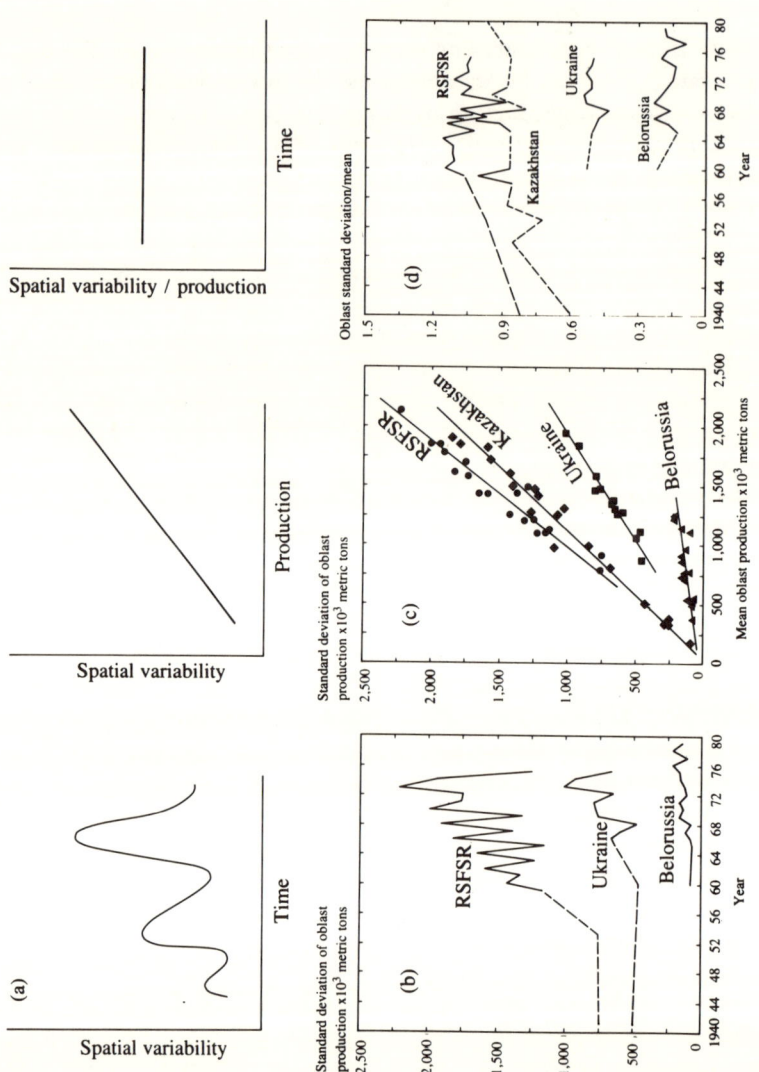

SOURCES: *Narodnoye Gospodarsvo Ukrainskoi:* Ukraine 1957, 1969, 1971, 1972, 1983. *Narodnoye Khozyaistvo Ukrainskoi:* Ukraine all other years. *Narodnoye Khozyaistvo Kazakhstanskoi:* Kazakhstan all years. *RSFSR v. Tsyfrakh:* RSFSR 1966. *Narodnoye Khozyaistvo RSFSR:* RSFSR all other years. *Narodnoye Khozyaistvo Byelorusskoi:* Belorussia all years.

NOTES: (a) The expected relationships between spatial variability, production, and time. (b) The spatial variability of cereal production within regions of the U.S.S.R. The standard deviation of cereal production in all oblasts of each region is plotted for each year for which there are data. The data for Kazakhstan, although following similar patterns, have been removed for clarity. (c) The spatial variability of cereal production related to average production levels within the U.S.S.R. For each year's data, the mean and standard deviation of

Woiwod 1980). Linear relationships have been established for a wide variety of species of plants and animals.

Evidence from the U.S.S.R. fits this general model well. The first test applied was to take the concept of the mean correlation field, as used by hydrologists to describe spatial patterns of precipitation within river catchments (Ward 1967, Hendrick and Comer 1970). When applied to patterns of Soviet grain production the mean correlation field is the correlation between the production of each oblast (political subdivision of a republic in the U.S.S.R.) and all others over a period of time. Dividing the data set into two time periods (table 4.1) shows that, in three regions, oblasts are decreasing similarly over time. Spatial variability increases over time in response to increased production (figure 4.2b). The rate of increase is a reflection of the inherent variability within the regions analyzed (figure 4.2c). The RSFSR includes a large area in the central U.S.S.R., stretching from the far north to the Caucasus. Belorussia, on the other hand, is a small region on the border of Poland, which has more uniform conditions. In all cases the increase in variability is linear with production and (figure 4.2d) confirms that variability is increasing in proportion with overall production. Variability between regions is examined below.

Annual Variability

As with spatial variability, if stochastic processes alone were operating, one would expect year-to-year variability in production to increase in proportion to increases in total production (figure 4.3a). Indexing the production to 1960 (figure 4.3b) facilitates a comparison of both the relative growth rates of production in the regions and the year-to-year variability. During the period 1960 to 1975, production data are available for the 104 oblasts in these four regions. The mean production of each oblast over this period is plotted with the mean deviation from its production trend. Although there is a considerable scatter (figure 4.3c), 74 percent of the variance in the mean deviation from trend can be explained by changes in mean production.

A comparison of absolute and relative annual variability through time is made difficult by the short and broken data runs. An attempt is made in

---

production of all oblasts are plotted. The regular increase in spatial variability is clear as is the different rate of increase depending on the inherent variability within the regions. (d) Spatial variability of cereal production relative to production through time. Although absolute spatial variability is clearly increasing (see b), it is increasing at no faster a rate than is production. In the RSFSR, the Ukraine, and Belorussia relative spatial variability may be falling slightly.

TABLE 4.1 Spatial variability in cereal production within Soviet regions

Region	Time Period[a]		
	Whole	Early	Late
RSFSR	0.38	0.16	0.18
Belorussia	0.93	0.95	0.83
Ukraine	0.66	0.56	0.49
Kazakhstan	0.54	0.52	0.41

Sources: See figure 4.2.
Note: The table indicates the mean correlation of every oblast with every other over all years, an early period, and a late period. The magnitude of the correlation coefficients reflects the degree of internal diversity within the region. Data limitations require the use of different time periods in each region.

[a]

	Early	Late
RSFSR	1940, 1953, 1959, 1960-65	1966-73
Belorussia	1960, 1965-81	1972-79
Ukraine	1940, 1960, 1965-69	1970-75
Kazakhstan	1940, 1950, 1953, 1955, 1958-61, 1965	1966-71, 1975, 1976, 1980, 1981

TABLE 4.2 Annual variability in Soviet cereal production through time

	$\Sigma(y-\hat{y})/(n-1)$[a]			$(\Sigma(y-\hat{y})\bar{y})/(n-1)$[b]		
Region	Early[c]	Middle[c]	Late[c]	Early[c]	Middle[c]	Late[c]
RSFSR	189.8	262.3	241.0	1.01	1.01	1.13
Belorussia	29.7	44.9	57.0	1.09	1.06	1.05
Ukraine	200.8	319.8	315.2	1.15	1.08	1.06
Kazakhstan	161.5	170.7	184.9	1.28	0.91	1.19

Sources: See figure 4.2.
Note: The three time periods are not continuous but have been arranged with overlaps to give an equal number of years in each time category.
[a] Average deviation from trend $\times 10^3$ metric tons for all oblasts in the region.
[b] Average relative deviation from trend for all oblasts in region.
[c]

	Early	Middle	Late
RSFSR	1940-1965	1962-1971	1966-1975
Belorussia	1960-1971	1968-1975	1972-1979
Ukraine	1940-1968	1966-1972	1969-1975
Kazakhstan	1940-1965	1958-1971	1966-1981

table 4.2. Each run of data for each region is broken into three time periods. These periods are not the same for each region because of differences in the regional data availability. The periods overlap to ensure that there are at least seven years in each period. The selection of the time divisions is made simply to ensure equal numbers of years in each case. Absolute variability increases in each region, although showing a slight drop in

FIGURE 4.3 Annual variability in Soviet cereal production

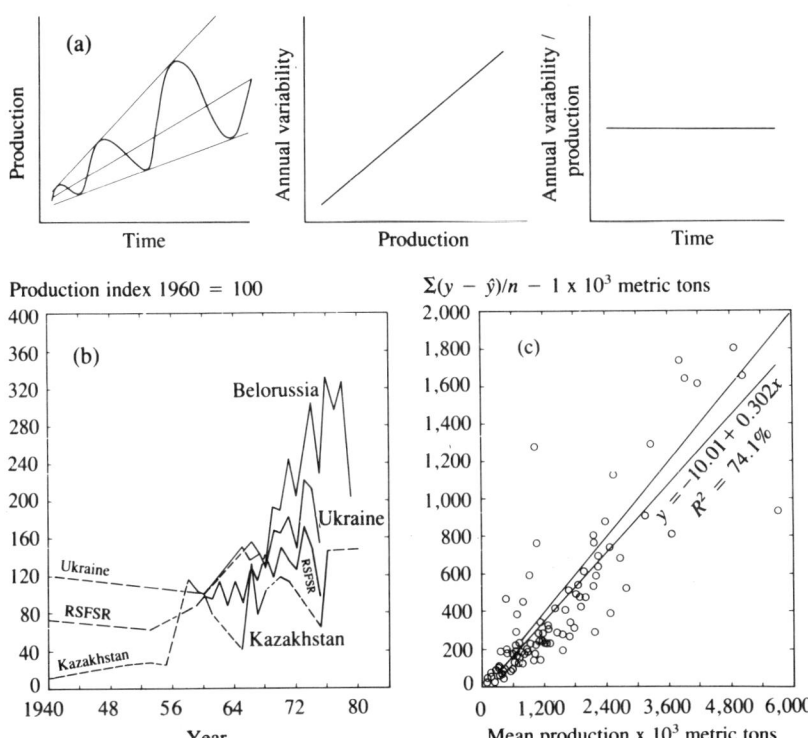

SOURCES: See figure 4.2.

NOTES: (a) The expected relationships between annual variability, production, and time. (b) U.S.S.R. regional cereal production (indexed to 1960), 1940-80. (c) Annual variability in cereal production related to mean production. Mean production for each oblast compared with its mean deviation from its trend. For each oblast the production trend through time is established using available data. The average deviation from this trend (ignoring the sign) is plotted with mean production for the same time period. The trends and mean production levels are established for 1960, 65, 66, 67, 68, 70, 71, 75.

the RSFSR and Ukraine between the middle and late period. As expected these increases are greatest where the production trend is steepest (figure 4.3b). Relative mean annual variability is shown by the second part of table 4.2 where the difference between the actual and predicted (trend) values of production are divided by the mean production for that period. Relative variability shows much smaller changes and indeed slight declines in three of the four regions. The statistical reliability of this analysis is not high because of the data problems and limited numbers of observations,

FIGURE 4.4 Diverging trends in Soviet regional cereal production

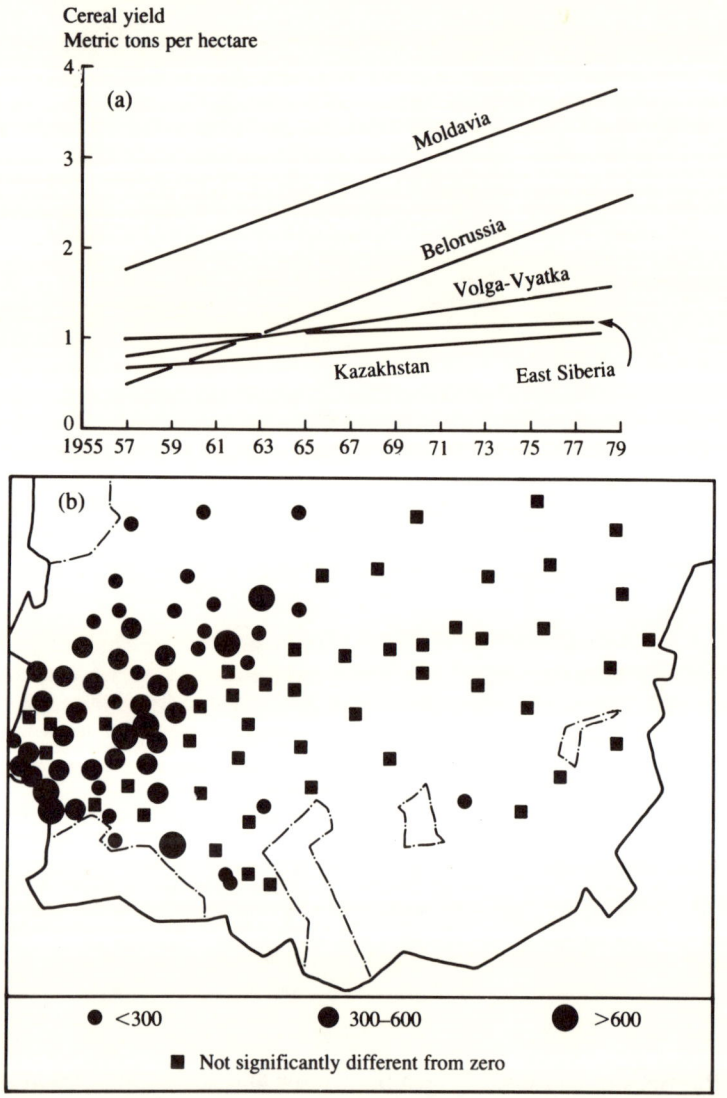

SOURCES: (a) Compiled from various Soviet sources by the Foreign Agriculture Service of the United States Department of Agriculture. (b) See figure 4.2.

NOTES: (a) Trends in cereal yields for a selection of Soviet economic regions. (b) The slopes (β coefficients) of the regression lines of cereal production through time for each oblast. The trends were established for the eight years as in figure 4.3 for which there are data for all oblasts. Over the majority of the country the slopes are not significantly different from zero (partly as a result of the small number of degrees of freedom). The contrast between the generally rapidly growing areas of the west and the stagnating east is striking.

but the results do fit closely to the relationships hypothesized in figure 4.3a.

Increases in spatial and temporal variability in the main Soviet grain production regions are no larger, and in some cases slightly smaller, than would be expected as a result of the increased levels of production. The situation and estimates for the future are complicated, however, by the effects of production conditions and rates of change in different production regions. It is necessary to look at variability between regions.

Variability between Regions

Changes through time in the production of different regions result from a combination of diverging trends in production and variability about those trends. Figure 4.4a shows differing trends of cereal yields for some economic regions in the U.S.S.R. Clearly, the rates of growth in cereal yields are very different and this will be the major determinant of production. The further east the slower the rates of growth. Figure 4.4b shows the slope values for the trend lines of production of each of the 104 oblasts in the regions under study. Over a large part of the country the slopes of linear trends are not significantly different from zero. In much of the western producing areas the rates in growth of production are considerable—although even here there are a number of oblasts that show little or no growth. These data, however, show a marked difference in the trends of production between the east and the west. Further evidence of this is provided by table 4.3

The establishment of trends in production data is complicated by the selection of appropriate start and finish dates. This becomes a major problem when the data run is short and when it includes some extreme years. Seven years of data (eliminating 1975 which was such a universally poor year that it would unrealistically reduce the production trends for such a

TABLE 4.3 Cereal production trends in Soviet regions

Region	R^2	Annual Increment ($\times 10^3$ metric tons)	Annual Increment as Percent of 1960 Production
RSFSR	0.58	3250	4.6
Belorussia	0.69	235	10.6
Ukraine	0.72	1323	6.1
Kazakhstan	0.08	438	2.3

Source: See figure 4.3.
Note: Trends calculated for seven of the eight years for which data are available for all oblasts in all regions.

FIGURE 4.5 Spatial contrasts in Soviet production

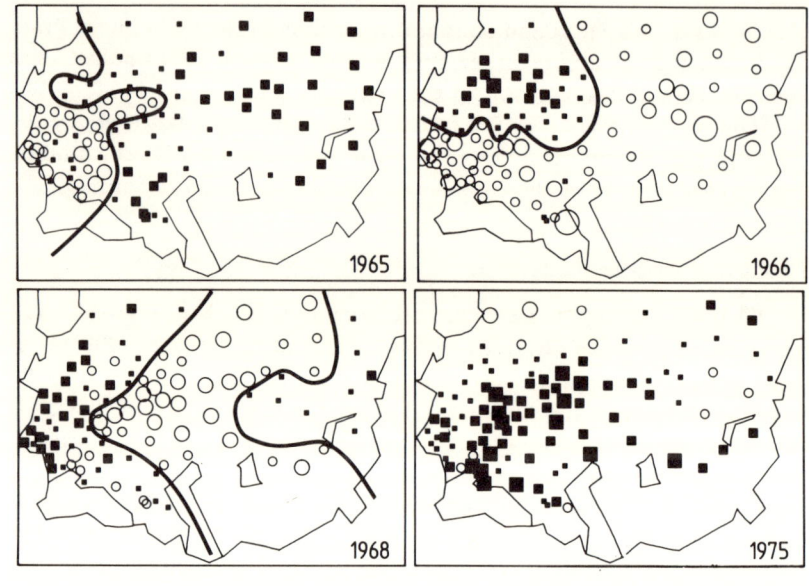

- ■ >2 standard deviations below mean
- ■ 1 to 2 standard deviations below mean
- ∙ 0 to 1 standard deviations below mean
- ○ >2 standard deviations above mean
- ○ 1 to 2 standard deviations above mean
- ○ 0 to 1 standard deviations above mean

SOURCES: See figure 4.2.

NOTES: Oblast deviations from trend for selected years. Deviations were measured even if the trend established for that oblast was not significantly different from zero. In such circumstances the deviations are essentially the same as deviations from the mean production over this time period.

short data run) show very different annual increments of production in the four regions, ranging from about 10 percent of 1960 production in the fast-growing western area of Belorussia to just over 2 percent per year in the slower growing Kazakhstan. As annual variability is related to overall production levels, so the effects of diverging trends will be accentuated by diverging variability about these trends.

Regional Compensation Effects

Overall production variability in the U.S.S.R. will be greatly reduced if, in one year, poor production in one area is compensated for by good production in another. An examination of the spatial pattern of each oblast's deviation from its trend shows that in 1966, for example (figure 4.5), conditions in the nonchernozem area of the northwest of the country were poor, and that production was well below trend—for many oblasts two or even three standard deviations below. At the same time, however, much of the rest of the country had production well above trend, especially in Kazakhstan and the southern RSFSR. In 1975 almost all oblasts were below trend—a fact which produced the disastrous overall production level for the U.S.S.R. that year (figure 4.1).

The main causes of these regional contrasts are climatic. There have been many studies of the interaction of climate and crop production in the U.S.S.R. (Desai 1981, Kogan 1981a,b, Berentsen 1982, Kogan 1983, Meshcherskaya 1983, Tarrant 1984a). Most have been based on some form of multiple regression analysis where a number of weather variables are regarded as the independent variables producing variations in the dependent variable, either production or yield. Such models have shown a high degree of statistical explanation of the annual variability in cereal production. Unfortunately, it is difficult to test these models outside the range of the data used to calibrate them. Soviet sources of agricultural data have been very limited recently and such models have had to be tested against Soviet production estimates derived from U.S. Department of Agriculture (USDA) and Food and Agriculture Organization (FAO) sources. These estimates are themselves based, at least partly, on the weather conditions during the growing season in the U.S.S.R., thus ensuring a reasonable fit of the regression models.

It is well known that plant growth, and therefore final production of grain, will be radically affected by weather conditions at critical times during the growing season (Mostek and Walsh 1981). This produces two complications. The first is that very detailed climatic analysis becomes necessary—using daily weather records if possible. This is difficult for a large area with many weather stations, and daily weather data for many Soviet stations have only recently become available in the West. The other complication is that the critical time or times will not be the same from one year to the next and from one area to another, which makes a time series analysis very challenging. Using very generalized data, this chapter presents just one illustration of the role of climatic variability.

Figures 4.6 and 4.7 show, for those weather stations reporting data over the period from 1951 to 1984, deviation of the mean spring and summer temperatures and the total spring and summer precipitation in 1965 and 1975 from their 35-year means. As most of the south and east of the Soviet grain growing area is in water deficit (Kelly et al. 1983), the combination of cool wet conditions would be expected to produce relatively good production, and conversely, hot dry conditions to produce poor produc-

72 *Evidence on Patterns of Changing Yield Variability*

FIGURE 4.6 Climatic factors in variability of Soviet cereal production, 1965

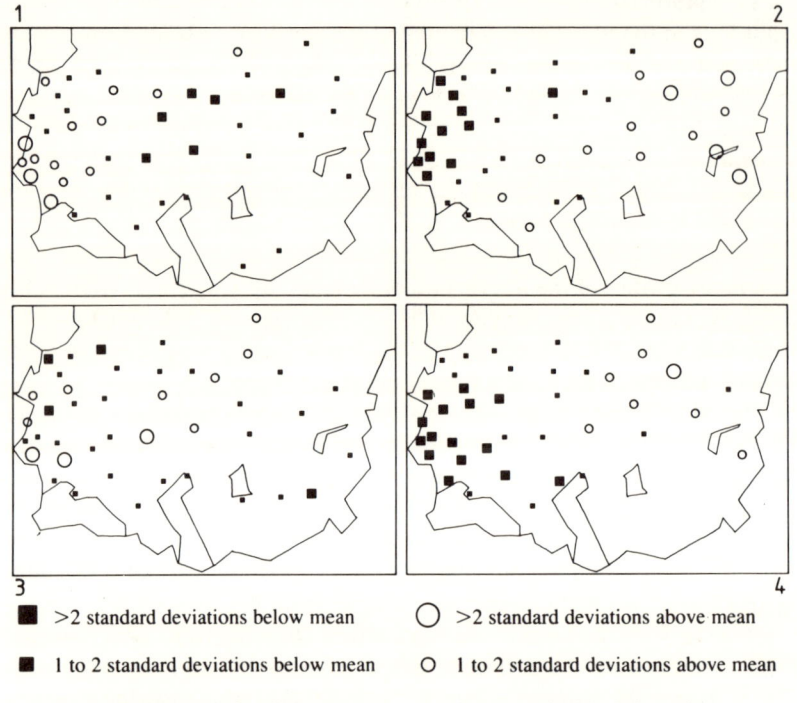

■ >2 standard deviations below mean   ○ >2 standard deviations above mean

■ 1 to 2 standard deviations below mean   ○ 1 to 2 standard deviations above mean

• 0 to 1 standard deviations below mean   ○ 0 to 1 standard deviations above mean

SOURCES: World weather records, U.S. Department of Commerce and Monthly Climatic Data for the World, NOAA, United States.

NOTES: (1) Precipitation in spring; (2) Temperature in spring; (3) Precipitation in summer; (4) Temperature in summer. Summer is defined as the months of June, July, and August and Spring as March, April, and May. For most of the weather stations the mean weather variables were established over the period 1951–83. Not all stations reported data for all months in all years, thus there is not an equal number of stations on all maps. In all cases weather variables showed no significant trends so are expressed as deviations from the mean.

tion. In 1965, when production in the west was above trend and production in the east below trend (figure 4.5) the spring and summer were generally cooler than average in the west, and hotter than average in the east. Precipitation distribution, although more spatially variable in the summer, generally reinforces this picture. In 1975 the very poor year for cereal production resulted from a very hot and dry spring and summer over most grain-growing areas (figure 4.7).

Variability in Soviet Grain Production 73

FIGURE 4.7 Climatic factors in the variability of Soviet cereal production, 1975

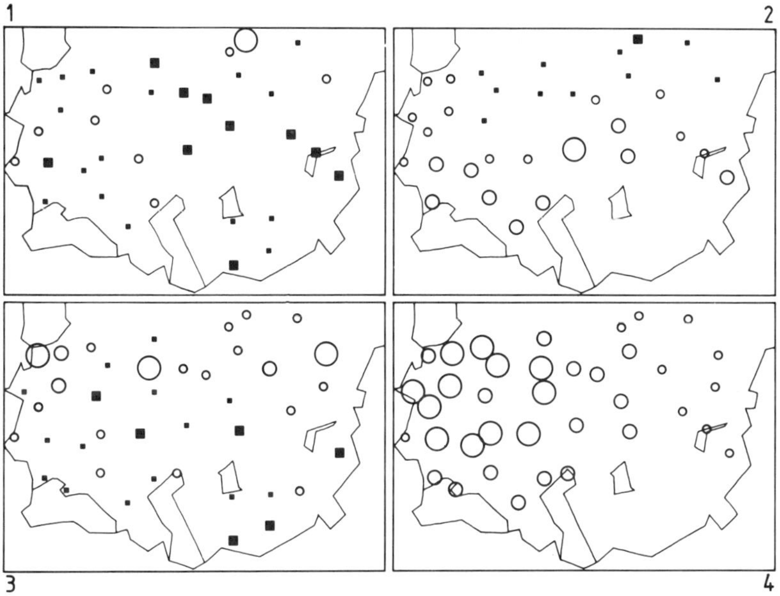

SOURCES AND DETAILS: See figure 4.6.
NOTES: (1) Precipitation in spring; (2) Temperature in spring; (3) Precipitation in summer; (4) Temperature in summer.

The Role of Regional Compensation Effects

In years when regional compensation effects do not work, there will be marked "blips," either upward or downward, from trend. These blips will tend to grow in size as production rises and variability increases. As there is a marked two-year cycle in Soviet production, once regional compensation is established, it will tend to continue in most years even if not specifically reinforced by contrasting climatic conditions. Comparing yields in Belorussia and Kazakhstan, for example, shows compensating yield changes in most years (figure 4.8a). Compensation is not confined to those years when production in one region goes up and in another, down. Winter wheat is mainly confined to the western parts of the cereal belt, while spring wheat is grown everywhere but concentrated in the east. The annual changes in production of wheat always lie somewhere between annual movements of winter and spring wheat (figure 4.8b). Years when winter and spring wheat production change in the same direction by a similar percentage are rare. In 12 of the years illustrated, winter wheat had the highest annual increase in production, and in 13 years, spring wheat pro-

74 Evidence on Patterns of Changing Yield Variability

FIGURE 4.8 Regional compensation effects in the Soviet Union

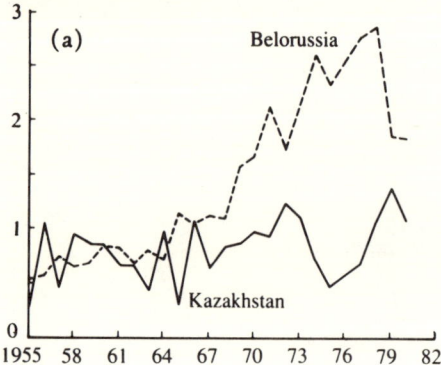

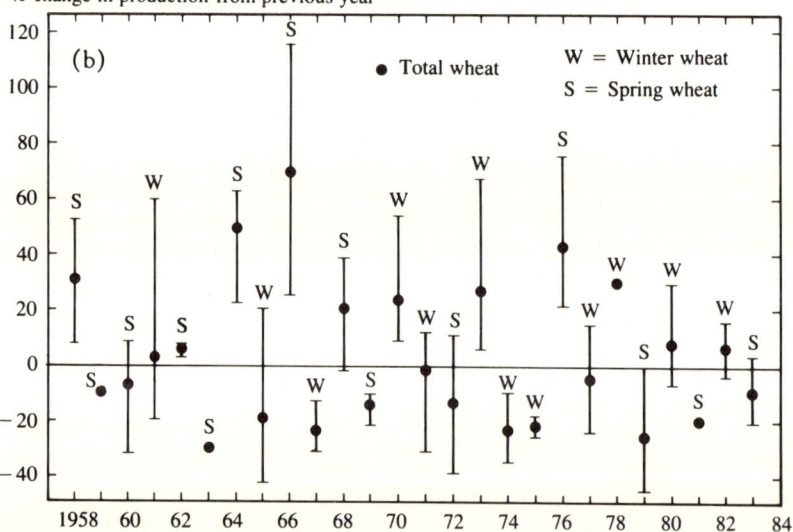

SOURCES: a. see figure 4.4a; b. see figure 4.1.

NOTES: (a) Cereal yields in Belorussia and Kazakhstan. Marked regional compensation can be seen, especially in 1965, 1971, and 1972. Even in the recent years with poor harvests the compensation has continued. (b) Percentage change in winter and spring wheat production over the previous year. The percentage change in total wheat production is usually between the two extremes of the winter and spring wheat (only the wheat crop with the fastest rate of growth is labeled). The compensation effect is not confined to years when one wheat crop increases and the other decreases.

duction grew fastest. As winter and spring wheat have different planting seasons, it is possible to induce these compensation effects by additional planting of the spring wheat crop if the winter wheat fails during the winter or early spring. The compensation effect between the two wheats is not entirely human induced, however, and the movements are often in the other direction.

Evidence has been presented (Nguyen 1985) that the regional compensation effects have reduced as intercrop and interregion yield correlations have increased. It is suggested that this is partly because of the introduction of common technologies throughout the Soviet Union and a policy of "sharing the shortage" of necessary inputs. This conflicts with Kogan's view (1983) of the very unequal allocation of inputs to agriculture. Figure 4.8b shows that the annual percentage change in winter and spring wheat production may have been unusually small recently (although representing a large volume of production) but, within that reduced variability, compensation between winter and spring wheat appears to be of continued importance.

Of greater significance is that regional compensation effects are eroded by strongly diverging trends in the cereal production in the western and eastern regions. As faster growing regions have increasing annual variability, and regions that are not growing have little change in their annual variability, total production soon fluctuates almost as greatly as production in the region with the steepest production trend, even with a complete coincidence between upturns in one region and downturns in the other. If production levels in regions with contrasting growing conditions are growing in parallel then the damping effect will remain constant. There is every reason to expect, therefore, that unless the trend of production in Kazakhstan and western Siberia improves, the production differences between east and west will increase and the annual variability in total Soviet production will grow faster than would be expected from the growth in total Soviet production alone.

Policy Implications

If livestock herds are not to be adjusted to the size of the cereal and other feedcrop harvest, annual variability becomes a determinant of the size of the import requirement, the size of the necessary buffer stock, or both of these. Marginal production conditions over much of the grain-growing area of the Soviet Union ensures that there is great annual fluctuation in yields and harvests—fluctuations that are probably relatively greater than in any other major cereal-producing country. As production increases, so will this annual variability, thereby increasing the uncertainties of the size of the Soviet import demand. These uncertainties will be accentuated by the diminishing importance of regional compensation effects if current trends continue. As imports are already close to port-handling capacity and there are obvious practical and financial limits to the size of security stocks, future shocks to the world cereal market are likely to follow a sharply reduced Soviet import need following a coincident upward movement in harvests in all Soviet grain-producing regions.

The Soviet Union obviously has a need to increase overall production and thereby to increase meat production. Meat consumption is still very low (Markish 1982, Hedlund 1984), and poor cereal harvests led to a downturn in cattle numbers and milk production in the late 1970s and early 1980s in spite of high levels of grain imports, and in sharp contrast to the demands of economic plans (USDA 1983c, 1984a, Tarrant 1984b). Although grain production may have recovered in 1985 (USDA 1984a), it will still be below the trend established from 1960 to 1980. Equally important, however, is that production increases should be achieved with the minimum increase in the annual variability that is already too great to be easily absorbed through the use of buffer stocks. Policies that are directed to stability are at least as essential as those directed at increased production. There are two regions where there is potential for rapid increases in production. The first of these is the nonblack earth region of the northwest—where increased production can be associated with land drainage and soil improvements (Rostankowski 1980). Unfortunately, much of this region has already shown very rapid improvements (figure 4.4) and a policy to accelerate the production trend even further, although it would certainly increase overall production, would also accelerate the end of effective regional compensation effects and sharply increase the annual variability of total Soviet production. The second region where there remains potential to increase production is in the dry east. Here new irrigation investment and more effective use of existing facilities would provide the increase (Micklin 1978). This increased production may bring with it increased variability. Provided that the variability moves, at least in most years, in a less extreme manner than in the west, it will represent a positive benefit. As production increases, so upturns in eastern harvests can compensate more fully for poor western harvests and vice versa. This provides the strongest case for the Soviet plans to divert rivers southward to the Aral Sea and lower Volga, and other less grandiose irrigation investments (Kelly, et al. 1983, Micklin 1983, Pryde 1983).

Conclusions

Absolute spatial and annual variability in Soviet grain production will continue to rise from already high levels. Absolute variability is higher than can be economically and practically catered to by buffer stocks, and imports are possibly near their maximum. Additional downward variability in production will have to be accommodated largely through further reduced consumption. The Polish food riots in the 1970s showed the Soviet government how dangerous such policies can be. If production varies sharply above trend, western exporting countries can expect an abrupt reduction in imports (USDA 1984a). Soviet import demands can be expected to be much more variable in the future with a great potential for market disruption (Kogan 1983).

Provided concerns over environmental damage can be overcome, there is likely to be continued pressure for river diversion schemes. Other policy and research efforts in agriculture are apt to be continued with increased urgency. These include the development of new techniques of fodder production as well as land improvement projects in the northwest. It is unlikely that further newlands remain to be developed—unless there is widespread increase in irrigation, which might come from the river diversion schemes.

There is no evidence that increased uniformity in the application of agricultural technology has led to significantly reduced spatial variation in production and, therefore, to increased annual variations. Access to agricultural technology is far from uniform and, together with the range of climatic conditions throughout the country, that ensures continued spatial variability.

Future changes in relative annual variability will be dependent on changes in relative spatial variability, itself dependent on changes in (a) scatter about trends in the different production regions, (b) the divergence of trends in different production regions, and (c) the compensation effects of deviations from trends within different production regions. There is no evidence for increased relative scatter about trends, but the trends themselves are sharply diverging. Therefore, although the compensation remains at present, its effectiveness is rapidly being reduced.

Diverging production trends will increase annual total harvest fluctuations relatively and absolutely, unless adoption of technology throughout the country can reduce the divergence of production trends, and thereby reduce spatial variability, maintain the effectiveness of regional compensation effects, and reduce annual variability. Of various possible scenarios, the most probable is that diverging trends in production between east and west will reduce regional compensation effects and produce greater than expected increases in annual variability.

5 Agricultural Planning Policy and Variability in Syrian Cereal Production

HUNG NGUYEN

Few countries experience such an extraordinarily high degree of variability in national cereal production as Syria. In 1986, for example, national barley production was only 15 percent of the previous year's production (Bakour 1984, p. 8). Such fluctuations are a long-standing phenomenon and originate largely from Syria's highly variable rainfall. There is evidence that the variability of national cereal production has increased in recent years, and this may be related to change in technology and agricultural policy.

This chapter examines recent changes in the patterns of variability in Syrian cereal production. Variance decomposition is used to identify the importance of various contributing factors to the increase in variability.

Background

Because of Syria's dry climate only about 3.4 million hectares are under cultivation while 2.5 million hectares of cultivable land are left fallow (Mukhitdinov 1974, p. 61). In areas receiving less than 250 millimeters (mm) of rainfall annually (which is the case for 60 percent of cultivable land), a two-year crop rotation system is adopted—the first year under grain, the second fallow. In areas receiving 400 to 600 millimeters annually (about 10 percent of cultivable land), a three-year crop rotation system is the common practice—the first year under wheat, the second under barley, and the third fallow. Rainfall occurs primarily during the winter, and the planting of winter crops depends crucially on the level of rainfall in November. El-Sherbini (1979, p. 145) has shown that the correlation between early and total rainfall is highly significant for every province of Syria. There has been a large increase in the area of irrigated wheat since the early 1970s and in the adoption of high-yielding Mexican wheat varieties. Barley remains an essentially rainfed crop. These two crops provide an interesting contrast for the study of production variability. Oats, maize, millet, and rice are excluded from this study as the time series for these crops are incomplete, and wheat and barley account for more than 97 percent of total cereal production in Syria. Data on areas, yields, and production for wheat and barley are available from 1950 to 1981. Data from 1950 to 1975 were provided by Nabil Khaldi, who collected them from original Arabic sources at the Ministry of Agriculture and Agrarian Reform. Data from 1976 to 1981 were taken from the Annual Agricultural Statistical Abstracts published by the Ministry of Agriculture and Agrarian Reform.

To take into account the various administrative reorganizations since 1960, the data are organized into nine units based on pre-1960 provincial boundaries. These provinces are: Damascus, Homs, Hama (currently Hama and Ghab), Latakia (currently Latakia and Tartous), Aleppo (currently Aleppo and Idleb), Hasakah, Euphrates (currently Raqqa and Deirez-Zor), Sweida, and Hauran (currently Dara). Apart from the coastal provinces of Latakia and Tartous, the rest of Syria is subject to a regime of low to intermediate rainfall. The driest areas are located in the northeastern provinces of Hasakah, Deir-ez-Zor, and Raqqa, along the Euphrates River and its tributaries, where most of the irrigated areas are also concentrated. The province of Quneitra was excluded from the analysis because it is small and unimportant in terms of cereal production and lies near the turbulent border with Israel.

The choice of time periods to be included in the analysis is very important as it can distort the results if not done carefully. Here a threefold partition of the 1950-81 period is adopted: nonland reform (1950-57 and 1962-64), land reform (1958-61 and 1965-70), and post-land reform (1971-81). This partition is based on the socioeconomic and political changes of the 1950-81 period. The prereform period from 1950 to 1957 was essentially a laissez-faire period. Land reform was launched in earnest during the union with Nasser's Egypt from 1958 and 1961, which witnessed a sharp drop in production resulting from droughts and from a large decrease in areas planted. While it could be expected that the irrigated areas would expand to take advantage of drought conditions during the land reform period, these areas also decreased precipitously, probably because of expropriations and disinvestment. A new regime in 1961 broke up the union with Egypt and ceased to enforce the land reform measures. Economic policies reverted to "business as usual." Land reform and socialization of agriculture were restarted in 1965, with the advent of a new socialist-oriented regime, and a relatively large cooperative sector was in place by 1970. While important features of the agricultural policy of the 1960s remained, particularly those related to price policies and grain procurement, the Asad period after 1971 was relatively stable in terms of changes in local institutional arrangements. The cooperative production sector, in particular, was gradually disbanded and became insignificant by the 1980s

TABLE 5.1 The mean and coefficient of variation of areas, yield, and production of cereals in Syria during the nonreform, land-reform, and post-land-reform periods

	Nonreform Period (1950–57 and 1962–64)		Land-Reform Period (1958–61 and 1965–70)		Post-Land-Reform Period (1971–81)	
Component/Crop	Average	CV	Average	CV	Average	CV
Production (thousand metric tons)						
Barley	498	0.36	382	0.51	712	0.54
Wheat	950	0.24	744	0.29	1,519	0.27
Total	1,445	0.27	1,125	0.34	2,216	0.35
Areas (10^3ha)						
Barley	590	0.10	700	0.26	969	0.16
Wheat	1,355	0.05	1,234	0.22	1,458	0.09
Total	1,945	0.04	1,935	0.19	2,428	0.11
Yields (t/ha)						
Barley	0.85	0.35	0.58	0.50	0.74	0.49
Wheat	0.70	0.25	0.61	0.27	1.04	0.28
Total	0.74	0.27	0.60	0.35	0.92	0.34

(Bakour 1984, p. 30). However, important policy initiatives with respect to the planning system were introduced in the 1970s and are discussed below.

Analysis of Detrended Data

As the deterministic, long-term trend in each variable needs to be removed in order to separate it from the short-term stochastic variation, the area and yield data for each crop and province were detrended by means of regression analysis (Hazell 1984). The residuals, centered on the mean areas or yields for each period, became the primary data for analysis.

Table 5.1 shows that area variability was particularly large during the land reform period for both barley and wheat, while yield and production variability also increased. Average barley area expanded, but yield dropped precipitously. Average wheat area decreased, probably because wheat is grown in the irrigated and more fertile areas, which were strongly affected by appropriations. It is more reasonable, therefore, to compare the post-land-reform period with the nonreform period since the economic and political disturbances of the land reform period probably compounded the destabilizing effects of unfavorable natural factors. Such comparison also provides a clear distinction between the two periods in terms of policy regimes and agrotechnology. It can be seen from table 5.1 that, while the average areas, production, and yields of cereals have increased since 1971 (except for barley yields), the coefficients of variation (cvs) of these variables have also increased appreciably.

Tables 5.2, 5.3, and 5.4 provide, respectively, a detailed picture of the changes in areas, yields, and production of barley and wheat in the more important producing provinces. Barley area increased most rapidly in the two northeastern provinces of Hasakah and Euphrates. A very large increase in the variability of barley area in one province, Euphrates, masked the relative stability of barley areas in other provinces. This situation probably reflected the severe labor shortages resulting from the reluctance of farmers to settle on newly reclaimed land in the Euphrates basin developed and controlled by the state. There was a remarkable decline in barley yields in every province. A sharp drop in the proportion of fallow to cultivated lands during the 1970s may have accounted for this decline in barley yields. The rural per capita amount of fallow fell from 0.74 hectares in 1970 to 0.45 hectares in 1975, and continued to decline up to 1982 (Bakour 1984, p. 18). Continuous production, instead of a barley-fallow rotation, can lead to a very large yield decline (Cooper 1983, p. 74).

The greater variability of Syrian wheat production in the 1971-81 period can largely be accounted for by increases in yield variability in the important producing provinces of Hasakah and Euphrates and by increased area variability in Hauran.

Decomposition Analysis

Total barley and wheat production increased by 54 percent between the nonreform and postreform periods (table 5.4). Using the decomposition procedure described in Chapter 2, area expansion was found to account for 58 percent of the increase in total barley and wheat production and yield increases for 48 percent (table 5.5). The increase in barley production is explained by area expansion; the average yield declined. The expansion of the barley area probably also occurred in more marginal areas, as the interaction term between changes in area and yield is negative. Most of the increase in wheat production is explained by an increase in mean yield.

The variance of total barley and wheat production increased by 296 percent between the nonreform and postreform periods (table 5.4). Table 5.6 shows the results from a decomposition of this change. Increases in the production variances of wheat and barley within provinces account for 11.0 and 5.4 percent, respectively, of the increase in the variance of their total production. The remaining increase (83.6 percent) can be attributed to increases in production covariances.

TABLE 5.2 Changes in the mean and variability of barley and wheat areas in Syria

Province	Average Area			Coefficient of Variation			
	First Period (10³ha)	Second Period (10³ha)	Change (percent)	First Period	Second Period	Change (percent)	F Ratio
Barley							
Hama	66	96	45.4	0.32	0.13	−57	0.40
Aleppo	235	269	14.5	0.10	0.06	−33	0.26*
Hasakah	94	248	163.1	0.53	0.22	−57	1.27
Euphrates	59	229	286.3	0.25	0.35	37	28.10*
Total Syria	590	969	64.2	0.10	0.15	55	6.45*
Wheat							
Hama	97	134	38.1	0.15	0.10	−32	0.86
Aleppo	294	373	26.9	0.14	0.10	−27	0.85
Hasakah	532	501	−5.8	0.17	0.09	−44	0.27*
Euphrates	122	172	41.0	0.27	0.26	−3	1.85
Hauran	87	72	−17.2	0.09	0.33*	268	9.20*
Total Syria	1,355	1,458	7.7	0.04	0.08*	98	4.52*

Note: First period: 1950–57 and 1962–64; second period: 1971–81.
*An asterisk denotes that the cv/variance in the second period is significantly different from that of the first period at least at the 5 percent level.

TABLE 5.3 Changes in the mean and variability of barley and wheat yields in Syria

	Average Yield			Coefficient of Variation			
Province	First Period (kg/ha)	Second Period (kg/ha)	Change (percent)	First Period	Second Period	Change (percent)	F Ratio
Barley							
Hama	998	755	−24.3	0.43	0.52	21	0.84
Aleppo	768	714	−7.0	0.51	0.43	−15	1.10
Hasakah	1,182	971	−17.8	0.34	0.60*	76	2.10
Euphrates	848	593	−30.1	0.38	0.65*	72	1.46
Total Syria	846	738	−12.8	0.35	0.49	40	1.50
Wheat							
Hama	727	1,367	88.0	0.42	0.29	−32	1.78
Aleppo	722	967	33.9	0.42	0.25	−39	0.67
Hasakah	758	1,050	38.5	0.28	0.40	45	4.50*
Euphrates	626	1,167	86.4	0.27	0.28	4	3.73*
Hauran	722	784	8.6	0.39	0.51	32	2.00
Total Syria	705	1,045	48.2	0.25	0.27	9	2.64

Note: First period: 1950–57 and 1962–64; second period: 1971–81.
*An asterisk denotes that the cv/variance in the second period is significantly different from that of the first period at least at the 5 percent level.

TABLE 5.4 Changes in the mean and variability of barley and wheat production in Syria

Province	Average Production (1,000 metric tons)		Change (percent)	Coefficient of Variation		Change (percent)	F Ratio
	First Period	Second Period		First Period	Second Period		
Barley							
Hama	66	72	10.4	0.51	0.57	10.0	1.47
Aleppo	184	191	3.8	0.55	0.44	−20.0	0.69
Hasakah	106	231	118.0	0.58	0.61	6.0	5.29*
Euphrates	52	129	145.1	0.53	0.67	27.0	9.74*
Total Syria	498	712	42.7	0.36	0.54	52.0	4.68*
Wheat							
Hama	69	181	162.3	0.40	0.29	−28.0	3.58
Aleppo	205	359	75.1	0.34	0.26	−23.0	1.82
Hasakah	395	523	32.4	0.26	0.39	47.0	3.82*
Euphrates	74	196	164.9	0.28	0.32	16.0	9.37*
Hauran	63	58	−7.9	0.41	0.69	65.0	2.33
Total Syria	950	1,519	59.9	0.24	0.27	13.9	3.30
Total barley & wheat	1,445	2,216	54.0	0.27	0.35	30.4	3.96*

Note: First period: 1950–57 and 1962–64; second period: 1971–81.
*An asterisk denotes that the cv/variance in the second period is significantly different from that of the first period at least at the 5 percent level.

TABLE 5.5 Components of change in the average production of barley and wheat in Syria: 1950-57 and 1962-64 to 1971-81 (percent)

Crop	Change in Mean Yields	Change in Mean Areas	Change in Area-Yield Covariances	Change in Interaction Term	Contribution of Crop to Change in Mean Production of Total Cereals
Barley	−35.3	190.2	−8.0	−46.9	27.3
Wheat	77.5	12.1	2.1	8.3	72.7
Total	48.4	58.0	−0.5	−5.9	100.0

Yield variances and covariances contribute 50 percent of the increase in the variance of total barley and wheat production. Of this amount, about one-fifth is due to changes in yield variances within crops and provinces, and most of the rest is due to increased covariances between provinces, both within and across crops.

A further decomposition of the changes in yield variances and covariances reveals that about one-half of their 50 percent contribution to the increase in the variance of total barley and wheat production can be attributed to increases in yield variances, whereas an autonomous increase in yield correlations, especially between provinces, accounts for another third of their contribution. Changes in yield covariances also contributed to the large interaction effect with changes in mean areas (43.7 percent), so that the role of higher yield correlations in destabilizing Syrian cereals production is large indeed.

Table 5.7 shows that the pattern towards more positively correlated yields between provinces was present for both barley and wheat. This increasingly synchronized pattern of yield variation also applies to the yield variation between barley and wheat (table 5.8).

The effects of changes in area variances and covariances are destabilizing, though small (4.7 percent) (table 5.6). Changes in area-yield covariances are stabilizing, however, and act to reduce the variance of total cereal production by 10.1 percent. Moreover, 70 percent of this reduction is due to an autonomous decrease in area-yield correlations, especially those between crops and provinces. On closer examination, most of this decline occurred in the correlations between areas sown to barley in one province and wheat yields in the same or other provinces.

Discussion

The increase in the variability of Syrian barley and wheat production between the nonreform and postreform periods can be attributed to three major sources: increased yield variances (especially for wheat), an increase

TABLE 5.6 Disaggregation of the components of change in the variance of total barley and wheat production in Syria: 1950–57 and 1962–64 to 1971–81 (percent)

Component	Change in Mean Yields	Change in Mean Areas	Change in Yield Variances and Covariances		Change in Area Variances and Covariances	Change in Area-Yield Covariances	Change in Other Interaction Terms[b]	Row Sums
			Pure Effect	Interaction Effect[a]				
Crop variances								
Barley	−0.38	4.35	−0.52	2.85	1.23	−0.98	−1.13	5.42
Wheat	0.52	0.98	10.24	−1.20	−0.81	2.12	−0.82	11.03
Total	0.14	5.33	9.72	1.64	0.43	1.14	−1.95	16.44
Intercrop covariances within provinces	−0.16	2.59	3.84	6.93	−0.97	−0.55	−0.19	11.49
Interprovincial covariances within crops								
Barley	−0.27	5.01	2.55	11.07	0.79	−2.83	−0.65	15.67
Wheat	−0.76	1.91	17.29	2.96	1.84	−1.17	−2.35	19.72
Total	−1.03	6.92	19.84	14.03	2.64	−4.00	−3.01	35.39
Covariances between different crops in different provinces	−0.27	7.33	17.19	21.08	2.57	−6.69	−4.53	36.68
Column sums	−1.32	22.18	50.59	43.68	4.66	−10.10	−9.69	100.00

[a]Between changes in mean areas and yield variances and covariances.
[b]Includes changes in the residual term.

TABLE 5.7 Yield correlations between provinces for barley and wheat in Syria

	Barley			Wheat		
Province	Hama	Aleppo	Hasakah	Hama	Aleppo	Hasakah
Aleppo						
Period I	0.54			0.58*		
Period II	0.89*			0.71*		
Hasakah						
Period I	0.13	0.49		0.47	0.71*	
Period II	0.62*	0.73*		0.48	0.58*	
Euphrates						
Period I	0.46	0.22	−0.04	0.66*	0.27	0.03
Period II	0.76*	0.92*	0.79*	0.62*	0.79*	0.85*

Note: First period: 1950-57 and 1962-64; second period: 1971-81.
*An asterisk denotes that the correlation is significantly different from zero at least at the 10 percent level.

TABLE 5.8 Yield correlations between barley and wheat in Syria

	Correlations between Wheat Yields in:			
Province	Hama	Aleppo	Hasakah	Euphrates
and Barley Yields in:				
Hama				
Period I	0.65*	0.31	0.67*	0.22
Period II	0.64*	0.79*	0.56*	0.71*
Aleppo				
Period I	0.37	0.57*	0.58*	0.03
Period II	0.71*	0.88*	0.78*	0.90*
Hasakah				
Period I	0.33	0.49	0.59*	0.00
Period II	0.66*	0.72*	0.74*	0.83*
Euphrates				
Period I	0.16	0.06	0.28	0.49
Period II	0.69*	0.82*	0.88*	0.92*

Note: First period: 1950-57 and 1962-64; second period: 1971-81.
*An asterisk denotes that the correlation is significantly different from zero at least at the 10 percent level.

in interprovincial yield correlations, both within and between wheat and barley, and a positive interaction effect between these two sources of change and area expansion.

With respect to the increase in the variability of wheat yields, the available evidence indicates that rainfall has not become more erratic. Nor is there evidence that price variability for wheat and barley has increased,

TABLE 5.9 Percentage of wheat areas planted to high-yielding varieties in Syria

Province	1974	1977	1980
Damascus	5	13	17
Hama	6	13	19
Aleppo	15	20	37
Euphrates	29	33	60
Hasakah	12	30	68
Syria	15	24	44

particularly as producer prices have been tightly controlled by the government since 1965. Rather, part of the increase may be due to the adoption of modern wheat varieties in nonirrigated areas of Syria. Table 5.3 indicates that the largest increases in the variance of wheat yields occurred in Hasakah and Euphrates provinces where the proportions of area planted to modern varieties were highest (table 5.9). Hasakah, in particular, had the lowest percentage of its Mexican wheat area irrigated (only 11 percent in 1980). On the other hand, 64 percent of total Mexican wheat area was irrigated in Hama, which showed the largest advance in wheat yield and a reduced cv (table 5.3). But, the variability of wheat yield also increased noticeably in the ancient province of Hauran in southern Syria, where Mexican wheat has not been adopted.

The increasingly synchronized pattern of yield variation across provinces, both within and between wheat and barley, also suggests that factors other than technology contributed to the increase in yield variability and yield correlations. It is hypothesized here that the system of agricultural planning evolved during the 1970s may have exacerbated the inherent instability of cereal production in Syria.

During the past 20 years of "socialist transformation" both the procurement prices of important crops, such as wheat and barley, and the domestic prices of nearly all important inputs have been centrally determined at the highest political level (El Akhrass 1983, p. 5). Purchase prices are announced prior to the planting season and are uniform in all producing areas for the same grade of crops. In principle, these prices are calculated to cover all costs of production and to allow producers a "profit margin" in accordance with planned expansion of these crops in the overall food security strategy. Moreover, the role of the state in planning agricultural production has grown significantly since 1970. Access to purchased inputs can only be acquired by means of Agricultural Bank credit which is granted only when farmers meet certain conditions set by the government (World Bank 1977, p. 211). Since 1975, these conditions have included the compliance by farmers with the detailed land use, crop rotation, and intensification schemes worked out in the Annual Plan (World Bank 1977, pp.

205-6). It is possible that, before this planning scheme became mandatory on a nationwide scale, it had been applied to provinces in the Euphrates basin where state control was strongest. According to the Plan, each province was given annual production quotas by crop, land type, and stability zone. Enforcement of these quotas is done by licensing, which, in principle, should give farmers access to credit and inputs, and by imposing severe penalties for noncompliance.

This quota system, reinforced by centrally determined prices and the state as the sole purchasing agent of cereals, probably led to greater yield variability and increased yield correlations across provinces. The detailed prescriptions of land use, crop rotation, and cultivation practices could substantially reduce the flexibility of farmers to respond to fluctuations in local weather conditions or input supplies, or to substitute between crops according to their preferences and risk assessments. There is some evidence to indicate that planned quotas on crop areas did go against farmers' preferences. For example, in 1977, the quotas for barley and Mexican wheat area were underfulfilled by about 10 percent while those for local wheat were exceeded by more than 40 percent (USDA 1980, p. 33). This system of fixed prices and quotas on crop areas probably accounts for the increases in the correlations of barley yields across provinces (table 5.7) and the correlations between barley and wheat yields between provinces (table 5.8).

The economic value of barley straw as animal feed could also be an important factor in explaining the increased correlation of barley yields. When expected yields for barley fall below a threshold level, the economic value of the straw may exceed the value (less harvesting costs) of the expected grain harvest. Consequently, farmers would rather let their animals graze their barley crops than harvest them (Mazid and Hallajian 1984). When barley grain prices are fixed but straw and livestock prices are not, the latter tend to move in an opposite direction to that of expected grain yields. Expectations of a poor harvest could, therefore, raise the grazing threshold through the barley-growing provinces, and reduce yields below the level that can be realized without grazing. The grazing thresholds could move up and down together across provinces and thus account for the increased correlations of barley yields.

If the above hypothesis is correct, it could be expected that deviations below trend would be more frequent or extreme during the second period. The skewness of barley yields indeed changed from negative (-1.1) to near zero (-0.3), while variances increased by 50 percent between the two periods. Negative deviations in barley yields may also be highly correlated with negative deviations in wheat yields because both are caused by the same weather factors (e.g., rainfall). In other words, barley yields tend to fall proportionately with the decline in wheat yields, a situation which was absent in the first period, when it could be expected that barley was a relatively more drought-resistant crop.

The increase in wheat yield correlations can probably be explained by the higher level of irrigation and the rationing of inputs, which spread shortages more evenly across planning units (Kornai 1982), rather than by changes in varietal diversity. Wheat areas in many provinces, with the exception of Damascus and Hasakah, were dominated by one or two local varieties in 1953 (World Bank 1955). Since modern varieties were planted on about 44 percent of the total wheat area in 1980, their introduction may have enhanced the level of varietal diversity.

Conclusions

The decomposition results support the hypothesis that agricultural planning policy, specifically the quota system, has played a pivotal role in inducing greater yield variability and correlation in Syrian cereal production since 1970. As a powerful instrument in expanding the area of favored crops, the crop and input allocation system may also have caused the highly destabilizing interaction effect between area changes with increases in yield variability and correlations. In view of the fluctuations in world barley prices and rising demand for barley as a feedgrain, this is a problem that requires more research.

Recent evidence indicates that the role of agricultural planners in directly affecting productivity at the local level could grow even more in the future. Since 1983, the government of Syria has been pushing for increased mechanization as a way of reducing unit production costs and maintaining "profit margins" without the need for large increases in procurement prices (American Embassy, Damascus 1984, p. 6). Clearly, planners' behavior in allocating agricultural machinery between regions will have a direct impact on local production performances and their correlations across provinces.

Finally, due to structural changes in demand patterns in Syria and the Middle East in general, barley is likely to receive even more policy emphasis in the future. The impact of this emphasis on national food security will warrant planners' careful attention.

6 High-Yielding Varieties and Variability in Sorghum and Pearl Millet Production in India

THOMAS S. WALKER

The International Crops Research Institute for the Semi-Arid Tropics (ICRISAT) invests heavily in screening and breeding for resistance to yield reducers. The benefits to this research are derived primarily from enhanced output, increased equity, and improved nutrition. In theory, improved yield stability from more pest resistant and stress tolerant varieties could also lead to reduced farm, regional, and national production variability.

Results from several studies suggest that variability in Indian foodgrain production has been increasing (Mehra 1981, Hazell 1982). Between 1954/55 to 1964/65 and 1967/68 to 1977/78 the coefficient of variation (cv) of detrended All India total cereal production increased by about 50 percent, from 0.04 to 0.059; the variance of All India production increased by 342 percent (Hazell 1982).

Hazell (1982) hypothesized that, if high-yielding varieties (HYVs) are a significant source of production variability, increased production variances within states should be large contributors to increases in the variance of cereal production. But his results show that only about 18 percent of the increase in variance of total cereal production can be accounted for by changes in crop production variances. The remaining 82 percent is explained by changes in the covariance components, particularly interstate covariances within crops, which contribute 41 percent to the change in variance in total cereal production. Changes in yield covariances were much more important than changes in yield variances. Hazell concluded that the increase in variability in India's cereal production between the two

---

This chapter owes a great deal to the inspiration of Peter B. R. Hazell; the perspiration of E. Jagadeesh, A. Pavan Kumar, and S. Lalitha; the interpretative insight of Hans P. Binswanger; discussions with several colleagues in the ICRISAT and All India Coordinated Crop Improvement Programs, including B. S. Rana and N. G. P. Rao; the support of Murari Singh in the use of weighted least squares in the GENSTAT statistical package; and secondary data collected by P. Parthasarathy Rao and K. V. Subba Rao.

periods cannot be attributed to HYVs but rather to other causes. He additionally drew the implication that there is very confined scope for yield-stabilizing varietal technologies to decrease production variability in Indian agriculture.

In a later paper comparing the U.S. and Indian experience, Hazell (1984) saw a greater role for HYVs to play in influencing yield covariances. He speculated that narrowing of the genetic base of maize hybrids has led to increased regional covariances and augmented production variability in maize production in the United States. This chapter presents statistical evidence from district-level data to show that diffusion of sorghum (or jowar) and pearl millet (or bajra) hybrids are positively associated with increased production variability in the major producing districts in India.

The Diagnostic Approach

The decomposition methods described in chapter 2 are relied on to identify components and sources of change in production variability in 48 sorghum and 40 pearl millet growing districts of India. Initially, the 50 most important producing districts for each crop were chosen based on the area estimates for 1981/82 (Government of India 1983). Information was not available for two sorghum and 10 pearl millet growing districts in Haryana and Uttar Pradesh. The remaining 48 sorghum districts contributed about 70 percent to both All India production and area; the 40 remaining pearl millet districts accounted for about 70 percent of area and 60 percent of production. Two 12-year intervals, 1956/57 to 1967/68 and 1968/69 to 1979/80, which correspond to pre- and post-green revolution periods for sorghum and pearl millet, were selected for analysis. District area and yield data from the state government season and crop reports were linearly detrended for each period and their residuals were centered on the mean for each period. Detrended area and yield data were multiplied to give detrended production data for each period.

For a given crop, the change in production variance can be partitioned into two broad components: (a) the sum of production variances within districts, and (b) the sum of interdistrict production covariances, and each of these can, in turn, be attributed to some 11 sources (Hazell 1982, p. 21; ch. 2).

Increased Variability in Sorghum and Pearl Millet Production

Variability in sorghum and pearl millet production increased both absolutely and relatively from the first 12-year period to the second. For sorghum the cv of production increased from 0.08 to 0.16 ($z = 3.45$, highly significant); for pearl millet the change was even more marked, from 0.11

to 0.34 ($z = 7.20$, highly significant). The variances increased by 4,000 and 1,670 percent, repectively, and were also highly significant.

Most of the major producing districts also experienced increased production variability. The cv and variance of production increased in 31 and 36, respectively, of the 48 sorghum-producing districts. Of the major pearl millet growing districts, 36 and all 40 were characterized by greater relative and absolute production variability, respectively.

Sources of Increased Production Variability

Increased production variance stemmed overwhelmingly from increased production covariance among major producing regions for both sorghum and pearl millet. More than 90 percent of the increase in production variance for both crops was attributed to changes in interdistrict production covariances (table 6.1). Changes in within-district production variance did not contribute appreciably to the changes in production variance. In a highly disaggregated analysis such as this one, this result is not surprising because, with the n variances, there are $n(n - 1)$ production covariances and their sum should increase with the sum of the production variances (Hazell 1984).

What is surprising is that these changes should be so dominated by changes in yield covariances. For both crops, changes in yield covariance

TABLE 6.1 Contribution of different sources to increased interregional covariance in sorghum and pearl millet production in India, 1956/57-1967/68 to 1968/69-1979/80

Source	Sorghum	Pearl Millet
	(percentage share)	
Change in mean yield	1.7	0.7
Change in mean area	3.1	0.6
Change in yield covariance	84.0	54.2
Change in area covariance	0.1	2.2
Interaction between changes in mean yields and mean areas	0.0	0.0
Change in area-yield covariance	−1.3	14.2
Interaction between changes in mean area and yield covariance	1.8	4.4
Interaction between changes in mean yield and area covariance	0.3	1.3
Interactions between changes in mean area and yield and changes in area-yield covariance	−0.8	6.0
Change in residual	6.0	8.5
Total	94.9	92.1

have been largely responsible for the increase in changes in production variance (table 6.1). Within each crop, the yields of sorghum and pearl millet have become increasingly covariate across districts, and this increased yield covariance has led to increased production variability.

Changes in area-yield covariance also accounted for an appreciable share (about 14 percent) of increased production variance in pearl millet. Farmers are apparently planting more area to pearl millet (bajra) in years when yields are higher. One explanation for this tendency is that many farmers, particularly in Gujarat, now have more water to plant irrigated summer bajra in more abundant rainfall years when rainfed yields are also heavier. A greater investment in irrigation and in HYVs has probably enhanced the potential for greater area-yield covariance. In contrast to bajra, little summer jowar (sorghum) is planted, and postrainy season (or rabi) sorghum is grown on residual soil moisture without irrigation.

The analysis thus far has raised the key empirical question: Why have sorghum and pearl millet yields become increasingly covariate over time across districts? There are several possible interrelated answers to this question although some are not amenable to measurement. Three potential causes are relatively easy to quantify: (a) changes in rainfall covariance, (b) changes in irrigated area, and (c) diffusion of HYVs.

The simplest hypothesis as to why detrended yields increasingly move together over time centers on changes in rainfall covariance. A severe drought, which Wolf Ladejinsky described as "never in a 100 years," occurred in 1972 in extensive sorghum and pearl millet growing tracts of peninsular India (Walinsky 1977). It is likely that such an extreme adverse rainfall event, where total annual rainfall in the affected districts was only 20–30 percent of the long-term average, would also be more covariate than more normal rainfall events.

Understanding the relationship between changes in irrigated area and yield covariance is more complex. Irrigation for a given level of technology makes the production environment more homogenous, thus reinforcing tendencies toward greater yield covariance. Irrigation also contributes indirectly to yield covariances by inducing greater adoption of improved varieties and hybrids, and better agronomic practices. Those district pairs having more irrigated area in the second period would be characterized by more covariate yields. Likewise, district pairs with greater differences in irrigated area in the second period are expected to have less covariate yields.

HYVs usually have a narrower genetic background than local varieties and landraces. For example, the bulk of HYV sorghum area in India is planted to four hybrids—CSH-1, CSH-5, CSH-6, and CSH-9—the last three being descended from the same male parent CS3541. Most of the commercially available pearl millet hybrids originate from closely related parents.

Although statistical evidence from secondary data is hard to find, it is also common knowledge that the first generation of pearl millet hybrids (HB-1, HB-3, and HB-4) were extremely susceptible to downy mildew resulting in significant economic losses in the early 1970s, after inoculum had built up on farmers' fields (Kanwar 1975). In response to those losses, farmers in several major producing regions reverted to local types and hybrid adoption rates plummeted. In the mid- and late-1970s, hybrid adoption again picked up as farmers accepted the second-generation hybrids which, at that time, were much less susceptible to downy mildew. Similar but atypical adoption patterns in producing regions as distant as Tamil Nadu and Maharashtra bear ample testimony to the problem of increasing production covariance caused by the release of supersusceptible cultivars (figure 6.1).

Sorghum production was not affected by such a cultivar susceptible source of risk as the downy mildew epidemic in pearl millet, but the 1971–

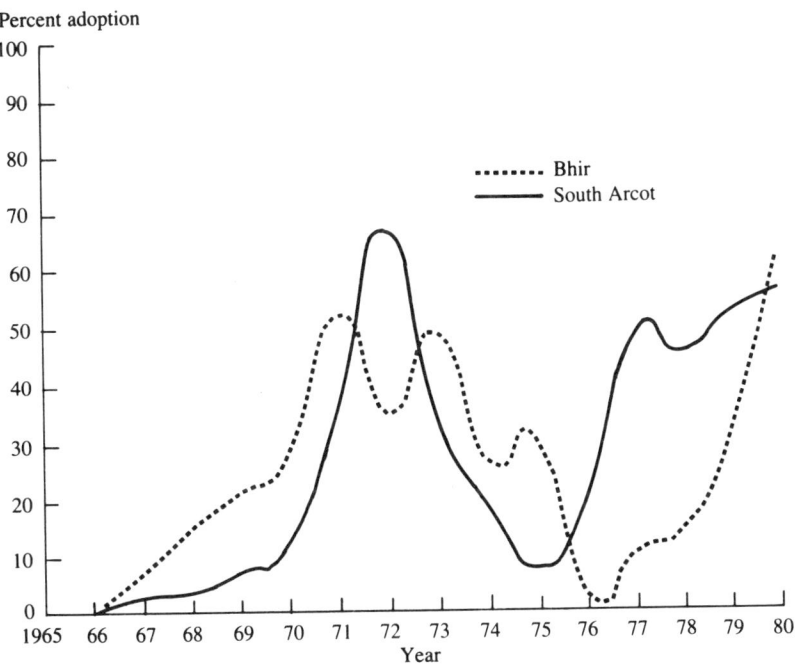

FIGURE 6.1 Adoption of pearl millet hybrids in Bhir (Maharashtra) and South Arcot (Tamil Nadu), 1966–1980

73 drought certainly slowed the uptake of sorghum hybrids in Maharashtra and northern Karnataka. Inspection of adoption curves suggests that the 1971-73 drought contributed to making the pattern of diffusion across sorghum-growing districts more covariate than it otherwise would have been.

The less tangible sources of changes in yield covariance are power and fertilizer shortages, and greater economic growth and development. Power "outages" and fertilizer shortages are an appealing explanation because more subsidized inputs in the form of electricity, fuel, irrigation water, and fertilizer were used in the second period, and because these shortages did occur cyclically and sporadically across regions (H. Ezekiel as cited by Hazell 1982). Their influence is expected to be much more significant for wheat and rice, which command a much larger share of these resources than do sorghum and pearl millet.

Economic development is also synonymous with increased covariance and interdependence. More literate and better educated agents have a greater capacity to process better quality information coming from more thoroughly linked factor and product markets. While the effects of these linkages are real, they are also difficult, if not impossible, to quantify.

Another potential explanation for higher yield covariances is that sorghum and pearl millet are increasingly grown on more marginal land. The marginal land hypothesis is, however, more consistent with increasing production variances within districts than rising production covariances between regions.

Data Description

To test the hypothesized role of rainfall, irrigation, and varieties in increasing yield covariances across districts, a regression analysis was undertaken. The analysis is based on district pairwise observations. Taking combinations of the 48 sorghum and 40 pearl millet districts two at a time gives 1,128 observations for sorghum and 780 for pearl millet.

The independent variables, pertaining to levels of HYV adoption (SUMADT and DIFADT), levels of irrigation (SUMIRR and DIFIRR), and changes in rainfall covariances (RFCOVCHG), are described in table 6.2 together with the dependent variable, the change in yield covariance (YCOVCHG). The rationale for having two regressors for each independent variable stems from the nature of the pairwise data set. For example, for any district pair it is to be expected that the genotypes in farmers' fields become more similar as HYV adoption increases because the HYVs are narrower in genetic composition than the local landraces that differ from district to district. Thus, a more positive change would be expected for a district pair with a (80,70) percent rate of adoption than another pair with

TABLE 6.2 Means and ranges of the data used to explain the increase in interregional yield covariance in sorghum and pearl millet production in India

Variable Name	Definition	Crop		Expected Sign
		Sorghum	Pearl Millet	
YCOVCHG	Change in yield covariance from the second period to the first (Mt^2)	4 (−43, 64)[a]	7 (−125, 169)	n.a.
SUMADT[b]	Sum of direct pairwise HYV area in percent of total area planted to the crop	40 (0.1, 111)	53 (0.0, 186)	+
DIFADT[b]	Absolute value of the difference in percent HYV area	17 (0.2, 60)	30 (0.0, 95)	−
SUMIRR[b]	Sum of district pairwise irrigated area in percent of total area planted to the crop	10 (0.0, 67)	8 (0.0, 51)	−
DIFIRR[b]	Absolute value of the percent difference in irrigated area	8 (0.0, 38)	6 (0.0, 28)	−
RFCOVCHG	Change in total rainfall covariances from the second period to the first	7	13	+

[a]Ranges are in parentheses.
[b]Mean value for each district for three cropping years from 1976/77 to 1978/79.

a (20,20) rate. The summed adoption rates would then be 150 and 40, and SUMADT should be signed positively. By the same token, an (80,20) pair should have more genetic variation than a (50,50) pair although the SUMADT is the same for both district pairs. For a given SUMADT more disparity in adoption rates within district pairs signals greater genetic variation and is expected to be accompanied by a reduction in the change in yield covariance. Hence, having two regressors leads to a more powerful test of the hypothesis that HYV adoption is responsible for increased yield covariance.

For about 78 and 66 percent of the sorghum and pearl millet district pairs, respectively, yield covariance increased in the second period. Wide ranging values for SUMADT and DIFADT reflect substantial interregional variation in HYV adoption. Large mean differences between SUMADT and SUMIRR also suggest that both sorghum and pearl millet hybrids have been planted exclusively in dryland agriculture. Positive values for RFCOVCHG confirm the suspicion that total annual rainfall was more covariate in the second period. Rainfall became more covariate in the second period for 68 percent of the sorghum and 75 percent of pearl millet district pairwise observations.

Empirical Results

To assign greater importance to those districts where more sorghum and pearl millet is grown, weighted least squares regression analysis is used. The weights are the mean proportions of area planted to the crop for each district pair relative to All India estimates of planted area during the last three cropping years of the second period.

The regression estimates reported in table 6.3 have very low explanatory power and suggest a noisy data set. The signs of the estimated coefficients, however, are generally consistent with expectations and, for the

TABLE 6.3 Estimated regression coefficients of the determinants of changes in interregional yield covariance in sorghum and pearl millet production

	Crop	
Variable	Sorghum	Pearl Millet
SUMADT	89*	110*
	(5.26)	(4.61)
DIFADT	−59*	−113*
	(−2.24)	(−3.84)
SUMIRR	100*	−462*
	(2.28)	(−3.40)
DIFIRR	−214*	108
	(−3.61)	(0.65)
RFCOVCHG	70*	14*
	(4.42)	(4.86)
Intercept	2,295	7,162
R^2	0.07	0.04

Note: t values are in parentheses.
*Indicates statistical significance at the 0.05 level.

most part, the coefficients are significantly different from zero at the 5 percent confidence level. Greater adoption of hybrids has increased interregional yield covariances in both sorghum and pearl millet production. More covariate rainfall events have also led to significantly more covariate interregional yields. For sorghum, change in irrigated area behaves as expected; however, irrigation leads to reduced interregional pearl millet yield covariances. This puzzling result could stem from the fact that irrigated pearl millet often entails only one or two applications of water and is largely cultivated where water supply is most uncertain. A closer look at changes in irrigated area by source may shed some light on this result.

Conclusions

Having shown that adoption of HYVs is positively correlated with, if not partially responsible for, increased sorghum and millet production variability, it would be facile but unwarranted to conclude that scientists in the sorghum and pearl millet All India coordinated crop improvement programs should have released hybrids and varieties with a broader genetic background and should have pursued a more regional or location specific release strategy to mitigate the adverse effect of increasing interregional yield covariance and rising production variability. Even with hindsight, it is impossible to say whether the benefits from following a more regional release policy and emphasizing selection and breeding from genetically more diverse populations would compensate for the productivity gains forgone from pursuing a more single-minded, national yield improvement strategy. Moreover, a judicious mix of international trade and storage policies can cost-effectively offset most, if not all, of the variability costs of increasing yield covariance. These issues are addressed more fully in part III of this book.

7 Variability in Wheat Yields in England: Analysis and Future Prospects

ROGER B. AUSTIN AND MICHAEL H. ARNOLD

This chapter presents data on variation in wheat yields in England and offers an assessment of the variation likely to be encountered in the future, given continued high levels of inputs. How yield stability might be modified by breeding and how the records from the U.K. may be helpful when considering likely changes in yields and their variability are discussed by Arnold and Austin (ch. 10).

The Partitioning of Variation

If the yields of wheat from a large number of individual fields are recorded over a period of years, variation can be partitioned into a number of different categories. In practice, complete sets of data that can be used to calculate the components of the total variation in yield are rarely available, and the best that can be done is to estimate the components from separate sets. A difficulty in making comparisons of variability is that mean yields can vary among different data sets, and the standard deviations are not independent of the means. Expressed as proportions of yield, that is, as coefficients of variation (cvs), they seem to be more constant for a given source of variation than the standard deviations themselves and so can conveniently be used for comparisons. Associations between means and their standard deviations are common in biology but the relationships are variable. Examples for animal populations are given by Taylor (1961).

Historical Trends in Wheat Yields and Their Variability

Records of wheat yields between 1200 and 1970 have been assembled by Stanhill (1976). Using these and more recent data, typical yields for the period from 1200 to 1980, together with the associated changes in agricultural practice, are summarized in table 7.1. Over the centuries, yield has

TABLE 7.1 Historical trends in English wheat yields

Period	Yield (t/ha)	New Features in Agriculture
1200	0.3–0.5	Open field system
1650	0.6	Enclosure, fallowing
1750	1.0	Seed drills
1850	1.8	Four course rotation
1920	2.1	Fertilizers, new varieties
1950	2.5	More fertilizers, herbicides
1980	6.5	More N fertilizer, short-straw varieties, fungicides

TABLE 7.2 Interannual variation in English wheat yields

Period	Average Yield (t/ha)	Standard Deviation of Yield (t/ha)	Coefficient of Variation
1832–59[a]	2.08	0.276	0.133
1880–1917[b]	2.12	0.179	0.084
1918–45[c]	2.25	0.167	0.074
1948–84[c]	4.18	0.492	0.118
1961–83	4.59	0.330[e]	0.072[e]

[a] Healy and Jones (1962).
[b] *Century of Agricultural Statistics* (1968).
[c] Ministry of Agriculture, Fisheries, and Food (1964–84).
[d] Time trends, where significant, removed by linear regression.
[e] For 1961–83, quadratic trend with time removed.

increased by 10–20-fold. Average yields of grain crops in semi-arid areas of the world today are similar to those obtained in England during the period from 1200 to 1850. Does the available evidence from England suggest that the variability of yield has changed over the centuries? Table 7.2 shows some results for national yields over a period when yields increased from an average of about two tons per hectare to over four tons per hectare. The results for 1832–59 are not strictly comparable with the remaining data because they include too great a proportion of fields outside the main cereal-growing area in England. Furthermore, yields were estimated from small samples. For the last ten years of the period 1948–1985, yields increased more rapidly than during the earlier period, and the trend in yield from 1948 was better fitted by a second degree polynomial in time. This reduced the cv of national yield from 0.118 (linear trend) to 0.101 (second degree polynomial), or to 0.088 when the data for the abnormally dry year of 1976 were excluded. Taking account of these features, no striking change in the interannual cv of yield is evident, though as the mean yield has increased substantially, the interannual variation in absolute terms has increased.

A more detailed examination of the interannual variation during the period 1948-85 was made by plotting the absolute values of the deviations of actual from fitted yields, expressed as a proportion of the fitted yields, against years.

The ordinate in figure 7.1 is a detrended coefficient of variation of yield (linear trend removed). Linear regression analysis of the 38 years' data showed that the cv had not increased significantly over the period. When the data for the abnormally dry year of 1976 were omitted, the regression was likewise not significant. Even if the analysis had indicated a significant trend, it would be impossible with these data alone to attribute the trend to any cause, for example, to a change in the variability of weather elements affecting yield, to differences in the varieties grown, or to altered management practices. As noted above, conclusions about trends in variability can be quite sensitive to an abnormally low yield and to the degree of polynomial used to eliminate the time trend. Furthermore, when calculations were done for the years 1961-83 (the period usually considered by Hazell and his colleagues, e.g., ch. 2), the large sampling errors of the variances were further emphasized. Thus, after fitting a second degree polynomial in time to the data for 1961-83, the interannual cv of yield was 0.072 (compared with 0.101 for the entire period). Taking all the available data from 1930-85, it would seem unwise to conclude that the cv of yield has shown any real trend with years.

Considering the period 1961-83, the best estimate of the cv of English wheat yields (0.072) is similar to the averaged values for the two periods 1961-71 and 1972-83 studied by Hazell (1985b) for several other countries (India 0.082, France 0.082, Mexico 0.089, and the Federal Republic of Germany 0.074). In other countries where wheat is grown in more variable environments and usually without irrigation, the cvs derived from Hazell's data in the same way are markedly greater (e.g., U.S.S.R. 0.149, Canada 0.137, Argentina 0.136 and Australia 0.187) (ch. 2).

Interannual Variation in Yield at Particular Sites

Because national yields are averages of those of a large number of individual fields, it may be expected that they will be much less variable from year to year than those from individual fields, which are subject to the effects of variable management, rotations, and weather. Table 7.3 shows that interannual variation in yield at particular sites is indeed greater than

FIGURE 7.1 U.K. wheat yields, 1948-1984

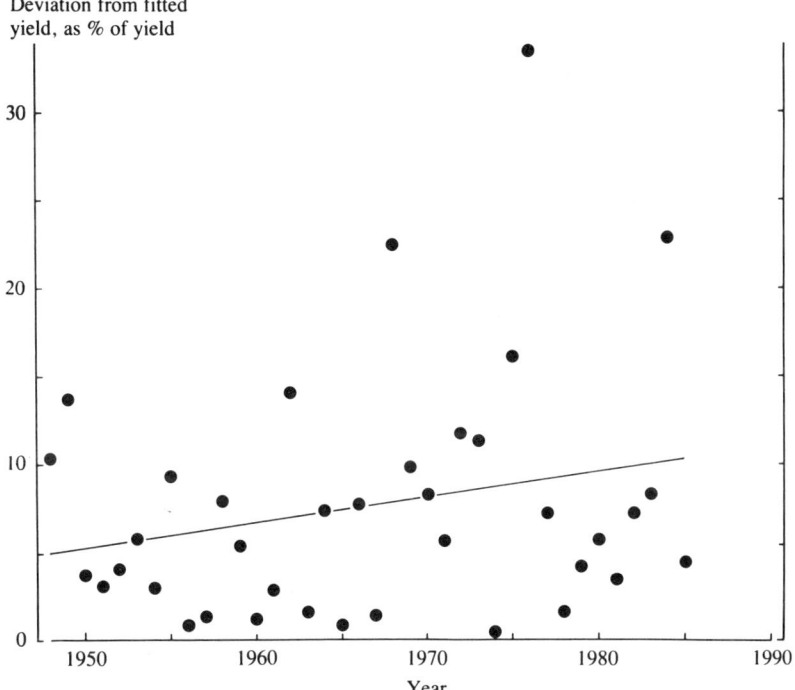

NOTES: Deviations from fitted yields, expressed as percentages of fitted yields, plotted against years. Fitted yields computed by linear regression of yield on years.

that in national yield. In general, as yields increase the standard deviation of yield also increases, but as a percentage of yield, it generally decreases. While the reasons for these trends in variability cannot be analyzed rigorously, some factors likely to be important are: winter rainfall, weeds, diseases, summer drought, and the weather at harvest time.

For the earliest records, all these factors are likely to have affected yield, and it is not surprising that the greatest variability was observed during these periods. For the Rothamsted data for 1852 to 1918, yields were somewhat less variable, especially on the plots that received mineral fertilizers or farmyard manure. However, winter rainfall caused considerable, but variable, leaching of soil nitrogen, originating from both farmyard manure and autumn-applied fertilizer. Also, weed infestations caused yield losses that varied with seasons. After 1950, the use of herbicides greatly reduced weed infestations thus reducing the variation in yield that they

TABLE 7.3 Interannual variation in wheat yields at individual sites in the United Kingdom

Site	Period	Average Yield (t/ha)	Standard[f] Deviation (t/ha)	Coefficient of Variation
Downton[a]	1225-1349	0.412	0.126	0.306
West Wycombe[a]	1211-1349	0.504	0.167	0.331
Broadbalk experiment, Rothamsted[b,c]				
1. Farmyard manure only (Plot 20)	1852-1918	2.43	0.406	0.167
2. Inorganic fertilizers (Plot 8)	1852-1918	2.51	0.513	0.204
3. No farmyard manure or fertilizer (Plots 3 & 4)	1852-1918	0.86	0.215	0.249
1. Farmyard manure only	1970-78	5.87	1.061	0.180
2. Complete inorganic fertilizer (N at 144 kg/ha)	1970-78	5.09	0.507	0.098
3. No farmyard manure or fertilizer	1970-78	1.70	0.286	0.168
Rothamsted[d] ley-arable experiment	1952-71	6.20	0.682	0.110
National Institute of Agricultural Botany[e]	1967-78	5.60	1.008	0.180

[a] Titow (1972).
[b] Fisher (1921).
[c] Dyke et al. (1983).
[d] McEwan (private communication).
[e] Talbot (1984).
[f] Linear trend removed, if significant.

caused. In well-fertilized plots, particularly where most of the nitrogen was applied in the spring, winter leaching of nitrogen as a source of yield variation was greatly reduced. The remaining uncontrolled factors causing variation in yield were the direct effects of weather on crop growth (e.g., severe winters, summer drought), the indirect effects (e.g., delayed sowing, poor weather during harvesting), and the effects of diseases. In recent years, cultivation systems have been developed which facilitate early sowing, and diseases are controlled by a combination of improved genetic resistance and the use of fungicides. It may be expected, therefore, that the interannual variation of yields on individual sites will decrease in the future, and may level out to about 0.1 times the mean yield. It seems very unlikely that it would ever be lower than the interannual cv of national average yields.

TABLE 7.4 Variation in wheat yields from field to field in the United Kingdom

Source of Data	Mean Yield Deviation (t/ha)	Standard Deviation (t/ha)	Coefficient of Variation
Liverpool surveys[a] (16 years between 1830 and 1859)	1.93	0.336	0.17
91 farms[b] (1934–38 in U.K.)	3.40	0.490	0.14
Huntingdonshire[c] (271 fields, 1971–78)	5.44	0.761	0.14
National Institute of Agricultural Botany[d] (1967–78)	5.70	0.912	0.16
ICI[e] survey (1980)	7.37	1.38	0.19

Note: Interannual variation eliminated.
[a]Healy and Jones (1962).
[b]Cochran (1939).
[c]Church and Austin (1983).
[d]Talbot (1984).
[e]Tinker and Widdowson (1983).

Variation in Yields from Field to Field

Results from some surveys are given in table 7.4. Field-to-field variation within a year is apparently fairly constant at 0.14–0.19 times mean yield. In biological terms, this variation results from the combined effects of variation in soil type, the variety grown, variations in cultural treatments (sowing rates, fertilizer rates, agrochemical use, etc.), as well as the effects of variations in weather, particularly rainfall. In commercial farming, it is impossible to ensure that cultural operations are carried out optimally, in part because of the scale of operations and in part because the optimal timing is dependent on future weather and can be determined only in retrospect from experimental results.

The component of field-to-field variation due to variations in cultural operations under modern farming conditions can be estimated approximately from the results of multifactorial experiments carried out between 1981 and 1984 at Rothamsted Experimental Station (Lester 1981, 1982, 1983; Rothamsted 1984). Results from these experiments, not presented in detail here, show that the average improvements in yield due to the best levels of individual factors were, as proportions of the mean yield: sowing date, 0.064; timing of the main application of nitrogen fertilizer, 0.066; amount of nitrogen fertilizer applied, 0.069; individual crop protection measures separately, 0.033. In these experiments the major factor affecting yield was the previous crop through its effect on the severity of take-all disease (*Gaumannomyces graminis*), which was much more severe when wheat followed barley than when it followed oats. The average variation above and below the annual mean yield due to this effect was 0.31 times the mean yield. These results are discussed elsewhere in this volume by Arnold and Austin (ch. 10).

Plant Breeding and Yield Variation

In the U.K., winter wheat breeding during the past 50 years has been based on selection under farming conditions that have been broadly representative of the total production area (Silvey 1978, 1981). Moreover, new varieties, whether bred in the U.K. or not, are recommended to farmers only after evaluation for three seasons over a wide range of localities. Stability is an important requirement for recommendation, in addition to potential for yield. A very close watch is kept to detect the development of new or more aggressive pathogens, and the variability in the yield that these could cause is counteracted by the breeding of resistant varieties and the use of new control agents. Analyses of genotype–environment interactions have tended to show that the new semidwarf varieties are more responsive in absolute terms to high levels of inputs than the taller old ones, indicating a reduction in stability (Patterson 1980). As table 7.2 and figure 7.1 show, variability of yield has increased in absolute terms, although the coefficient of variation of yield has shown no marked trend with years. It is the view of experienced agronomists and breeders in England that the cv of yield may decrease in the future as farmers become more familiar with the requirements of the new varieties and the management of the higher input systems introduced in the past 20 years.

8 Variability in Wheat and Barley Production in Southeast England

PAUL WEBSTER AND NIGEL T. WILLIAMS

Previous work using aggregate data (Hazell 1982, 1984) has indicated that higher levels of production are often associated with increased variability in yields and increased interregional yield correlations. The purpose in this study is to examine whether there is evidence to suggest that the same is true in a sample of farms from Southeast England.

Data Sources

The study is based on information from the *Farm Management Survey*, which is an annual and continuing survey into farm incomes in the U.K. The data come from the southeastern region of the U.K. and consist of production, yield, and area planted of wheat and barley for identical farms over a period of 21 years (Williams et al. 1984).

Analysis was restricted to those farms that had grown the particular crop every year during the periods surveyed. The final groups consisted of 16 wheat growers and 18 barley growers. Thirteen growers appeared in both groups. All wheat growers had grown some barley during the period; all barley growers had grown some wheat during the period. Thus, while the changes in the structure of production will be discussed largely on a crop basis, it should be remembered that these changes were often taking place on the same farms. One effect of the requirement for the crops to be grown in every year was that farmers moving into or out of production had to be excluded. To this extent the results may understate the changes taking place.

Changes in production were measured between two periods, namely 1964–74 and 1975–84. While this division was made pragmatically on the basis of the availability of the data, the second period had two particular characteristics: first, it followed the U.K.'s accession to the European Economic Community in 1973, and second, it coincided with the period of increasing availability and adoption of fungicides to control cereal diseases. Since the first year of the second period, 1975, was a severe drought year in the region, results are also reported after excluding 1975 from the analysis.

Changes in areas sown and yields of wheat and barley reflect both short- and long-term influences. The area and yield data were detrended using a generalized least squares estimating procedure (ch. 2).

Changes in Wheat and Barley Production

Table 8.1 shows the changes in total wheat and barley production on the two groups of farms between the periods 1964–74 and 1975–84. Wheat production increased by 87 percent while barley declined by 2 percent. Wheat yields improved almost twice as rapidly as barley yields for these farms.

The individual farm results (not shown) show that all but one of the farmers increased their areas of wheat while the majority (11 of 18) reduced their areas of barley. All but one of the wheat farmers increased their yields (by up to 50 percent). The single farmer who did not was already performing particularly well in the first period. All but one of the barley farmers increased their yields (by up to 45 percent).

Table 8.1 also shows the change in variability of yields as measured by the coefficient of variation (cv). Both wheat and barley show significant increases (of 32 and 45 percent, respectively, even when the 1975 data are excluded). The magnitude of the cv for the wheat group is comparable with Austin and Arnold's (ch. 7) estimate at the national level. On the basis of individual farms, the average coefficient of variation of yield in the group moved from 0.153 to 0.157. While the change was not significant, the absolute level is also comparable with Austin and Arnold's estimate for variability at particular sites.

Using the decomposition methods described in chapter 2, over half the additional wheat production was found to come from an increase in area sown, while one-third came from improved yields. Almost all the remainder arose from the interaction of yield and area, with the change in the area-yield covariances being negligible. When the drought year of 1975 was excluded, the results were largely similar.

With such a small change in production of barley (-2.3 percent, table 8.1) no significance could be attached to its decomposition results, which are not reported.

Decomposition of Changes in the Variability of Production

Table 8.2 shows the results from the decomposition of the changes in the variance of wheat production between the two periods. More than two-

TABLE 8.1 Changes in the mean and variability of wheat and barley production on two groups of farms in Southeast England: 1964-1974 to 1975-1984

Item	Wheat			Barley		
	First Period[a]	Second Period	Change (percent)	First Period	Second Period	Change (percent)
Average production (t)	3,101	5,808	87.3	3,036	2,967	−2.3
Average yield (t/ha)	4.1	5.3	29.3	3.6	4.2	15.8
Average area planted (ha)	47.0	66.4	41.1	47.1	40.0	−15.1
Coefficient of variation						
Production	0.110	0.163	48.2	0.122	0.135	10.6
		(0.118)[b]	(7.3)		(0.126)	(3.2)
Yield	0.055	0.089	61.8	0.053	0.104	96.2
		(0.072)	(30.9)		(0.077)	(45.3)
Area sown	0.100	0.108	8.0	0.096	0.073	−24.0
		(0.089)	(−11.0)		(0.085)	(−11.4)
F ratios						
Production		7.4*			1.2	
Yield		4.5*			5.1*	
Area sown		2.3			2.4	
Number of farms		16			18	

[a] The first period is 1964-74; the second is 1975-84.
[b] Figures in brackets refer to results when 1975 is excluded from the second period.
*An asterisk denotes that the variance in the second period is significantly different from that of the first period at the 5 percent level (two-tailed test).

TABLE 8.2 Components of change in wheat production variance on 16 farms in Southeast England: 1964-1974 to 1975-1984 (percent)

Variance Component	Source of Change						
	Change in Mean Yields	Change in Mean Areas	Change in Yield Variances and Covariances	Change in Area Variances and Covariances	Change in Area-Yield Covariances	Change in Interaction Terms	Change in Residual	Row Sums
Sum variances within farms	11.33	3.82	4.71	3.78	2.06	2.35	−0.56	27.49
Sum interfarm covariances	7.69	3.28	11.17	9.64	13.28	30.64	−3.18	72.52
Column sums	19.02	7.10	15.88	13.42	15.34	32.97	−3.73	100.00

thirds of the increase in variance of wheat production came from increased production covariances between farms. Nearly 16 percent of the increase in variance in wheat production was due to changes in yield variances and covariances. The smaller part (4.7 percent) was due to increases in yield variances within farms, while the larger part (11.17 percent) was due to increases in yield covariances between farms. Of this 11.17 percent, a further decomposition showed that about half (55.1 percent) was due to increases in yield variances alone and the rest would not have occurred without an autonomous increase in interfarm yield correlations. While wheat yield variability within farms increased, so did the correlation of yields between farms.

A similar analysis was carried out for the barley farmers but, bearing in mind the small and nonsignificant change in the production variability (table 8.1), it was difficult to attach much weight to the decomposition results. Changes in within-farm yield variances appeared to be more important in explaining changes in production variability for barley than for wheat.

The analysis shown in table 8.2 was repeated with the drought year of 1975 excluded. The results were stable for wheat but less so for barley. Despite the fact that the increase in production variability was not significant, there was a significant increase in yield variability for barley.

Looking at the individual farm results, figure 8.1 indicates that 12 of the farmers showed significant (at the 10 percent level) increases in yield

FIGURE 8.1 Number of sample farms showing change in variability of wheat and barley yields in Southeast England, 1964-1974 to 1975-1984

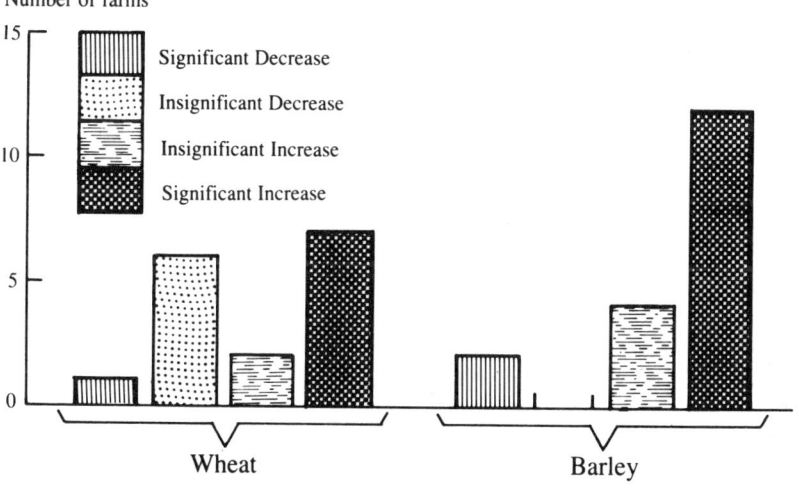

TABLE 8.3 Interfarm yield correlations of wheat and barley significantly different from zero on selected farms in Southeast England

	1964-74		1975-84	
Crop	Positive	Negative	Positive	Negative
		(percent)		
Wheat[a]	22.5	5.0	33.3	1.7
Barley[b]	26.1	2.6	23.5	2.6

Note: Significance defined at the 10 percent level or better (one-tailed test).
[a] Percent of 240 correlations between 16 farms.
[b] Percent of 306 correlations between 18 farms.

variability of barley while two showed significant decreases. This contrasts with the position for wheat where only seven farmers showed significant increases in yield variability with one showing a significant decrease.

Further analysis of the individual results showed that, in terms of their contribution to changes in group production variability, two farmers stood out. Both had expanded their wheat production markedly. One had expanded his area sevenfold and had doubled his yield per hectare over the 20-year period. There were insignificant changes in the variability of his wheat and barley yields. The other farmer had also expanded his area of wheat (by about three times), but had first increased and then decreased his area of barley. He was one of the four farmers in the groups to show significant increases in the variability of both wheat and barley yields. Over the past six years he had hired a crop management consultant to help with his cereal production decisions.

Table 8.3 shows the percentage of between-farm yield correlations significantly different from zero for both periods. The number of positive correlations increased for wheat, but for barley there was a slight decline. The number of negative correlations dropped for wheat but remained constant for barley. For wheat, this suggests that the distribution of correlation coefficients has become more skewed toward the positive region, while there seemed to be a slight reduction of variability in the correlation coefficients for barley.

In summary, there were increases in the cv of production of 48 percent for wheat and of 11 percent for barley when the periods 1964-74 and 1975-84 were compared, though the increases were considerably smaller when the drought year 1975 was excluded. The cv of yield increased by 63 percent for wheat and 96 percent for barley. However, changes in yield variances and covariances accounted for only about 16 percent of the increase in production variability for wheat. Increases in within-farm yield variances were more important than increases in between-farm yield correlations as contributors to overall production variability. More barley producers than wheat producers showed significant increases in yield variability. Wheat yields between farms became more positively correlated. Barley yields showed a slight decline in the number of positive correlations.

Sources of Change in Variability

Why have wheat yields become more variable on these farms and at the same time more highly correlated between the farms? Why is there a tendency toward lower between-farm correlations for barley? Is there a pattern to these changes in variability? A complete answer would require detailed study of cropping decisions over the 21-year period, which is beyond the scope of the present investigation. However, some hypotheses may be generated and investigated.

Cereal Varieties

Silvey (1978, 1981) has reviewed the contribution of better varieties over the period 1947 to 1979. She attempted to partition the contribution of "variety" and "other factors" (such as fertilizer, herbicides, fungicides, pesticides, growth regulators, better timing, etc.) to yield increases. Between 1967 and 1979 she estimated that about three-quarters of the yield increase for wheat was due to better varieties while one-quarter arose as a result of the "other factors." Wheat, therefore, might be regarded as less dependent on input supplies than barley.

The second period, 1975–84, saw the introduction of the semidwarf wheat varieties whose shorter straw allowed increased nitrogen uptake. Patterson (1980), using trials data between 1976 and 1979, showed that these varieties were more "sensitive" to changes in site than the longer strawed varieties. On the better soils, their yield advantage was greater compared with the longer strawed varieties.

A further explanation of increased between-farm covariability might be that farmers were using fewer varieties in the second period. Analysis of national data relating to the popularity of cereal varieties (Rothamsted Experimental Station 1984) showed no significant reduction in the numbers of varieties achieving 10 percent or more of the U.K. market either for wheat or barley. No wheat variety during 1975–84 matched the record of Capelle in the 1964–74 period when it was never less than 16 percent of the market and achieved 65 percent in 1968. For barley, following the earlier decline of Proctor, only Zephyr (at 45 percent in 1968) achieved anything like Capelle's level of prominence. Changes in cereal varieties per se do not seem to have had a strong impact on yield variability.

FIGURE 8.2 Nitrogen application per hectare, England and Wales, 1974-1984

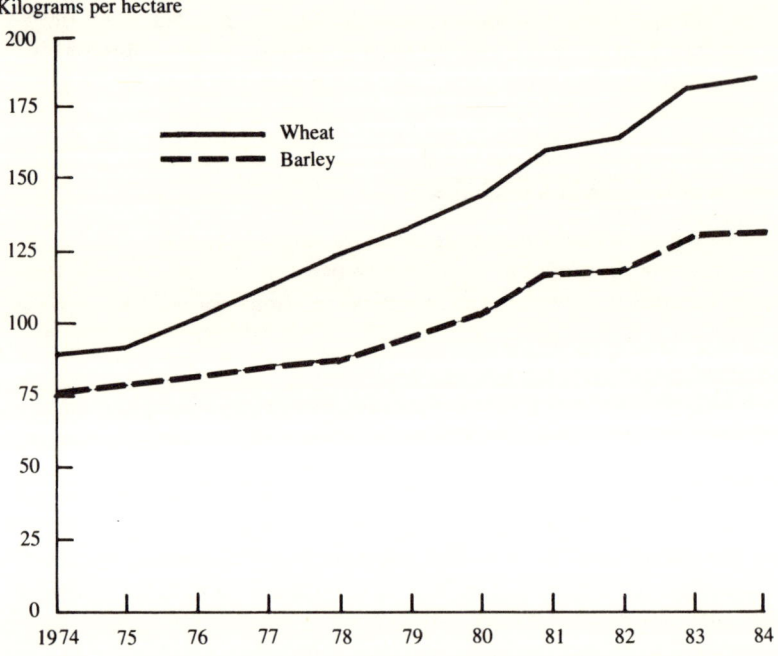

Fertilizers

Figure 8.2 shows the levels of nitrogen applied to wheat and barley crops. While there has been a steady increase, the data do not support the hypothesis of increased variability of input levels induced by changes in price of either nitrogen or wheat. Even the rise in fertilizer price following the increase in oil prices during the 1970s seems to have had little impact.

Fungicides

A particular feature of the changing cereal technology since World War II has been the progressive uptake of chemical inputs. In the 1950s and 1960s, herbicides and insecticides became available and were part of the accepted technology throughout the study period. As such, these last two categories of chemical inputs seem unlikely to have had much impact on the variability of yields.

The first fungicides only became available for commercial use on cereals in 1970 (King 1977). Figure 8.3 shows the rapid uptake of these materials. By 1982, 82 percent of winter wheat crops and 77 percent of winter barley crops were being treated (Cook 1982). For wheat—which was pre-

FIGURE 8.3 Fungicide application on cereals, England and Wales, 1970-1984

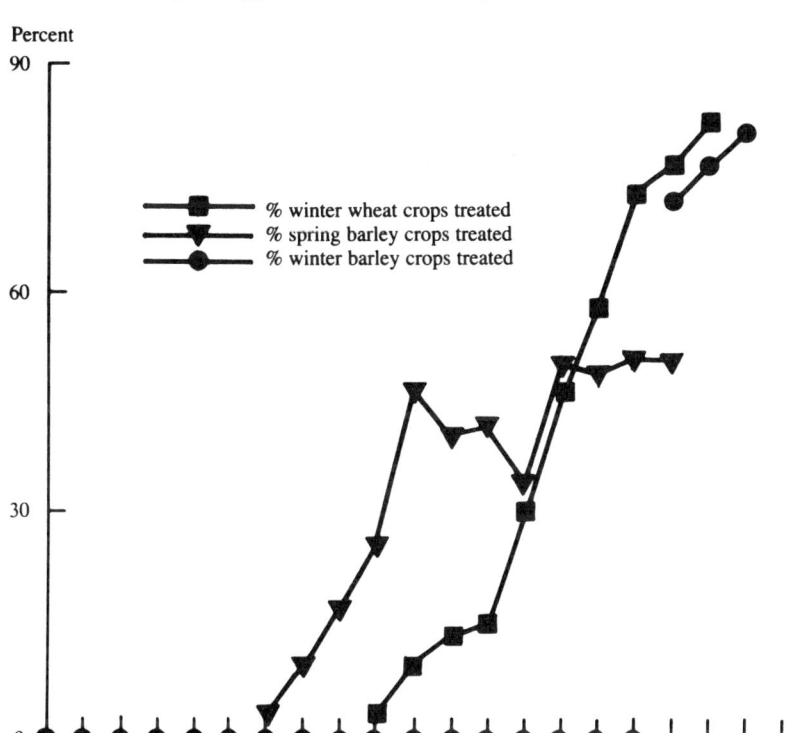

SOURCES: King (1977), Cook (1982).

dominantly winter sown throughout the period—the adoption of fungicides coincided with an apparent upsurge in yield levels after the drought years of 1975 and 1976.

In contrast, the effect of the availability of fungicides for barley was to change a largely spring-sown crop into a winter-sown one. With fungicides available to control mildew in the autumn, it became possible for better yields to be gained from the new winter-sown varieties (figure 8.4). This change may explain the greater level of within-farm variability observed for barley. During the second period, the barley crop became a more heterogeneous mixture of winter- and spring-sown crops. This change may also explain the reduction in the number of significant positive correlation coefficients seen in table 8.3.

The effect of fungicides is to reduce losses from cereal diseases, which in the U.K. are highly dependent upon weather. Since weather affects all

FIGURE 8.4 Fungicide use and the change to winter-sown barley, England and Wales, 1969-1984

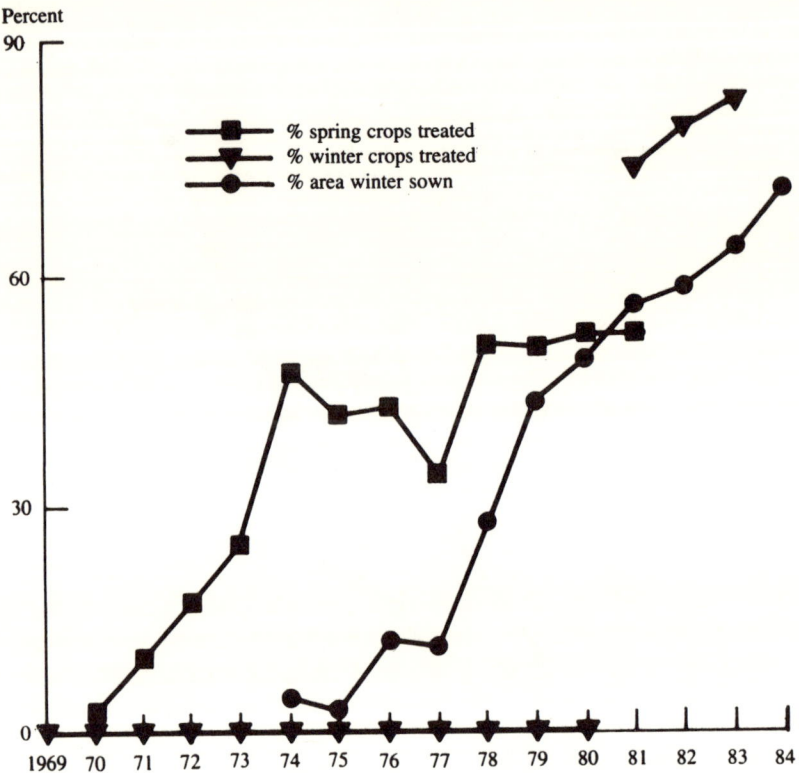

NOTE: Treatment data are for England and Wales (King 1977, Cook 1982); area data are for Southeast England only (unpublished "Farm Management Survey" data, 1974-84).

farms this perhaps explains the increase in between-farm covariance for the wheat growers.

The discussion so far has emphasized changes in the major variable inputs (varieties, fertilizers, sprays). Other developments have also contributed to improved yields. Growth regulators have recently become popular and autumn sowing dates for winter cereals have moved some weeks earlier. Farmers are better able to control the production process more readily while improvements in machinery have enabled better timing of cultivations, sprays, and fertilizer.

A plausible hypothesis might be that the impact of these developments has been to increase the number of controlled inputs at the expense of the number of uncontrolled inputs. Farmers perhaps have to face fewer random factors. As one wheat grower put it: "These days you know that if you make a mistake or if the weather is bad, it is going to be reflected in your yield. But twenty years ago you never really knew why your yield was what it was. With hindsight, there were always half a dozen things that went wrong, but we didn't know what they were or what we could do about them. And so we didn't bother about them."

While further work is needed before this hypothesis can be accepted, it appears to go some way to explaining the results of the earlier analysis. It could also be used to suggest that within-farm crop variability is unlikely to decline until crop growth becomes independent of many more factors, and that between-farm correlation of yields is likely to increase. Finally, neither of these sources of variability seems likely to have a major impact on the variability of production as a whole.

9 Variability in Winter Wheat and Spring Barley Yields in Bavaria

G. FISCHBECK

Winter wheat and spring barley are the predominant cereals grown in Bavaria. As a result of continuous improvements in varieties and agronomic practices, and because of the minimum price support policies practiced by the federal government, and later the European Economic Community, the crops have remained attractive to farmers and yields have increased substantially. Average winter wheat yields increased from 2.25 tons per hectare in 1950 to 6.32 tons per hectare in 1984, and spring barley yields increased from 2.21 tons per hectare in 1950 to 4.28 tons per hectare in 1984. The performance of these two crops, together with the availability of reliable state yield data (from the Besondere Enteermittlung scheme), make them a good case study of the relationship between yield increase and yield variability.

Methods

Measuring yield variability is inherently difficult because it is not easy to separate the effects of random events, such as weather, from the short-term impact of new varieties or changes in agronomic methods. Fitting trends to shorter time series helps capture the effects of technological change, but the trend estimates are more sensitive to unusual weather events. While fitting trends to longer time series reduces the sensitivity of results to weather, it is more likely to assign some technology-induced changes in yields to random causes. As a compromise, in this chapter yield trends were estimated for consecutive sequences of 10-year periods between 1950 and 1984. That is, trends were fitted for the periods 1950-59, 1951-60, 1952-61, and so on. The estimated trend coefficients (b) and

---

The cooperation of G. Pommer, who provided yield data from the farming systems trial at Puch, and of J. Bergermeier and A. Penger, who did the computing, is gratefully acknowledged.

TABLE 9.1 Coefficients of regression and standard deviation for kernel yield of winter wheat and spring barley in Bavaria in 10-year periods, 1950–1984

	Winter Wheat		Spring Barley	
Period	b (kg/ha/yr)	sd (kg/ha)	b (kg/ha/yr)	sd (kg/ha)
Decade beginning				
1950	67	24	50	9
1951	113	38	71	17
1952	108	39	46	26
1953	137	36	64	28
1954	145	36	69	28
1955	112	34	72	28
1956	59	45	15	40
1957	40	46	10	43
1958	54	48	29	46
1959	52	48	47	49
1960	59	49	77	52
1961	84	42	79	51
1962	108	46	74	50
1963	128	43	106	47
1964	142	41	117	46
1965	156	40	132	43
1966	94	37	70	36
1967	31	34	8	31
1968	32	34	12	31
1969	57	35	16	31
1970	48	36	18	31
1971	31	31	−42	16
1972	71	26	−27	19
1973	73	26	−26	19
1974	112	29	−7	24
1975	194	35	43	32

standard deviations of the residuals (sd) are reported in table 9.1.

As expected, the estimated b and sd values vary markedly from one 10-year period to another, so the results were smoothed by taking 10-year moving averages (figure 9.1).

Results

Winter wheat yields increased consistently over the period 1950–84 at an annual rate of over 60 kilograms per hectare per year (kg/ha/yr) (figure 9.1). However, the rate of increase has declined modestly over the years. Yield increases for spring barley started at much lower rates, increased to

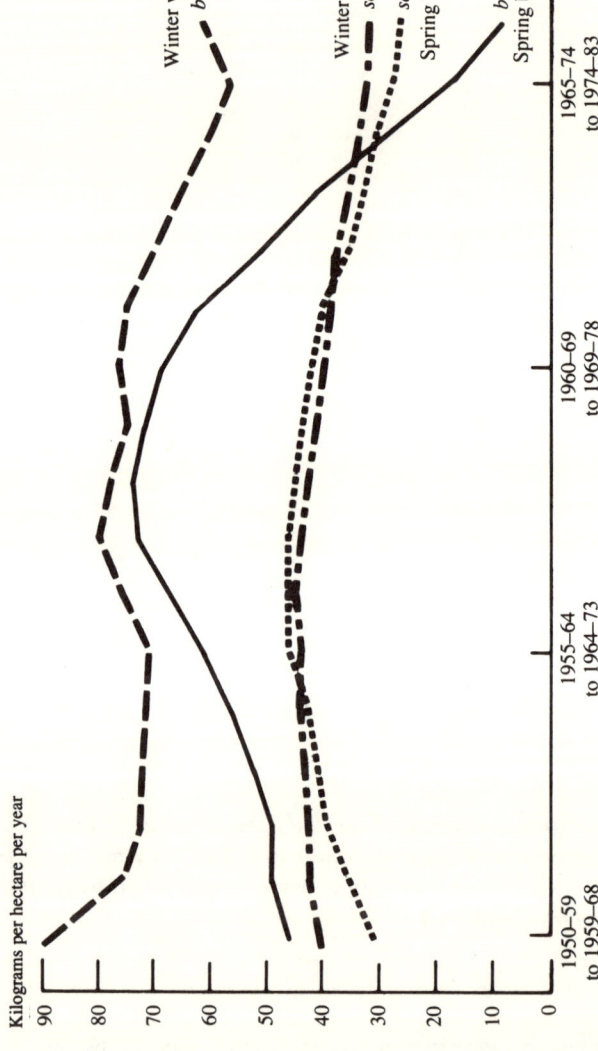

FIGURE 9.1 Changes in yield increase and yield variation of winter wheat and spring barley in Bavaria, 1950–1984

NOTE: Changes in yield increase are shown by moving averages of regression coefficients (b) for yield upon time for 10-year periods. Changes in yield variation are shown by moving averages of standard deviations of regression coefficients (sd) for 10-year periods.

rates comparable to those for wheat at midperiod, and then declined to almost zero by the end of the period.

Changes in yield variability, as measured by *sd* have been almost identical for the two crops (figure 9.1). There was a modest increase in the early years, especially for spring barley in the mid-1960s. This decline in variability occurred even though average yield increased for both crops.

Figure 9.2 shows the actual yield of each crop over the period 1960 to 1978. There is a very close correlation between their yields ($r = 0.93$), suggesting that a common factor, probably weather, is primarily responsible for yield fluctuations. But there are other factors which need to be considered, especially if the decline in variability is to be explained.

A major goal in breeding efforts for both crops has been increased resistance to lodging, though progress was more rapid with winter wheat than spring barley. This resistance has allowed the more intensive use of nitrogen, but again more so on winter wheat than spring barley, especially as the latter has been pushed onto more marginal lands, and intensive fertilizer application is detrimental to malting quality. In the mid-1960s, the first growth regulator (CCC) also became available to reduce straw length, and this was effective on wheat but not barley. As average wheat yields surpassed four tons per hectare in the early 1970s, it became economical to apply fungicides to control diseases in the dense plant stands promoted by high fertilizer application. Taken together, these developments explain most of the widening gap between winter wheat and spring barley yields. They also suggest that improved agronomic practices can be effective in reducing the impact of weather on yield variability, even as significant advances in average yields are attained. This view is considerably reinforced by the similar levels of yield variability for the two crops in recent years (figure 9.1) even though winter wheat yields were growing much faster than spring barley yields.

An alternative way to analyze the yield data from Bavaria is to split the 1950 to 1984 period into two roughly equal periods (1950 to 1966 and 1967 to 1984), and then to compare the trends and change in variability between these periods. The results of this analysis are reported in table 9.2.

The trend in winter wheat yields changed little between the periods 1950-66 and 1967-84, but the trend in barley yields fell sharply. The coefficient of variation also declined for spring barley but changed little for winter wheat. But, as should be expected from figure 9.1, these results are unlikely to be robust if alternative time periods are chosen. This is illustrated in table 9.2 by including results for the period 1956 to 1975. Although the results are relatively robust for winter wheat, the yield trend and cv are much higher for spring barley than in other periods. The results from this type of analysis can, therefore, be misleading, and the use of moving averages as reported earlier is a more reliable method of analysis.

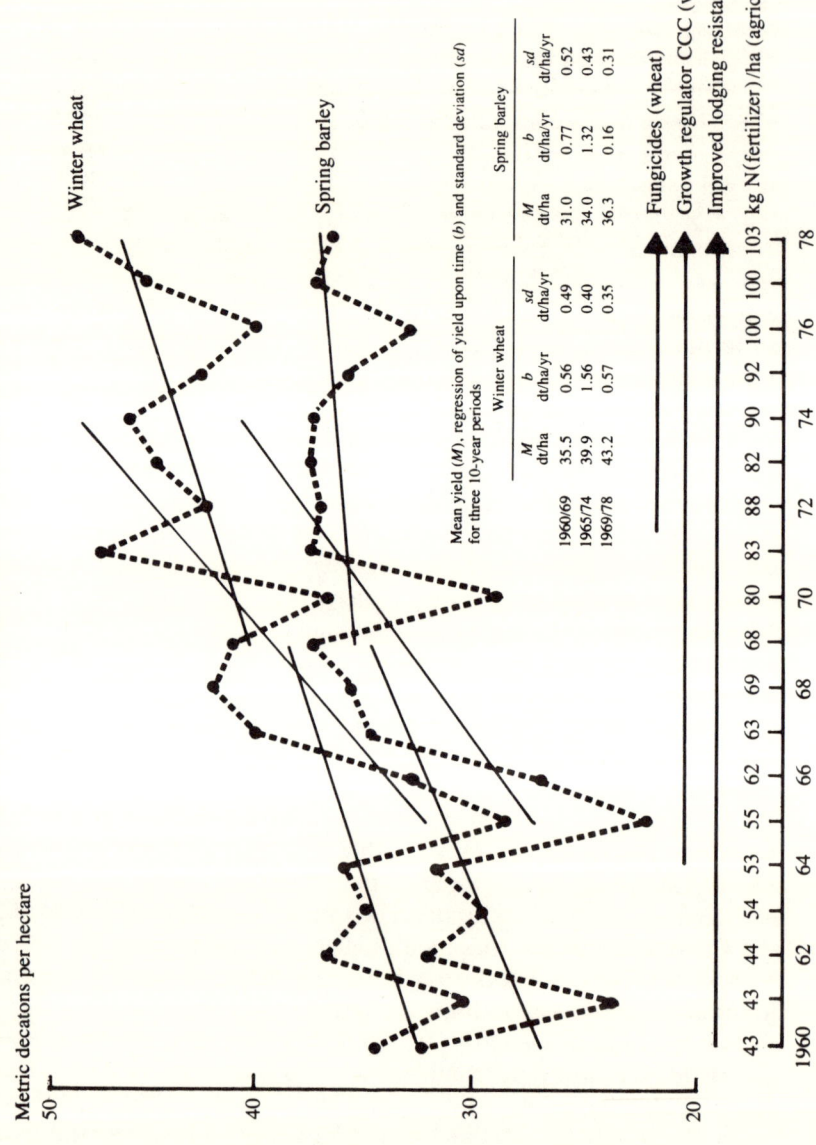

FIGURE 9.2 Mean yield of winter wheat and spring barley in Bavaria, 1960–1978

Metric decatons per hectare

TABLE 9.2 Changes in the mean and variability of winter wheat and spring barley yields in Bavaria, 1950-1966, 1956-1975, and 1967-1984

Period	Average Yield		Trend in Yield		Coefficient of Variation	
	Winter Wheat	Spring Barley	Winter Wheat	Spring Barley	Winter Wheat	Spring Barley
	(t/ha)		(t/ha/yr)			
1950-66	2.92	2.63	0.071	0.035	0.15	0.12
1967-84	4.58	3.60	0.093	0.015	0.14	0.08
1956-75	3.64	3.13	0.093	0.065	0.17	0.16

Experimental Data

More specific insights into how breeding for higher yield may affect yield variability can be obtained from data from one of the experimental farms of the Bayerische Landesanstalt für Bodenkultur und Pflanzenbau. This trial was laid out in 1965 with the purpose of demonstrating the major differences between traditional and modern methods of crop production. Since 1974, progenies of a very old landrace of spring barley and, since 1978, one of the early cultivars of winter wheat, have been included in the trial. Kernel yields obtained under different farming systems within the 11 six-year trial periods are summarized in table 9.3. The recent cultivar Caribo outyielded the old cultivar Tassilo by 10 percent in the no-input farming system and by 26 percent in the present day system. In the case of spring barley, the landrace outyielded the cultivar in both low-input farming systems (by about 5 percent), while, with the present day farming methods, the yield of the modern cultivar was 24 percent higher than the landrace. The landrace barley does well in low-input environments because its longer straw provides better competition against weeds.

The coefficient of variation generally decreased with the yield increase in higher input systems, although it was typically lower for the old cultivars or landrace compared with modern cultivars in all farming systems (the only exception was spring barley grown with high inputs). A more detailed examination of the yield data by year (not presented in table 9.3) reveals that large yield differences between the two wheat cultivars in the more favorable years was largely responsible for the higher cv of the modern cultivar (Caribo), while low yields for the spring barley cultivar (Carina) in low-input systems was responsible for its higher cv. The experiment, therefore, demonstrates not only the higher yield potential of modern cereal cultivars but also the need for better growing conditions for its realization.

TABLE 9.3 Mean and variability of kernel yield of old cultivars (O) or landraces and modern cultivars (M) of winter wheat and spring barley in different crop management systems in Bavaria[a]

Management System[a]	Winter Wheat[b]						Spring Barley[c]				
	O (t/ha)	M (t/ha)	Ratio M/O	O (cv)	M (cv)		O (t/ha)	M (t/ha)	Ratio M/O	O (cv)	M (cv)
I	2.11	2.33	110	0.236	0.294		1.27	1.19	94	0.325	0.445
II	2.54	3.05	120	0.240	0.256		1.61	1.53	95	0.390	0.445
III	4.24	5.41	126	0.150	0.198		3.16	3.93	124	0.235	0.225

Source: Puch. Exp. Station of Bayerische Landesanstalt für Bodenkultur und Pflanzenbau.
[a]Crop management system—Rotation: fallow, winter wheat, spring barley
Inputs: I—no inputs; II—15 t/ha manure added to winter wheat; III—N,P,K fertilizer, herbicides, and other protective chemicals as needed.
[b]Winter wheat cultivars: O = Tassilo (released 1930) and M = Caribo (released 1968).
[c]Spring barley cultivars: O = Landrace (Nurnberg 1832) and M = Carina (released 1971).

PART II

Plant Breeding and Yield Variability

10 Plant Breeding and Yield Stability

MICHAEL H. ARNOLD AND ROGER B. AUSTIN

In the continuing debate on whether or not modern high-yielding varieties of cereals have contributed to the observed increased variation in yield, there is often some misconception about the aims of plant breeders, the methods they use, and what they can achieve. This chapter outlines some of the underlying principles from the plant breeding standpoint and discusses the possibilities and limitations of the contribution of plant breeding to greater stability of yield.

The plant breeder is constantly creating genetic variation and altering, by selection, the mean expression of a wide range of heritable characters. The expression of complex characters, particularly yield, is heavily influenced by environmental conditions. Furthermore, because all of the traits that contribute to yield may not be positively correlated among themselves, material selected for high yield in one environment may perform relatively poorly in another. If released for general production, such material might well contribute to increased yield variability. Consequently, it is normal practice to evaluate material over a range of locations as early as practicable in the breeding process. Advanced material is also usually evaluated over two or more successive seasons. In both sets of circumstances, differential responses can be quantified statistically as the interaction terms in an analysis of variance, typically comprising some or all of the following components:

Source of variation:
    Varieties (genotypes) $V(G)$
    Locations L
    Years Y
Interactions:
    Locations × years LY
    Varieties × locations VL ⎫
    Varieties × years VY ⎬ Genotype-environment (GE)
    Varieties × locations
       × years VLY ⎭

Only the second type of interaction (*VL*) can be exploited—by breeding varieties for specific localities—but only if the *VL* component is consistently greater than the other two components of the genotype-environment (*GE*) interaction. In practice, these conditions seldom exist within a single production area and the breeder usually seeks to maximize yielding ability and minimize genotype-environment interactions when comparing potential new varieties with established ones. It is this strategy and various refinements of it that have become known as breeding for stability, as well as yield.

In order to analyze, and hence to predict, the response of a variety to different growing conditions, it is necessary to define and quantify the environmental variables. To do this directly is both difficult and time-consuming and beyond the resources of most plant-breeding programs. However, it can, to a limited extent, be done indirectly, by using the mean performance of a range of genotypes as an estimate of the production potential of a given environment or locality. Estimates of varietal responses to a range of environments can then be obtained from the regression of the mean performance of each variety at each location on the mean of all varieties at the same locations. The analysis can be expanded to include seasons, either averaged over localities (if the data set is orthogonal), or separately. Comparisons among varieties and their implications for variability can then be made visually from the slopes of the regression lines. This type of analysis was first proposed by Mooers (1921) and developed by Yates and Cochran (1938). It was adopted by some plant breeders but, because it was regarded as a routine procedure, examples of its application to practical plant breeding were not usually published. It was, for example, used in a cotton breeding program developed during the 1950s in Uganda by H. L. Manning (Arnold and Innes 1976). Here the aim was to ensure that new varieties would show improvements over the whole range of growing conditions, particularly those characteristic of the small farmer.

Further impetus to the use of this type of analysis was provided by Finlay and Wilkinson (1963). From their analysis of extensive data on barley yields in Australia, they suggested that the regression coefficient itself might be used as an estimate of stability. Values of less than unity would represent more stable and those greater than unity, less stable, varieties. By plotting estimates of stability against mean yields, they described the broad adaptation to various types of environment of the 277 varieties they studied.

Regression analysis is attractive because it facilitates a simple visual presentation of complex results. Consequently, it has been extensively used and, following Finlay and Wilkinson's (1963) paper, featured prominently in published accounts of genotype-environment interactions and breeding for yield stability. The analysis has its limitations, however, especially when the data represent only a small sample of genotypes and when the environments (localities and years) are not fully representative of those to which the varieties will be exposed in production. Moreover, as Eberhart and Russell (1966) pointed out, the deviations from regression may be as important as the regression itself.

The methods currently available to plant breeders for the assessment of stability have been reviewed by Westcott (1986, 1987). Among these, various forms of multivariate analysis have shown some advantages over simple regression analysis, but they are difficult to interpret and have not yet been routinely adopted in breeding programs, although they have been extensively used to analyze large data sets. Consequently, multivariate analyses have so far had little impact on decisions made by plant breeders, or on the nature of varieties released into production.

Whether the methods of quantifying it are adequate or not, stability is only one of the many selection criteria that the breeder has to consider. The importance attached to it, relative to all the other attributes required in a successful variety, will vary greatly with local circumstances. In the present context, we consider the extent to which plant breeders might be expected to influence yield variability through the characteristics of the varieties they release. The analysis is based on data for wheat in the U.K. reported by Austin and Arnold (ch. 7).

The Magnitude of Genotypic Contribution to Yield Variability

When considering the effects of genotype on yield variation, it is instructive to simulate the consequences for variation in yield of a number of factors, each of which may be controlled by both genotypic traits and environmental factors. The average effects of individual factors on the yield of wheat in the U.K. are commonly of the order of 5 to 10 percent. Using these values, a binomial model can be used to calculate the cvs of yields of wheat from farmers' fields, assuming the factors influence yield independently. Suppose a population of identical fields (in terms of the amount of wheat they yield per hectare) is divided into two groups, in one of which a single factor operates so as to give a 5 percent increase in yield. The coefficient of variation (cv) of yield of the total population of fields would be 0.025. If two factors operate independently, giving four yield classes, the cv would increase to 0.035. Calculations can be done for any combination of factors having any desired effect, and some results are shown in table 10.1. In this binomial model, as the number of factors causing variation in yield increases, the distribution of yields closely approaches normality. In the few cases where yields from a sufficiently large number of fields have been recorded, the distribution has been found not to be significantly different from normal. One example is given by Tinker and Widdowson (1983) for

TABLE 10.1 Coefficients of variation of yield computed for hypothetical cases

Number of Factors	Effects of Each Factor[a]	
	H/L = 1.05	H/L = 1.10
1	0.025	0.050
2	0.035	0.071
3	0.043	0.087
4	0.050	0.100
6	0.061	0.122
8	0.071	0.144
10	0.079	0.158

[a]Ratio of high yield to low yield for each factor.

wheat yields in England in 1980, where the mean yield was 7.37 tons per hectare (t/ha) and the cv 0.188; the distribution was normal and showed no skewness or nonnormal kurtosis.

In reality, yield is influenced by many factors, each having a continuous distribution of effects and interactions. Clearly, it would never be possible to identify all the factors influencing yield in individual fields or to quantify their effects and interactions with other factors. While the binomial model is obviously a simplification, it is useful for illustrating that the observed variability of yield can be a consequence of the effects of a considerable number of factors, each having a relatively small effect. For example, a combination of 10 factors each having a 5 percent effect and five having a 10 percent effect would produce a cv of yield of 0.137.

Calculations of this kind suggest that, in the U.K., the contribution of the plant breeder to changes in the observed cv for yield in a given production area is likely to be small. To illustrate this conclusion, suppose that the "basal" cv in yield is 0.137, which results from the effects of the factors described above. Suppose that the entire area is then sown to a new variety such that a 5 percent advantage in yield previously obtained on only one-half of the fields is eliminated and also that the variety is resistant to two diseases, each of which previously reduced yield by 5 percent in one-half of the fields. The cv of yield would then become 0.130, a reduction of 0.007, which would be very difficult to detect statistically. But mean yield would be increased by 7.5 percent, a difference that might be detectable in production figures if it persisted for a few years, bearing in mind that the interannual variation in yield is about 7 percent.

Supporting evidence for this conclusion about the contribution of varieties to yield variation comes from analysis of 174 variety trials with winter wheat from 1967–78 at 20 locations (Talbot 1984). The components of variance are shown in table 10.2. The percentage of the total variance at-

TABLE 10.2 Components of variance in 174 winter wheat trials during 1967–1978

Source of Variation	Variance (t/ha)²	Percentage
Varieties (V)	0.099	7.2
Centers (localities) (L)	0.104	7.5
Years (Y)	0.055	4.0
LY	0.976	70.9
VL	0.007	0.5
VY	0.022	1.6
VLY	0.113	8.2

Source: Talbot (1984).

tributable to the effects of variety and its interactions with locations and years is 17.5. This figure may be compared with that derived from the analysis given above, in which a variety having the characteristics mentioned would decrease the variance of yield by 10 percent (the cv of yield being reduced from 0.137 to 0.130). Considering the simplifications and approximations entailed, these values, 17.5 and 10.0 percent, are consistent with each other and support the conclusion that the growing of varieties with more stable yield and greater disease resistance would raise yield but would have only a marginal effect on variation in yield.

Of course, this conclusion would be incorrect if, for example, a disease developed that had a major effect on yield over a large proportion of the area. The development of a variety resistant to this disease would increase yield and reduce its variability. Again, taking a basal cv of 0.137, a factor reducing yield by 46 percent (the loss due to take-all in the Rothamsted example cited by Austin and Arnold ch. 7) on one-half of the cropped area would increase the cv in yield to 0.327 and reduce mean yield by 23 percent. In modern agriculture, where a close watch is kept to anticipate the development of new or more aggressive pathogens and to develop control measures and resistant varieties, it is very unlikely, though not impossible, that such variation would occur.

Relevance to Other Environments

Clearly, the extent to which it might be possible for new varieties to contribute to changes in yield variability will differ greatly among regions. The problem of stability is particularly acute under conditions of rainfed agriculture in the semi-arid and semi-humid tropics. In these environments, reducing the risk of crop failure will often be as important as increasing the yield potential.

To achieve greater stability, it is desirable first to understand its physiological basis in relation to the main environmental variables (Dowker 1971, Arnold and Innes 1984). The breeding of improved varieties, better adapted to variable environments and with more stable performance, can then be put on a more scientific basis. In many circumstances improved varieties remain the most cost-effective means of increasing yield and reducing the risk of crop failure. The breeding strategies needed are, however, different from those in the U.K., where continually rising standards of crop management have permitted the breeders to exploit the genotype-environment interaction for high levels of inputs without detectable effects on yield stability.

11 Modern Rice Varieties as a Possible Factor in Production Variability

W. RONNIE COFFMAN AND T. R. HARGROVE

Rice varieties have probably changed more in the past 20 years than in the previous 20 centuries. Dalrymple (1985) states that high-yielding varieties (HYVs) of wheat and rice have spread faster and more extensively than any other technological innovation in the history of Third World agriculture. Concurrent with this, Hazell (1984a) has shown a decrease in production stability in some areas. This chapter examines modern rice varieties as a possible factor in production variability.

Ancestry of Modern Rice Varieties

The development of high-yielding varieties of rice and wheat has averted the "time of famines" predicted in the 1960s by global food watchers such as Paddock and Paddock (1967). As in other crops, however, widespread adoption of a relatively few improved rice varieties, many of which are genetically related, has steadily reduced the genetic diversity of the crop. The first example of this phenomenon was the rapid adoption of hybrid maize varieties in the United States about 40 years ago, and the subsequent loss of most of the variation in traditional germplasm (Brown and Goodman 1977). While many of the traditional rice varieties have been collected (the International Rice Research Institute, IRRI, has preserved more than 75,000 accessions), few are still grown by farmers in the irrigated areas where high-yielding varieties have made the greatest impact. About 40 percent of the world's rice land is planted to high-yielding varieties (HYVs).

In 1914, a variety called Cina (also Tjina) was introduced from China into Indonesia where it became the most popular variety in Indonesian farms because of its photoperiod insensitivity, yield, and grain quality (Meulen 1950, Parthasarthy 1972). In 1934 plant breeders in Indonesia made the cross Cina/Latisail, from which Peta and other popular cultivars were selected. In 1962 Peta was used as the female parent in a cross with

Dee-geo-woo-gen, a stiff-strawed variety from China whose genes have given semidwarf stature to almost all of the semidwarf rice varieties grown in the Third World today. IR8 was selected from that cross and released to farmers in 1966. IR8 had high-yield potential, mainly because its short, stiff straws allowed it to produce heavy panicles of grain without falling over; it tillered profusely; and it was insensitive to photoperiod.

The green revolution in Third World rice production was triggered by the dramatic farmer adoption of IR8 and subsequent semidwarf varieties together with improved management practices and the introduction of economic incentives to stimulate adoption. Hunger would have been more widespread without the improved rice varieties. Asia's population has increased by 53 percent from 1951-60 to 1971-80 (U.N. 1983). But average rice yields in Asia for 1971-80 were 42 percent higher than in 1951-60 and total production rose 77 percent. Asia's land area planted to rice increased only 25 percent during that period (Barker and Herdt 1985).

Plant breeders also adopted IR8 and other Peta derivatives as parents in their hybridization programs. In the 1970s and 1980s, hundreds of new locally developed semidwarfs replaced IR8; most of the new varieties were bred by scientists in national rice breeding programs, from crosses in which the early semidwarfs such as IR8 were used as female parents. Components of the cytoplasm are inherited through the female parents, so varieties with Cina as their ultimate maternal ancestor probably carry similar cytoplasm.

In 1975, the ancestry of improved varieties released by national rice breeding programs in 10 Asian nations were surveyed. About 42 percent of the newest varieties were maternal progeny of Cina. The study was updated at most of the same breeding centers in 1984, and 46 percent of the newest varieties were Cina progeny (Hargrove, Cabanilla, and Coffman 1985). For widely grown varieties, 33 percent in 1975 versus 34 percent in 1984 traced maternally to Cina.

Thirty-eight percent of a sample of the female parents used in 106 crosses made in 1983/84 were maternal progeny of Cina—implying that many of the varieties that will be selected from those crosses and released in the late 1980s will also carry similar cytoplasm. (Using conventional plant breeding, development of a modern rice variety takes four to seven years.)

The parentage of the 15 IR varieties named in the Philippines (IR8 through IR42) was traced in 1980. All were from crosses made at IRRI involving 11 parents that traced to 18 original farmer varieties from eight countries. All traced maternally to Cina (Hargrove, Coffman, and Cabanilla 1980).

The 1985 release of IR64 and IR65 brought the total of named released IR varieties to 29. The 14 varieties named since IR42 trace to 28 farmer varieties, including 10 that were not in the ancestry of the first 15 varieties. IR64 is a descendant of 20 original farmer varieties from eight countries (figure 11.1) (IRRI 1985a). Eight of the 14 subsequent varieties were maternal progeny of Cina (figure 11.2).

The 1970 epidemic of southern corn leaf blight in the U.S. maize crop is the only recorded pest epidemic that was conditioned by cytoplasmic uniformity. However, research shows that cytoplasm conditions both resistance and susceptibility to pests in other crops (Harland and King 1957, Mercado and Lantican 1961, Nagaich et al. 1968, Rath and Padmanabhan 1972, Mahill and Davis 1978, Akohas 1983). Although no weakness in Cina cytoplasm has been detected, the specter of the maize epidemic lingers on. The resources to respond to such an emergency in rice-growing Asia are far more limited than in the United States. A widespread epidemic in Asian rice could mean famine.

It should also be mentioned that most of the semidwarf rice varieties outside of China carry the same dwarfing genes—those of Dee-geo-woo-gen (Aquino and Jennings 1966; Coffman, Kaufman and Heinrichs 1977; Foster and Rutger 1978).

The common ancestry of modern cultivated varieties of rice does not necessarily imply that they contribute to increased production variability. In fact, it could be argued that many modern varieties such as IR64 have a very diverse parentage and could be expected to perform well under a wide range of environmental conditions.

In this chapter, some varietal characteristics that affect production stability are examined; changes brought by the introduction of modern varieties are discussed; and some programs to transfer production-stabilizing traits from traditional rices into improved varieties are described.

Varietal Characteristics Affecting Yield Stability

Several broad groups of varietal characteristics affect yield stability. Perhaps the most important are agronomic traits such as photoperiodism, growth duration, height, tillering, and grain dormancy. Pest resistance (diseases, insects, weeds) is almost certainly a factor and stress tolerance (drought, flood, adverse soils, adverse temperatures) is probably important in some cases.

Agronomic Characteristics

Agronomic characteristics are too numerous to review in detail but a few are of obvious importance in considering production variability.

PHOTOPERIODISM/GROWTH DURATION. Over centuries, farmers in tropical Asia selected thousands of site-specific varieties that responded to photoperiod. Those varieties flowered at about the same date regardless of

FIGURE 11.1 Twenty landraces, or traditional rice varieties, from eight nations in the genetic ancestry of IR64, released in May 1985

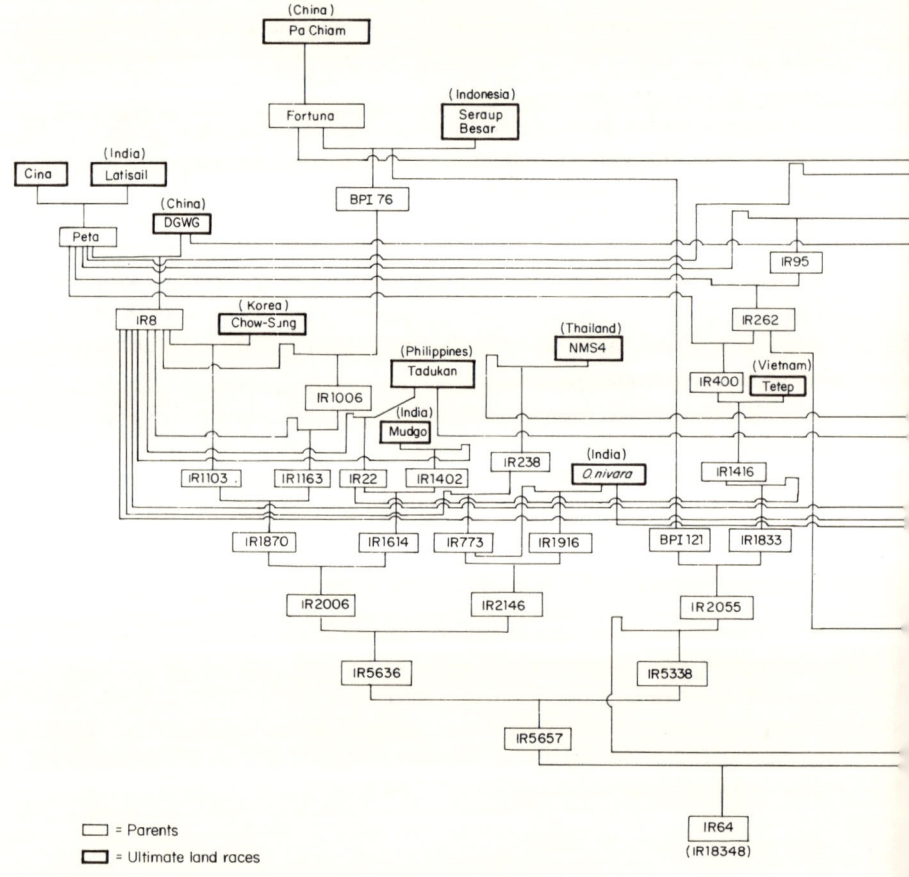

NOTE: Female parents are always on the left; males on the right.

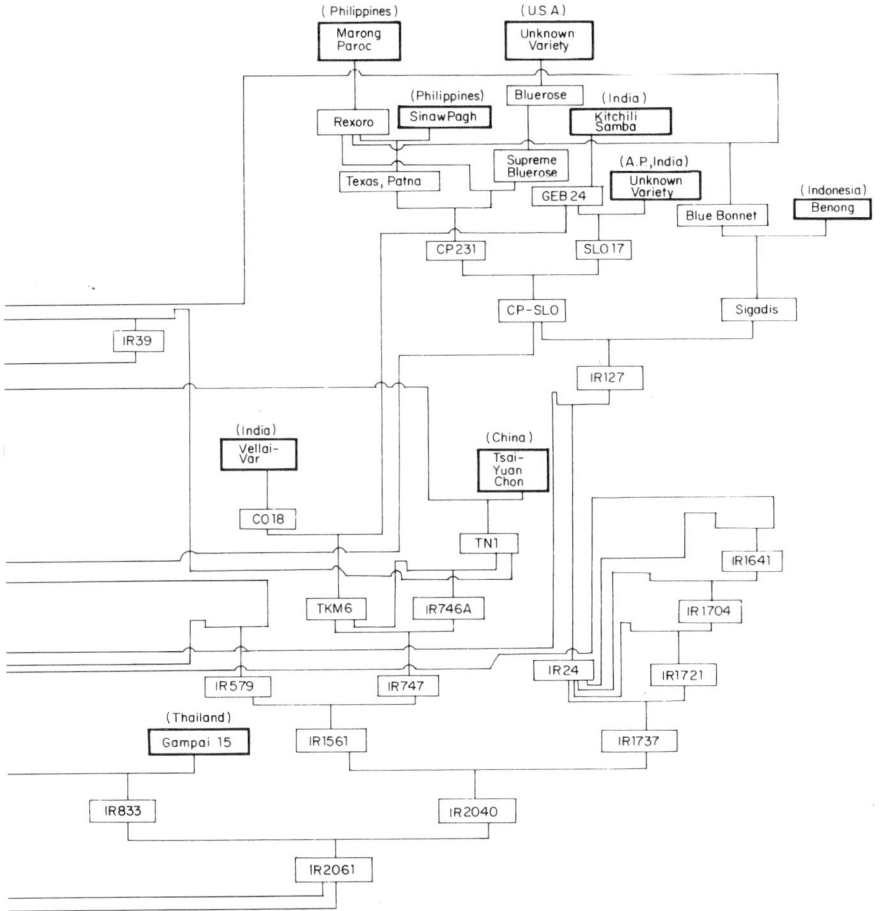

FIGURE 11.2 Maternal derivation of IR varieties

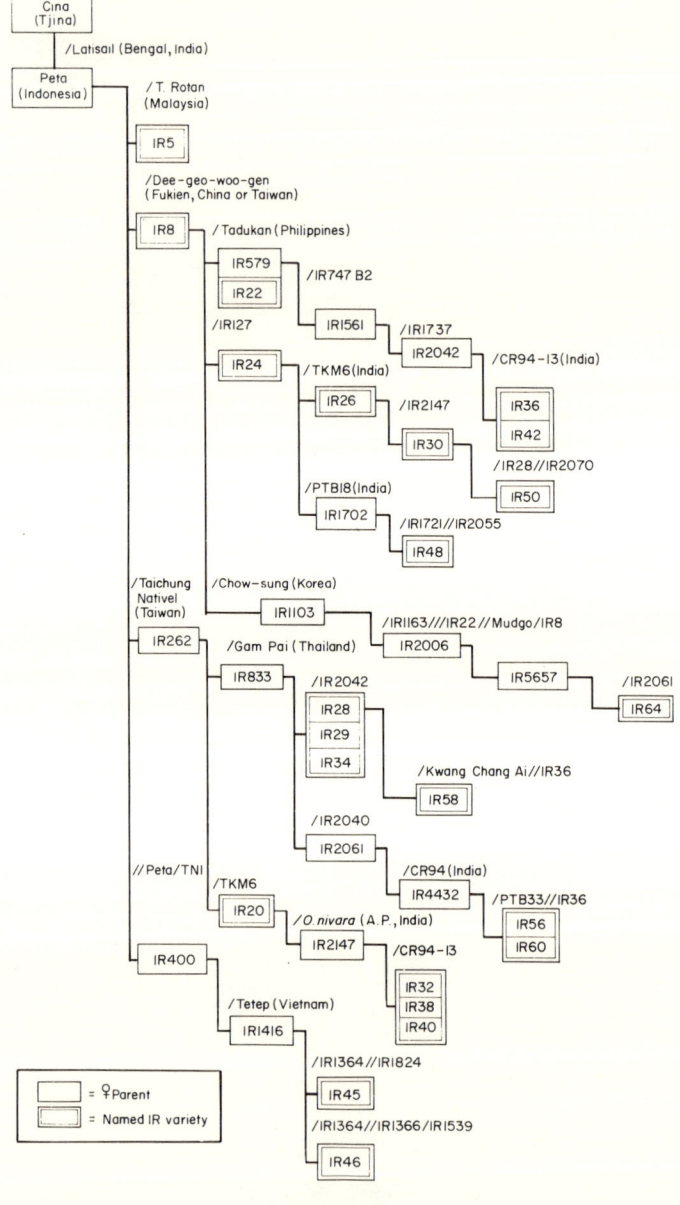

NOTE: Female parents are in boxes on the left; male parents on the right.

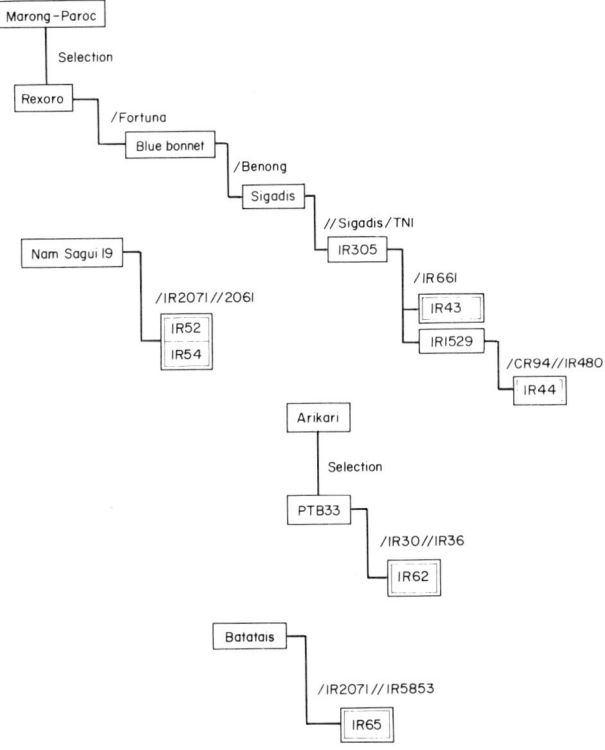

when they were sown. Because the rice plant is most vulnerable to stress during its reproductive growth phase, the photoperiod sensitive traditional varieties entered reproduction at the peak rainfall period, when risks were minimal. The varieties then ripened after the rains stopped.

Some traditional varieties, such as Cina, were selected for photoperiod insensitivity and were popular, particularly in irrigated areas, because they could be grown at any time of the year. Plant breeders combined the photoperiod insensitivity of Cina, with other desirable traits to give varieties such as Peta, which later led to IR8.

IR8's photoperiod insensitivity and its shorter, fixed growth duration allowed farmers in many latitudes to grow it at any time of the year. It also meant higher returns to farmers in irrigated areas by allowing them to grow two or even three rice crops where they previously grew only one crop. IR36, reportedly grown on some 12 million hectares (IRRI 1982), is the most prominent example of the popularity of early maturing HYVs of rice.

But the flowering or harvest of varieties that mature in a fixed period after seeding can coincide with natural calamities such as typhoons or droughts. A shortage of water or labor can prevent a farmer from transplanting within 30 days after seeding, or the crop may flower during a drought. Of course, this can sometimes happen with traditional varieties too. It may be offset by the fact that staggered planting of modern varieties, as dictated by the availability of labor, would result in staggered maturity and possibly reduce the vulnerability of the crop to unfavorable climatic factors.

The fixed growth duration of modern varieties may give them less "buffering capacity" than the photoperiod sensitive traditional types— even though the climate or the labor supply might be directly responsible for production variability.

Rice breeding objectives were determined in the 1975 and 1984 breeder surveys by randomly selecting crosses from current hybridization records and asking each breeder to describe in detail the reasons for using each parent (figure 11.3). Preferred growth duration was the third most common objective (after yield potential and grain quality). Early duration was a breeding objective in 49 percent of the 1975 crosses and increased to 59 percent of the 1984 crosses. Eleven percent of the 1984 crosses were for intermediate, and 2 percent for late, growth duration. Thus, most HYVs released in Asia probably will continue to be early maturing and day length insensitive.

HEIGHT. Reduced plant height is the most obvious trait of a modern rice variety. This improves the harvest index (ratio of grain to straw) and allows the plant to remain standing under heavy doses of nitrogen fertilizer. It is this characteristic that is responsible for most of the production gains of the green revolution.

FIGURE 11.3 Comparison of breeding objectives, 1984 and 1975

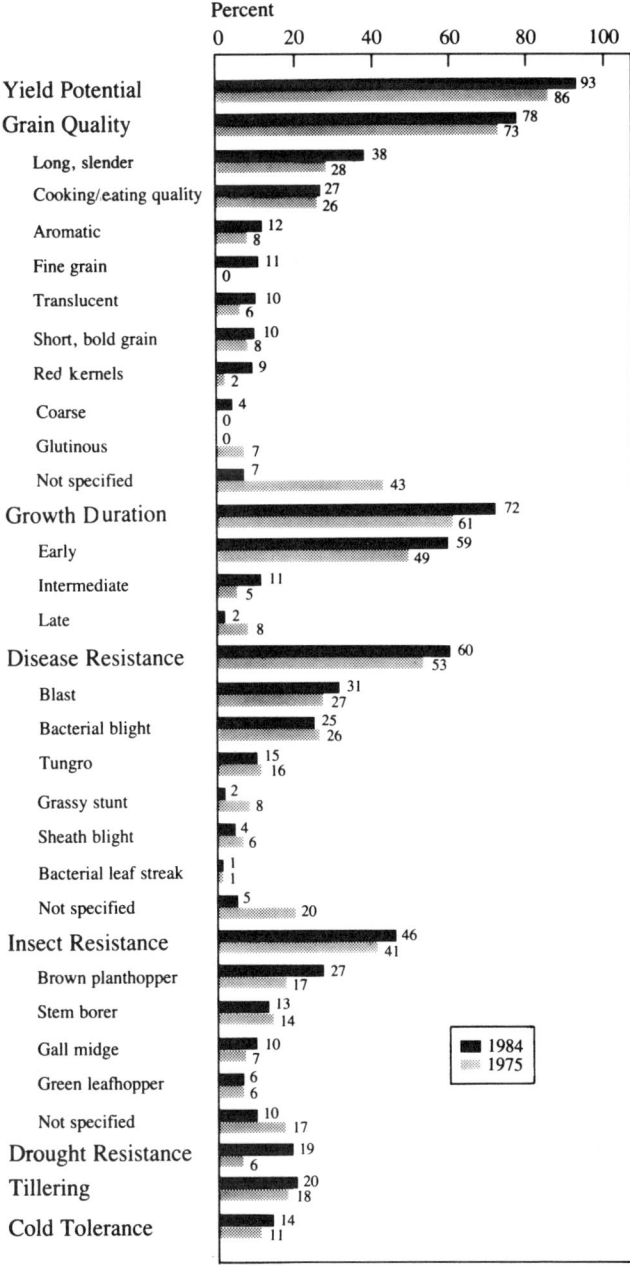

However, drought during the vegetative growth stage may shorten the height of semidwarf plants well below optimal levels, decreasing their ability to cope with subsequent floods and weed growth.

Although most new varieties released by national rice programs continue to be semidwarfs, there was a shift toward the release of taller varieties in the 1984 breeding survey. In 1975, 69 percent of new varieties were semidwarf (<130 cm) and 25 percent were intermediate statured (130–160 cm) or tall. In 1984, 54 percent of new varieties were semidwarfs, and 31 percent were intermediates or talls.

TILLERING. Modern varieties tiller heavily under optimal conditions, producing a larger number of smaller panicles than traditional types. But during a serious drought, such varieties often "hay off," producing much fodder but little grain. Traditional varieties, under drought stress, may be able to fill their smaller number of panicles and produce a relatively respectable grain yield.

DORMANCY. If untimely rains come at crop maturity, the grain dormancy of most traditional rice varieties prevents grain germination and causes subsequent loss. This trait has not always been retained in modern varieties.

Pest Resistance

Rice breeders, entomologists, and pathologists can claim many successes in the incorporation of pest resistance into modern varieties (Coffman, Khush, and Kaufman 1978; Khush and Coffman 1977). Although IR8 had little genetic resistance to insects or diseases, IR20, released in 1969, replaced IR8 in many areas because of its genetic resistance to pests (Pathak, Beachell and Andres 1973). IR26, released in 1973, had a broader spectrum of pest resistance and soon replaced IR20. Several modern HYVs carry built-in resistance to as many as a dozen common rice pests.

But more than 600 known diseases, some with numerous physiological races, attack the Third World's rice crop; its insect pests may be nearly beyond counting. The traditional varieties were selected for resistance to or tolerance of their local biological environments. Modern rice varieties are selected in less than a decade (IR36 was developed in five years), sometimes on experiment stations where the biological environment has been dramatically altered by the use of pesticides. Modern varieties are often resistant to specific pests, for which they were specifically screened, but resistance to additional pests is usually a matter of luck. It seems unlikely that such varieties could have spectra of pest resistance comparable to those of traditional types.

Breeders now have at their disposal an impressive system of international testing, permitting them to expose promising cultivars to a wide range of environments in a short period of time and to monitor the biological environment (IRRI 1985b). This may offset the disadvantages of the short time frame in which modern varieties are developed.

INSECTS. Major insect pests contribute to production variability and modern varieties are at least indirectly involved. The brown planthopper (BPH) is an interesting case study. The initial introduction of modern varieties, with their additional production potential, combined with government subsidies for insecticides, made it profitable for farmers to apply insecticide. The heavier tillering modern varieties provided a denser plant canopy and a moist, shaded environment that was favorable for the brown planthopper (IRRI 1973). The broad spectrum insecticides initially recommended (and still on the market and subsidized in many developing countries) destroyed natural enemies, such as spiders, that prey on brown planthopper eggs and larvae. In many areas, devastation of natural enemies caused a resurgence of the brown planthopper. Insecticides themselves became the major cause of an insect problem.

In reaction to severe brown planthopper (BPH) outbreaks in the early 1970s, IRRI and other institutions screened and released brown planthopper resistant varieties such as IR26. Their brown planthopper resistance was soon overcome, however, by the emergence of a new Biotype 2 of brown planthopper. Varieties resistant to Biotype 2 have been developed and have proved somewhat more stable—but they, too, will probably eventually break down to still other biotypes.

DISEASES. The potential for a widespread disease epidemic among modern varieties, based on a cytoplasmic similarity, has been discussed under "Ancestry of Modern Rice Varieties."

WEEDS. Modern rice varieties are clearly less competitive with weeds than traditional types because they are shorter, and their leaves are more erect. Therefore, shortages of labor, herbicides, or cash for herbicide purchase at critical times could contribute to production variability. A slight shift toward the release of taller varieties was discussed under "Height." The responding plant breeders, particularly in southern India, Sri Lanka, and Bangladesh, often cited better weed competition (as well as a high price for straw as animal fodder or fuel) as a reason for this shift.

Drought Tolerance

Modern rice varieties are generally less tolerant of drought than are traditional types. The modern varieties are bred to produce the maximum amount of grain under optimal conditions; thus, they do not develop the thick, deep root system needed for drought tolerance. The development of IR52 at IRRI illustrates the feasibility of breeding improved varieties with drought tolerance (IRRI 1981). The maximum yield potential of such varieties, however, is probably somewhat lower than that of modern varieties with less drought tolerance.

Flood Tolerance

Tall, traditional varieties are naturally more flood tolerant than semidwarfs because they are less easily submerged. Traditional deep water rice varieties have the capacity to elongate as the water rises and thus keep their panicles above the water. A few low-yielding traditional rices can actually tolerate complete submergence and survive for as many as 10 days under floodwater. Most modern rice varieties have no flood tolerance and are quite vulnerable to flooding.

Breeding elongation capacity or submergence tolerance into modern varieties is an objective of scientists at IRRI, and in Thailand, Bangladesh, and other programs. RD19 and sister lines, grown by farmers in Thailand and Burma, are progeny of crosses made in Thailand of modern and traditional deep-water varieties. They have limited ability to elongate in rising floodwaters. RD19 yields well in water as deep as 100 centimeters (cm) versus a maximal tolerable depth of 25–30 centimeters for conventional modern varieties.

Tolerance of Adverse Soils

Many traditional varieties evolved on soils with poor mineral nutrition. But modern varieties have often been selected on experiment stations with superior soils. While this may place modern varieties at a disadvantage in certain areas, there is no reason to expect that it should be a factor in production variability.

Rice scientists are crossing traditional varieties that can tolerate saline, acid sulfate, alkaline, or other adverse soils with modern varieties, hoping to bring such areas into higher rice production. IR36 has low levels of tolerance to salinity, alkalinity, iron toxicity, and other soil problems (IRRI 1982). In contrast, IR42 has tolerance of salinity, alkalinity, and other stresses (Ponnamperuma 1979).

Tolerance of Adverse Temperatures

Temperature tolerance is of minor importance in the major rice-growing areas of tropical Asia. It is important in other selected regions, however, and could be an important factor in production variability.

LOW TEMPERATURE. Korea is a key rice-growing area where modern varieties have been widely adopted and where varieties must have tolerance to low temperature. Modern japonica/indica varieties now widely grown in Korea—products of crosses of local japonica (temperate) with indica (tropical) varieties—outyield their japonica predecessors but are less tolerant of low temperatures (Kwak et al. 1984).

In 1980 an unusual cold spell struck the Korean rice crop, which caused poor panicle exertion. That led to an epidemic of neck blast. The importation of large quantities of rice was necessary in 1981. The planting of japonica/indica hybrids dropped from 79 percent of Korea's rice land in 1979 to 32 percent in 1982 (Chang 1984).

Improved cold-tolerance varieties are also needed in mountainous areas of Asia where cold air or cold irrigation water stunts the growth of most modern varieties. Himali and Kanchan, improved varieties with cold tolerance, have been released for farmer cultivation in Nepal. Similarly, Himalaya I and II have been released in Himachal Pradesh, India. All are progeny of crosses of IRRI and traditional cold-tolerant varieties.

HIGH TEMPERATURE. High temperatures ($>35°C$) during flowering adversely affect most modern varieties (Mackill and Coffman 1983). Traditional varieties with heat tolerance are still grown in limited areas where high temperatures may occur at flowering. Traditional varieties with heat tolerance have been identified and crossed with modern varieties. Some progeny of those crosses appear promising but no improved varieties with heat tolerance have been released yet.

Discussion

Rice is the lifeblood of Asia. About 55 percent of the world's people live in Asia, where 92 percent of the world's rice is grown and consumed. Population is increasing rapidly in the rice-growing countries, creating an annual increase of 3 percent per year in demand for rice (Barker and Herdt 1985).

Rice production, at a low and stagnant level, is probably more stable with traditional varieties than with the improved varieties that have replaced them in many areas. But to suggest that Asian farmers abandon modern varieties and return to their low-yielding traditional varieties is unrealistic. Asia has virtually no arable land available to put into rice cultivation. Without high-yielding varieties, Asia would starve, or become a beggar for the maize, soybeans, wheat, sorghum, and rice grown in the more developed countries.

Consider the Philippines. If Filipino farmers had not adopted new rice varieties and technology, it is safe to assume that rice yields would have remained at previous levels of about 1.2 tons per hectare, and that the increased rice needed to feed the expanded population of the Philippines would have had to be grown on an increased area of rice land, or imported. The 1981 population required 6.8 million metric tons of milled rice. To grow that much rice at previous yield levels would have required 5.6 million hectares of rice land. The Philippines has only 3.5 million hectares of land for rice growing (Vega 1983).

However, modern varieties are not perfect. This chapter has pointed out specific weaknesses of the new varieties, and potential hazards that could result from an erosion of genetic diversity. It has also described how rice scientists are working to incorporate production stability traits, such as pest resistance and tolerance of drought, deep water, and adverse soils, from hardy but traditional varieties.

Rice scientists have an obligation to diversify the genetic base of improved varieties, and to transfer traits that give traditional varieties their production stability, into new and constantly evolving improved varieties for farmers in adverse environments.

12 Possible Genetic Causes of Increased Variability in U.S. Maize Yields

DONALD N. DUVICK

In contrast to the previous 30 years, the trend line for U.S. maize yields has risen continually since 1930. The rate of gain in yield increased sharply in the mid-1950s, going from about 57 kilograms per hectare per year (kg/ha/y) (1930-55) to about 133 kilograms per hectare per year (1955-85) (figure 12.1).

Visual inspection of the data indicates increased variability around the trend line during the latter time period (1955-85), particularly since about 1970. Average U.S. yields in 1970, 1974, 1980, and 1983 fell markedly below the trend line, and yields in 1972, 1979, and 1982 were noticeably above the trend line. However, regression analysis does not agree with visual analysis, for the coefficient of variation around trend for the period 1930-55 was 0.114, whereas for the period 1955-85 it was 0.100. Because yields in the 1930s were so much lower than those in the 1970s, it may be more difficult to notice the proportionately large deviations from trend in the early years of the 1930-55 period, for example, the below trend values in 1934, 1936, and 1947.

Hazell (1984) has calculated that changes in yield variances and covariances account for most of the increase in the variance of total cereal production in the United States, when comparison is made between the periods 1950-66 and 1967-80. He points out that variance in maize yields accounts for much of this increase, further noting that 60 percent of the increase in variance for maize is due to an increase in correlation of yields between states. He suggests that a narrowing of genetic base for maize may have been responsible for the increase in interstate correlations and thus for the increase in the variance of maize production.

Visual inspection of U.S. maize yields in the period 1950-85 shows that yields did tend to show less deviation from trend in the first half of the period (1950-66) than in the second half (1967-85). Regression analysis agrees with visual observation, showing that the coefficient of variation around trend for 1950-66 is 0.060, whereas that for 1967-85 is 0.105.

FIGURE 12.1 Annual average grain yield of U.S. maize, 1930–1985

SOURCE: USDA, *Agricultural Statistics*.

NOTE: Straight lines indicate linear regressions of yield on years for 1930–1955 ($r^2 = 0.79$) and 1955–1985 ($r^2 = 0.86$).

The purpose here is to describe and analyze possible causes of increase in year-to-year variability of U.S. maize yields in the past 15 years. Possible genetic causes will be given particular attention.

Weather and Disease-Related Causes of Annual Yield Variability

Personal recollection plus weather and crop records (as in the "Weekly Weather and Crop Bulletin," U.S. Department of Commerce and U.S. Department of Agriculture) make it easy to describe salient environmental causes of the major deviations below or above trend line since 1930. Corn Belt-wide droughts seared the nation in 1934, 1936, 1980, and 1983. Excessive rains and cold weather in 1947 delayed planting dates by as much as six weeks, thereby putting the crop at a serious disadvantage throughout the rest of the growing season. A mid-July drought compounded the problems for the 1947 maize crop. Abnormally wet and cool weather in the spring of 1974 delayed planting throughout the Corn Belt; then a hot, dry spell in July caught much of the maize crop at the sensitive flowering stage; and finally a succession of early autumn freezes cut yields short in the northern half of the Corn Belt. The infamous southern corn leaf blight (*Helminthosporium maydis*), aided by a season ideally suited for its spread, was responsible for most of the low yields in 1970. The blight was devastating in the southeastern United States and in the southern and eastern portions of the Corn Belt but caused few or no problems for maize in the western and northern portions of the Corn Belt.

The unusually high average maize yields of 1972, 1979, and 1982 were associated with favorable weather during the maize flowering period. In 1972 and 1982, spring weather was wet and cool, delaying maize planting throughout the Corn Belt, whereas the spring of 1979 was warm and dry. The common and most important factor in these three high-yield years was that, during July, moderate temperatures and sufficient soil moisture were available during the critical tasseling and silking period.

Genetic uniformity clearly was the cause of widespread yield reductions in 1970. Up to 80 percent of U.S. maize was based on T cytoplasm, specifically susceptible to the T race of southern corn leaf blight (Tatum 1971). That the susceptible gene or genes were contained in the cytoplasm rather than in the nucleus made the uniformity no less dangerous, as the virulent fungus spread across the eastern part of the nation, aided by an abnormally wet summer that favored germination and spread of the disease spores. Hybrids without T cytoplasm were clearly not affected by the disease, so the consequences of uniformity for the susceptible cytoplasm were undeniable.

It is less easy to demonstrate nationwide if recent increases in genetic uniformity have intensified weather susceptibility of maize hybrids. Were the nation's hybrids more uniformly susceptible to drought in 1980 and 1983 than in previous hot, dry years? Were they more susceptible to the cool, wet spring, droughty summer, and early autumn frosts of 1974 than they would have been in similar previous seasons? Maize yields did drop precipitously in the drought years of 1934 and 1936, and in the cool, wet spring season of 1947. Conversely, U.S. maize yields reached new highs in 1942 and 1948, with abundant summer rains and moderate July temperatures. It is very difficult to match nationwide or even Corn Belt-wide weather records over a series of maize-growing seasons in order of environmental severity. Thompson (1969), however, attempted to calculate the effects of weather variables on Corn Belt maize yields, finding that July rainfall and temperature have the greatest association with abnormally high or low maize yields. High rainfall and normal temperatures in July are associated with high yields, and hot, dry July weather is associated with low yields. Preseason precipitation, June temperature, and August rainfall and temperature are also important variables (Thompson 1984, French and Headley ch. 22).

The chances are that weather is the overriding cause of annual variation in U.S. maize yields. It seems likely, however, that variations in maize culture could amplify or decrease the effect of weather, and so it is worthwhile to look at various inputs to maize culture, including genetic inputs, and to speculate as to whether or not they show trends that agree with the hypothesis that increased genetic uniformity of U.S. maize is another major cause of increased variability in U.S. grain yields.

Important Changes in U.S. Maize Culture since 1930

Probably the most important input to U.S. maize culture since 1930, outside of breeding contributions, has been the enormous increase in use of synthetic nitrogen fertilizer. The rate of consumption of nitrogen fertilizer, although rising continually since 1930, went up precipitously in the mid-1950s. Total U.S. use in 1980 was six times as great as in 1955. The time curves for consumption of synthetic nitrogen fertilizer and for U.S. maize yields are almost identical, breaking sharply upward in the mid-1950s, climbing smoothly until the 1970s, and then both becoming somewhat erratic (Duvick 1984a).

This is not to imply a one-to-one correspondence between nitrogen usage and maize yields, but there is no doubt that much of the increase in maize yields since about 1955 is due to increased use of nitrogen fertilizer. One study (Cardwell 1982) attributes 19 percent of the yield gains in Minnesota maize since 1930 to increased use of nitrogen fertilizer. The nation's maize is now fertilized at extremely high levels, giving it the ability to make maximum yields whenever environmental conditions are favorable. It also is probably grown under much more uniform conditions, particularly with respect to nitrogen nutrition, than it was before the 1950s.

A further enhancement of the ability of the maize crop to use good weather and high nitrogen supplies for high yields is the now universal practice of high-density planting. Maize plant population density is nearly three times as great as it was 50 years ago and is nearly twice that of the 1950s. High plant populations plus high levels of nitrogen fertilizer have greatly increased the possibility for extremely high yields, providing that the weather is favorable.

Other important inputs have been improved weed control, particularly through herbicides, and better precision and timeliness of planting and harvesting, with improved machinery and greater use of power. Early planting, the norm since 1970, is conducive to higher yields in most seasons, and planting dates in the Corn Belt have been advanced since 1930 by almost a month, from late May to late April. Planting also is spaced within a much shorter period than it used to be. Planting records and visual inspection have shown that very large percentages of the U.S. Corn Belt now tend to be planted at about the same time, most typically during two or three rain-free periods of a few days each. Thus, throughout the season, most maize plantings are at about the same stage of development across the entire Corn Belt.

Genetic Uniformity among U.S. Maize Hybrids

Several surveys of usage of public inbred lines, sponsored by the maize seed trade, allow inferences to be made about genetic uniformity of U.S. maize hybrids. Zuber and Darrah (1980) list the most widely used public inbred lines in each survey according to use exceeding 3 percent of need. In 1956, 1964, 1970, 1975, and 1979 the numbers of these lines were 9, 13, 7, 6, and 3, respectively.

The six most widely used inbreds in 1956, 1964, 1970, 1975, and 1979 were used in hybrids representing 20, 41, 71, 38, and 42 percent of total need, respectively. Using a smaller class size, the two most widely used inbred lines in 1956, 1964, 1970, 1975, and 1979 were used in hybrids representing 13, 27, 29, 22, and 28 percent of total need (National Academy of Sciences 1972, Zuber and Darrah 1980).

These three comparisons indicate very little or at most only a weak trend toward increasing use of only a few inbred lines. Rather, it appears that, since at least 1956, the industry has tended to concentrate on a few outstandingly good public inbred lines.

Because hybrid pedigrees are not disclosed by the seed maize companies, it is not possible to state positively what is the concentration of identical (or very similar) hybrid pedigrees across the nation in any one year. There is also no objective way to determine whether or not privately developed lines are increasingly supplementing the public lines, and how genetically divergent they may be from the widely used public lines. ("Public" lines are developed by publicly supported institutions, such as the land grant universities and their experiment stations.)

Zuber and Darrah did note, however, that about 28 percent of hybrid seed production in 1979 was of hybrids made up of only private lines, and about 24 percent of 1979 seed production was of hybrids that contained only public lines (Zuber and Darrah 1980). The remainder of hybrid seed production was of hybrids made up of both private and public inbred lines. Thus, there is the probability that significant use of private inbred lines supplemented the use of public lines. The private seed industry has continually increased its research potential through the years, and it is reasonable to suppose that, during the past 15 or 20 years, significantly increased use has been made of privately developed inbred lines, different to some degree from the most popular public lines.

There is some belief that private maize inbred lines are not really different from public ones, that the private lines typically are changed from the public lines just enough to allow their developers to claim difference.

My personal experience and my conversations with other members of the private maize-breeding establishment, say that this is not so. There would be no utility in making such minor changes since relatively unchanged inbred lines would not give genuinely different hybrids, and so no chances for competitive advantage in hybrid performance could exist. If one wishes to use a public inbred line, it is much easier (and legally permissible) to use the line without change. Public inbreds are widely used without change and acknowledged as such.

One can safely state that private inbred lines differ from each other, and from public ones, as much as the public lines differ from each other. Certainly, some privately developed inbred lines belong to unique families and give hybrids with unique, significantly different performance.

I have close knowledge of the U.S. hybrid maize industry, going back about 35 years, and am well acquainted with industry members whose experience goes back before 1930. It is well known to us that, from the very beginning of use of hybrid maize in the United States, the industry concentrated on use of only a few inbred lines at one time. (The lines were heavily used because they gave clearly superior hybrids.) Our "trade" knowledge agrees well with the results of the successive inbred usage surveys. This is not to say that concentration may not now be increasing, nor should one believe that this means such concentration is necessarily good for stability of the nation's maize production. But concentration on a few inbred lines is not a new phenomenon.

Another item of trade knowledge may bear on the question of uniformity of genotype in the U.S. maize-growing regions. Since about 1965, single-cross hybrids (with two inbred parents) have replaced double-cross hybrids. About 88 percent of the hybrid seed produced in 1979 was single cross (Zuber and Darrah 1980). Since the mid-1960s there has always been at least one (usually two or three) outstandingly popular single-cross hybrid(s), grown across a wide section of the Corn Belt. Sometimes the most popular hybrids have been made of public inbreds (according to trade knowledge), sometimes they have been made of private inbreds, and sometimes they have had one public parent and one private parent. The important point is that they have dominated maize plantings in those maturity zones where they are adapted. Even the most successful of these hybrids has, however, covered no more than about 5 percent of the surface planted to maize (personal estimate).

The difference between maize production before and after the mid-1960s is that, although there may be no more concentration on use of a small number of inbreds than previously, the tendency now is for plantings to concentrate on specific, successful single-cross combinations, rather than on several permutations of inbred combinations, as is possible when half-a-dozen superior inbreds are used in various combinations of four to make double-cross hybrids. Thus, relatively small numbers of specific single-cross hybrid genotypes are planted widely across the nation. In technical terms, both specific and general combining ability now have the opportunity to interact with environment, whereas, in earlier years, general combining ability interactions were the predominant kind.

The fact that specific single-cross hybrids are now very popular testifies that their performance is superior to that of the double-cross hybrids. The movement to single-cross hybrids does not mean the nation's maize production is placed in jeopardy. It may mean, however, that there is more tendency for maize yields to vary synchronously across the Corn Belt and the nation, as environmental inputs vary from season to season.

Another change since the mid-1960s is that farmers outside the Corn Belt, specifically in the southeastern, midsouth, and southwestern parts of the United States, have moved strongly toward use of Midwest-adapted hybrids. The hybrid M017 × B73, for example, is not only grown across the entire southern half of the Corn Belt, but it is also widely grown on the high plains of Texas, in the midsouth states of Kentucky and Tennessee, in California, and in Kansas. Thus, there is more uniformity of genotype between widely separated states than there used to be. These non-Corn Belt states, however, contribute only a small amount to total U.S. maize production.

Yield Stability of Modern U.S. Hybrids

Yield stability over varying environments is an important contribution of hybrid genotype. For example, if hybrids of recent vintage are generally less stable than those of earlier eras in reaction to stress environments, U.S. maize production could well be more variable from year to year than it used to be. In the past few years several researchers have made comparisons of hybrids from different eras, starting with hybrids first grown in about 1930 (Hallauer 1973; Russell 1974, 1984, Duvick 1977, 1984b; Castleberry, Crum, and Krull 1984). These studies allow one to look for trends in yield stability as well as for maximum yielding ability, as hybrid pedigrees have changed through the years.

All of the hybrid era experiments have shown that modern hybrids are greatly improved in stress resistance, over those of earlier eras. Improvement has been linear for resistance to heat and drought, to stalk rot diseases and second generation European corn borer (*Ostrinia nubilalis*), to barrenness (female sterility brought on by dense plant populations or drought), and to premature death (a syndrome with unknown cause that results in reduced yield and excessive stalk breakage). Newer hybrids have stronger roots. They are better able to withstand nitrogen deficiency as well as excessive nitrogen fertilization. They require essentially the same amount of time to reach maturity as older hybrids; flowering dates and grain moisture levels at harvest have not changed through the years.

The result is that new hybrids outyield the old hybrids in all environments. Yield gains have been continuous and essentially linear since 1930, when comparisons are made in average growing seasons. In all era experiments, the data indicate that breeding improvements are responsible for over 50 percent of maize yield gains since 1930. Other inputs, such as more fertilizer and better weed control, are responsible for the other 50 percent.

The yield advantage of the new hybrids is greatest when environmental conditions are most favorable. When environmental factors are severely limiting, as in drought, the new hybrids outyield the old ones, but by a smaller margin. It is likely, therefore, that present-day hybrids introduce the possibility of greater year-to-year variation in U.S. maize yields than used to occur, since they can expand their yields so much further in environmentally favorable seasons. When environmental factors are overwhelmingly limiting, the fallback in yield of the new hybrids is correspondingly greater than it would have been for the older hybrids, even though the new hybrids, under poor conditions, yield more than the old ones.

Conclusions

Several changes in maize cultural practices in the United States, especially in the Corn Belt, have come about in the past 15 to 20 years, all acting to accentuate year-to-year variability in maize yields. Advances in mechanization have resulted in more synchronous planting dates. Corn Belt-wide weather changes thus affect most of the crop at the same stage, increasing the chances of widespread weather effects on yield.

Use of high rates of nitrogen fertilizer, high-density planting, and hybrids adapted to these potentially stressful treatments have greatly raised yield potentials in favorable years. (Hybrids of the early eras actually suffer yield loss with high density, high nitrogen regimes.) When environmental factors are limiting, the fallback from maximum yields is correspondingly greater even though yields are not less than would have been achieved in the same unfavorable seasons with low plant density, lower fertility, and older hybrids.

Although modern hybrids are greatly improved in resistance to environmental stress, farmers are continually testing them at their limits, by continually increasing planting rates, as hybrids are improved in stress resistance. Thus, it is possible that on-farm yield variability is not much less than it was with old hybrids and old cultural methods, even though individual farmers' average yields are much greater now than they were 20 or 30 years ago.

Although there is no trend toward increased dependence on a few favored inbred lines, there has been a change, over the past 20 years, toward widespread plantings of a relatively small number of single-cross hybrids rather than of a somewhat larger number of double-cross hybrids with an equally small genetic base. This change has probably increased Corn Belt-wide uniformity of reaction to climatic variables.

Although average yields of U.S. maize are clearly higher than they used to be, the amount of year-to-year variation in U.S. average yields can be expected to be greater precisely because of the means by which yields have been raised. The nation's maize farmers have individually adopted the best means for achieving high maize yields and they have all made similar choices, thus bringing much greater uniformity in cultural practices to U.S. maize farming.

An important consideration is whether this uniformity will, in the future, bring about disastrously low yields that could have been prevented by a greater diversity in cultural practices. For example, southern corn leaf blight, race T, could have been avoided, in hindsight, if T cytoplasm had not been used so extensively. On the other hand, it is likely that damage from the 1974 late summer freezes in the northern Corn Belt could not have been prevented by any reasonable change in cultural practices, including changes in hybrids.

It is not likely that nationwide epidemics of disease or insects will disastrously affect the maize crop as did southern corn leaf blight, race T. There is much more genetic variation, in nuclear genes, among the country's hybrids than was afforded by the 80 percent concentration of T cytoplasm genes. Further, frequent turnover in hybrids (average life is about seven years) gives further opportunity to avoid buildup of any hybrid specific disease or insect (Duvick 1984c).

The superior modern hybrids favored by most farmers do the best possible job of producing high grain yields under all environmental conditions. Early planting places the maize crop in the best stage for escaping the hot, dry conditions of midsummer. (If planted early, it is more likely to flower before damaging midsummer heat. Heat and drought during flowering can cause female sterility and thus irreversibly lower maize yields by large amounts.) There would be no point in placing some fraction of the nation's maize plantings at higher risk every year just in order to have a wider range of planting dates. It is not likely that farmers will forgo the opportunity for top yields in environmentally favorable years just to make sure that the drop in yield will be less in poor growing seasons. They especially would not make this choice if they knew (as experimental data show) that, in very poor seasons, modern hybrids with modern cultural practices will outyield old style hybrids with old style cultural practices (Duvick 1984b).

Maize breeders are, however, continually working to develop more stable, high-yielding hybrids. Also, farming practices are changing toward less tillage and more crop rotation. This change may bring some greater degree of stability to maize yields, if it helps the crop do a better job of withstanding environmental stress. For example, farm experience and experimental data show much less drought-induced yield loss in maize following soybeans than in maize following maize.

I expect that any changes in U.S. maize farming practices will be made in concert. The tendency for the nation's maize plantings to be handled like one big farm will continue. Reactions to varying climatic conditions will be amplified, and some measure of instability in year-to-year national expectations for maize yields must continue. This may be the price that must be paid for high average yield in the long term.

13 Yield Stability in Bread Wheat

W. H. PFEIFFER AND H. J. BRAUN

Despite impressive increases in basic food production that accompanied the green revolution, critics claim that the widespread use of high-yielding technologies has increased the risk profile of millions of Third World farmers. Their primary concern is a reliance of farmers on new varieties and farming systems that are somehow inherently less stable than traditional cultures and modes of production. Increased production thus comes at the expense of greater variability.

At least one study (Hazell 1985b) indicates the opposite; a comparison of global wheat production data for the 1960s and 1970s shows that production variability for wheat has actually declined over time. Moreover, the main wheat-producing countries in the developing world (for example, India and Pakistan) experienced drastic decreases in wheat production variability on a country-by-country basis. Since Centro Internacional de Mejoramiento de Maiz y Trigo (CIMMYT) related wheat germplasm occupies approximately 45 percent (some 45 million ha) of the area devoted to bread wheat in Third World countries, it can be inferred that it played a role in this shift to greater production stability.

CIMMYT's wheat-breeding strategy is designed to develop broadly adapted germplasm that performs exceptionally well in one or more ecological regions and that performs well under both high- and low-input conditions. CIMMYT strives to develop germplasm that features high yield stability.

Concepts and Approaches

Sources of yield instability can be classified as spatial, temporal, and system dependent. Spatial variability results when a cultivar is grown at

---

Special thanks are due to Drs. S. Rajaram and A. Klatt for their helpful and timely review of this manuscript, and to CIMMYT Information Services, especially to Mr. T. Harris, for assistance in editing and preparation of graphics.

different locations. Location-specific environmental factors, such as soil type, general climate, endemic diseases, and pests, will vary from one location to another and will cause yield variability. These characteristics tend to be distinctively different between geographically separate locations and, hence, of a predictable nature (Allard and Bradshaw 1964). This predictability enables plant breeders to target their research on specific environmental factors.

Temporal variability occurs when a given cultivar is grown over a number of seasons. The environmental factors contributing to this kind of variability tend to fluctuate from one year to the next (such as the amount and distribution of precipitation) and are thus less predictable. In general, this source of variation cannot be integrated as well into the plant breeding process.

System-dependent variability occurs when a given cultivar is grown under different farming systems. The factors contributing to this type of variation include the various aspects of the production process controlled by farmers: crop rotations, levels of mechanization and irrigation, and the amounts and types of fertilizer, herbicides, insecticides, and fungicides applied to the crop. All these factors can result in yield variability from one farming system to the next, but they can also decrease variability by modifying the natural environment. From a plant breeding point of view, and within the constraints imposed by the availability of production inputs, system-dependent variability is largely predictable.

The three sources of variation described above tend to be interdependent. For example, precipitation strongly influences the incidence of certain fungal diseases, which in turn can be controlled by fungicides. This fact carries with it implications for the approach used in evaluating yield stability.

A Biological Approach

One approach to the investigation of yield stability involves the definition of environments in terms of their underlying biological factors and their individual contributions to the observed variability. This approach would be ideal if there were a feasible method for incorporating the nearly infinite number of influential environmental factors into the analysis.

A Practical Approach

A more practical approach to the investigation of yield stability entails an evaluation of the total environment, without identifying the specific environmental factors affecting yield stability. Thus, the overall production conditions prevailing at a given site during a given crop cycle are denoted as an environment. In this approach a single location can constitute, over a 15-year period, as many as 15 environments. An environment's production potential can be measured by the mean yield of all genotypes tested in that environment. In addition, the yield of the highest yielding variety in each environment gives an indication of the maximum production potential.

Research Methods

The analysis presented here is based on data from the First to the Fifteenth International Spring Wheat Yield Nurseries (ISWYNs), which were distributed by CIMMYT from 1964/65 to 1978/79 and grown in sites representative of the major wheat-growing environments. The ISWYN is a standardized international yield nursery consisting of three replications of 49 spring bread wheat varieties and advanced lines, plus one local check. Since local checks frequently were not identified by cooperators growing the trials or were CIMMYT cultivars, they have not been used in most computations.

The genotypes were subdivided (according to their origins) into four different groups defined in detail by Braun (1983) and Pfeiffer (1983):

Group I: CIMMYT-bred cultivars released directly by national crop improvement programs;

Group II: Initial crosses made by CIMMYT, but at least one further selection made in a national program;

Group III: Locally developed cultivars with CIMMYT germplasm in their pedigrees;

Group IV: Locally developed cultivars without CIMMYT germplasm in their pedigrees.

Most of the models used for the investigation of yield stability are based on an assumed positive linear relationship between the performance of a variety and better growing conditions (that is, it is assumed that varieties will yield more grain as the general production potential of the site increases, taking into account all production constraints). The regression model used was a combination of those developed by Perkins and Jinks (1968), Wright (1971), and Utz (1972).

More specifically, the site means are shown on the X-axis, and the variety yields are shown on the Y-axis (figure 13.1). The yield of a given variety at each site is used to calculate a regression line through the points that represent the performance of the respective genotype in each environment. The slope of this regression line measures the individual response of the variety to better growing conditions. The line that represents the average response of all entries included in the analysis has a slope of unity (a 45 degree line). Thus, an above-average yield response is indicated if the slope of the variety regression line is greater than one (Varieties 1 and 2 in figure 13.1); the greater the slope, the higher the responsiveness of the variety.

FIGURE 13.1 Response of four hypothetical varieties to higher productivity levels

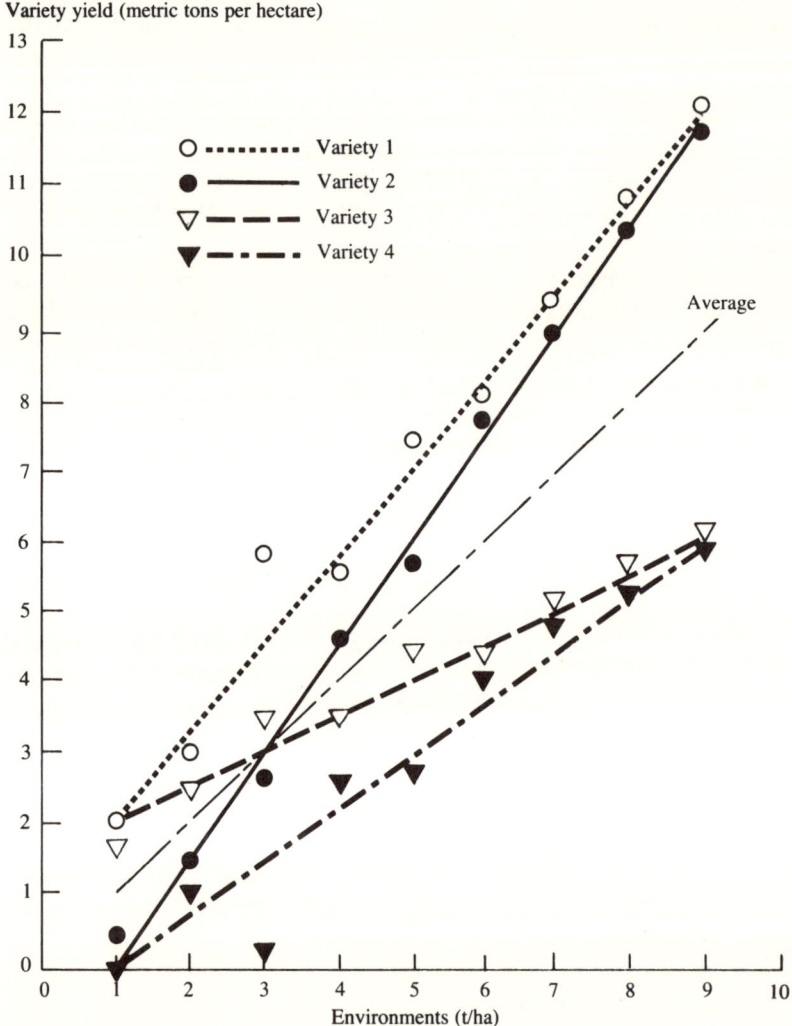

CIMMYT seeks Variety 1 types; Variety 2 types are rejected because they are low yielding in poorer production environments, and Variety 3 and 4 types are less responsive to improving conditions.

The sum of the squared deviations from the regression line (ch. 10) is used to describe yield instability. This indicator can be misleading. To identify the best performing varieties across sites, both the variety mean and the parameters for stability and response must be considered.

A high-yielding variety (HYV) is said to have acceptable yield stability if (a) the mean yield is significantly higher than the average yield across sites, (b) the slope of the regression line is greater than or equal to unity, (c) the sum of the squared deviations is small, and (d) the yield in the environment with the poorest production conditions exceeds or equals the average of all entries. This combination implies superior yield performance across the entire environmental range.

Research Results

An indication of the adoption of the genotypes can be obtained from table 13.1. As the proportion of CIMMYT developed Group I and II genotypes increased from 45 percent in the Sixth ISWYN to 65 percent in the Seventh ISWYN, with a corresponding decrease from 47 to 29 percent of the locally developed varieties (LDVs) in Group IV, the ISWYN grand mean increased by about 30 percent. This was due to the replacement, on a global level, of low-yielding commercial cultivars with broadly adapted Group I and II genotypes. Figure 13.2 gives a more detailed picture of the mean yields, coefficients of regression, and yield stability parameters for the four groups of genotypes. The broad variation evident in figure 13.2 illustrates that each group contains high-yielding, highly responsive, and stable genotypes. Since the large number of genotypes prohibits their consideration on an individual basis here, the general response patterns of the groups are emphasized.

Yield Performance

A comparison of the yield performance of the four groups clearly indicates the yield superiority of Group I genotypes in each ISWYN. Thus, Group I superiority is independent of the change over time in the composition of the nurseries. Across the ISWYNs, yield differences remained constant (in absolute terms); the relative yield differences between groups decreased as the ISWYN mean yields steadily increased. Across the 15 ISWYNs, the following relationship among the groups holds: Group I has statistically significantly higher yields than the entries in Group II; Group II has significantly higher yields than Group III; and Group III has significantly higher yields than the varieties in Group IV.

RESPONSIVENESS TO BETTER GROWING CONDITIONS. Similarly distinct results (clear group-specific differences) have been obtained for the regression coefficients (b). The means of the b values of all four groups are significantly different. The genotypes of Groups I and II show an above-average-to-high responsiveness to improved production conditions, whereas the cultivars of Groups III and IV are below average in their responsiveness (figure 13.2b). A high positive correlation (0.84) between the

TABLE 13.1 Proportion of genotypes in international spring wheat yield nurseries from 1964-1965 to 1978-1979

Group	ISWYN Number														
	1	2	3	4	5	6	7	8	9	10	11	12	13	14	15
I	6	11	15	16	15	10	14	12	12	14	25	24	23	25	27
II	3	2	5	7	6	12	18	18	18	24	12	12	15	14	8
III	—	—	3	3	3	4	3	2	4	4	7	5	6	4	11
IV	15	11	26	23	25	23	14	17	11	7	5	8	5	5	3
No. of entries	24	24	49	49	49	49	49	49	49	49	49	49	49	48	49
No. of locations (environments)	34	47	61	63	63	60	66	81	69	68	65	76	76	71	73
ISWYN grand mean (t/ha)	2.7	2.8	2.8	2.9	2.6	2.8	3.6	3.6	3.9	3.5	3.8	3.9	3.3	3.5	3.8

FIGURE 13.2 (a) Distribution of mean yields, (b) coefficients of regression, and (c) yield stability parameters for four groups of genotypes across International Spring Wheat Yield Nurseries (ISWYNs) 1 through 15

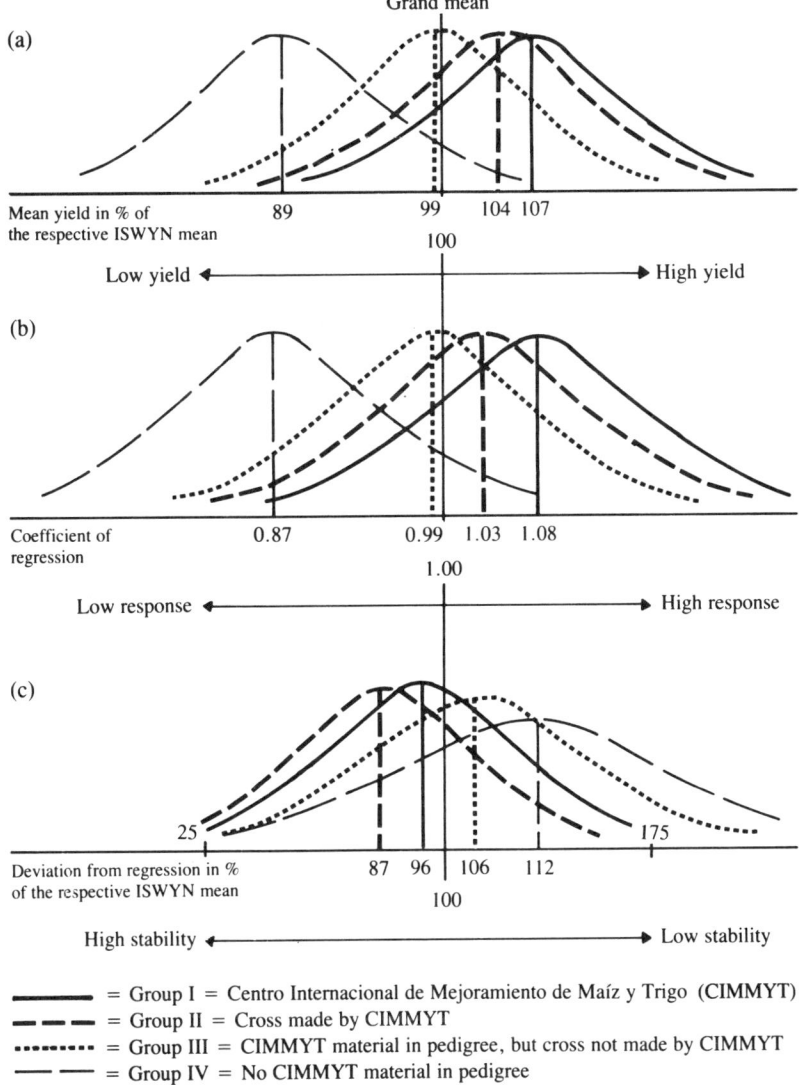

mean yield of the varieties and their regression coefficients was obtained so that seemingly high yield performance across environments can be obtained only by using highly responsive varieties.

HIGH-YIELDING VERSUS LOW-YIELDING VARIETIES. The strength of this correlation implies that above-average mean yields and below-average regression coefficients rarely occur together. When production conditions are poor, yields are low for all varieties. In the low-yielding environments, the differences in yield between high-yielding varieties (HYVs) and locally developed varieties (LDVs) are small. The low regression coefficients associated with locally developed varieties, which some people interpret as resulting from superior yield performance in poor environments, are due to their poor yield expression in high-yielding environments. Thus, HYVs can be characterized both as input efficient and input responsive.

Some "idealists" would opt for varieties having complete stability, such as could be depicted by a horizontal line in figure 13.1. They argue that such varieties are feasible as well as preferable. Such completely stable varieties cannot exist, however; they would have to perform outside the possible range in the low-yielding environments. Exceptionally high yields in low-yielding environments are possible only when disease is the cause of the low yields. A given variety can respond to improving production conditions in one of only four ways, the extremes of which are shown in figure 13.1.

Widespread opinion holds that HYVs do not perform well under low input conditions. Occasionally, genotypes with high regression coefficients produce high yields when production conditions are very favorable and below average yields in poor environments. In this analysis, such cases generally reflect the susceptibility to specific diseases present at the location, rather than the lack of input efficiency, per se, in the genotype.

Figure 13.3 illustrates the analysis of an input efficient and input responsive variety, Veery "S." It has high genetic yield potential and exhibits superior yield performance across the entire range of environments. Its yield is better than the mean of all entries in nearly all environments. Its regression coefficient is not much higher than that for the mean of all entries, but its yield is consistently above the mean yield of all entries.

YIELD STABILITY. It is evident from figure 13.2c that each of the four groups contains genotypes having stable yields, as well as some having unstable yields. Stability analyses of the data show that Group II is significantly more stable than Groups I, III, and IV. Group I genotypes have the same mean stability as Group III and are significantly more stable than IV. However, considering yield stability alone when examining these four groups is not sufficient to decide what is and what is not a "good" genotype; by our definition, good genotypes must combine high yield stability

FIGURE 13.3 Yield of Veery "S" in the 73 environments of the 15th International Spring Wheat Yield Nursery (ISWYN)

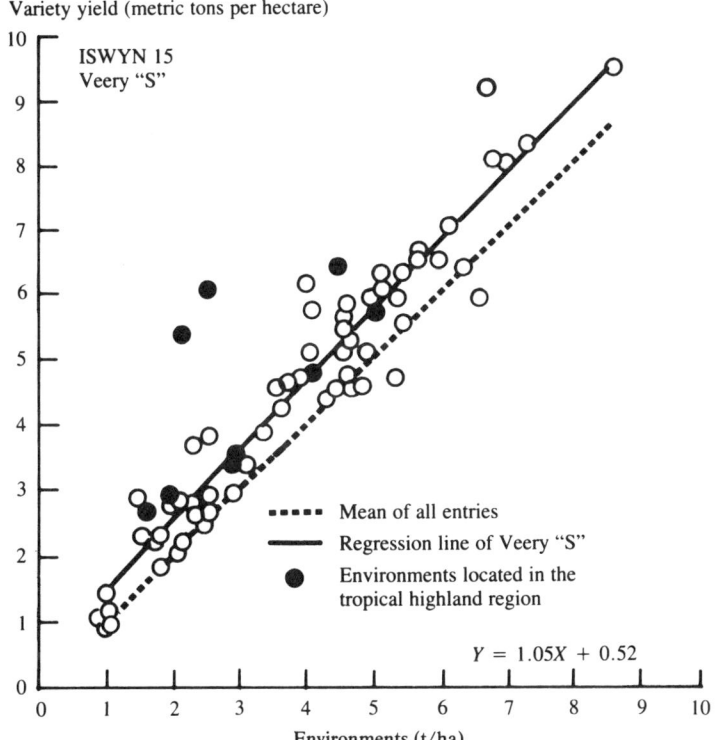

SOURCE: Pfeiffer (1983).

with high yield potential, high input efficiency, and high input responsiveness.

This tendency for higher instability in the Group IV entries is caused, to a certain extent, by a high proportion of genotypes in the group with low yield stability due to late maturity, photosensitivity, or some vernalization requirement. The grand mean might, therefore, be somewhat biased. Furthermore, that Group II shows a slightly higher yield stability than Group I may be misleading, since the yield stability of some outstanding Group I genotypes is underestimated (as is discussed later).

Since critics state that HYVs are less stable than locally developed varieties, the relevant question is whether the high mean yields of the HYVs are correlated with yield stability. In fact, a significant correlation on a global level between mean grain yields and yield stability parameters has been found in nine of 15 ISWYNs. The average correlation coefficient is negative (-0.46, significantly different from zero at the 1 percent level). Low deviation from the regression line indicates genotypic yield stability; therefore, a negative correlation of these two factors suggests that genotypes with high mean yields exhibit a high yield stability, a conclusion that holds true not only on a global basis, but also on a regional basis and for groupings of similar environments.

In special cases, using the sum of squared deviations from the regression line to characterize yield stability can be misleading. For instance, Veery "S" has a low yield stability when expressed as the sum of squared deviations, but it significantly outyielded other entries across all locations.[1]

In figure 13.3, the solid points indicate environments where there was either a high incidence of major diseases or specific requirements for adaptation. Note that three of these points lie far above the regression line for Veery "S" (the solid line), indicating the superior performance of the genotype at those specific sites. These large deviations distort the results, causing a high sum of squared deviations from the regression line, which implies a low yield stability. If these points are omitted from the analysis, Veery "S" also has high yield stability.

Performance on a Regional Level

A comparison was made between the four germplasm groups on a regional basis and on the basis of groups of specific environments. This comparison highlights the influence of the site-specific adaptation of the locally developed cultivars in Groups III and IV.

The ecologically different regions of Asia and the tropical highlands are compared in figure 13.4. The tropical highlands region includes environments above 2,000 meters elevation in Africa, and in Central and South America. The wheat-producing areas in the tropical highlands are disease "hot spots," making diseases one of the primary determinants of yield.

In figure 13.4, the data indicate superiority of the respective best Group I or Group II entries, both across years and regions. Three general trends are obvious for the Asian region: first, Group I entries in ISWYNs 1 through 4 outyielded all other groups by far; second, in ISWYNs 5 through

---

1. To overcome the disadvantages of the "sum of squared deviations" as a stability parameter, CIMMYT is developing a new parameter similar to the one suggested by Jensen (1976). The "distance" between the yield of the highest yielding line at each location and the yield of a given variety is used to characterize the "total (or entire) performance" of a variety, including its mean yield, responsiveness, and yield stability. Using such a parameter will place Veery "S" in the first position among top performing genotypes.

FIGURE 13.4 Relative yield performance of the respective highest yielding genotype (variety) in the Asian and tropical highlands regions

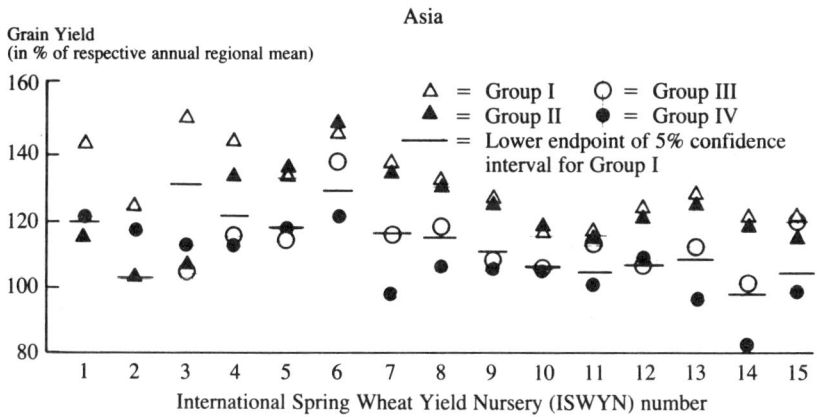

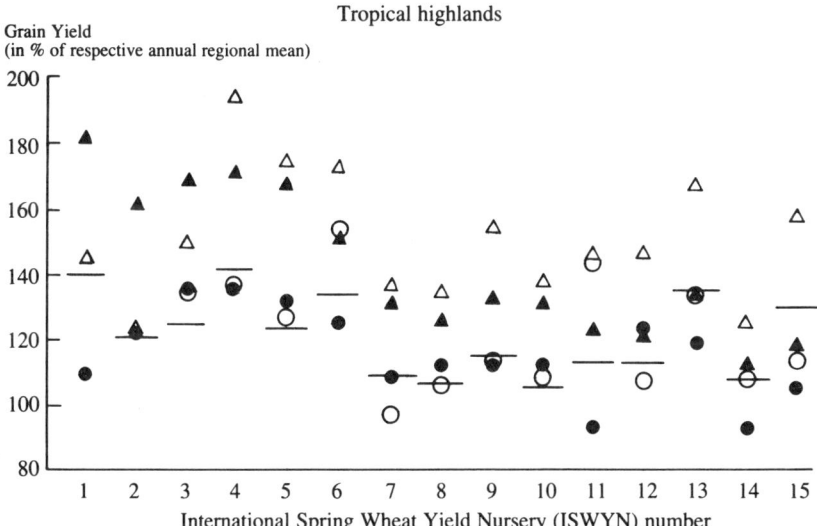

SOURCE: Pfeiffer (1983).

NOTE: Group I: CIMMYT-bred cultivars released directly by national crop improvement programs. Group II: Initial crosses made by CIMMYT, but at least one further selection made in a national program. Group III: Locally developed cultivars with CIMMYT germplasm in their pedigrees. Group IV: Locally developed cultivars without CIMMYT germplasm in their pedigrees.

9, a clear improvement is seen in the Group II genotypes; and third, in ISWYNs 10 through 15 a clear trend can be seen toward the greater success of locally developed (Group III) materials.

A different pattern in the progress toward wheat improvement for the tropical highlands can be observed. In ISWYNs 1 through 3, materials selected for stripe rust resistance (from Colombia and Ecuador) showed the best performance in this region. Beginning with ISWYN 4, Group I entries with excellent stripe rust resistance were available (e.g., Tobari 66), but these varieties did not respond to improvements in fertility and gave relatively low yields in high-yielding environments. Over time, this limitation was eliminated by incorporating better responsiveness in materials resistant to stripe rust; these improved lines were available in subsequent cycles.

At the same time, emphasis was given to introducing better resistance to *Septoria* spp., a limiting disease in the tropical highlands. Varieties such as Pavon 76, which combine the needed disease resistance with high yield potential and high input responsiveness, were the result of this breeding effort. These varieties still give good performance across a global set of environments, as well as in specific areas.

Finally, a new performance level was reached in ISWYN 15 with genotypes stemming from spring times winter crosses. Veery "S" (which carries the 1B/1R translocation) significantly outyielded all other entries across all locations included in the 15th ISWYN. In the tropical highlands, it was the best performer by far; it was also the top-yielding line in the South American lowlands, the irrigated areas of northwest Mexico, the southern United States, and under rainfed conditions in the northern United States and Canada. In the Middle East region, Veery "S" yielded slightly lower than the top yielder, and in the Asian region its yield was not significantly different from the top performer. The outstanding performance of the Veery lines indicated by this analysis has since been verified in ISWYNs 16 through 20.

Performance in Different Groups of Environments

Groups of environments were formed using such criteria as their mean yield level and according to various production constraints, such as heavy incidence of disease. These groups can be further divided into subgroups (e.g., low-yielding disease environments or low-yielding disease-free environments).

Figure 13.5 shows the relative performance in ISWYN 15 of the CIMMYT line Veery "S," the best respective locally developed variety (LDV), and the longtime check variety Siete Cerros, a CIMMYT-developed cultivar included in this and all previous ISWYNs. The lower 5 percent confidence bound for the top yielder is shown by the solid horizontal

FIGURE 13.5 Relative grain yield of the CIMMYT variety Veery "S," the best locally developed variety (LDV), and the longtime check variety Siete Cerros in eight different environmental groupings for the 15th International Spring Wheat Yield Nursery (ISWYN)

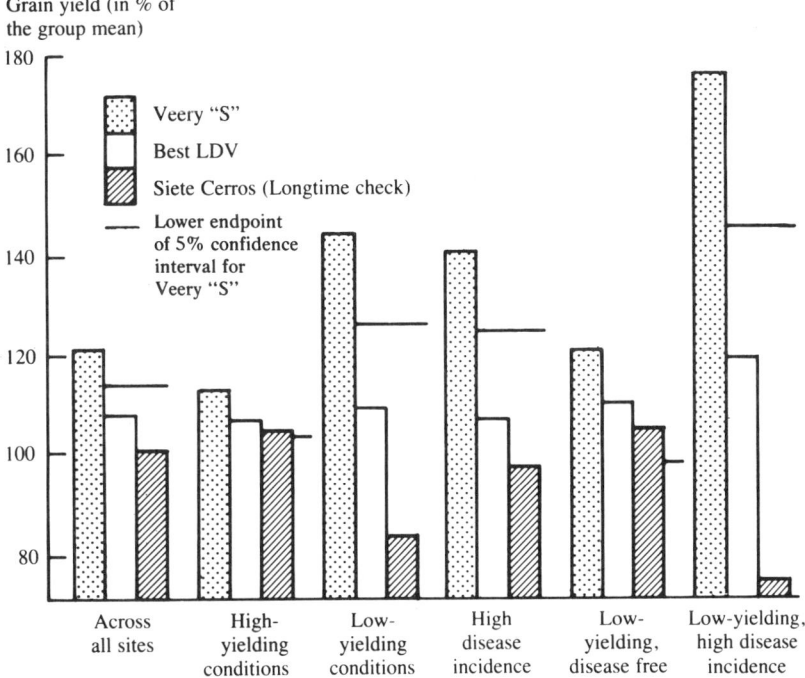

SOURCES: Braun (1983) and Pfeiffer (1983).

lines. The yield advantage of the new varieties compared to the standard check and the locally developed varieties is expressed in the significantly higher yields across the total of 76 environments. While a decisive advantage was not achieved in the high-yielding environments, an increase in the yield potential of the recently bred cultivars is obvious and proved to be statistically significant in individual high-yielding environments, such as Northwest Mexico. The superiority of the new varieties was not as evident in the low-yielding, disease-free environments. However, yields under poor conditions have improved by about the same relative amount compared with yields in high-yielding environments.

The reason for the outstanding yields obtained in environments with disease stress can often be found in the good yield potential of such sites when disease-resistant varieties are grown. In contrast to the "real" low-yielding environments (e.g., drought-afflicted environments), some of the disease environments are fertile enough to permit very good yields. In such cases, the disease resistance of a variety is the most important factor enabling it to profit from additional inputs, such as water and nutrients. A variety cannot produce yields above a certain limit associated with the absolute amount of the yield-determining input factors. Therefore, from the biological point of view, it is not possible for one variety to show much better absolute yields at the lower end of the environmental range if the yields are limited by the availability of inputs.

Verifying the Yield Stability of High-Yielding Varieties

System-Dependent Stability

Experiments conducted at the Sonora Experiment Station in northwest Mexico provide verification of many of the foregoing statements. Two old, tall cultivars (Yaqui 50 and Nainari 60, released in Mexico in 1950 and 1960, respectively) were compared to 12 CIMMYT advanced lines to evaluate promising advanced lines for their yield dependability in differing simulated environments.

The experimental design was a complete factorial, 3 moisture regimes × 3 nitrogen levels × 2 weed levels:

Moisture regimes:
No moisture stress: seeding irrigation plus five supplementary irrigations,
Terminal drought: seeding irrigation plus one supplementary irrigation at crown root initiation,
Relieved drought: seeding irrigation plus one supplementary irrigation at heading;
Nitrogen levels: 0, 75, and 150 kg of N/ha;
Weed levels: weedy and weed free.

Veery "S" and the highest yielding CIMMYT advanced lines produced yields under water stress, zero input, weed-free, and weedy conditions that were at least as high or higher than those given by the old cultivars (figure 13.6). Under higher input levels, significantly higher yields were obtained with the recently developed genotypes.

Figure 13.7 shows the nitrogen response curves of the two old cultivars and Veery "S." The bold lines show the response to nitrogen across the three different moisture regimes and the two weed conditions. The thin lines show the response under weed-free, fully irrigated conditions. The superiority of Veery "S" at all nitrogen levels shows clearly. The input efficiency of Veery "S" at the zero nitrogen level is higher than that of the old cultivars, and its response to additional amounts of nitrogen is also

FIGURE 13.6 Input efficiency of old and new varieties under differing production conditions

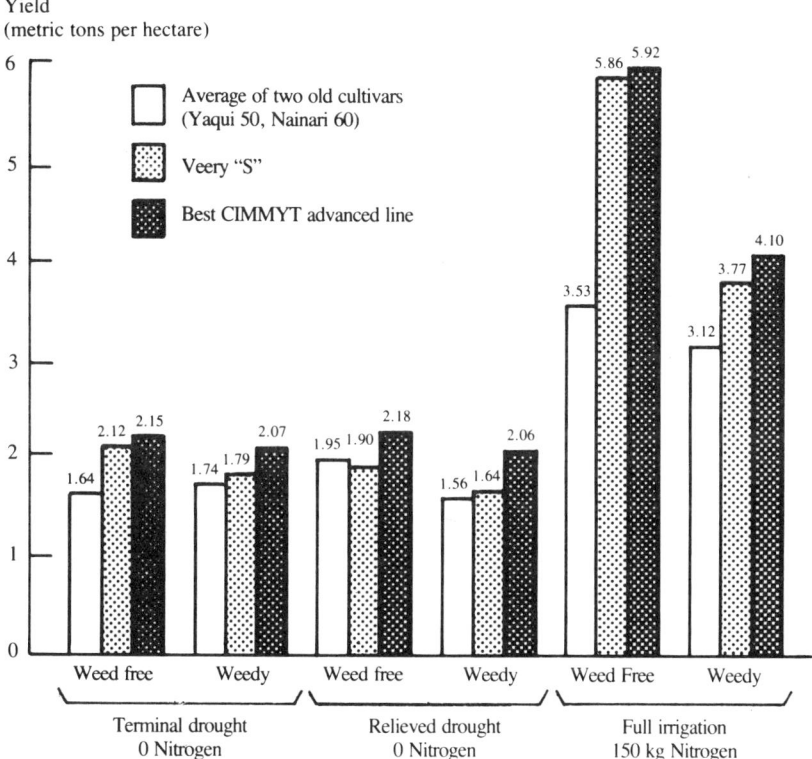

greater. Furthermore, the response lines for Veery "S" indicate that it can physiologically use more than 150 kg/ha of nitrogen. The application of 150 kg/ha of nitrogen exceeds the yield maximizing levels for the two old cultivars.

Temporal Stability

Farmers, of course, cannot provide completely stable environments for their crops. Hence, annual changes in environmental conditions cause fluctuations in yield. Adding to the variability caused by this set of unpredictable factors is the damage caused by birds, rodents, and hail.

In accepting that yields must fluctuate from one year to the next, it is clear that the evaluation of temporal yield stability cannot be based on constant yields across years. Rather, an acceptable variety should main-

FIGURE 13.7 Nitrogen response curves of Veery "S" and two old cultivars

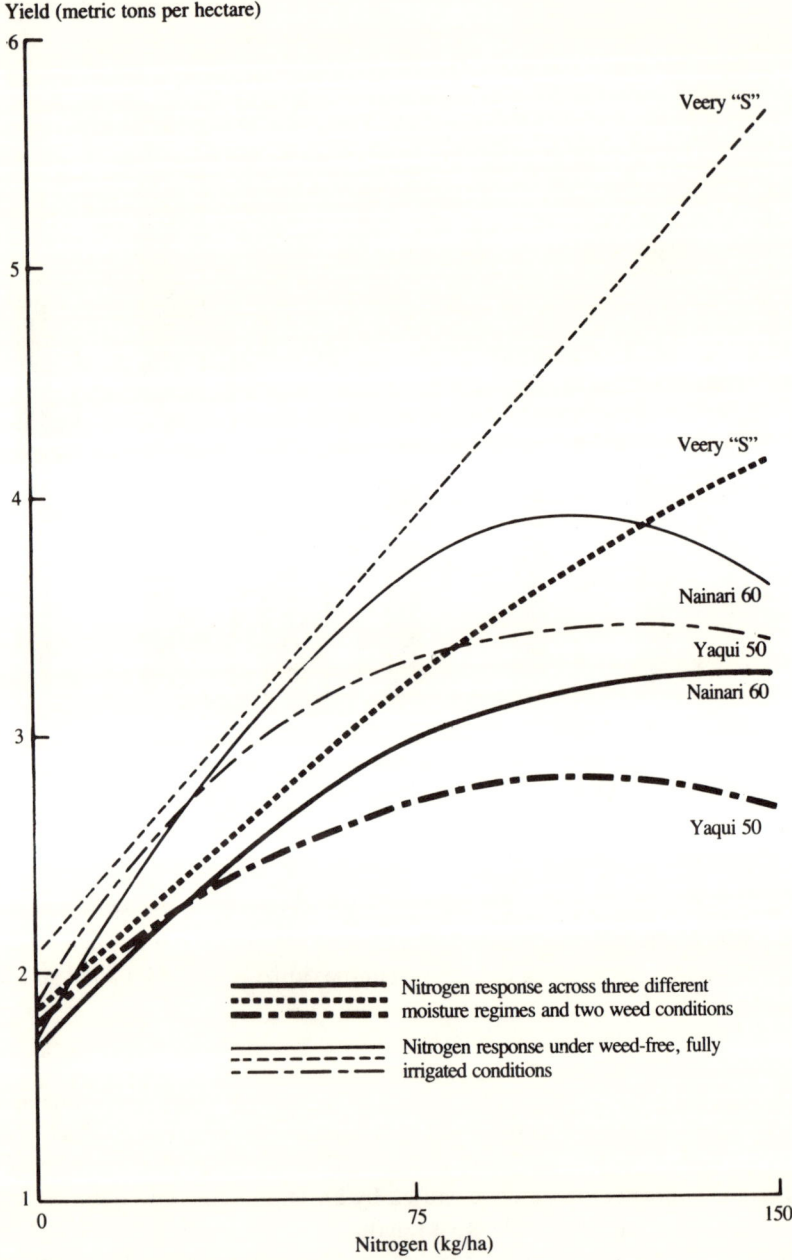

TABLE 13.2 Correlations between parameters from one year to the next for a common set of genotypes and environments

ISWYN	Mean Yield	Regression Coefficient	Yield Stability Parameter
1/2	0.98	0.85	0.59
2/3	0.94	0.85	0.76
3/4	0.96	0.88	0.77
4/5	0.97	0.89	0.54
5/6	0.96	0.89	0.55
6/7	0.96	0.95	0.54
7/8	0.93	0.92	0.60
8/9	0.96	0.89	0.66
9/10	0.92	0.82	0.83
10/11	0.99	0.92	0.90
11/12	0.83	0.79	0.85
12/13	0.78	0.83	0.91
13/14	0.90	0.89	0.62
14/15	0.92	0.94	0.85
Average correlation	0.92	0.87	0.72

Note: All correlations significantly different from zero at the 1 percent level (Pfeiffer 1983).

tain its ranking with respect to the desirable traits of high yield potential, input responsiveness, and yield stability when evaluated over time.

Table 13.2 presents the correlations of stability parameters from one year to the next for a common set of genotypes and environments analyzed from ISWYN 1/2 through ISWYN 14/15. The fact that the correlations are very high indicates that the ranking of the genotypes remained basically constant. These genotypes have both high spatial and temporal yield stability. The corresponding average correlations for mean yield in the tropical highland region, Asia, and the Middle East (0.83, 0.87, and 0.90, respectively) indicate that this result holds true on a regional level.

An explanation of the high spatial and temporal yield stability found in this analysis is that CIMMYT's wheat improvement research involves shuttling experimental germplasm between two primary locations in Mexico having very different environmental conditions. These locations comprise near optimum and heavy disease stress environments, and materials must perform well in both environments to be advanced. In addition, materials are tested in a number of other locations in Mexico that, collectively, are representative of many of the wheat production environments found around the world. In addition, each year CIMMYT advanced lines undergo global multilocation testing in over 100 countries. Thus, within Mexico, breeding can be done for a broad spectrum of diseases and environmental stresses, while screening and testing on a global basis expose materials to a wide range of differing environmental conditions.

Future Challenges Confronting Wheat Breeders

Perhaps most importantly, the gains made so far must be maintained. Plant breeding is always a dynamic process. The resistance of a given variety to a specific disease will likely fail over time as new bioraces of the disease pathogen appear. Not only must the resistance be maintained, but breeders should also strive to make it more durable, as has been done in the case of stem rust.

For other diseases, such as *Helminthosporium,* root rots, and *Fusarium* head scab, or for environmental stresses such as aluminum toxicity, heat, and saline soils, the breeding challenges remain. CIMMYT wheat breeders are only now identifying sources of resistance and tolerance and are just beginning to incorporate these traits into good agronomic types. Success in this effort will help to reduce the variability of bread wheat production as more marginal areas come under wheat cultivation.

For low-yielding environments, significant progress has been achieved and further improvements can be expected though, as always, only in small incremental steps. The stability of production is input dependent rather than genotype dependent and can only be increased significantly by compensating for environmental factors with increased inputs, since a breakthrough in genotypic input efficiency has a very low probability.

The CIMMYT Wheat Program's approach will continue to be one of combining input responsiveness with input efficiency in broadly adapted genotypes having high genetic yield potential. The objective is to develop a range of materials as broadly adapted as Veery "S" but possessing the traits needed to provide maximum yield stability in selected production areas.

14 Genetic Improvement and the Variability in Wheat Yields in the Great Plains

C. JAMES PETERSON, V. A. JOHNSON,
J. W. SCHMIDT, AND ROBERT F. MUMM

Plant breeders have long recognized the importance of cultivar stability over a range of environmental conditions. Most of the world wheat crop is produced in semi-arid, rainfed environments, such as the Great Plains of the United States, which are subject to wide fluctuations in climate, disease pressures, and precipitation over and within growing seasons. Soil types and production practices, such as tillage methods, rotation practices, weed control, fertilization, and management equipment, may also vary widely within regions. Cultivars must have the potential to maintain competitive yields in various suboptimal environments as well as to respond to more favorable conditions or increased inputs.

Cultivar stability has been defined as the ability to produce the yield expected at the level of productivity of the respective environment, that is, a cultivar which shows no genotype-environment (GE) interaction (Becker 1981). A stable cultivar would not contribute to variance in productivity over a region; in practice, cultivars show wide variations in stability.

Evaluation and selection of cultivars over wide ranges of environments are essential if stability and wide adaptation are to be identified. The Northern and Southern Regional Performance Nursery (NRPN and SRPN, respectively) programs were initiated in the Great Plains over 50 years ago by the U.S. Department of Agriculture (USDA) and state experiment stations as a response to breeders' concerns for evaluation and selection of cultivar stability, yield potential, and adaptation.

Many researchers have evaluated gains in wheat productivity and contributions of cultivar development to increased yields (Russell 1973; Silvey 1978; Sim and Araji 1981; Schmidt 1984; Feyerherm, Paulsen, and Sebaugh 1984). It has been difficult, however, to evaluate changes in cultivar stability, cultivar responses to variation in environmental conditions, and genetic contributions to production variance over time. The NRPN and SRPN provide an opportunity to evaluate such trends and to examine cultivar performance in relation to long-term check cultivars and contributions to increased variability in wheat yields.

Materials and Methods

Yield data from the NRPN and SRPN from 1959 to 1984 were examined. The nurseries comprised experimental hard red winter wheat cultivars developed by breeders and agronomists with the USDA/Agricultural Research Service (ARS), state experiment stations, and private industry.

Experimental cultivars were usually included in the nursery for two years and the top-yielding ones were often later released for commercial production. Long-term check cultivars were included annually in the nurseries for comparisons of cultivar and nursery performance over years. The check cultivars Kharkof and Scout 66 were grown in the SRPN and Kharkof and Warrior in the NRPN. Kharkof is an old cultivar considered to have adequate winter hardiness and wide adaptation and is representative of the Turkey Red wheat originally introduced to the Great Plains.

Cultivars in the SRPN were grown primarily at locations in the southern Great Plains (Texas, Oklahoma, New Mexico, Kansas, Colorado, and Nebraska). Cultivars in the NRPN were grown primarily in the northern region (Nebraska, Montana, South Dakota, North Dakota, Wyoming, Minnesota, and Alberta).

The total number of locations and cultivars varied from year to year for each nursery but did not exceed 40 cultivars and 32 locations in the SRPN or 32 cultivars and 22 locations in the NRPN. Nurseries were evaluated in randomized complete block designs at each location, usually with three replications. Seeding rates, dates, row spacing, and fertilization were different at each location and conformed to local practice.

Data from 11 and 9 locations in the SRPN and NRPN (table 14.1), respectively, which reported nursery yields for nearly every year from 1959 to 1984, were used for calculations of yield trends and variance in productivity. These locations were representative of the diverse environmental conditions of each region and were used to reduce the effects of annual variation in numbers of evaluation sites. The nurseries were grown under dryland conditions with the exception of the SRPN at Ft. Collins, Colorado.

Yield gains attributed to improved production practices and cultivar development were calculated from annual nursery means. Genetic contributions to increased yields were calculated by expressing annual nursery mean yield as a percent of the yield of Kharkof, the long-term nursery check cultivar. The genotype–environment (GE) interaction mean square was calculated for each year using a multilocation analysis of variance as an estimate of variance in productivity of the nursery cultivars. Check cul-

TABLE 14.1 List of Locations in the Southern and Northern Regional Performance Nurseries from which yield data were used for calculation of trends in yield and variance in productivity

SRPN	NRPN
Chillicothe, Texas	North Platte, Nebraska
Stillwater, Oklahoma	Alliance, Nebraska
Cherokee or Lahoma, Oklahoma	Sheridan, Wyoming
Garden City, Kansas	Archer, Wyoming
Colby, Kansas	Preshoor or Highmore, South Dakota
Hays, Kansas	Moccasin or Havre, Montana
Ft. Collins, Colorado	St. Paul, Minnesota
Springfield, Colorado	Waseca, Minnesota
Akron, Colorado	Lethbridge, Alberta, Canada
North Platte, Nebraska	
Alliance, Nebraska	

tivar yields were not included in calculations of annual nursery mean yields and mean squares for genotype-environment interactions.

Regressions of check cultivar mean yields on an environmental index of nursery means from each location (Eberhart and Russell 1966) were calculated for each year as an indirect measure of changes in cultivar response to environmental variation. Data from all possible locations were used in the regression analyses to provide a wider environmental index, to increase the number of observations for regression, and to improve estimates of b values. Regression analyses were used to determine significance of trends over years for all parameters.

Results
Genetic Contributions to Increased Production

Mean yield of the SRPN grown at 11 locations from 1959 to 1984 has increased linearly (significant at the 1 percent level) at 56 kg/ha per year and increased from an average of 2,100 kg/ha in 1959 to 3,500 kg/ha in 1984. The 67 percent increase in yield resulted from cultivar development and improvements in production practices, such as weed control, equipment for improved nursery management, and increased fertilization.

The proportion of yield increase in the SRPN attributed to genetic improvement was determined by expressing the annual nursery mean yield as a percent of that for Kharkof. Since the long-term check and experimental cultivars were treated alike, effects of cropping practices, soil fertility, and weather variables are reduced. Mean yield of experimental cultivars in the SRPN increased linearly (significant at the 1 percent level) from 111 percent of the check in 1959 to 139 percent in 1984. A 25 percent improvement in yield, or 31 kg/ha per year, was attributable to genetic improvement and breeding efforts. Genetic contribution to increased yield accounted for 55 percent of the total yield gain. There was little indication of a yield plateau in the nursery.

Mean yield of the NRPN grown at nine locations from 1959 to 1984 has also increased linearly (significant at the 1 percent level) at 56 kg/ha per year from an average of 1,800 kg/ha in 1959 to 3,200 kg/ha in 1984. Improved production practices, cultivars, and increased fertilization contributed to the 77 percent total increase in yield.

Genetic contributions to increased yield in the NRPN were less than those in the SRPN. Mean yield of experimental cultivars in the NRPN did not increase significantly from 1959 to 1984, when expressed as a percent of that for Kharkof. Stem rust (*Puccinia graminis* f. sp. *tritici*) was a major factor in the nursery averages from 1959 to 1965 with resistant experimental cultivars gaining an advantage over Kharkof. From 1966 to 1984, a linear (significant at the 1 percent level) increase in yield of experimental cultivars from 103 percent to 117 percent of Kharkof occurred, and disease was not a major problem. This corresponds to a 14 percent increase in yield, or 22 kilograms per hectare per year, from 1966 to 1984 that was attributable to genetic improvement. Only 40 percent of the total yield improvement in the NRPN was attributable to genetic gains in these years. The harsh climate of the northern Midwest is believed to have limited genetic gains because of major requirements for winter hardiness and drought tolerance in commercial cultivars. Many difficulties encountered in evaluating germplasm in the highly variable environmental conditions are also responsible for limiting gain from selection for yield. Improvements in production techniques have had a major impact on yield gains in the northern region.

Genetic Contributions to Production Variability

Yield stability over a wide range of environmental conditions is an important criterion in the development of cultivars for the Great Plains. The interaction of genotypes and environments indicates ranges in adaptation as well as relative production stability of experimental cultivars over moisture and temperature variations. Baker (1969) suggested that the production stability of a cultivar is inversely proportional to the sum of squares for genotype–environment interaction attributable to that cultivar. In a uniform performance nursery, the trends in production stability attributable to cultivar development and genetic improvement can be measured by trends in the magnitude of the genotype–environment interaction mean square.

The genotype–environment interaction mean square associated with cultivar stability over 11 locations in the SRPN showed a linear (significant

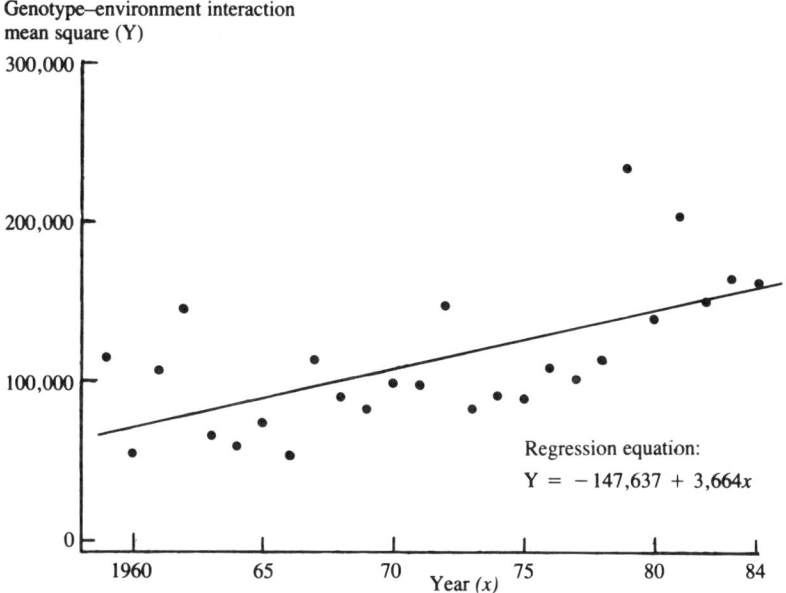

FIGURE 14.1 Mean squares associated with the interaction of genotype and environment effects on yield of cultivars in the Southern Regional Performance Nursery, 1958-1984

at the 1 percent level) increase from 1959 to 1984 (figure 14.1). The mean square increased 134 percent in 26 years. The significant contributions of cultivar development to increases in yield also appear to have contributed to increased instability or variance in levels of productivity of cultivars in the nursery. Recent cultivars appear to be less stable over a wide range of environments and have narrower areas of adaptation than those in the past.

Trends in the genotype-environment interaction mean square over nine locations in the NRPN follow a quadratic response from 1959 to 1984 (figure 14.2). Varying disease pressures and differential cultivar responses contributed to relatively high levels of production instability among the cultivars from 1959 to 1965. The genotype-environment interaction mean square showed a linear (significant at the 1 percent level) increase from 1966 to 1984 after disease pressures were reduced. The mean square increased 300 percent in those 19 years. Breeding and development of cultivars for the northern Great Plains region contributed to a dramatic increase in instability or variance in productivity of cultivars in the NRPN. Many recent experimental cultivars in the NRPN have good productivity but insufficient winter hardness for the northern plains conditions. This,

FIGURE 14.2 Mean squares associated with the interaction of genotype and environment effects on yield of cultivars in the Northern Regional Performance Nursery, 1958-1984

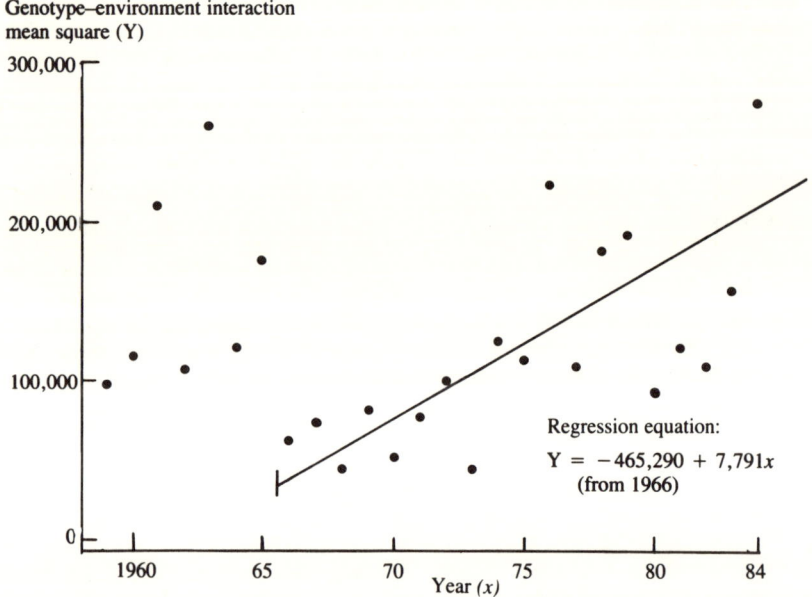

along with a narrowing of adaptation of the cultivars, may contribute to increases in instability and the genotype-environment interaction mean square.

While the absolute magnitudes of the genotype-environment variances have increased over years, they have changed little when expressed as a function of the increasing nursery mean yield levels. If the genotype-environment interaction mean squares are expressed as a coefficient of variation (cv), they have remained relatively stable at about 13 percent in the SRPN and have increased slightly from about 10 to 15 percent in the NRPN. There were no trends in the absolute magnitude of variances associated with either of the main effects of environments or genotypes.

Trends in Varietal Response to Environmental Variation

Parameters from regression analyses of cultivar yields on an environmental index (the nursery means in a particular set of environments) have been used by many researchers as a measure of cultivar stability (Finlay and Wilkinson 1963; Eberhart and Russell 1966; Johnson, Shafer, and Schmidt 1968; Stroike and Johnson 1972; Schmidt, Johnson, and Stroike 1972; Schmidt et al. 1973; Worrall et al. 1980; ch. 10).

FIGURE 14.3 Coefficients (*b* values) from regression of check cultivar yields on nursery mean yields at locations in the Southern Regional Performance Nursery, 1959-1984

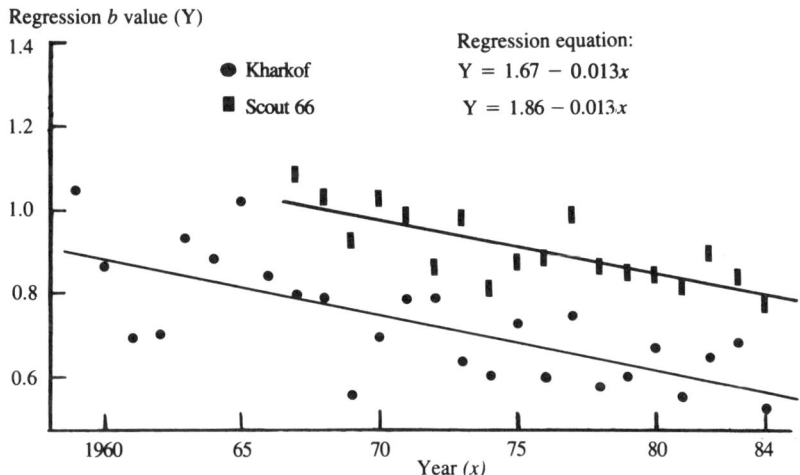

Trends in average cultivar response to environmental conditions and constraints in the SRPN and NRPN can be evaluated indirectly in terms of changes in relative responses of the long-term check cultivars (figure 14.3). Stability and environmental responses of the nursery checks would not be expected to change over years. However, stability parameters are based on average environmental response of cultivars included in a nursery and may vary for a check cultivar if cultivars in the nursery are changed. Changes in stability parameters of the checks over years, therefore, indicate changes in average response to environment. Yearly regressions of the yield of Kharkof on the nursery mean yield at each location in the SRPN shows a linear (significant at the 1 percent level) decrease in the b values for Kharkof from 0.90 in 1959 to 0.60 in 1984 (figure 14.3). Similarly, the regression b values for the secondary check Scout 66 have decreased linearly (significant at the 1 percent level) from 1.00 in 1967 to 0.80 in 1984. Trends in deviation from regression were not evident.

In 1959, experimental cultivars in the SRPN expressed a small yield advantage over Kharkof, which increased slightly with improving environmental yield potential. In 1984, experimental cultivars expressed a large yield advantage over Kharkof in high-yielding environments, but the yield advantage diminished rapidly as the environmental yield potential decreased. A major portion of the genetic contributions to increased yield since 1959 has been from increased cultivar yields as expressed in favorable or nonlimiting environments. Genetic contributions to increased yield in

FIGURE 14.4 Coefficients (*b* values) from regression of check cultivar yields on nursery mean yields at locations in the Northern Regional Performance Nursery, 1959-1984

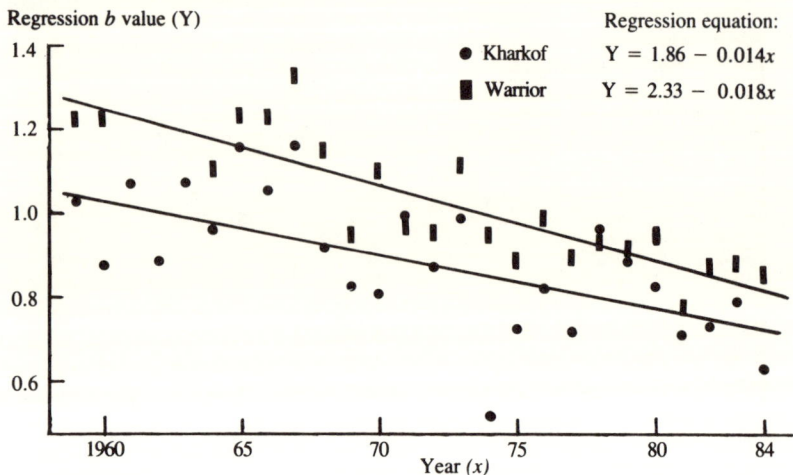

marginal or highly stressed environments have been limited. Decreasing regression values of the two long-term checks are an indication of increasing genetic yield potential of cultivars in the southern Great Plains since 1959.

In the NRPN, yearly regressions of the yield of Kharkof on the nursery mean yield at each location also show a linear (significant at the 1 percent level) decrease in the *b* values for Kharkof from 1.03 in 1959 to 0.68 in 1984 (figure 14.4). The *b* values for the secondary check, Warrior, have decreased linearly (significant at the 1 percent level) from 1.27 in 1959 to 0.82 in 1982. Genetic yield potential of cultivars in the northern Great Plains has increased substantially since 1959 and a large portion of the genetic contributions to increased yield has been from increased yield in favorable or nonstress environments. Yield increases attributable to cultivar development in marginal or stress environments have been minimal.

Discussion

Plant breeding and cultivar development have made significant contributions to increased yield in the Great Plains. An average yield increase of 56 kg/ha per year in the SRPN from 1959 to 1985 was shown with 55 percent of the gains attributed to genetic contributions. Improvements in production practices have had a somewhat greater impact on yield gains in the NRPN than cultivar development. Genetic contributions account for

40 percent of the 56 kg/ha per year yield increase in the NRPN from 1966 to 1984. These estimates are comparable to wheat yield gains reported by Russell (1973) in Australia, Silvey (1978) in England, Sim and Araji (1981) in the western U.S., Kuhr et al. (1985) in an international performance nursery, and Schmidt (1984) in nine regional performance nurseries across the United States.

Cultivar yield responses to environmental variations have changed from 1959 to 1984, and variance of productivity associated with the interaction of cultivars and environments has increased. Cultivars appear to have become less adapted to production over wide ranges in environmental conditions. A portion of increased genetic gains in yield has come from narrowing the adaptation of cultivars, thus maximizing yield potential in smaller production areas by exploitation of genotype-environment interactions. Variance of total production over a region may not significantly increase with proper deployment of more narrowly adapted cultivars while achieving maximum yields, but these cultivars may be less stable and more sensitive to yearly fluctuations in weather, moisture, and production inputs.

The increased cultivar genotype-environment interactions and narrowing adaptation may relate, in part, to an increase in genetic diversity amongst elite experimental lines. Increased cooperation in and dissemination of germplasm on an international basis has allowed breeders to incorporate many diverse genetic materials into their programs. Over a wide production area, the use of many diverse and narrowly adapted cultivars, as opposed to a few widely adapted cultivars, may substantially reduce the potential of genetic vulnerability to disease and insect pressures.

The genetic yield potential of cultivars in the Great Plains has increased significantly and contributed to yield gains in the region. Most of the genetic contributions to increased yield in the SRPN and NRPN have come from increased productivity of cultivars in more favorable or higher yielding environments. Little genetic improvement in yield of cultivars under marginal or highly stressed environments was indicated. Currently grown cultivars have increased potential to take advantage of favorable environmental conditions and production inputs. However, under unfavorable conditions or if inputs are withdrawn, yield advantage of newer cultivars may be significantly reduced, thus contributing to increased production variance over a diverse region. The differences in production levels between favorable and unfavorable environments have been widened as a consequence of cultivar development and increased genetic yield potential.

The limited yield gains in marginal or stressed environments are an indication of difficulties encountered in breeding for stress tolerance. Genetic variation for stress tolerance is available, but limited, and progress is difficult in these low heritability environments with overriding environmental constraints. Some new crop management techniques may be needed to derive greater benefits of plant breeding efforts in marginal areas.

Finlay (1968), based on extensive adaptation tests, believed that yield stability and yield potential are more or less independent of each other. Heine and Weber (1982) found no strong correlation between stability parameters and yield in 20 years of winter wheat trials. Walton (1968) suggested that maximum stability in cultivars has been sacrificed to maximize yield potential and that the two characteristics are negatively correlated. Results from the regional nursery trial tend to support Walton (1968) and the suggestion by W. J. R. Boyd that "there may be an adaptive advantage in mediocrity" (personal communication, J. W. Schmidt 1983), especially if wide adaptation is critical. It is unrealistic, however, to suggest that breeders sacrifice high yield and responsiveness for wide adaptation and increased stability in a new cultivar. Trends in cultivar response to environments in the Great Plains indicate that breeders must carefully consider any trade-offs between maximum yield, stability, and ranges in adaptation during cultivar development and evaluation.

Trends in regional cultivar performance discussed here represent average responses of the experimental cultivars entered in the nurseries and general trends in cultivar development. In certain cases, individual cultivars in recent nurseries may have combined excellent stability with increased yield potential. To put all this in context, it must also be recalled that grain yield and stability are only two of many criteria involved in cultivar selection and release.

15 Yield Stability of CIMMYT Maize Germplasm in International and On-Farm Trials

H. N. PHAM, S. R. WADDINGTON, AND J. CROSSA

Most of the maize in developing countries is grown by subsistence farmers who are working in extremely difficult maize production environments. These farmers have little grain to spare for the market after meeting their families' needs, and so most lack the means of investing heavily in irrigation, fertilizer, pesticides, and other modern means of coping with the depredations of diseases, insect pests, and the vagaries of the weather. Nor do those farmers have a strong incentive for making such an investment, since many do not grow the high-yielding, input-responsive maize varieties that would enable them to take maximum advantage of purchased inputs. In contrast to the situation in wheat production, developing country maize farmers are, by and large, still growing the old, established landraces. In 1983 the Centro Internacional de Mejoramiento de Maiz y Trigo (CIMMYT) estimated that about 5 percent of the entire maize-growing area in the Third World countries was planted to varieties developed by national researchers using germplasm from the Center's Maize Improvement Program.

When grown in favorable environments under good agronomic management, there is no doubt that modern varieties of lowland tropical maize give higher grain yields than do older types. The emphasis placed by CIMMYT on reducing plant height and tassel size has not only reduced the tendency for tropical lowland materials to lodge when given fertilizer,

---

This chapter is the result of a collaborative effort and represents work done by many people. The authors appreciate in particular the contribution of numerous cooperators in national programs who carried out the Experimental Variety Trials and the on-farm trials. Results of on-farm trials conducted in Ghana, Guatemala, Haiti, and Mexico were supplied by Drs. G. Edmeades, A. C. Hibon, A. F. E. Palmer, A. Violic, M. Yates, and Ing. H. S. Cordova. Those from trials carried out in Paraguay were provided by Ings M. Ozaeta and A. Lopez P. Many colleagues offered valuable suggestions. Thanks are due, in addition, to R. F. Mumm of the University of Nebraska, who wrote the computer program used to analyze part of the data presented here.

but has greatly improved the efficiency of their partition of assimilate to grain while crop biomass has remained the same at optimum plant densities (Fischer and Palmer 1984, Johnson et al. 1986).

Although improved tropical maize is now widely available around the world, the high grain yield potential of such material is often one of the less important considerations that enter into a small-scale farmer's decision about a variety. Other factors include grain color, cooking quality, taste, milling properties, ease of shelling and shelling percentage, forage yield, and resistance to ear rots and insect pests, both while the ear is on the plant and later in storage. Subsistence farmers are also interested in reduced variability of grain yield. Characteristics that contribute to greater stability include tolerance to water stress and extreme plant densities, and resistance to diseases and insect pests. The CIMMYT Maize Program is attempting to satisfy many of these requirements in addition to boosting grain yield. Currently, for example, it is pursuing a dual approach to the protection of the ears of lowland tropical maize against disease and insect pest damage. As well as introducing genetic resistance, researchers are improving the husk cover of normal materials and endosperm hardness of maize with improved protein quality (Paliwal and Sprague 1981, Sprague and Paliwal 1984, CIMMYT 1985). Other approaches being followed to improve yield stability include improvement of drought resistance (Fischer, Johnson, and Edmeades 1983), tolerance to barrenness at high plant densities, and greater nitrogen fertilizer use efficiency.

This chapter offers an analysis of yield stability of CIMMYT germplasm. A genotype is generally considered stable if its grain yield varies little from year to year at a given location or varies little across locations within a "mega-environment" to which the genotype is adapted in a broad sense. This view is in agreement with the concept of yield stability as defined by Eberhart and Russell (1966) and by Perkins and Jinks (1968). Some authors, such as Binswanger and Barah (1980), divide this definition into two components: concern with temporal variation (stability) and with spatial variation (adaptability).

The study is divided into two parts. The first attempts to gauge the effects on yield stability of the various procedures that make up CIMMYT's population improvement and international testing scheme. The approach taken is to analyze the performance in multilocational testing of experimental varieties (EVs), derived from four CIMMYT populations. The findings of this analysis cannot answer with complete satisfaction questions about the yield stability of high-yielding varieties. The point that remains to be clarified is whether materials will also perform well under the more difficult and variable conditions of farmers' fields.

The second part of the study attempts to answer that question by analyzing the yield and yield stability of improved maize varieties in comparison with traditional varieties in farmers' fields under their wide range of environments and management practices. It also examines how improved genotypes perform relative to traditional ones when grown under higher levels of inputs and management.

Yield stability is analyzed according to the technique (ch. 10) described by Eberhart and Russell (1966, 1969) and Hildebrand (1984). With this technique, a stable variety can be defined as one having a regression slope (b) of 1.0 suggesting that it can exploit favorable environments and, more importantly, a small deviation from the regression (s^2_d), indicating that it will respond very predictably in a given environment. It is further assumed that, in a stable variety, it is desirable to have a high mean yield and a large intercept on the y-axis (indicating that the variety yields well in low-yielding environments). The authors are well aware that this simple method has limitations as a tool for assessing stability. Its biological and statistical drawbacks have been pointed out by various authors, including Baker (1969), Knight (1970), Witcombe and Whittington (1971), Hill (1975), and Binswanger and Barah (1980). Partly for that reason, Center researchers are starting to work with another technique for measuring yield stability (Crossa and Deutsch 1985, Westcott 1987).

CIMMYT's Population Improvement and International Testing System

Of the many ways of providing high-yielding, stable germplasm, the CIMMYT Maize Program has chosen one that involves the development and improvement of broad-based gene pools and populations in conjunction with international distribution and testing of varieties derived from this germplasm. The Program manages 23 normal and 10 quality protein maize (QPM) advanced populations (according to the scheme illustrated in figure 15.1) that are superior in yield and other attributes. In the course of the improvement cycle, 250 full-sib families of a particular population are tested, along with six local checks, in International Progeny Testing Trials (IPTTs) at up to six locations around the world (including one of CIMMYT's stations in Mexico). In a given year, about 15 populations are tested.

The results of these trials are used in two ways. First, based on information provided by trial cooperators, CIMMYT scientists select the best 50–60 families in a population for within-family improvement, recombination, and regeneration of new progenies in each population for the next cycle of improvement. The second use of International Progeny Testing Trials results is for development of experimental varieties; most of these are derived from the ten best families at each location and others from the

FIGURE 15.1 Steps in population improvement and experimental variety development, evaluation, and use

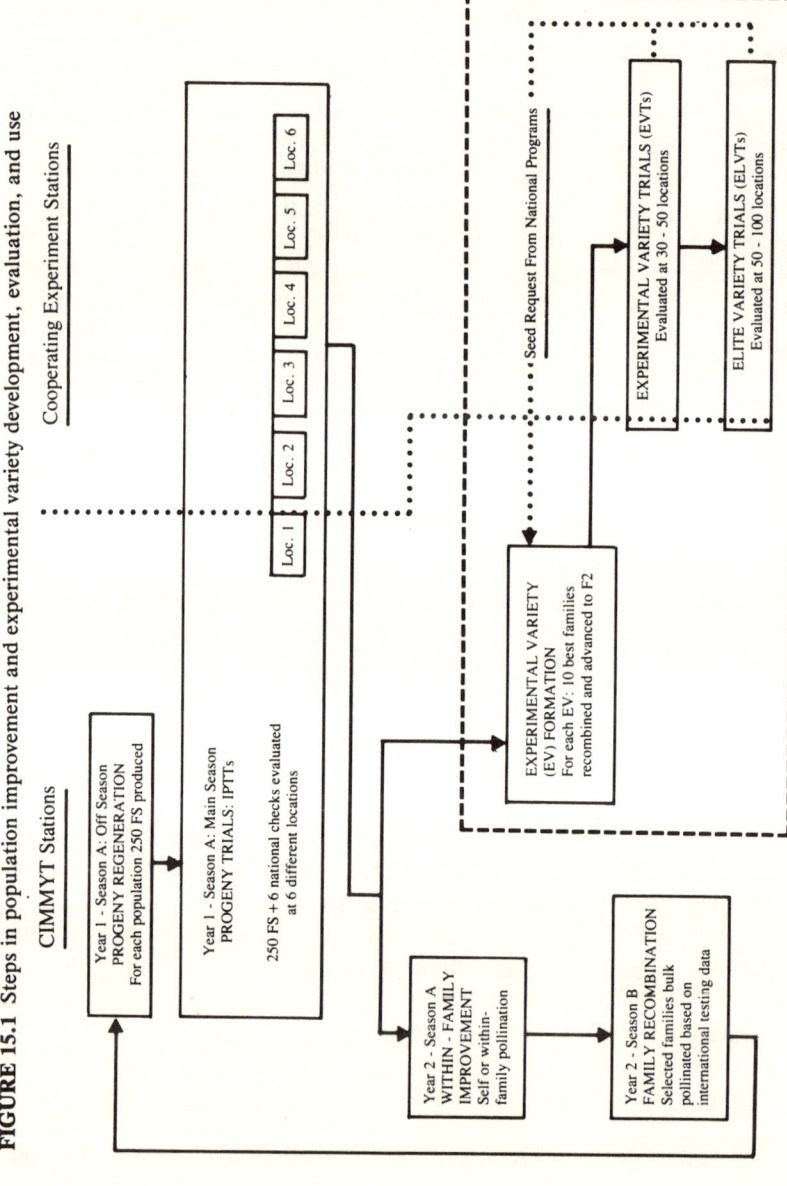

NOTE: FS refers to full sibs; IPTTs are International Progeny Testing Trials.

ten best families across locations. In the formation of these varieties, selected families are crossed in all possible combinations and then advanced to the synthetic-1 stage by bulk pollination.

The experimental varieties are tested by cooperators in national research programs in Experimental Variety Trials (EVTs), each of which is conducted at 30-50 locations and compares the experimental varieties with two local checks and two reference entries. The trials are distributed mainly according to cooperators' requests and conducted for the most part at experiment stations of participating national maize programs. After data analysis CIMMYT scientists select the best varieties in yield and yield stability for Elite Variety Trials (ELVTs), which are carried out at 60-80 locations in much the same way as the Experimental Variety Trials.

All trial cooperators receive summaries of the test results and can obtain seed at any stage of the testing scheme for breeding, further testing, or seed increase and variety release. Over the past ten years, CIMMYT and its trial cooperators in national programs have developed over 800 experimental varieties through this system, and by 1984 about 120 varieties based on CIMMYT germplasm had been released by 29 national programs.

Grain Yield and Yield Stability of Experimental Varieties in Multilocational Testing

This part focuses on grain yield and yield stability parameters of experimental varieties developed from the following randomly selected populations: Populations 21 (Tuxpeño-1) and 43 (La Posta), which are late-maturing white materials, and Populations 32 (ETO Blanco) and 49 (Blanco Dentado-2), which are intermediate-maturing white materials. The experimental varieties were formed over two or three consecutive cycles of population improvement during the period 1979-84. Experimental varieties from Populations 32 and 49 were tested in Experimental Variety Trial 14B (tropical lowland, early-intermediate, white) from 1982 to 1984 and those from Populations 21 and 43 in Experimental Variety Trial 12 (tropical lowland, late, white) from 1979 to 1984.

The total number of entries per trial ranged from 14 to 30, including newly formed experimental varieties plus the two local check varieties and two reference entries. Different experimental varieties were tested each year and, for any given trial, the local checks varied from one test location to another. The same reference entries were included over the entire six-year period of testing. The experimental varieties in a particular testing cycle of a given population entered the Experimental Variety Trials in one or, more often, two test years. The reason a few were tested only in one year is that data from some International Progeny Testing Trial locations arrived later than others; these trials are grown at a wide range of locations both north and south of the equator in different growing seasons, and their results are the basis for formation of the experimental varieties. Data from locations with a large experimental error were excluded from the analysis. The data reported here came from trials conducted at 17–41 sites, but the majority were carried out at 30–35 locations in Central, North, and South America; East, West, and southern Africa; South and Southeast Asia; and the Middle East.

One condition for deriving pertinent regression parameters and hence for making predictions about the performance of crop varieties is an adequate range of values over test sites for the character being measured. Without exception, all the trials reviewed in table 15.1 have a quite wide yield range. In Experimental Variety Trial 14B, for example, which was conducted at 36 locations in 1983, means for grain yield ranged from 1.2 to 7.2 tons per hectare (t/ha). The number of testing environments (17–41) was more than sufficient for making regression estimates.

Four salient points are evident from the data on the experimental varieties. First, within a given cycle of population improvement, there were always some outstanding experimental varieties in terms of grain yield. In the improvement of Population 32, for example, Poza Rica 8032 was superior for grain yield in cycle n, and three experimental varieties—Los Baños (1) 8232, San Jeronimo 8232, and Poza Rica 8232—were superior in cycle $n + 1$ (table 15.1). Varieties from Population 43 also gave high yields in various cycles, including Across 7843 and La Maquina 7843 in cycle n, San Andres 8043 and Ilonga 8043 in cycle $n + 1$, and Suwan 8243, Across 8243, and Ferke 8243 in cycle $n + 2$.

A second notable point is that the experimental varieties tested in the Experimental Variety Trials had regression slopes equal to or significantly greater than 1.0 (table 15.1). Experimental varieties with a slope significantly greater than 1.0 and low mean yields are not included in the Elite Variety Trials. Such varieties respond well in good environments but give less than desirable results in poor environments. Since the variety trials are normally conducted at research stations and supplied with adequate levels of inputs, only those experimental varieties with a unit regression slope are included in the Elite Variety Trials as a means of ensuring that the selected varieties are sufficiently adapted to farmers' conditions, in addition to being stable.

The third point is that experimental varieties in the later cycles were just as stable as those in the earlier cycles. This is indicated by their deviation from regression, which, according to Eberhart and Russell (1969), is the more important of the two parameters for judging the stability of genotypes. This third conclusion is evident from the data in table 15.1, which lists grain yields and stability parameters of maize varieties developed from

TABLE 15.1 Grain yield and stability parameters of maize varieties in consecutive cycles of selection tested in 1979–1984

Test Entry	Year Tested	Yield (t/ha)	b	s_d^2
INTERMEDIATE-MATURING MAIZE				
EVs from Population 32				
Cycle n				
Poza Rica 8032	1982	4.39	1.153*	0.132*
Cotaxtla 8032	1982	4.17	1.037	0.073*
Alajuela 8032	1982	4.16	1.089	0.177*
Across 8032	1983	3.92	1.031	0.111*
Ilonga 8032	1983	3.90	1.067	0.083*
Cycle $n+1$				
Los Baños (2) 8232	1984	4.28	1.118	0.048
San Jeronimo 8232	1984	4.25	0.977	0.041
Poza Rica 8232	1984	4.23	1.072	0.075*
Los Baños 8232	1984	3.93	1.006	0.020
EVs from Population 49				
Cycle n				
Mexico 8049	1982	4.13	0.952	0.082*
Cycle $n+1$				
Rattray-Arnold (1) 8149	1983	4.11	0.995	0.089*
Across 8149	1983	4.08	0.984	0.057*
Poza Rica 8149	1983	4.06	0.948	0.039*
Ikenne 8149	1983	4.06	1.052	0.033*
Ikenne (1) 8149	1984	4.53	0.917	0.052
Gandajika 8149	1984	4.31	1.060	0.050
LATE-MATURING MAIZE				
EVs from Population 21				
Cycle n				
Across 7721	1979	4.49	1.026	0.000
Gandajika 7721	1979	4.45	0.975	0.000
San Andres 7721	1979	4.27	1.053	0.122*
San Andres 7721	1980	5.01	0.942	0.049*
Cycle $n+1$				
Maracay 7921	1980	5.29	1.047	0.000
Cotaxtla 7921	1980	5.27	1.018	0.079
Poza Rica 7921	1980	5.20	0.921	0.000
Across 7921	1982	5.31	0.997	0.025
Los Diamantes (1) 7921	1982	5.04	0.921	0.055*
Cycle $n+2$				
Rattray-Arnold (1) 8121	1983	4.76	1.031	0.020
Poza Rica 8121	1983	4.73	0.993	0.008
Across 8121	1983	4.43	0.094	0.044
Jardinopolis 8121	1983	4.70	1.015	0.000
Omonita (1) 8121	1983	4.46	1.013	0.004
Potchefstroom 8121	1984	5.15	0.919	0.140*

TABLE 15.1 Continued

Test Entry	Year Tested	Yield (t/ha)	b	s_d^2
EVs from Population 43				
Cycle n				
La Maquina 7843	1979	4.90	1.207*	0.000
Poza Rica 7843	1979	4.86	1.105	0.162*
Across 7843	1980	5.47	1.083	0.418*
Ejura (1) 7843	1980	5.27	1.077	0.128*
Cycle $n+1$				
San Andres 8043	1982	5.36	1.147*	0.084*
Across 8043	1982	5.27	1.056	0.017
Cotaxtla 8043	1982	5.18	1.104*	0.036
Los Diamantes (1) 8043	1982	5.10	1.068	0.052*
Ilonga 8043	1983	4.95	1.037	0.147*
Kwadaso 8043	1983	4.83	1.069*	0.027
Cycle $n+2$				
Suwan 8243	1984	5.51	1.114	0.017
Across 8243	1984	5.40	1.059	0.068*
Ferke 8243	1984	5.38	1.022	0.004
Ikenne 8243	1984	5.34	1.076	0.143*
Sta. Rosa (1) 8243	1984	5.33	1.155	0.059
Ferke (1) 8243	1984	5.32	1.154	0.118*
Catacamas 8234	1984	5.25	1.033	0.015
Catacamas (1) 8234	1984	5.06	1.038	0.000
Ikenne (1) 8234	1984	5.06	1.079	0.072*

*Asterisks denote significant difference from unity for b and from zero for s_d^2 at 5 percent level.

different populations. Based upon their deviations from regression, experimental varieties from Population 32 at cycle $n+1$ were generally more stable than those from the same population at cycle n. Two experimental varieties from Population 49—Ikenne (1) 8149 and Gandajika 8149—out of the six tested were stable at cycle $n+1$ having both unit regression slopes and small deviations from regression. The only experimental variety derived from Population 49 in cycle n was unstable, with large, significant deviations from regression.

The same general trend occurred among the late-maturing experimental varieties derived from Population 21; those from later cycles were just as stable as ones from earlier cycles. Two experimental varieties out of the three tested in cycle n were stable, four out of five in cycle $n+1$, and five out of six in cycle $n+2$ (table 15.1). There were, however, no definite trends over cycles in the grain yields of these experimental varieties.

Experimental varieties from population 43 were similar in stability to those from population 21. In the most recent cycle ($n + 3$), five experimental varieties out of the nine tested showed small deviations from regression and had regression slopes not significantly different from 1.0.

These findings should be of interest to scientists in national programs, who prefer to select not just the highest yielding experimental varieties but those which give high grain yields and possess yield stability parameters of unit regression slopes and small deviations from regression. The varieties are also judged according to insect pest and disease resistance and agronomic characters such as maturity, husk cover, and standability. Varieties can be selected on the basis of these criteria at any cycle of selection.

The fourth point is that, in every cycle of selection, there were some high-yielding, stable experimental varieties. In the most recent cycle, likely candidates for further testing of intermediate-maturing varieties include Los Baños (1) 8232 or San Jeronimo 8232 from Population 32, and Ikenne (1) 8149 or Gandajika 8149 from Population 49. Candidates among the late-maturing varieties would probably include Rattray-Arnold (1) 8121, Poza Rica 8121, or Across 8121 from population 21, and Suwan 8243 or Ferke 8243 from population 43. These are typical of the high-yielding, stable varieties chosen for the Elite Variety Trials.

The presence of high-yielding, stable varieties in every cycle of selection is perhaps a result of developing broad-based maize germplasm and subjecting it to international testing. The practice of sending breeding nurseries and variety trials mostly to research stations, where the materials are grown under adequate management, results in the selection of genotypes that, judging from their regression slopes, are more responsive to higher levels of inputs. A second practice favoring stability is to select only full-sib families that have performed well across testing environments to be recombined for the next cycle of improvement.

Another feature of the approach to population improvement also has some bearing on yield stability. All the populations and experimental varieties derived from them are grouped broadly according to adaptation, maturity, and grain color. Thus, Populations 21 and 43 are tested in tropical lowland areas, and the late-maturing, white grain varieties generated from them are tested in the variety trial EVT 12 under essentially the same environmental conditions. Likewise, Populations 32 and 49 and the corresponding Elite Variety Trial (14B) include early to intermediate-maturing white maize, and each is tested in the same zone of adaptation.

It would perhaps have been better to judge the success of this approach by testing the improvement cycles of the populations at many locations. Such a large undertaking would have required more time than was available for the preparation of this chapter. Even so, data from this study do provide evidence that at every cycle of selection there are some high-yielding, stable experimental varieties and that their high yield potential and stability are maintained and in many cases improved over cycles of selection.

Stability of Improved Varieties in On-Farm Testing

Some of the experimental varieties tested in international trials are adopted and released directly by national programs. More often, however, these materials are incorporated into the national breeding effort, undergo further changes, and are used in various ways to develop varieties or hybrids. There may thus be a considerable difference between the germplasm national researchers receive and the material based upon it that finally reaches farmers. For that reason and, perhaps more importantly, because there is usually a great difference in developing countries between nursery management at experiment stations and crop management in farmers' fields, it is essential to consider the performance of improved varieties in on-farm trials to reach a satisfactory conclusion about their yield performance and stability.

Over the past ten years or so, CIMMYT has accumulated results from a large number of on-farm trials by working closely with many national maize programs in the testing of improved varieties at the farmers' level of management and under improved agronomic technologies in farmers' fields. Among the countries where Center researchers have participated in on-farm work are Bolivia, Colombia, Costa Rica, Ecuador, Ghana, Guatemala, Haiti, Honduras, Mexico, Pakistan, Panama, Tanzania, Thailand, and Zaire. In spite of the volume of this research, it is still difficult to compile good data on genotype performance in farmers' fields that are suitable for stability analysis, though such results are becoming more readily available. The problem with much of the currently available data is that stability analysis was not included in the original planning of the research. Frequently, the number of sites included is not sufficient, and the nonexperimental variables are set at levels other than those of the farmers.

This part presents results and conclusions from some of the trials for which it is possible to gain indications on yield stability in improved and local varieties. The term "improved" here denotes varieties that are developed according to the methods described and are adapted to the megaenvironment in which they were tested. The term "local" denotes the farmers' variety. In the trials described here, this was usually a landrace that had not been developed by modern breeding methods. In most trials no attempt was made to include pooled seed of local materials or to provide participating farmers with a representative local variety. Therefore, the local variety across sites was, in most cases, not one but several different varieties.

The trials and locations were selected on the basis of trial type, the availability of data, and the authors' confidence in the data. The trials were carried out not only in farmers' fields, but also at the farmers' agronomic input and management level, unless this was an experimental variable. In most cases the trials were managed by the researcher. The economic analyses were done according to methods described by Perrin et al. (1976).

All the variety trials reported (except those in Mexico) had a randomized complete block design with three or four replications at a site. The trials involving management and agronomic inputs in addition to varieties were in most cases not replicated at a site, so s^2_d values could not be calculated for those trials. All grain yields reported are adjusted to a grain moisture content of 15 percent.

Variety Trials

In table 15.2 the grain yield and yield stability of improved varieties are compared with those of local varieties in nine sets of on-farm variety trials conducted in five countries. In all cases, except Guatemala, sites with mean yields as low as 0.5-1.4 tons per hectare were included in the analyses.

Mean grain yields across sites for improved varieties were usually greater than for local materials, and in no case was yield lower than that achieved by local varieties. The slope (b) in the Eberhart-Russell analysis was almost always steeper for the improved varieties, but very few crossover interactions were found between improved and local materials. Deviations from regression were similar for the two types of materials.

To illustrate these general points, data are presented from Paraguay, Ghana, and the Mexican state of Guerrero.

PARAGUAY. In 24 trials conducted during 1984 in eastern Paraguay, Suwan 8027 gave an overall better yield than the local variety; it was more productive in both good and poor environments and for all practical purposes no less stable than the local variety (figure 15.2). The other two improved varieties were not significantly higher yielding than the local one. One of those varieties (Population 66), though not significantly higher yielding, performed well under both conditions. The slope of the Paraguayan improved variety (Guarani V-311 B) indicated that it may perform more poorly than the local one in the poorest environments.

GHANA. A series of variety trials were conducted in Ghana over three years (1981-83) at 74 sites in all. The varieties tested were of 110- to 120-day maturity and generally met the requirements for 75 percent of Ghana's major season maize production area.

The local varieties were poorer yielding than the improved varieties during all three years and in all environments, including the low-yielding

TABLE 15.2 Summary comparison of improved maize varieties with farmers' local varieties in on-farm variety trials, where inputs and management are at the farmer level

Country and Year	Mean Grain Yield of Improved Varieties Across Sites[a]	Slope of Improved Varieties	Deviations from Regression of Improved Varieties	Crossover Interaction Between Improved and Local Varieties Across Sites Where Tested
Guatemala, 1976	30% of varieties greater, all other same	Generally steeper	Similar	No[b]
Guatemala, 1977–78	All greater	Generally similar	40% of varieties similar, all others smaller	No[b]
Paraguay, 1984	33% of varieties greater, all others same	Slightly steeper	Similar	No
Haiti, 1983	Same	Slightly steeper	Slightly larger	No
Mexico				
Veracruz, 1973–80	Same	Similar	Slightly larger	No
Guerrero, 1984–85	Greater	Steeper	Similar	No
Ghana, 1981	All greater	All steeper	All smaller	Yes, at sites with mean yield 1.5 t/ha
Ghana, 1982	All greater	All steeper	All smaller	No
Ghana, 1983	All greater	All steeper	All smaller	No

[a] Only statistically significant differences are noted.
[b] At no site did the mean yield fall below 2.5 t/ha.

FIGURE 15.2 Linear regressions of variety yield on the mean grain yield at a site for three improved maize varieties and the local variety in eastern Paraguay, 1984

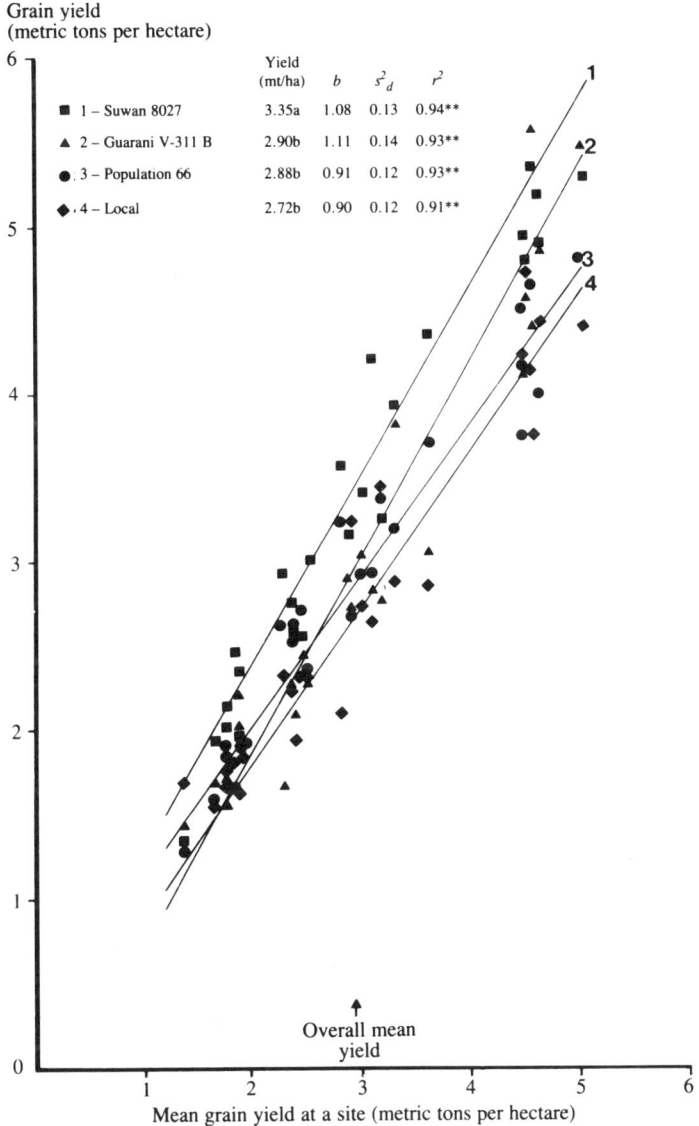

NOTE: Mean yields with the same letter are not significantly different from each other at the 5 percent level according to Duncan's multiple range test. ** denotes significant at the 1 percent level.

FIGURE 15.3 Linear regressions of variety yield on the mean grain yield at a site for seven improved maize varieties and the local variety at 18 sites in Ghana, 1983

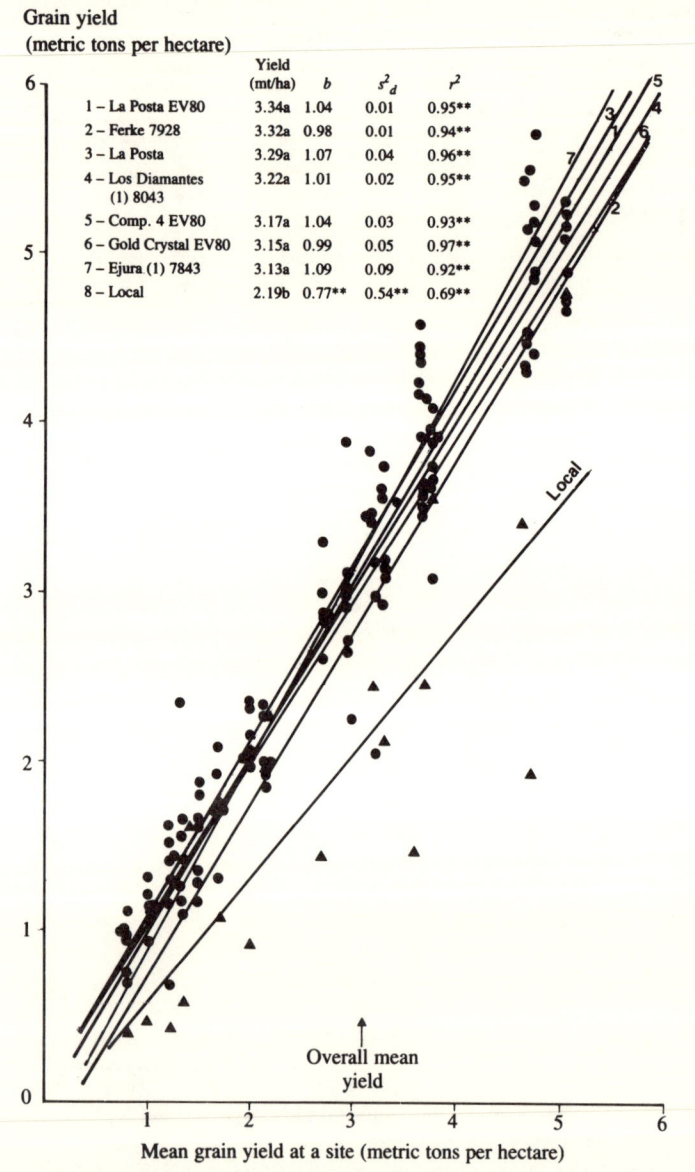

NOTE: Mean yields with the same letter are not significantly different from each other at the 5 percent level according to Duncan's multiple range test. ** denotes significant at the 1 percent level.

sites in 1983, a drought year. There was no evidence of a crossover between the local variety and the improved ones. Improved varieties gave greater benefits at the higher yielding sites, as illustrated for 1983 in figure 15.3. Slopes for local varieties were significantly less than unity in two out of the three years, deviations from the regression s^2_d were significant only for the local variety. A feature of the data is the small amount of variation in type of response between the improved varieties studied.

MEXICO. In a total of 14 trials grown on farmers' fields in Guerrero during 1984 and 1985, the Mexican variety V455—derived from Population 22 (Mezcla Tropical Blanco) and selected at Poza Rica in 1978—consistently outyielded the local variety grown by farmers at both low- and high-yielding sites (figure 15.4). As was the case in the trials discussed previously, differences between the improved and local varieties were greater at the better sites. The average grain yield improvement with V455 was 0.68 tons per hectare above the average of 1.92 tons per hectare for the local variety. The two materials were very similar in phenology.

Variety and Agronomic Inputs Trials

Farmers are able to modify maize yields by altering the levels of agronomic inputs, such as seeding rate and fertilizer, and by their management of the crop. Better agronomy is the primary way in which farmers can hope to improve production levels. It is, therefore, of great importance to gain an idea of how improved maize varieties behave in comparison with local varieties when more advanced production technologies are used.

Two examples illustrate the differences commonly encountered between improved and local varieties when grown at the farmers' level of management and at higher levels in farmers' fields.

MEXICO. A series of on-farm trials was conducted at 26 site-year combinations in Veracruz state from 1973 to 1980. The results show that, in this mega-environment, the performance of the improved variety (Tuxpeñito), compared with that of the local variety, depended on the level of agronomic inputs and management.

In these trials yield was improved only when a level of agronomic inputs and management higher than that of the farmers was employed with either the local variety or the improved one (figure 15.5). There was, however, a response crossover between the two varieties at the higher input level. The improved variety was better able to take advantage of the higher inputs than the local one, at the higher yielding sites. Even though the local variety gave a greater average yield across all sites with a higher level of inputs than with the farmers' inputs, its advantage was small at the highest yielding sites. This was due mainly to lodging of the tall local variety with the higher level of inputs. The Tuxpeñito and higher inputs com-

FIGURE 15.4 Linear regressions of variety yield on the mean grain yield at a site for V455 and the local variety at 14 sites in Guerrero, Mexico, 1984 and 1985

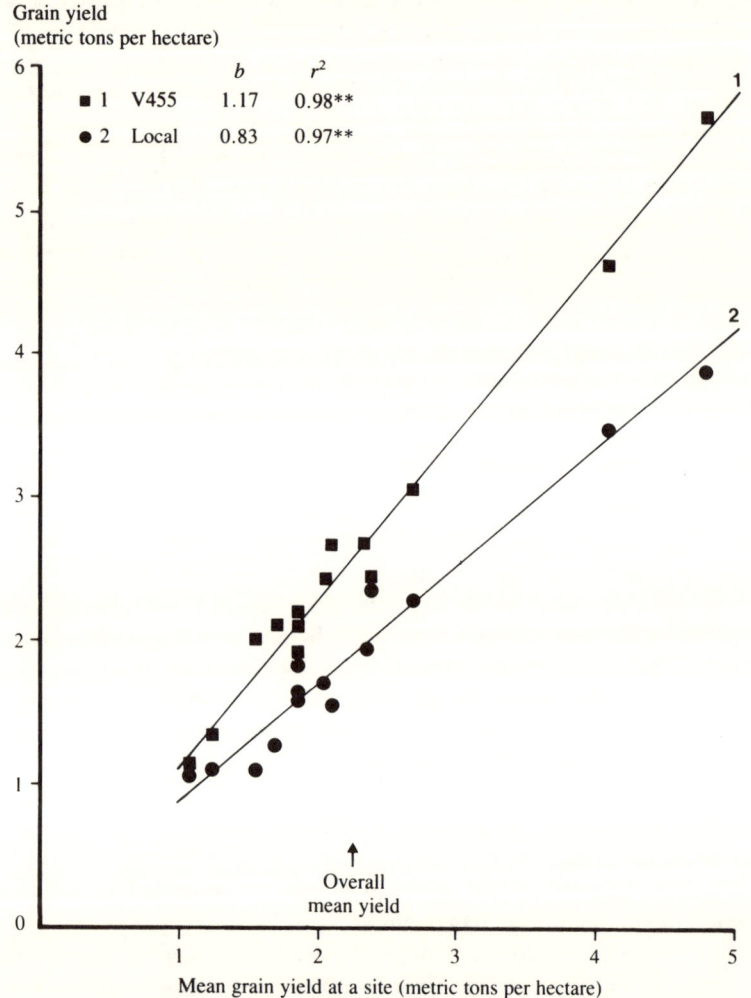

NOTE: Mean yields with the same letter are not significantly different from each other at the 5 percent level according to Duncan's multiple range test. ** denotes significant at the 1 percent level.

FIGURE 15.5 Linear regressions of variety/input treatment yields on the mean grain yield at a site for four variety/input treatments at 26 sites in Veracruz state, Mexico, 1973–1980

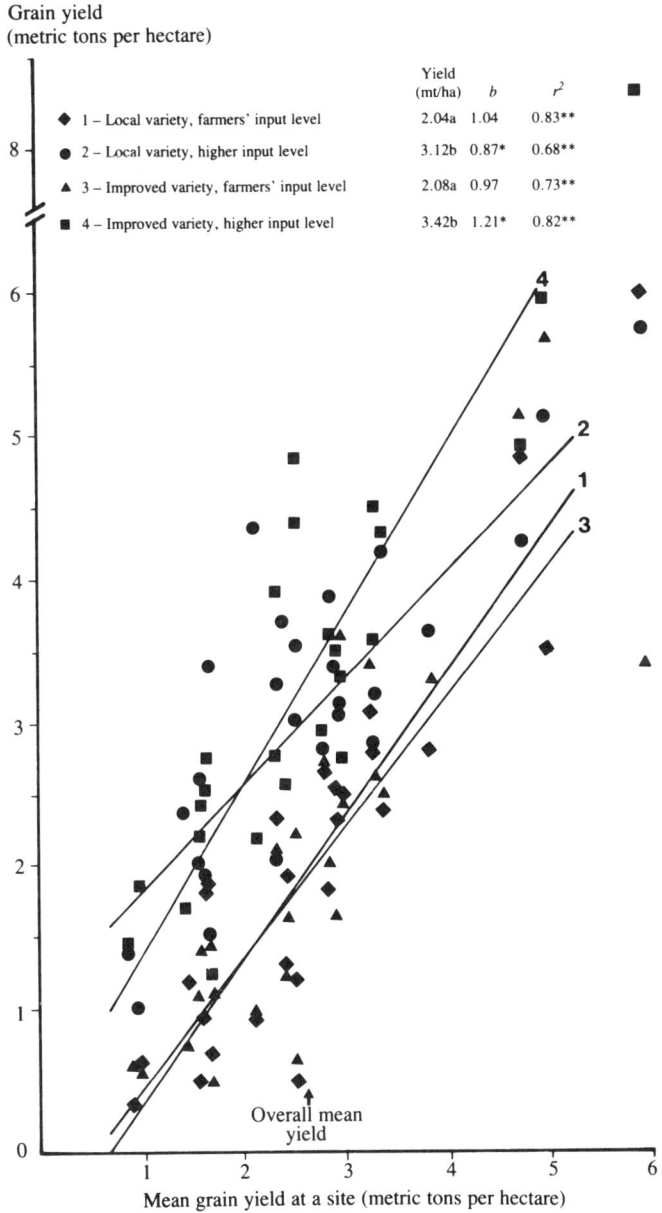

NOTE: Mean yields with the same letter are not significantly different from each other at the 5 percent level according to Duncan's multiple range test. ** denotes significant at the 1 percent level.

TABLE 15.3 Grain yield and stability parameters for six variety × N fertilizer combinations at seven sites on the Cayes Plain, Haiti, 1983

Variety (N Treatment)[a]	Mean Grain Yield[b] (t/ha)	Slope	s_d^2
Chicken Corn (0N)	1.70 d	0.78	0.029
Chicken Corn (40N)	2.10 bc	0.63	0.116
La Maquina 7827 (0N)	1.81 d	1.24	0.010
La Maquina 7827 (40N)	2.38 a	1.22	0.041
La Maquina 7928 (0N)	1.90 cd	1.04	0.157
La Maquina 7928 (40N)	2.28 a	1.09	0.064

[a] Kilograms per hectare.
[b] Mean yields with the same letter are not significantly different from each other at the 5 percent level according to Duncan's multiple range test.

bination gave the highest net benefit and a high marginal rate of return (MRR) on the investment.

HAITI. In a 3 × 2 factorial trial with four replications, an improved and a local variety were tested with and without added nitrogen (N) on the Cayes Plain during 1983. The varieties were Chicken Corn (local variety), La Maquina 7827, and La Maquina 7928 and the fertilizer treatments were zero and 40 kilograms nitrogen per hectare as urea. Added nitrogen and variety improvement had statistically significant effects on yield (table 15.3), but effects were smaller than in previous trials in Haiti because of drought. The marginal rate of return for Chicken Corn at 40 kilograms nitrogen per hectare, compared to zero nitrogen, and that for La Maquina 7827 at 40 kilograms nitrogen per hectare were well above the estimated minimum rate of return for landowners using free-market urea to adopt the improved technology. With or without added nitrogen, the improved varieties were more responsive in the better environments than Chicken Corn and yielded no less at the lower yielding sites. To raise grain yield thus requires improved inputs and management as well as a variety that can respond effectively to those inputs.

Demonstration and Verification Trials

THAILAND. In a verification trial grown at 25 sites during 1984, the farmers' varieties and cultural practices were compared with three improved technology "packages." Yield gains and some reduced costs brought about by a treatment that included an improved variety and a high level of management more than covered the investment. The improved technologies were equally advantageous across the wide range of environments studied (figure 15.6).

FIGURE 15.6 Linear regressions of input "package" yield on the mean grain yield at a site for four input packages at 25 sites in Thailand during 1984

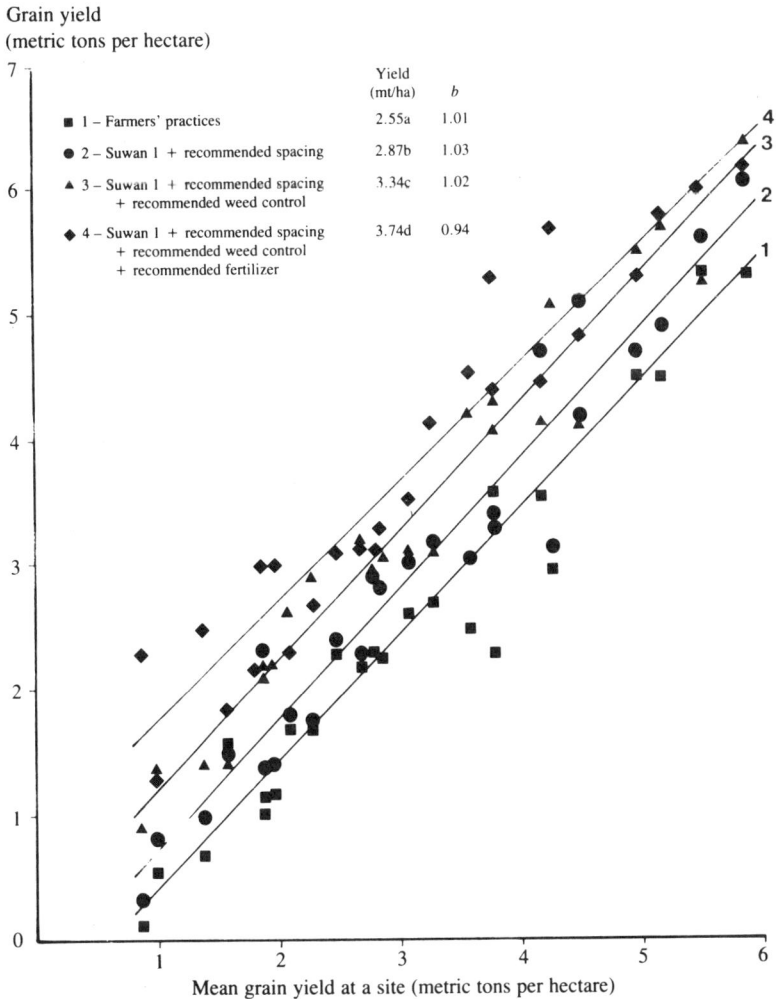

NOTE: Mean yields with the same letter are not significantly different from each other at the 5 percent level according to Duncan's multiple range test. ** denotes significant at the 1 percent level.

GHANA. Evidence from Ghana showed that higher levels of inputs and management, coupled with an improved variety, favorably affected yield across all environments studied and reduced the risk of economic failure of the investment. The trial was grown at 199 sites throughout the maize-producing zones of Ghana in 1982 and at 219 sites in 1983, a drought year.

TABLE 15.4 Yield, slope, and economic data for three packages of inputs at 418 sites in Ghana, 1982-1983

Package	Mean Grain Yield[a] (t/ha)	Slope[b]	Net Benefit (thousand cedis/ha)[c]	Marginal Rate of Return (MRR)[d] (percent)
1982				
Farmers' level (A)	1.96	0.82*	3.7	
Intermediate level (B)	3.36	1.09*	5.3	381 B versus A
High level (C)	3.84	1.08*	6.1	272 C versus B
1983				
Farmers' level (A)	1.57	0.65*	10.4	
Intermediate level (B)	2.63	1.13*	15.6	593 B versus A
High level (C)	3.14	1.22*	18.3	430 C versus B

[a] Within each year, the means in this column are significantly different from each other at the 5 percent level according to Duncan's multiple range test.
[b] An asterisk denotes that the slope is significantly different from 1.0 at the 5 percent level.
[c] cedis = Ghana's currency.
[d] For 1982, the minimum rate of return was estimated to be 100% and for 1983, 135%.

In both years the intermediate- and high-level packages gave yields above that of the farmers' level at both the poorest yielding sites (as low as 0.25 t/ha) and the highest yielding sites (over 6 t/ha in 1982) (table 15.4). Yield responses were greater, however, at the higher yielding sites. In both years marginal rates of return were considerably higher than the estimated minimum rates of return required for adoption by farmers of either of the two improved technologies.

In 1983 the risk involved in using each of the three levels of technology was estimated as the percentage of sites where no net benefits accrued from the adoption of an individual technology level. The failure rate for the farmers' level of technology was 9 percent, with the two higher technology levels failing in only 6 percent of cases.

Conclusions from the On-Farm Trials

It would not be difficult to find cases in which the performance of modern maize genotypes has been inferior to that of older local materials in developing countries, particularly since maize is grown in such numerous and diverse environments around the world. In many of those cases, though, the improved genotype has been found wanting not because it was innately inferior to the local variety, but because it was poorly adapted to the mega-environment in which the comparison was made. All the results reported here were from well-designed and conducted research programs in which well-adapted improved genotypes were compared with local varieties. Results similar to those reported here have been obtained in Honduras, Panama, Tanzania, and Pakistan.

The overall conclusions are as follows:

1. When tested in mega-environments to which they are adapted, modern improved varieties give higher yields than the farmers' local varieties. In the trials discussed here, improved varieties generally gave higher grain yields than local varieties in farmers' fields, many of which received relatively low levels of inputs (fertilizer, water, etc.) and were poorly managed.

2. The largest differences between local and improved materials are observed in the better (higher yielding) environments, and there is little evidence that improved varieties perform worse than local ones even in the worst environments studied. There was little evidence of a response crossover for the two types of variety. In contrast, many local varieties respond poorly to better environments, being unable to take advantage of the good weather, high soil fertility, high inputs, and good management that characterize those environments.

3. The yields of modern improved varieties across a given set of environments within a mega-environment seem to be more predictable than for local varieties. Thus, not only are improved varieties more responsive to good environments than local ones, but their response is more consistent. Increased deviations from the regression for local varieties is in part due to the use of different local varieties by farmers.

4. The yield advantage of modern varieties over local ones can usually be increased by raising the level of management and agronomic inputs. Farmers are able to improve the environment in which they grow maize through the addition of inputs (such as fertilizer and insecticide) and by good management of the crop. Since improved varieties are usually better able to take advantage of this extra investment, they can thus be regarded as an incentive for farmers to raise their level of inputs and to improve their management of maize.

16 Variability in the Yield of Pearl Millet Varieties and Hybrids in India and Pakistan

JOHN R. WITCOMBE

The possibility that open-pollinated varieties may be more stable in yield than hybrids has been much discussed. Over a number of years and across many locations in India and Pakistan, open-pollinated varieties and hybrids have been tested in the International Crops Research Institute for the Semi-Arid Tropics (ICRISAT) International Pearl Millet Adaptation Trial (IPMAT) (table 16.1). Consequently, it is possible to examine whether the customary procedure of selecting among the best entries on mean yield data is satisfactory. It is also possible to analyze the relative stability of hybrids and varieties and to examine the consistency of any differences over years.

Several statistical techniques have been developed to analyze the interaction of genotypes and environments. Apart from techniques that use analysis of variance, regression analyses have been used for the purpose of studying interactions (Yates and Cochran 1938, Finlay and Wilkinson 1963, Eberhart and Russell 1966, Perkins and Jinks 1968). These regression methods are essentially the same, as the mean squares for the major components of variation are identical in all cases. Although such analyses have been extensively used, they have various limitations, some of which have been pointed out by Knight (1970), Witcombe and Whittington (1971), Anderson (1974b), Binswanger and Barah (1980), and Arnold and Austin (ch. 10).

In these analyses the average yield of all the genotypes in an environment is termed the environmental index and is used as an assessment of

---

This chapter would not have been possible without the help of the cooperators who have grown the trials, and their vital role is gratefully acknowledged. The International Pearl Millet Adaptation Trial reports of 1979 and 1980 were prepared by Dr. Anand Kumar. Drs. Anand Kumar and K. N. Rai have coordinated the trials of IPMAT in different years.

I am grateful to Mr. M. N. V. R. Rao for his assistance in analyzing the data, and to Dr. Tom Walker for his suggestions in the analysis of the data from an economist's viewpoint.

TABLE 16.1 Summary of International Pearl Millet Adaptation Trials

Year	Number of Entries Analyzed	Hybrids	Varieties	Number of Locations Analyzed
1979	19	7	12	14
1980	19	8	11	19
1981	18	7	11	15
1983	21	8	13	17
1984	23	9	14	18

Note: Trial not held in 1982.

that environment. The individual yield data of the entries are then regressed on the environmental indices, giving three main parameters that describe the performance of each entry; namely, (a) the mean yield, (b) the regression coefficient of the entry (average for all entries in the analysis is one), and (c) the remainder mean square (RMS) of each individual regression. The remainder mean square accounts for the deviation from the regression line and indicates how well an individual entry meets the linear model. The size of the remainder mean square indicates the degree of unpredictability of yield of an entry and lower values are desirable. Eberhart and Russell (1966) subtract a constant, which is a measure of inexplicable environmental variation, from the remainder mean square. The value thus obtained is termed s_d^2 and bears a simple relationship to the remainder mean square. The derivation of the remainder mean square is discussed and partially accounted for by Witcombe and Whittington (1971).

The regression analysis of variance also partitions the variance into its components, and the relative contributions of environment, genotype, and genotype-environment interactions can readily be seen (ch. 10). Regression analyses have particular limitations when economic criteria are considered. Accordingly, two further analyses are made below using methods used more often by economists than plant breeders.

Comparison of Selection for Yield in Different Environments

To examine the patterns in high-, average-, and low-yielding environments the values for yield, regression coefficient, and s_d^2 of the entries have been plotted for the mean of the environments, and for the predicted yields in the highest and lowest yielding environment in each year of the IPMAT trials (figures 16.1 to 16.5). In this way the predictive value of the linear model has not been extrapolated beyond the range of the experiments, and in all years, except 1983, the lowest yield was about 600 kg/ha, which is typical of the average yield of farmers' fields in many regions of India.

FIGURE 16.1 Relationship of regression coefficients, yield, and s_d^2 values in (a) highest yielding environment, (b) average of environments, and (c) lowest yielding environment, International Pearl Millet Adaptation Trial, 1979

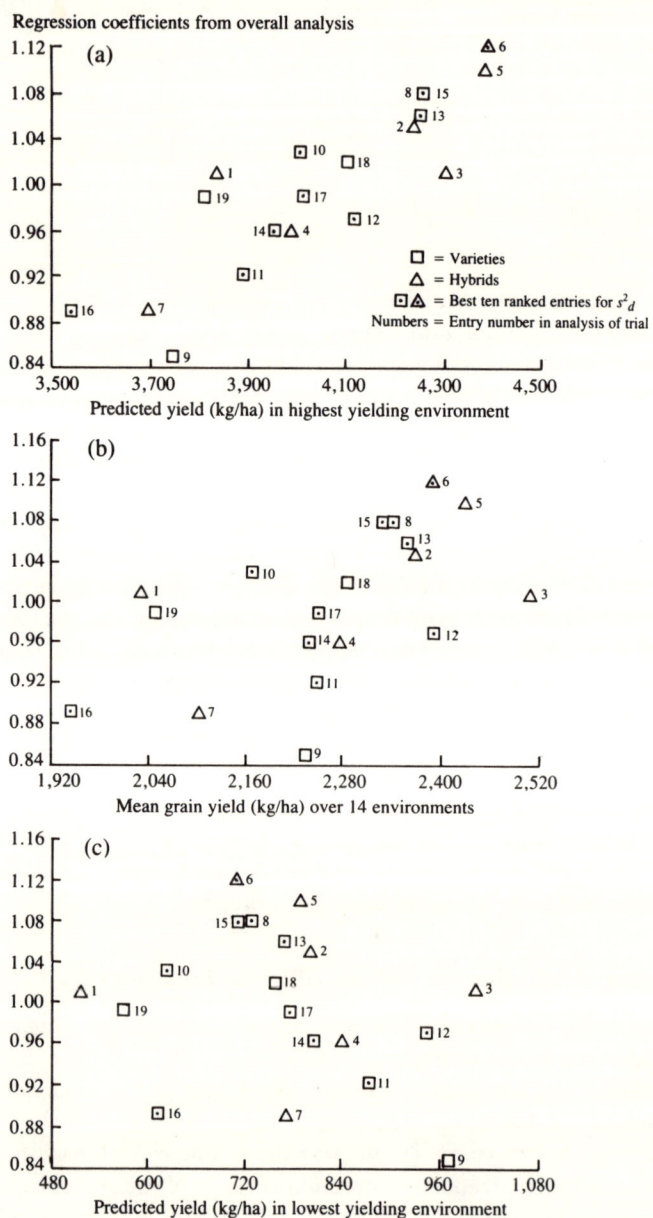

FIGURE 16.2 Relationship of regression coefficients, yield, and s_d^2 values in (a) highest yielding environment, (b) average of environments, and (c) lowest yielding environment, International Pearl Millet Adaptation Trial, 1980

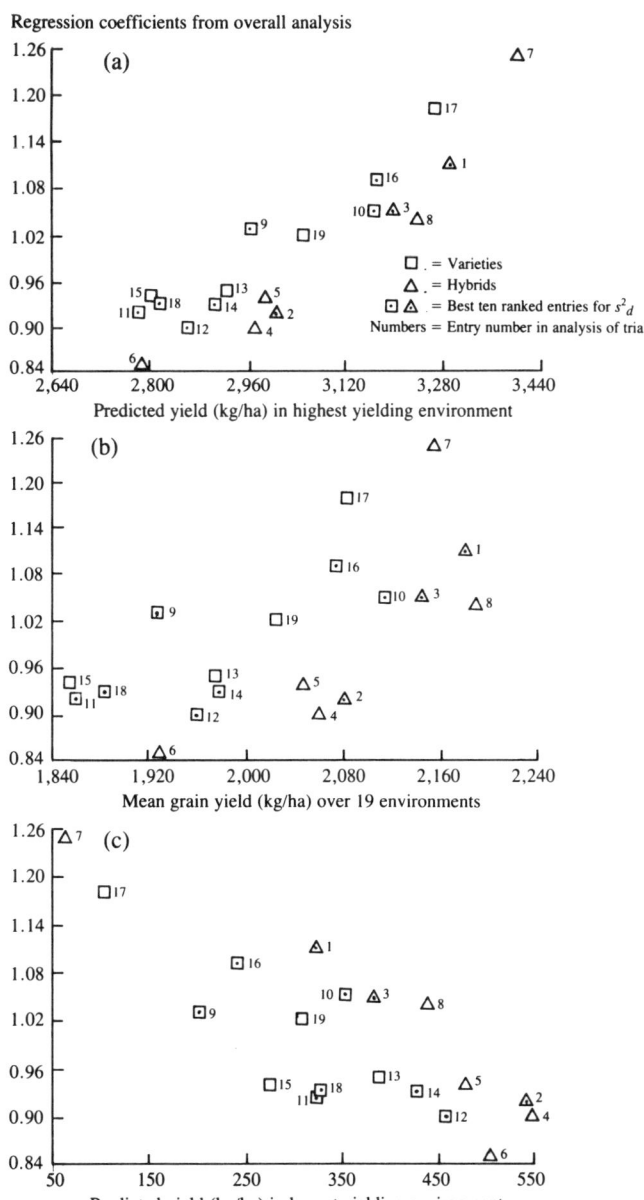

FIGURE 16.3 Relationship of regression coefficients, yield, and s_d^2 values in (a) highest yielding environment, (b) average of environments, and (c) lowest yielding environment, International Pearl Millet Adaptation Trial, 1981

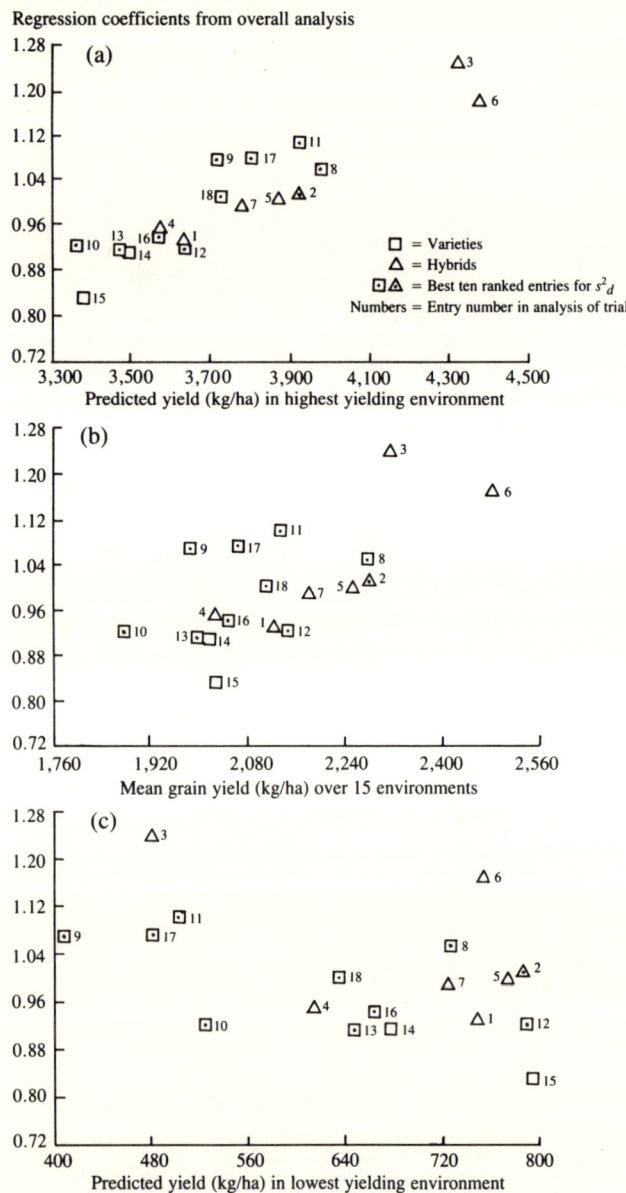

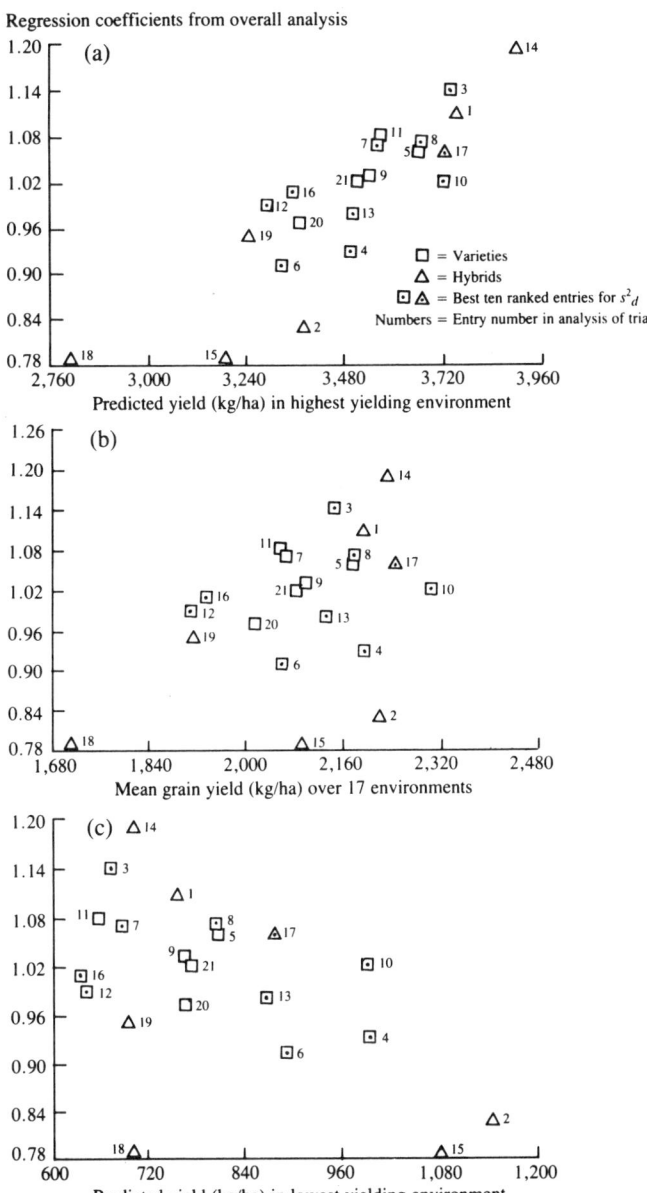

FIGURE 16.4 Relationship of regression coefficients, yield, and s_d^2 values in (a) highest yielding environment, (b) average of environments, and (c) lowest yielding environment, International Pearl Millet Adaptation Trial, 1983

FIGURE 16.5 Relationship of regression coefficients, yield, and s_d^2 values in (a) highest yielding environment, (b) average of environments, and (c) lowest yielding environment, International Pearl Millet Adaptation Trial, 1984

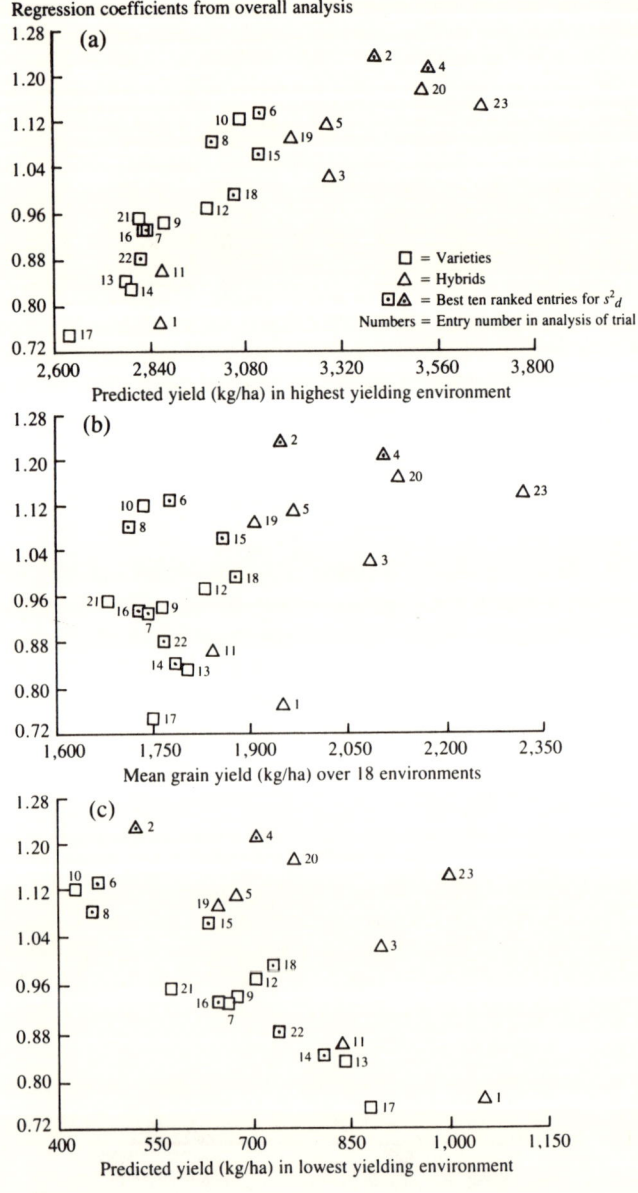

The selection of the best entries, which can be promoted to the next stage in the testing scheme, is a most important consideration. How do the top-yielding entries vary between the environments? Clearly, there are large differences in the ranking of entries between the highest yielding and lowest yielding environments and usually the top two entries are not common in these two extreme environments. Of more interest is the comparison between the average-yielding environment and the predicted performance in the lowest yielding environment of the experiment. In three of the five years there is a common entry in the two highest yielding entries in these two environments (hybrid 3 in 1979; variety 10 in 1983; and hybrid 23 in 1984) (table 16.2).

Within these top two entries can selections be made for varieties in preference to hyrids, and can high-yielding entries be selected with low s_d^2 values? If selection is made in the lowest yielding environment then in three out of five years a variety can be chosen, and in three out of the five years an entry with a low s_d^2 value. In the mean-yielding environment a variety can only be selected in one of the five years, and there is little difference in the stability of the entries (table 16.2).

The data can also be examined by selecting only the single best entry rather than the top two to see how the highest yielding entry over all environments performs in the lowest yielding environment, or vice versa (table 16.3). A marked contrast between these environments can be seen, and in only one year is the highest yielding entry the same. However, it would appear that selection based on the mean of environments is more reliable for selecting entries that perform well in the poorest environment than vice versa. In the former case the worst yield rank is 6, but in the latter it is 13.

Comparison between Hybrids and Varieties

In general, the hybrids are higher yielding, differ little from the varieties in their regression coefficients, but are, on average, less stable for the s_d^2 values (figures 16.1 to 16.5). These conclusions are confirmed by the mean values of these parameters for hybrids and varieties (table 16.4).

Since the varieties have lower s_d^2 values, the hybrids should be examined for the importance of the deviations from the regressions as a source of variability. Therefore, the amount of genotypic variability in the experiments has been related to the amount of variability between environments (table 16.5). The environment is by far the largest component of variation, the interaction of the genotypes with the environment the next largest, and the difference between genotypes the smallest. When the genotype–environment (GE) interaction is considered, the variation due to the differences in regression coefficients is invariably much smaller than that due to the remainder mean square. Since the varieties are superior to hybrids in relation to the deviations from the regression (s_d^2 values), it is possible that

TABLE 16.2 Characteristics of the two highest yielding entries in the mean and lowest yielding environments

| Year | No. of Entries | Mean Environments ||||||| Lowest Environment |||||||
| | | First ||| Second ||| First ||| Second |||
		Entry	Rank Slope	Rank s_d^2	Entry	Rank Slope	Rank s_d^2	Entry	Rank Slope	Rank s_d^2	Entry	Rank Slope	Rank s_d^2
1979	19	H 3	10	16	H 5	18	15	H 3	10	16	V 9	1	14
1980	19	H 1	16	3	H 8	12	13	H 2	4	6	H 4	3	12
1981	18	H 6	17	14	H 3	18	13	V 15	1	16	V 12	5	5
1983	21	V 10	11	2	H 17	14	9	H 2	3	18	V 10	11	2
1984	23	H 23	20	23	H 20	21	18	H 1	2	13	H 23	20	23

Note: H = hybrid, V = variety.

TABLE 16.3 Yield and stability characteristics of highest yielding entries averaged over all environments and in the lowest yielding environment

Year	No. of Entries	Mean of Environments			Lowest Yielding Environment	
		Yield Rank	Regression Rank	s_d^2 Rank	Predicted Yield Rank	Type
1979	19	1	10	16	1	H
1980	19	1	12	13	6	H
1981	18	1	17	14	5	H
1983	21	1	11	2	4	V
1984	23	1	20	23	2	H

Year	No. of Entries	Lowest Yielding Environments			Mean of Environments	
		Predicted Yield Rank	Regression Rank	s_d^2 Rank	Actual Yield Rank	Type
1979	19	1	10	16	1	H
1980	19	1	3	12	9	H
1981	18	1	1	16	13	V
1983	21	1	3	18	4	H
1984	23	1	2	13	6	H

Note: H = hybrid, V = variety.

TABLE 16.4 Mean yields, s_d^2 values, and regression coefficients for hybrids and varieties

Year	Mean Grain Yield (kg/ha)		Mean s_d^2		Mean Slope	
	Hybrids	Varieties	Hybrids	Varieties	Hybrids	Varieties
1979	2,300	2,240	163,500	61,200	1.02	0.98
1980	2,100	1,970	62,800	33,100	1.01	0.99
1981	2,240	2,260	118,000	33,200	1.04	0.97
1983	2,070	2,110	158,000	51,000	0.97	1.02
1984	2,030	1,770	62,200	40,200	1.07	0.96

TABLE 16.5 Sources of genetic variation relative to environmental variation standardized to one hundred

Source	1979	1980	1981	1983	1984
Genotype (= mean values)	2.2	1.5	4.1	2.8	6.6
GE[a] (linear = b values)	0.6	1.0	2.5	1.1	1.9
GE (deviation = s_d^2 values)	14.9	12.8	16.3	19.7	19.0

[a]GE = genotype–environment interaction.

TABLE 16.6 Entries selected on basis of complex criteria of yield and stability

	Mean of Environments	Lowest-Yielding Environment		
Entry	Rank for Yield	Rank for Yield	Rank for s_d^2	Rank for Slope
1979 V 12	3	3	2	7
1980 V 10	5	10	1	13
1981 H 8	4	6	7	12
1983 V 10	1	4	2	12

Note: H = hybrid, V = variety.

the selection of varieties may reduce crop yield variability. When stability for both s_d^2 and higher than average yield are the selection criteria, varieties predominate, even though hybrids would most frequently be selected solely on the basis of average yield. This predominance of varieties is demonstrated by the selection of entries on the basis of a selection index where entries have to be higher yielding than average, both overall and in the lowest environment, and have a lower s_d^2 value than average. In all cases the entry selected was a variety, although in 1984 it was impossible to make a selection using these criteria (table 16.6).

What is not clear is how the superior stability of varieties translates into real terms for the farmer. How, in a specific location does a low s_d^2 reduce the variation from year to year (the temporal variation) compared with a low regression coefficient? How large a reduction in mean yield can be accepted to select an entry with a lower s_d^2? The answers to these questions are important but unattainable from a regression analysis. Binswanger and Barah (1980) have pointed out that regression analyses are not suitable for studies on risk effects, and instead they have used a mean variance analysis where reduction in temporal variation (or improvement in adaptability) can be traded off against reduced yield. However, their analysis, unlike regression analysis, cannot predict the behavior of the genotypes in different environments.

FIGURE 16.6 Mean yield and standard deviation of the entries in the International Pearl Millet Adaptation Trial, 1983

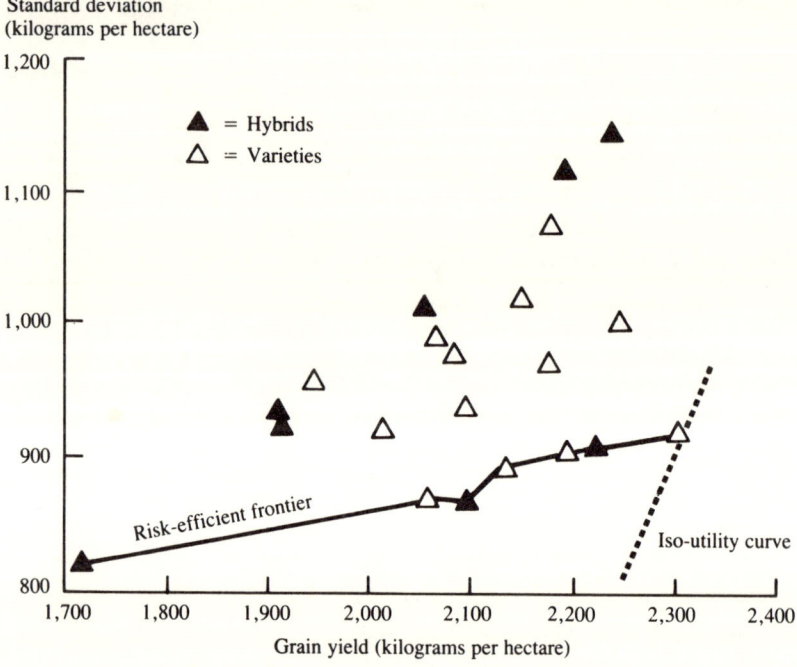

The variance analysis of Binswanger and Barah (1980) was carried out for all five years for the entries in IPMAT, 1983. The analysis essentially plots the standard deviation against mean yield using the same scale for both axes (figure 16.6), and it assumes (somewhat arbitrarily) that entries of equal utility lie on an iso-utility curve with a slope of 2.0 for representative risk-averse farmers. Such an iso-utility curve is indicated in figure 16.6. In each year a line is drawn connecting the risk-efficient entries, that is, those that for a given level of yield performance have the lowest standard deviation. That line maps a risk-efficient frontier and it is also indicated in figure 16.6. The best entry must lie on this frontier, and it is chosen with regard to the iso-utility curves. In no year was an entry chosen other than the one that was highest yielding over all environments. Thus, in no case did the improved stability of the varieties over the hybrids compensate for their lower yield.

Stochastic dominance techniques (Anderson, Dillon, and Hardaker 1977) can also be used to help to predict a risk-averse farmer's choice of varietal types. A stochastic dominance analysis was carried out on pooled data for hybrids and varieties as separate groups on predicted yield in the

FIGURE 16.7 Cumulative probability and predicted yield in the lowest yielding environment in the International Pearl Millet Adaptation Trials, 1979, 1980, 1981, and 1983

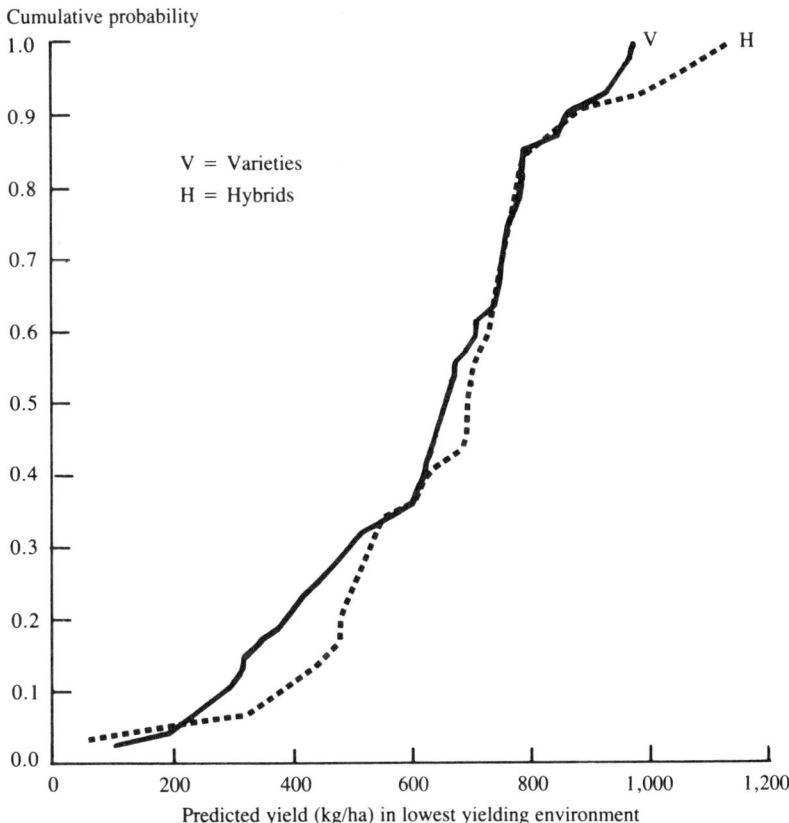

lowest yielding environment in 1979, 1980, 1981, and 1983. Data from 1984 were omitted because the hybrids in that year are qualitatively different from those in the earlier years. A focus on the lowest yielding environment is justified because it is more likely to represent farmers' field conditions than the other locations. Over most of the range in predicted yields in the lowest yielding environments, hybrids were superior to varieties (figure 16.7). For example, the cumulative probability that a variety would yield less than 400 kg/ha was about 0.2 while the same estimate for a hybrid was about 50 percent lower at 0.1. Because the two distributions crossed at the lowest yield interval, stochastic dominance analysis did not give a clear prediction as to whether risk-averse farmers would prefer hybrids to varieties, but the estimated cumulative yield distributions do not indicate that the genetically more broadly based varieties as a group are more stable yielders than hybrids in the most adverse production environments in the trials.

Conclusions

Although there were big differences between the lowest and mean-yielding environments it is possible, when only the two highest yielding entries are considered, to select in most years an entry which is common in both environments. Indeed, in three of the years the highest yielding entry across all environments was also one of the two highest yielding entries in the lowest yielding environment. Moreover, good performance over all environments appears to indicate good performance of an entry in the low-yielding environment, whereas the reverse does not always apply. This is generally an encouraging result for the plant breeder in terms of selection procedure, as entries which perform well in both average and low-yielding environments possess a certain measure of stability.

Although regression analyses are helpful in testing and selection procedures, to obtain an overall picture of how stability and mean yield are to be traded off, other analyses are required. The mean variance analysis showed that, in all years, no entry was selected other than on the basis of its mean yield. A stochastic dominance analysis showed that, in general, varieties would not be preferred to hybrids, even though varieties show superior stability in other analyses. It thus appears that these analyses demonstrate that the typical breeder's procedure of selecting among the highest yielding entries across environments is satisfactory. Such an emphasis will usually select entries that perform well in poor environments and would tend to be chosen by risk-averse farmers.

The best entry in 1983 is V 10 (figures 16.4b and c, 16.6), which is an ICRISAT millet variety ICMV 81111, derived from an advanced cycle composite. It has both high yield and superior stability. Variety 10 was in the All India Coordinated Millets Improvement Project (AICMIP) trials of the mid-1980s; in the 1984 AICMIP Initial Population Trial, it was the top-performing entry with a yield about 15 percent better than the released variety that is both high-yielding and stable is a desirable alternative to a hybrid, particularly in view of varieties' simpler seed multiplication procedures and reduced susceptibility to ergot and smut. Moreover, individual hybrids in India have proven to be most unstable in yield from year to year due to their rapid increase in susceptibility to downy mildew. There is every reason to expect that the more genetically diverse variety would become susceptible in a less rapid and spectacular manner.

PART III

Input Management and Yield Variability

17 Fertilizer and Crop Yield Variability: A Review

JAMES A. ROUMASSET, MARK W. ROSEGRANT,
UJJAYANT N. CHAKRAVORTY, AND
JOCK R. ANDERSON

Manufactured fertilizers, especially those rich in nitrogen, have often been accused of causing unfavorable changes in variability of yields of field crops. The likely mechanisms were broached in the introduction to this volume (ch. 1). The topic is explored here in a more detailed manner from both methodological and empirical perspectives. The empirical evidence is diverse but, unfortunately, not yet rich in agroclimatological context. A complicating feature to challenge the would-be reviewer is a likely nonneutral interactive effect between the method of investigation and findings on the sign and magnitude of marginal variability and risk effects.

In an earlier review of related phenomena, Anderson, Dillon, and Hardaker (1977, p. 147ff) distinguished two broad approaches to studying such problems of riskiness of response to varying levels of controlled inputs: a "gross approach" where the effects of individually measured stochastic uncontrolled variables such as soil moisture are not explicitly modeled, and an "analytical approach" where some or all of the stochastic variables are so modeled. This broad distinction still seems to be useful, although recent methodological advances require more informative classifications within these categories.

Methodology

Gross Approaches to Estimation

The general problem in gross estimation is to describe and measure variability in yield as a function of managed plant nutrients, without directly including stochastic variables in the estimation process. Several approaches have been taken. The most straightforward is to observe time-series variability of yield at several levels of nutrients and to summarize the data in various informative ways.

Most straightforwardly, Day (1965) in his pioneering work estimated directly the first four moments of the probability distribution of yield with unbiased sample estimators of the Pearson system of density functions. Roumasset (1974) and Barker, Cordova, and Roumasset (1976) modified the procedure by introducing a stage of hand smoothing the probability density functions (PDFs) in a way that combined the estimated moments with additional subjective information about the shapes and limits of the distributions. Mendoza (1980) refined the techniques further, replacing hand smoothing with a maximum likelihood procedure, and applying the technique to a cross-section of time-series data on management trials. Thattil (1980) applied a similar technique to Philippine data on cropping patterns.

More indirectly, because he was particularly concerned with situations with very few data (that he described as "sparse"), Anderson (1973) employed a data-smoothing process based on first using the sparse data as unbiased estimates of fractiles and then inferring smooth cumulative distribution functions (CDFs) from which the first few moments and other summary statistics could be derived. He used such statistics directly as dependent variables in ordinary least squares (OLS) regression analysis. To the extent that variance of yield is dependent on fertilizer, this method will not account for heteroscedasticity, causing inefficiencies in the estimation. The ultimate in sparseness of observed data was the work of Anderson and Hamal (1983), who used peasants' purely subjective probability distributions of yield at three levels of nitrogen fertilizer.

The most recent work in this style is that of Antle (1983a,b) who developed efficient generalized least squares (GLS) techniques to estimate the responsiveness of the first few moments to varying inputs. A first application of these techniques to crop fertilizer processes has been made by Antle and Crissman (1986).

Considerable work has also been done on risk analysis confined to the first two moments, namely the mean and variance. In these somewhat restrictive approaches, two distinctive sets of methods have been used. While these are not mutually exclusive, applications to date have essentially regarded them as such.

The more traditional set is based on the random coefficient model of Swamy (1970). Here generalized least squares estimates are used for both the mean response function and for a variance–covariance matrix for the regressions, and from this, variance of crop yield can be predicted for given levels of fertilizer. This method was utilized in a crop fertilizer context by Young and Mount (1979) and has been applied by Smith and Umali (1985).

The less traditional mean variance analysis is based on conceptualizing (following Just and Pope 1978) a rather general heteroscedastic error term, as in:

$$Y = f(F) + h^{1/2}(F)u,$$

where u is a conventional disturbance with zero expectation and unit variance so that mean yield is $E(Y) = f(F)$ and variance of yield is $\text{Var}(Y) = h(F)$, and the functional forms f and h can be different and flexible in modeling marginal mean and variance effects. Just and Pope (1979) illustrate their multistage nonlinear generalized least squares method of estimating the parameters of the model by an analysis of some of Day's (1965) data. Related estimation methods, although not involving crop fertilizer processes, have been developed and applied by Griffiths and Anderson (1982) where data are cross sections of time series. An application by Farnsworth and Moffitt (1981) of the Just-Pope methods to input management of Californian cotton revealed that fertilizer (mixed nutrients) reduced yield variability.

Analytical Approaches to Estimation

The distinguishing feature of explicit inclusion of some stochastic variables as real variables in explanatory equations is somewhat arbitrary, and recent applications (for example, by Rosegrant and Roumasset 1985) that feature elements of both gross and analytical approaches serve to blur the distinction even further. There are, however, several intuitively attractive aspects and some insights to be gained by attempts to model stochastic effects more explicitly and directly, variously illustrated by Byerlee and Anderson (1969), de Janvry (1972), Ryan and Perrin (1973), Roumasset (1976), Talpaz and Taylor (1977), and Rosegrant and Herdt (1981).

The analytical approach to risk specification is composed of two processes: first, measuring the production or response function, including observed stochastic variables; and second, estimating the joint probability distribution associated with the stochastic variables. The major advantages over the gross approach are that the analytical approach improves understanding of the causal factors underlying yield variability and permits generalization of the production function and fertilizer effects to different environments. Potential problems with this approach include the failure to allow for omitted stochastic variables, and the restrictions placed on the interaction between controlled inputs and the stochastic elements of production. A natural compromise is to use the analytical approach to account for measurable variables and the gross approach for remaining sources of variation.

Byerlee and Anderson (1969) analyzed the effects of fertilizer on yield variability of wheat, attributing yield variability to the amount of growing season rainfall. De Janvry (1972), in a study of optimal fertilization under risk for maize and wheat in Argentina, combined rainfall variables into a single weather index. The risk effects of weather on potato yields were analyzed by Ryan and Perrin (1973) using a yield response function including applied nutrients, soil characteristics, rainfall, and temperature.

These studies estimated probability distributions for the stochastic variables based on data from weather stations and experiments. Roumasset (1976), in a study of fertilizer and risk in Philippine rice production, introduced alternative techniques for eliciting from farmers the probability distribution of various damage states. One such technique relates the "village" probability distribution to sample farmers' perceptions about the actual occurrences of various sources of damage over the previous three years. The other uses a "consensus" approach to estimating the probability and severity of major sources of damage, including a residual category of "other damages." The village-specific probability distributions were then used to adjust a "no-damage" production function estimated from experimental data to one applicable to on-farm reality.

Rosegrant and Herdt (1981) expanded the number of stochastic variables incorporated in the production function for rice, including moisture stress, insect damage, pest damage, solar radiation, and typhoon damage and introduced simulation techniques to estimate probability distributions for the stochastic variables in different agroclimatic environments.

A limitation of the analytical approaches described above is the representation of unmeasured stochastic inputs in the production function by a homoscedastic error term. Rosegrant and Roumasset (1985) incorporated a heteroscedastic error term similar to the Just–Pope specification, combined with explicit representation of observed stochastic variables, to achieve a more general approach. Smith et al. (1984) employed a similar method in their analysis of rainfed rice in the Philippines.

Comparison of Results

Although there have been several studies assessing the impact of fertilizer on yield variability and risk, it is difficult to make firm generalizations based on the results. This is partly because the different methods and styles of presenting results do not permit direct comparison of results across the studies. More importantly, the agroclimatic coverage of the studies has been very limited. This limitation appears to be largely due to data availability. Only rice in the Philippines has been studied enough to permit broad generalizations, primarily because of the detailed yield response and agroclimatic data collected by the International Rice Research Institute (IRRI) in both experiment station and on-farm trials.

Nevertheless, it is worthwhile to review the available results. This section reviews the impact of fertilizer on yield variability and its implications for fertilizer use under risk, and discusses the even more limited information available on the effect of fertilizer on the higher moments of yield distributions.

Fertilizer, Yield Variability, and Risk

There are two related questions regarding the impact of fertilizer on yield variability and risk. First, does use of fertilizer increase the variability of crop yields? Second, is the increase (if any) in variability large enough relative to increases in expected yields from nitrogen use to reduce substantially the optimal fertilizer use under risk averse preferences relative to risk neutral optimal fertilizer use?

Empirical generalization at this stage seems possible only for the important nutrient nitrogen. It is hoped that comparable information will soon be assembled for other major nutrients, which in some areas are more important than nitrogen. Table 17.1 summarizes the available information on the impact of nitrogen fertilizer on mean yields, variance of yields, and the resulting optimal levels of nitrogen under risk-neutral and moderately risk-averse decision rules. Supporting the early work on the effect of nitrogen on mean and variance of maize yield in the United States by Fuller (1965), Colyer (1969), and Tollini and Seagraves (1970), most of the studies cited found that nitrogen increases yield variance. In most cases, the elasticity of variance with respect to nitrogen is usually higher than the elasticity of mean yield with respect to nitrogen in the economically relevant range of nitrogen use (especially around the optimal levels of fertilizer use).

In the studies using analytical approaches, the elasticity of yield variance usually increases as the level of nitrogen increases. However, there is a decline in the elasticity of yield variance with increase in nitrogen for the studies using a gross approach. It is unclear whether these differences are due to implicit restrictions imposed by the method and functional forms utilized in the studies or to environmental effects. Additional research into this issue would be useful.

Antle and Crissman (1986) found nitrogen to be variance increasing in Philippine rice production the first two years of the study but variance reducing thereafter. They attribute this shift to a learning process following adoption of modern varieties and increases in fertilizer use, by which farmers improve crop care practices associated with nitrogen use. This possibility demonstrates the importance of experimental design in drawing inferences about variability. Controlled experiments that allow only fertilizer to vary will overestimate the extent to which risk-averse farmers should (or will) decrease fertilizer below the risk neutral optimum since they abstract from the possibility of adopting variance-reducing inputs and cultural practices. If fertilizer increases the sensitivity of yield to moisture stress, it is natural to expect (or to recommend) the farmer to be more careful in water management. If fertilizer increases susceptibility to insect

TABLE 17.1 Elasticity of mean and variance of yield with respect to nitrogen fertilizer and optimal nitrogen use with risk-neutral and risk-averse decision preference

Publication Source	Crop	Nitrogen Level (kg/ha)	Elasticity of Yield Moments with Respect to N		Optimal Nitrogen Use (kg/ha)		Reduction Due to Risk (percent)
			Mean	Variance	Risk Neutral	Risk Averse	
A. *Gross Approach*							
Anderson (1973)	Wheat, Australia	40	0.14	0.22			
		80	0.06	0.19	52	47	10
Smith and Umali (1985)	MV rainfed rice, Philippines normal[a]	40	0.28	0.36			
	gamma[a]	80	0.16	−0.08	42	35	17
Antle and Crissman (1986)	MV rice, Philippines 1975–76	11[b]	0.16	0.22			
	1977–79	21[b]	0.25	−0.35			
B. *Analytical Approach*							
Byerlee and Anderson (1969)	Wheat, Australia	20	0.08	0.44			
		40	0.04	0.62	20	14	30
Ryan and Perrin (1973)	Potatoes, Peru	100	0.10	0.20			
		200	0.17	0.35	220	160	60
Roumasset (1976)	MV rice, Philippines						
	Village 1	40	0.49	0.49			
		80	0.16	0.32	67	67	0
	Village 2	40	0.22	0.45			
		80	0.03	0.06	44	41	7

Study	Category						
	Village 3	40	0.19	0.37	19	19	0
		80	0.00	−0.01			
Rosegrant and Herdt (1981, 1985)	MV rice, Philippines						
	Irrigated	40	0.20	0.29	67	55	18
		80	0.19	0.42			
	Rainfed	40	0.14	0.31	42	30	29
		80	0.10	0.30			
Smith et al. (1984)	MV rainfed rice, Philippines						
	Wet season	40	0.16	0.24	45	43	4
		80	0.10	0.48			
	Dry season	40	0.15	0.26	41	40	3
		80	0.10	0.48			
Rosegrant and Roumasset (1985)	MV rice, Philippines						
	Good irrigation, dry season	40	0.20	0.03	124	112	10
		80	0.24	0.36			
	Average irrigation, dry season	40	0.19	0.12	104	88	15
		80	0.21	0.54			
	Average irrigation, wet season	40	0.14	0.06	60	56	7
		80	0.13	0.49			
	Rainfed, wet season	40	0.13	0.14	48	40	17
		80	0.10	0.59			

[a] Yield distribution assumed to be a normal or gamma distribution as specified.
[b] Reported elasticities computed at mean input levels, expressed in pesos per hectare. Figures given are estimated mean nitrogen use given prevailing prices.

damage, increased pest control is indicated. It is possible that if complementary inputs are adjusted to optimal levels, fertilizer does not increase variability (Farnsworth and Moffitt 1981; Hanus and Schoop, ch. 21). But, pooled cross-section/time-series data may underestimate the elasticity of variance relative to fertilizer, if inputs have been freely chosen by farm operators and if there are significant differences in managerial ability. Relatedly, as indicated by Watson and Anderson (1977), cross-section data may substitute poorly for more pertinent time-series data in quantifying yield variability.

Alternatively, negative variance elasticity may be the result of low levels of nitrogen use. Rosegrant and Roumasset (1985) found nitrogen to be variance reducing at levels of nitrogen use up to 16–32 kg/ha in three of the four environments analyzed, shifting to variance increasing thereafter. Finally, negative variance elasticity may simply be a statistical accident resulting from inadequate information on the probability distributions of the stochastic variables.

How relevant is the effect of nitrogen on variance for optimal nitrogen use under risk aversion? One series of experimental studies to measure farmer risk preferences in developing countries has been completed, including work by H. P. Binswanger in India, D. A. Sillers in the Philippines, W. Grisley in Thailand, and T. S. Walker in El Salvador; the results are summarized by Binswanger and Sillers (1983). The studies consistently showed that most farmers are moderately risk averse. It is not known whether the relative uniformity of risk preferences is due to uniformity in underlying sources of risk aversion or to uniformity in the way that the interview techniques influenced the subject's perceived reference point.

Table 17.1 also summarizes the impact of moderate risk aversion on optimal fertilizer use relative to risk neutral (profit-maximizing) nitrogen levels from the available studies. Several of these analyses, including Rosegrant and Herdt (1981), Smith et al. (1984), and Rosegrant and Roumasset (1985), explicitly used utility functions and moderate risk preference parameters derived from the series of studies cited above. For the other studies, we have attempted to represent comparable degrees of risk aversion.

The results show that reductions in optimal nitrogen use due to moderate risk aversion are modest, usually ranging from 0 to 30 percent compared with risk neutral optimal nitrogen levels. Even a 30 percent reduction may represent a modest absolute decrease of only 10 kg/ha. Based on the available studies, the variance-increasing nature of nitrogen is typically not large enough to cause large reductions in optimal levels of nitrogen for moderately risk-averse farmers.

The Impact of Fertilizer on Higher Moments of Yield Distribution

As can be seen by a Taylor's series expansion of an expected utility function, skewness can have a substantial impact on expected utility, especially for utility functions with both concave and convex segments. Given its relative importance (Day 1965; Anderson, Dillon, and Hardaker 1977) and the unreliability of estimating higher moments, the primary attention here is to skewness.

Fertilizer appears to have different effects on skewness under different conditions. Roumasset (1976) suggests, based on Day (1965) and on data collected from rice trials at experiment stations in the Philippines, that under experimental conditions, yield distributions become more negatively skewed at higher levels of nitrogen. Conversely, Rosegrant and Roumasset (1985) suggested that, for data collected from farmers fields, yields become more positively skewed at higher nitrogen levels.

This raises the issue of how hypotheses concerning fertilizer and the shape of frequency distributions might be tested. Antle (1983b) and Antle and Crissman (1986) propose estimating the moments of frequency distributions as functions of the inputs. This substitutes for estimating stochastic production functions since an estimated frequency distribution can be found for each vector of inputs. Moreover, using a Taylor's series approximation, the moments may be entered directly into an expected utility function for the purpose of estimating optimal input levels.

The justification for estimating moments independently is that there is often no information about the shape of the density functions. However, if the family of distributions (such as generalized gamma, beta, etc.) can be identified, then the parameters of the density functions should be estimated, rather than their moments. It seems plausible that estimating variance in the absence of skewness (for example, with a Just–Pope error term) would tend to overestimate variance, the more so the further skewness differs from zero. This hypothesis could, of course, be investigated analytically or with a Monte Carlo sampling approach.

The sensitivity of the estimated density function to specification errors is probably greater for the gross approach. In the analytical approach, empirical distributions of the measurable stochastic inputs are usually used, and the possibility of misspecification then arises mainly with the unmeasurable stochastic inputs.

Summary and Conclusions

There has been a tendency in the literature to assume that fertilizer causes substantial increases in yield and income variability, with the corollary that the riskiness of fertilizer use causes substantial reductions in farmer use of fertilizer relative to profit-maximizing levels (Rangaswami 1982). The studies summarized here, however, indicate that, although the effect of nitrogen fertilizer on yield variance is typically positive, it is not large enough to cause major reductions in fertilizer use for moderately risk-averse farmers.

Based on the several studies for Philippine rice, this conclusion appears robust for lowland rainfed and irrigated rice in the humid and semi-humid tropics, an agroclimatic region accounting for much of South and Southeast Asian rice production. However, evidence for other crops, technologies, and agroclimatic regions, while consistent with these results, is too fragmentary to be conclusive. The lack of evidence on the relationship between fertilizer, yield, variability, and risk for other regions and crops can contribute to continued incorrect inferences regarding the underlying causes of input choices by farmers. This, in turn, can lead to incorrect policy decisions. Given the potentially high cost of such decisions, there should be a concerted effort to collect the detailed farm management and agroclimatic data needed to analyze the impact of fertilizer on variability and risk. The highest priority should be given to the more important semi-arid crops, where interactions between fertilizers and environments may be quite different from those for humid and semi-humid rice.

Lacking data on distribution functions for unfavorable environments, observers of farmers' "failure" to adopt new technologies in such areas have sometimes inferred that farmers put too much weight, from a social point of view, on the lower tail of the distribution. Another possibility is that the bulk of the profit distribution function gets sufficiently lowered under adverse environments to render new technologies suboptimal, even for a risk-neutral farmer. A third possibility, highlighted by Antle and Crissman (1986), is that new technologies are initially risk increasing but become risk reducing once farmers have learned appropriate risk management strategies. The tendency for these disparate explanations to be confounded in policy discussions underscores the importance of careful modeling of the role of fertilizer (and other inputs) in decision making.

For policy purposes, it is not enough to know the nature of the risk fertilizer relationship in specific environments with controllable inputs held fixed. Implications for a research and extension strategy and for economic policy will also depend on the sources of risk. Information about the role of stochastic inputs in the relationship is needed in order to determine the environmental domain of particular results. Information about substitutability or complementarity of controllable and stochastic inputs is also needed in order to prescribe the role of fertilizer reduction as a risk management strategy vis à vis pest and disease control, water management, spacing, tillage, and other cultural practices. Ideally, evaluation of alternative risk management strategies should be based on an experimental design that allows for appropriate variation in several risk-reducing inputs.

18 Irrigation and Crop Yield Variability: A Review

SUSHIL PANDEY

This chapter examines whether or not an expansion in irrigation stabilizes foodgrain production. A substantial increase in irrigation investment in many developing countries in recent times can be considered to be due to the widely held belief that irrigation not only increases production, but also reduces variability by enabling better control over the environment. However, empirical evidence indicates that the relationship between irrigation and stability is not straightforward. Barker, Gabler, and Winkelmann (1981) have identified the tendencies of average yield, standard deviation, and coefficient of variation to increase with irrigated area in South and Southeast Asia. But in East Asia (Japan, South Korea, and Taiwan), absolute variability in yield is lower even though the proportion of area irrigated is much higher. According to Mehra (1981), irrigation has both stabilizing and destabilizing effects in different states of India.

Irrigation is not a uniform input—various sources of water differ in the stability of their supply and in the efficiency of their distribution (i.e., timing, quantity, etc.). Hence, for studying stability, it is essential to disaggregate the irrigated area or quantity of irrigation according to the source of irrigation. Similarly, measures of stability need to be obtained for both "with" and "without" irrigation while keeping everything else constant. Irrigation also induces more intensive cropping practices and crop substitution that make it difficult to disentangle the effects of irrigation. Some of these complex issues are addressed here.

Measurement of Water as an Input

Of all agricultural inputs, water is unique in its overwhelming importance to plant growth. Water is used by crops on a continuous basis from sowing to harvest. Irrigation is required where rainfall is inadequate or too poorly distributed to satisfy the requirements of crops for water.

In comparison to other inputs (such as fertilizers) whose response to yields has been widely studied, crops were traditionally considered to have unique water requirements determined by climatic variables (Doorenbos and Pruitt 1977). Where water requirements are fully satisfied, variations in yields could only be attributed to changes in the use of other inputs or to uncontrollable factors. However, modern literature is replete with evidence that crops do respond to differential applications of water (Stewart et al. 1975, Hexem and Heady 1978). Irrigation as an input into the production process must, therefore, be measured in terms of quantity of water used by crops rather than by classifying whether or not a piece of land is irrigated. A large part of the variation in annual yield may be merely due to variations in the quantity of irrigation applied. An appropriate question to ask is whether or not increased use of irrigation brings stability to food production.

Irrigation tends to be special also in the sense that it is not only the total seasonal use, but also the distribution over the growing period that critically determines yield. Response to irrigation is generally higher in the reproductive phase of cereal growth. Even though the same total quantity of water may have been used by crops, yields can differ drastically, depending on the seasonal distribution of water use. Not only are the production functions "dated," but also their effects are typically interactive.

The observed variability in crop yields may thus be due largely to a particular time pattern of water use rather than to the provision of irrigation as such. Downey (1972) found that, for the same level of water use, yields can vary between 40 and 95 percent of the potential value depending on the seasonal distribution of water use. It is thus possible for different irrigated plots to have different variabilities in yield merely as a result of differences in the distribution of water use over the growing season.

Thus, irrigation, as an input, is properly measured as at least a two-dimensional variable—the total quantity and the seasonal distribution. The relationship between irrigation and yield variability cannot be examined properly without removing the confounding effects that may have been caused by differences in the type and pattern of irrigation.

How should irrigation best be measured? A definition of irrigation as the act of applying water to plants implies that the quantity of water is an appropriate measure of irrigation. But this measure may not, biologically speaking, be very meaningful because it is not the quantity of water applied but the quantity actually used by crops that more closely determines yield. Whereas water is usually applied in discrete quantities, it is used by crops continuously over time. Agronomists and others have used the concept of moisture stress to measure the effect of irrigation on yields. A crop is considered to be suffering from moisture stress if the physiological processes in the plant cells are adversely affected by a deficiency of water. Depending on the researchers' objectives and orientation, different proxies for moisture stress have been used: such as soil moisture content (Music, New, and Dusek 1976; Morgan, Biere, and Kanemasu 1980), soil moisture tension (Taylor 1952), evapotranspiration deficit (Doorenbos and Kassam 1979), and leaf water potential (Meyer and Green 1981). Irrigation affects moisture stress by altering the soil moisture available to plants. Even if the quantity of irrigation and its distribution over time are constant, moisture stress and yield can vary depending on the moisture-holding characteristics of the soil and the plants' capabilities to regulate water uses.

The measurement of water as an input into the production process has often been treated simplistically by analysts. Irrigation has been considered as a homogenous input and its effects judged irrespective of the timing of irrigation, quantity of water applied, soil types, and crop-specific factors. This practice may be explained variously by a lack of data or a lack of appreciation of the mechanisms through which irrigation affects yields. With so many important attributes of irrigation ignored, it is hardly surprising that observations on the effects of irrigation on yield variability have been confusing and often contradictory.

Production Variability and Irrigation

The effects of irrigation on plant yields were discussed above. If farmers are assumed to know the optimal irrigation schedule and to be able to meet this schedule with available technology and water, the variability in individual plant yields must generally decrease with increased irrigation. The lower tail and mean of the probability distribution of yields will shift rightwards with more irrigation. To examine the effects of irrigation at the farm level, it is essential to model the decision-making behavior of farmers. Optimal doses of inputs such as irrigation, fertilizer, labor, and so forth are likely to be jointly determined. Irrigation, by increasing the marginal productivity of other complementary inputs, such as fertilizers and labor, encourages more intensive cropping practices.

Intensification is indicated by a more rapid diffusion of an improved "package" involving modern varieties in irrigated areas (Herdt and Capule 1983). However, with intensified cropping, the reduction in absolute yield in unfavorable years (due to environmental conditions other than those associated with soil moisture) can be expected to be much larger. Hence, changes in cropping practices induced by irrigation likely result in an increase in the absolute variability of yield. Whether or not relative variability will also increase is an empirical question.

Variability in total production is due to the combined and often joint effects of variabilities in yield and area. Which of these two is more important is likely to depend on whether the crop under consideration is grown in the dry or rainy season. In the case of crops that are grown mainly in the rainy season (e.g., rice in India), variability in yield is likely to be more significant than the variability in area. The area of these crops depends mainly on the expected (or normal) rainfall pattern and the expected availability of irrigation. If expectations are not realized, it is the yield per unit area that must adjust. To the extent that some complementary inputs are committed before the water supply is known, annual variability in yield could conceivably be higher with irrigation than without. The stabilizing effect of irrigation may, however, override such effects and the matter, on balance, is an empirical issue.

In the case of dry season crops, area variability may be the more important component because area is adjusted to account for changes in the availability of water. The quantity of water available is sometimes known at sowing time and, in years of perceived scarcity, it may be more profitable to cultivate a smaller area intensively than to lose water by spreading it thinly over a larger area. The extent of adjustment will depend on the yield response to water, irrigation efficiency, and other relevant factors. (Vaux and Pruitt 1983).

Whether or not irrigation increases stability depends on the stability of the water supply itself. If the supply of water is stochastic, the resultant increase in variability in both yield and area as farmers adjust their production plans will almost certainly increase instability in production. This relationship has been empirically verified by Rao (1968), Mehra (1981), and Dhawan (1985) using irrigation data from various states of India. In the Punjab, where tubewells are the most common means of irrigation, the coefficients of variation (cvs) of yield and production were the lowest. In contrast, variability was highest in Gujarat and Tamil Nadu, which are mostly irrigated by shallow wells and tanks. Because of the higher level of dependence on current rainfall, the supply of water from these sources is more unstable than from tubewells.

Similarly, a part of the increase in the variance of foodgrain production in India has been attributed to variability in irrigated area caused by power outages (Hazell 1984). Variability is expected to be low in situations where the level of water control is high, such as in irrigation systems fed by a perennial source of water and backed by adequate storage structures to even out fluctuations in water supply. This was speculated to be one of the reasons for greater yield stability in East Asia compared to South and Southeast Asia (Barker, Gabler, and Winkelmann 1981). If the level of control over water increases in the course of economic development, it may be hypothesized that variability imparted by irrigation will decrease as countries develop.

It is useful to distinguish between variability at the farm and system levels. At the system level, variability for the whole of the irrigation project is considered. Where the source of water supply is privately owned, the system and the farm level variabilities are generally equivalent. However, in a publicly owned irrigation system serving several or many farmers, variability in yield will also depend on the rules for distributing water among the farmers. In a continuous irrigation system, variability of yields on the farms located near the head end can always be expected to be lower than at the tail end. However, if a rotational system of irrigation is effectively used, variability in yield is likely to be more or less uniform throughout the system. Depending on the relative shares of area irrigated in the head and tail ends, the systemwide variability may increase or decrease as a result of changeover from a continuous to a rotational irrigation system. Based on a simulation study of the Philippines, Rosegrant (1986) found the systemwide variability in yield to be higher in a rotational system of irrigation.

The magnitude of the effects of a stochastic supply of water on yield variability also depends on the quantity of water applied per unit area. Where the water requirements by crops are nearly satisfied, an increase in the variability of water supply is likely to have a smaller effect on the variability of yield. This is due to the relative "flatness" of the yield response function at high levels of water application (Pandey 1986). On the other hand, if water is thinly spread such that production occurs at the relatively "steep" portion of the yield response curve, the effect of increased variability in water supply on the variability of yield will be much higher. This is one of the reasons for a higher variability in yield at the tail end than at the head end in a continuous flow system of irrigation (Rosegrant 1986).

Availability of irrigation encourages multiple cropping and a shift from less to more water-responsive crops. Evidence from India indicates that farmers substitute rice for sorghum when irrigation is available (Jodha 1979). If, in the course of irrigation development, crop combinations that are negatively or weakly correlated give place to those that are strongly and positively correlated in their yields, total production will be more unstable than before. Nadkarni and Deshpande (1982) suspect that such changes in crop combination may have resulted in increased variability in foodgrain production in India. Even if the cropping combinations remain unchanged, an increase in covariance between yields over a wider area can result in an increase in aggregate variability. Irrigation, by making the environment more homogeneous, tends to increase the yield covariances. This may be one of the reasons for increased production variances in India (Hazell 1982; Walker, ch. 6).

Models for Measuring Variability

The discussion in the previous sections highlights the multitude of factors that need to be considered in modeling the effects of irrigation on yield and its variability. A frequent, albeit rather naive, approach has been to estimate a single-equation production function with water as one of the inputs. Apart from the biological inadequacy of such models, Just and Pope (1978) have shown that production functions with either additive or multiplicative error structures restrict the marginal response of variance of yields to inputs to be constant or increasing, respectively.

Antle (1983b) has more recently proposed a flexible moment-based approach and has devised efficient estimators of the parameters. The approach is flexible in that it does not impose restrictions on the functional relationships between decision variables and the moments of the probability distribution of output. This method has seemingly not yet been applied to measuring the effects of irrigation on production variability. If water use can be assumed to be exogenously determined, and a biologically meaningful index for measuring it is available, a moment-based approach is certainly desirable. However, the discussion above indicates that these conditions are unlikely to be satisfied.

Plant growth processes are dynamic and interactive, and decisions on input use are sequential. According to Antle (1983c), the production model can be formulated as a sequence of interlinked steps. Each step can be defined as an individual production stage whose output feeds forward to the next stage. Depending on the state of crop growth, farmers are assumed to revise their decisions about input use at each stage, so that input use is endogenously determined. Yield formation can then be satisfactorily modeled as a system of equations rather than a single equation. Antle (1983c) has discussed various types of information feedback and the corresponding optimization problems.

Going a step further, it might be said that purely econometric approaches to the estimation of production relationships that are complex, stochastic, dynamic, and interactive are bound to be operationally infeasible. Such problems can satisfactorily be studied by using the tools of systems modeling (Dillon 1976). A biophysical simulation model of plant growth can be used as a tool for evaluating production relationships. Such models will minimally consist of a climate submodel, a submodel describing various processes influencing plant growth and a submodel specifying the decision-making behavior of the farmer. In this framework, the farmer is considered to be interactively controlling plant growth through control or decision variables. While conventional optimization techniques cannot be used in this framework for deriving optimal control policies, this seems to be a small price to pay for improving realism. Anderson (1981) has discussed the basic principles for using such models to study production relationships. This advocacy of systems modeling is not to deny the value of econometric estimation of submodels within such more ad hoc specifications as illustrated by Rosegrant (1986).

An earlier section mentioned that it is the intensity and distribution of moisture stress, not the quantity of water applied, that determines the yield. However, quantity of water applied, rather than moisture stress, is usually the decision variable. A link between the decision variable (irrigation) and moisture stress can be established by using a submodel for water use by plants. The biophysical mechanisms involved can be modeled to any desired degree of accuracy. Similarly, interaction between various inputs can be allowed for by linking a fertilizer submodel, a pest submodel, and so forth to the overall model. The model may be run on an hourly, daily, or weekly basis, and the effects of alternative control policies on various parameters of the yield distribution can be examined. For a review of the application of simulation models to agriculture, see Anderson (1974a).

Of course, the conventional production function is a highly reduced form of a biophysical simulation model. With increasing knowledge of the biophysical processes governing plant growth, the use of simulation for evaluating alternative management strategies can be expected to be more widespread (Musser and Tew 1984, Trapp and Walker 1985). Recently, such models have been used for deriving optimal irrigation policies by English (1981), Boggess et al. (1983), and Pandey (1986). Where a larger number of policy alternatives at each stage are to be evaluated, biophysical simulation models can be linked to an optimization routine (such as dynamic programming) for deriving an optimal decision policy (Dudley 1971). These simulation models are ideally suited for isolating the effects of irrigation from other variables that may change simultaneously in reality (e.g., Rosegrant 1986).

Measuring Variability at the Aggregate Level

Given that irrigation is a nonhomogeneous input, measures of the effect of irrigation on variability at the aggregate level may not be very useful. Besides, factors other than irrigation (such as changes in input supplies, prices, etc.) may be more important in explaining variability at the aggregate level. Analysis using disaggregated data classified according to the type of irrigation will certainly be more enlightening. However, such data are not readily available. Keeping aside for the moment the aggregation issues involved in a cross-country comparison of production relationships, estimation of the Just and Pope (1978) type of production function at the aggregate level is hampered by lack of data on other inputs. Carlson (ch. 19) discusses some of the data related problems.

In his study of instability of foodgrain production in India, Hazell (1982) found that 41 percent of the increase in variance in production is explained by changes in interstate covariances within crops. Possible narrowing of the genetic base as a result of the diffusion of high-yielding varieties was considered to be one of the reasons for increase in the interstate covariances. It was speculated that a part of the increase in covariance may have been due to the supply of irrigation being more covariate across states. In a more disaggregated analysis using 48 districts growing sorghum and 40 districts growing pearl millet in India, Walker (ch. 6) found that the percentage of area irrigated had a significant positive effect on changes in interdistrict yield covariances. This result indicates that irrigation has a destabilizing effect on aggregate output. Similar results have also been obtained for Sri Lanka (Chandrasekar 1986).

Conclusions

Empirical evidence on the effects of irrigation on production variability at the aggregate level is as yet as inconclusive as it was when Barker, Gabler, and Winkelmann (1981) assembled their evidence. One of the reasons for this may be the treatment of irrigation as a homogeneous input. The effect of irrigation depends on the quantity applied, the timing of application, stability of water supply, water distribution rules, plant characteristics, and so forth. The conventional production function approach, although less costly, is inadequate for studying production relationships which are dynamic, interactive, and stochastic. A biophysical simulation model linked up with a farmer decision model is suggested as a more satisfactory tool for evaluating the stability effects of irrigation at the farm level.

19 Pest-Resistant Varieties, Pesticides, and Crop Yield Variability: A Review

GERALD A. CARLSON

This chapter discusses the role of pest-resistant crop varieties in changing cereal (especially rice) production variability. The genetic approach to pest control in most countries is part of the spread of modern varieties. Pest resistance is one of the important traits upon which cereal varieties are selected. However, it is not possible to examine the effects of resistant crop varieties without also considering irrigation, fertilizer, labor, farm size, and background (unknown) sources of production variability that are linked to weather and pest development.

Grain Crop Pests and Production Variability

There are economic and biological features of agriculture, especially some related to pest control, that may influence crop production variability at the field and more aggregate levels.

Long-term changes in pest populations in a given area are frequently associated with changes in cropping patterns (rotations of crops and crop varieties, multiple cropping, intercropping, time of planting, crop-free periods, varietal choices, etc.). Also, changes in other farm inputs, such as fertilizer and irrigation, are known to influence pest buildup (Kenmore 1979, Penaranda et al. 1985). Soil characteristics are also critical in influencing pest development, especially for nematodes, weeds, and soil insects. These pests are generally less variable in number from year to year than are foliar pests.

Pest populations, particularly foliar pathogens (rusts, mildews, blasts, smuts) and some insects, are influenced by weather events before and during the growing season. Weather-induced pests can give rise to positive covariances in crop damage and yields across sizable regions. Other weather events such as flooding can delay planting and expose crops to uniform, unusual pest conditions. Important insect pests of grain crops, such as brown planthopper, armyworm, grasshoppers, and locusts, can be influenced by distant weather events since these pests are highly mobile. An important feature of weather and pests of rainfed grain crops is that many pest species are enhanced by the same weather that encourages high crop yields. That is, moist conditions that improve grain-growing conditions also increase pest severity for most foliar pathogens. Consequently, adequate pest control is more profitable in wet than dry years given a fixed price for the final product.

Pest Resistant Crop Varieties

The most important farmer-controlled inputs affecting pest damage in grain crops are hand weeding (X_1), resistant crop varieties (X_2), pesticides (X_3), cultivation (X_4) and pest control information (X_5). In many developed countries, cultivation and herbicides have replaced hand weeding. As indicated above, weather (W) and other inputs such as irrigation (X_6) and fertilizer (X_7) can influence pest development. M represents the probability distribution of pest level or pest damage, though other features of pests such as duration of attack and crop susceptibility and resistance to pest controls also define pest threat in terms of crop damage (Carlson 1984).

A farm profit (R) function with a known vector of input prices ($\underline{r}'$) and output price is:

$$R = P_y Y(X_1, X_2, \ldots X_8, W, M) - \underline{r}' \underline{X},$$

where P_y is product price, X_8 is all other fixed and variable production inputs and $\underline{r}'\underline{X}$ represents total cost of all inputs. Assuming no price risk at the time that the input allocations are made is certainly less than realistic for inputs in developing countries where they can often be highly variable in supply at any price. However, the simplifying assumptions of known prices and a utility function related to only the first two moments of the observations of profit give simple optimal (utility maximization) conditions for use of a pest control input, such as resistant variety seeds, as:

$$\partial E(Y)/\partial X_2 = r_2/P_y + H P_y \, \partial V(Y)/\partial X_2,$$

where $E(Y)$ is expected yield, $V(Y)$ is variance of yield and H is a risk aversion coefficient that is positive for a risk averse person. r_2/P_y is the relative price of the new variety. Additional fertilizer and credit expenditures may also be major components of this type of technology change, but these are ignored here. The final term is an extra component of costs, which will be negative if an input such as a resistant variety reduces yield variance ($\partial V(Y)/\partial X_2 < 0$). Similar conditions can be obtained for the other pest control inputs.

In the above model the interaction between inputs such as irrigation and fertilizer and the optimal level of pesticides or crop resistance are thought to occur mainly through the effect of irrigation and fertilizer on the level of pests in the area. Interactions can also occur because pest-resistant crop varieties may have higher marginal products for water and fertilizer inputs. This has been especially true for many of the modern rice varieties. Usually, new crop varieties incur a trade-off in achieving disease and insect resistance that results in varieties being released that have lower yields than conventional varieties when the incidence of pests is below average (Carlson and Main 1976).

In the above model there is considered to be a continuum of crop resistance available, which farmers can receive by selecting among various crop varieties. With considerable genetic variation in a given pest species and with both horizontal and vertical resistance objectives in breeding programs, such varietal choices are indeed becoming available (Hooker 1979). However, the varietal choices are, in fact, frequently limited, and farmers must achieve the optimal mix of resistance by allocating some land to resistant and some to nonresistant varieties. Just and Zilberman (1983) have investigated credit constraints, costly adoption, farm size, and risk aversion features on the allocation of land between modern and conventional inputs. Only a few empirical applications of this type of model are available. Marra and Carlson (1984) have investigated double cropping of wheat and soybeans in the United States over the past 15 years, and Lazarus and Swanson (1983) examined the effects of allocation of land and pesticides for corn rootworm control using variations of their model. The distinguishing feature of these models is that the allocation of land to the pest-resistant crop is explicitly assumed to provide both direct pest damage reduction and diversification possibilities in product markets. Diversification to other crops with higher income elasticities and export potential is now very important for rice producers in many countries (Gonzales 1984).

Adoption of modern grain varieties that are pest resistant has the potential of reducing farm income variability compared with using traditional varieties that suffer variable pest damage. However, in most cases traditional varieties are not grown where they are frequently damaged by pests. More importantly, use of resistant varieties over wide areas can induce diseases and insects to adapt and mutate. Selection pressure is placed on pest organisms by planting resistant varieties. The higher the proportion of resistant varieties that are grown in an area, the faster are mutation and the appearance of new biotypes of the pests. Such "human-directed evolution" is most clearly documented for rusts and other fungal diseases of grains (Vanderplank 1968). For many major grain diseases and insects, there are breeding programs to provide an inventory of new varieties by crop region (IRRI 1979).

Pesticides

Pesticides are an increasingly important input in controlling pests. Yet, use of insecticides in food grains is of minor importance relative to their use in other crops such as cotton, fruit, and vegetables. In the United States for 1982, only about 18 percent of all domestic insecticides were applied on maize and all other grain crops (USDA 1983a). For the 1971-82 period, only the following percentages of the area in these crops were treated with any insecticides: maize, 36; sorghum, 30; rice, 21; wheat, 8; and other small grains, 3. Herbicide use is much higher on U.S. foodgrains, with the percentages of area treated for the same crops being: maize, 88; sorghum, 52; rice, 92; wheat, 40; and other small grains, 37 (average of three surveys) (USDA 1983a).

The impact on the variability of crop production from pesticide use has been examined by several agricultural economists. This work was reviewed by Carlson (1984) and eight studies are summarized in table 19.1. Only the study of Lazarus and Swanson (1983) included analysis of a food grain. In four out of five studies, pesticides reduced profit variability. In the Lazarus and Swanson study, crop rotation was found to reduce income variability, while continuous maize cropping combined with use of pesticides increased income variability. Most of the income variability reduction in the maize-soybean study came from reduction in variability of pest damage, and only a small part from enterprise diversification.

Several of the studies in table 19.1 considered the nonsymmetrical nature of the pest damage probability distributions, and the authors utilized objective functions other than those involving only the mean and variance. In each case where skewness is considered, distributions of pest damage were positively skewed with low probabilities of very high losses. Objective functions with methods for consideration of skewness seem appropriate for cropping problems involving pest control (Carlson 1970, Antle 1983b, 1986).

There are numerous studies on determining the optimal timing and dosage rates for pesticides or minimum pest densities that justify pesticide treatment. The concept of adjusting pesticide use to potential pest density (in its various forms) is known as the economic threshold (Feder 1979; Reichelderfer, Carlson, and Norton 1984). Use of thresholds versus alternative decision criteria will give different levels of variability and average returns (Feder 1979). Herdt, Castillo and Jayasuriya (1984) used experimental data on Philippine rice to evaluate changes in income variability from following economic threshold, next higher, or maximum protection strategies. In the case of moderately resistant varieties, they found that the economic threshold strategy was dominant (first-degree stochastic) for all income levels. The maximum protection strategy became more

TABLE 19.1 Sources of risk, utility formulation, and evidence on marginal risk effects of pest control inputs

Publication Source	Measured Sources of Risk[a]	Utility Formulation(s)[b]	Crop(s)	$\partial V_\pi / \partial X_i$, Marginal Risk Effects Found — Pesticides	$\partial V_\pi / \partial X_i$, Marginal Risk Effects Found — Other
Carlson (1970)	$M\ k$	EV, DA	Peaches	—	Monitoring (—)
Carlson (1979)	M	EV, SD	Cotton	?	Monitoring (—)
Cochran and Robison (1982)	M, Y	EV, SD	Apples	—	Monitoring (?)
Feder (1979)	$M\ d\ k$	$M\text{-}P\text{-}S$	None	—	
Hall (1977)	M	EV	Citrus, cotton	?	Monitoring (—)
Lazarus and Swanson (1983)	$M\ d\ P_y\ Y\ P_s Y_s$	EV	Maize, soybeans	+	Rotation (—)
Moffitt et al. (1982)	M_1, M_2	EV, SD	Soybeans	?	Monitoring (—)
Musser, Tew and Epperson (1981)	$\underline{M}$	EV, SD	Vegetables	—	Monitoring (?)

[a] M = pest density (M refers to multiple pest species, M_1 is scout observation, M_2 is area forecast); d = damage per pest; k = percent pest reduction; P_y = crop price; Y = yield of substitute crop; $\underline{Y}_s$ = yield of substitute crop; P_s = substitute crop price.
[b] EV = expected profit-variance of profit; SD = stochastic dominance analysis; $M\text{-}P\text{-}S$ = mean-preserving-spread; DA = disaster avoidance.

attractive than the economic threshold at higher income levels for rice varieties that are more susceptible to insects.

Four of six of the studies of table 19.1 that investigated the effects of pest density information showed reduced variability in agricultural income with higher levels of pest monitoring. However, it is easy to show that it is possible to increase income variability by following inaccurate forecasts of pest damage (Moffitt et al. 1982; Reichelderfer, Carlson, and Norton 1984). Pest density and pest biotype (or race) monitoring for determining crop resistance in a given field is often quite expensive. This is particularly true in situations with poor roads and few pest control specialists. With uniform crop conditions across farms, it is possible to provide regional pest forecasts. Farmers with larger farms can afford to hire monitoring and advisory specialists or to develop their own pest-monitoring abilities. In some developing countries, the possibilities of size economies in pest density information and pesticide application, and possible human hazards from pesticide application have led government agencies to conduct pesticide applications in farmers' fields. In many cases, the complexity of control with pesticides, along with the high local managerial requirements (dosage, material, and timing considerations), has reinforced the emphasis given to pest-resistant crop varieties.

Problems in Empirical Estimation

There are data-related and conceptual problems in estimating stochastic models of production that incorporate pest management variables such as levels of pesticide use. There are differences in such models between the perspective of the farmer and that of an analyst examining historical records of farms or larger aggregates. Farmers have the advantage of knowing local values for input prices (r_i), their resource endowments ($r'X$), and probably estimates of the production elasticities of the inputs that they have observed being used at variable levels in their or neighbors' fields. Their knowledge of the marginal contribution of inputs to output variability (Anderson and Griffiths 1982) may also be extensive if cross-sectional variation in input use (X_i) and in sources of background variation, such as pest density or soil moisture, are easily observed by farmers. Farmers are restricted in their ability to gauge the marginal variability effects for input use practices that are spatially uniform and for exogenous sources of risk such as pests and weather, which are at similar levels over wide areas and over long periods of time. It has also been found that farmers with more farming experience and higher levels of human capital are better able to estimate parameters of pest control random variables (Pingali and Carlson 1985).

The analyst has the advantage of greater computational capacity and specific estimation techniques, such as (a) adjustments for contemporaneously correlated observations, and (b) weighting procedures for sample data with unequal variances as indicated by the estimation techniques described by Just and Pope (1978, 1979). Biologists have also contributed in this area by finding units of measure of random events occurring at one location that are highly correlated with crop conditions over wider areas, and with improved sampling techniques and technologies (pest traps, pheromones, moisture probes, etc.)

Because crop production takes many months, there are often chances to make some input adjustments to changing weather and pests over the growing season (Antle 1983a). Crop status is linked between periods and farmers can protect crops more if expected product prices rise or apply less insecticide than usual to protect a crop thought to have reduced yield potential. In foodgrain cropping such dynamic considerations are probably more important for modification of planting schedules and multiple cropping decisions than they are for varietal decisions and pesticide scheduling.

An empirical test of the effects of input use on rice production variability was attempted using country-level data. (More micro data were not available for all major inputs and output variability.) Coefficients of variation (about trend) for yield and total production were compiled for 13 Asian rice growing countries for the 1961-82 period. Pakistan, Philippines, and China had the largest reduction in variability between these two decades, while Malaysia and Taiwan had sizable increases in total production variability. A linear model relating input use to variability of output was estimated much as other researchers have done for cross-country production functions (Hayami and Ruttan 1985). Lower use of nitrogen fertilizer, higher use of improved varieties, and a higher proportion of area irrigated were associated with countries and time periods with lower total production variability. (Chapters 17 and 18 present more detail on irrigation and fertilizer and their relationship to variability.) The negative association between use of pest resistant varieties and yield variability warrants more investigation because biologists have noted the possibility of high fluctuations in yield associated with pest adaption to pest-resistant varieties (IRRI 1984).

Pesticide and Crop Price Changes

There are frequently no consistent time-series data on pesticide use and prices for many regions and countries, including developed countries. Suitable indexes of pesticide prices and quantities depend upon being able to detect changes in product quality and changes in quantity due to technical change and pesticide resistance by pests. Quantity measurements are complicated since adding weight of active ingredients across chemical types can be misleading. For example, synthetic pyrethroid insecticides are

TABLE 19.2 Export price ratios of pesticides for rice and wheat

Period	Pesticides/Rice[a]	Pesticides/Wheat[b]
1961-1963	108	—
1964-1966	103	—
1967-1969	83	—
1970-1972	90	93
1973-1975	56	88
1976-1979	73	114
1980-1982	71	117

Sources: FAO (1962-1982), USDA (1950-1982). Index values = 100 in 1970-71.
[a] Japanese pesticide price index ÷ Thailand white rice price index; 1981 and 1982 use Hong Kong pesticide prices.
[b] Canadian pesticides index ÷ Canadian crop price index.

often used at the rate of 0.1 kilograms per hectare (kg/ha), while others are used at 10 times that rate for the same insects. Unit area pesticide treatments are not comparable across pesticides because of widely different numbers of treatments per crop season. These problems are most severe for insecticides and least severe for herbicides, although there have been major technical changes in the latter as well.

The long-run trend in pesticide prices compared with the general price level has been downward, much as for fertilizer. Table 19.2 presents an attempt to form two pesticide–crop price ratios. The first utilizes Japanese pesticide prices and Thailand export prices for rice. Japanese domestic prices for rice are much higher than international rice prices (USDA 1984b). The pesticide mixture in the pesticide price ratio is similar to that primarily used in rice culture. The second time series is for Canada and reflects export prices of compounds primarily used in temperate climate wheat production, mostly (90 percent) herbicides. The pesticide price ratio for rice production is generally declining with sharp declines in the late 1960s and mid-1970s. The wheat production pesticide price ratio declined with the rapid increase in wheat prices in the early 1970s, but there has since been a steady rise.

The rising price ratio in wheat pesticides certainly will not encourage rapid increases in pesticide use. On the other hand, the long downward trend in pesticide prices relative to rice has probably encouraged more use of pesticides in rice. More accurate data collection efforts could greatly enhance ability to determine the role of pesticides in rice production. Most efforts to evaluate the impacts of pesticides in rice have had to rely on a use or nonuse measure (Mandac and Flinn 1983, Feder and Slade 1984). Very large quantities of insecticides are being used in rice production, and the consequences for pest control and production stability should be evaluated.

Conclusions

This survey of biological and economic literature indicates that there have been reductions in production variability seemingly associated with the use of pesticides and field monitoring for pest density. However, there are biological theories and case examples where intensive production with high levels of fertilizer, modern varieties, irrigation, and pesticides can be unstable.

Farmers may devote pest control resources to decrease variability of output; many of these resources are only qualitatively different from the usual production inputs. Farmers generally accept higher levels of income variability in return for sufficiently higher mean levels of income.

Most cereal farmers have relied on labor, mechanical, and genetic approaches to pest control. Relatively higher pesticide-to-wheat price ratios since 1976 may predispose little increase in pesticide use for wheat. However, the constantly falling prices of pesticides relative to rice encourage more pesticide use in many rice-producing countries. Poor price and quantity data for pesticides at both the aggregate and microlevels hinder analysis in this area.

Periods of subsidized fertilizer prices, credit that is linked to use of modern varieties, and price supports for rice have increased rice production dramatically in the past two decades. Now there are large stocks of domestic rice in countries such as Indonesia, which has traditionally been a large rice importer. Rice farmers are currently experiencing depressed prices. At the same time, there is more variability in rice production. Increased use of irrigation and adoption of pest resistant cereal varieties appear to be helping countries cope with instability in the production system. More attention to the combined effect of input use on stability and mean output is needed.

20 Yield Stability and Modern Rice Technology

JOHN C. FLINN AND DENNIS P. GARRITY

The nature of modern rice technology and its inherent implications for increasing or decreasing rice yield stability are discussed in this chapter. First, the evidence of whether rice production stability in aggregate has increased in Asia with the adoption of modern varieties (MVs) is reviewed. Second, experimental data are examined to determine whether the components of modern rice technology are likely to stabilize or destabilize yield. Third, farm data are used to provide some insights on the impact of higher input technology, when managed by farmers, on yield distributions. Fourth, research strategies that are likely to result in second-generation modern varieties and methods of crop management having higher productivity and stability than first-generation modern varieties or traditional rice varieties are reviewed.

Here, older varieties (OV) include traditional varieties and older improved varieties such as Peta and BE-3. These are commonly tall, photoperiod sensitive, and not very responsive to modern agronomic practices. Some varieties with traditional plant types have also been improved to exhibit characteristics intermediate between modern and older varieties; these intermediate varieties (IVs) include Pelita and Pankaj.

It is useful to distinguish between first- and second-generation modern variety rices. The first-generation modern varieties, typified by IR8, had the capacity to utilize fertilizer effectively. However, they were of long duration, and lacked broad spectrum disease and insect resistance. The second-generation modern varieties retain this fertilizer responsiveness and, in addition, are of short duration, and have multiple insect and disease resistance, high yield potential, and improved grain quality. IR8, for example, has a fixed 130-day growth duration; the first really short duration modern variety, IR36, matures in 110 days; more recent varieties, such as IR58, mature in 100 days. This means that second-generation modern varieties use less water, are exposed to field hazards for a shorter period, and most importantly from a food security viewpoint, can be har-

TABLE 20.1 First-period coefficients of variation and their changes in production, area, and yield of rice in eight major rice-growing countries for periods before and during modern variety rice adoption

Country	Period First	Period Second	First-Period cv (and Percentage to Second Period) Production	First-Period cv (and Percentage to Second Period) Area	First-Period cv (and Percentage to Second Period) Yield
Bangladesh	1959–73	1974–84	0.077 (−56*)	0.034 (−52)	0.056 (−58*)
Burma	1959–76	1977–84	0.067 (−21)	0.045 (−17)	0.037 (4)
China	1959–77	1978–84	0.028 (15)	0.021 (37)	0.026 (37)
India	1959–73	1974–84	0.083 (15)	0.018 (61*)	0.072 (37)
Eastern	1959–70	1971–82	0.122 (3)	0.024 (25)	0.108 (−1)
Southern	1959–68	1969–82	0.051 (132*)	0.015 (410*)	0.036 (66*)
Northern	1959–69	1970–82	0.122 (−7)	0.057 (61*)	0.086 (−2)
Indonesia	1959–67	1968–84	0.051 (4)	0.034 (−50)	0.014 (207*)
Philippines	1955–65	1966–84	0.032 (−84*)	0.040 (−30)	0.050 (−88*)
Sri Lanka	1959–75	1976–84	0.146 (−64*)	0.126 (−51)	0.098 (−60*)
Thailand	1955–65	1966–84	0.147 (−55*)	0.093 (−55*)	0.071 (−36)

Source: *FAO Production Yearbook*, various issues.
Note: Coefficients of variation are computed from means and standard errors of residuals from second-order polynomial time trends except when time trend not significant.
*An asterisk denotes a change that is significant at the 5 percent level.

vested early enough to allow farmers to plant and harvest another crop during the same rainy season. (See also Coffman and Hargrove, ch. 11.)

Rice Production Stability in Asia

The rate and extent of modern variety adoption vary markedly among (and within) Asian countries, as do policies that influence modern variety adoption (price policies, irrigation investment, research, extension, etc.). Therefore, the choice of periods for time trend analysis must be country specific and based on structural shifts in modern variety adoption or major policy changes. Table 20.1 reports changes for eight Asian countries between periods defined by changes in rice policies, programs, and modern variety adoption. On this basis, yield variability may have increased in Burma, China, India, and Indonesia in aggregate but decreased in Bangladesh, the Philippines, Sri Lanka, and Thailand. Although Burma and Indonesia may show slight increases in yield variability, the first period in each case was characterized by stagnant low yields, while the recent period of modern variety adoption exhibits large and, in most cases, continuing yield increases.

The same picture emerges on a regional basis within India. Rice production variability has not markedly increased in eastern India where yields remain stagnant, but has increased in the north and the south where rice productivity has dramatically increased.

A problem with the trend analysis reported is that methods (and quality) of collecting and reporting national statistics may vary considerably over time and between countries. Therefore, part of the apparent change in variability may be due to changes in data collection practices as opposed to shifts in productivity. Also, trend analysis is not an appealing technique to analyze changes in production and in its components (area and yield) because factors that cause variability are not identified, measured, or included in the analysis. Ray (1983) examined variability in Indian agriculture and showed that weather and price variables were significant determinants of yield and production stability in rice production. However, variables associated with technological change—for example, modern variety adoption and irrigation rate—were not explicitly included in the analysis. Clearly more rigorous analysis is necessary to estimate the impact of technological change on stability parameters.

Component Technology and Yield Stability

Coffman and Hargrove (ch. 11) and Carlson (ch. 19) discuss how the morphology of modern varieties influences the comparative yield stability of modern and older varieties. This discussion is not duplicated here but examples are provided of the association between modern variety traits and yield stability. Traits examined are: (a) evidence of varietal adaptability over space and its relationship to stability within locations, (b) performance under water stress conditions, (c) pest resistance, and (d) fertilizer responsiveness.

Stability and Adaptability

Much of the success of modern rice varieties is attributed to the benefits of multilocational testing, which has led to the identification of widely adapted cultivars. Adaptability may be important to crop improvement scientists, but breeding for wide adaptability also has associated costs. Because selection is based on multilocation performance, cultivars selected may not necessarily be the best for any specific location where they are recommended. The performance of a genotype at a site over time is measured in terms of yield stability, while the performance of a genotype across locations is measured in terms of adaptability (Evenson et al. 1981).

Plant breeders place considerable confidence in the multilocation testing process as a means of selecting new cultivars. Of course, final genotypic selection is not based on multilocation performance within a single year. Cultivars are normally selected as varieties only after at least three years of testing. But advancement of cultivars within a selection program does depend primarily on multilocation, within-year results.

It is implicitly assumed that adaptability is highly correlated with stability. Whether or not this is true is a central issue in the effectiveness of the breeding process in producing genotypes that have stability as well as high yield. Optimization of crop improvement research in identifying stable cultivars may depend on this correlation. If this is not so, the acceptance of multilocation performance as a proxy for time-series performance in cultivar selection requires re-examination.

There is a considerable body of literature for the major cereal crops on the interaction between genotype and environment. This work received strong impetus from Finlay and Wilkinson (1963) and Eberhart and Russell (1966). However, these and similar studies make little distinction between the concepts of stability and adaptability. Evenson et al. (1981) used analysis of covariance to test whether the two parameters were related, using a set of rice genotypes selected from the first three years of irrigated rice yield trials of the International Rice Testing Program (IRTP) (IRRI 1980), and several years' results of similar trials conducted by the All India Coordinated Rice Improved Program (AICRIP).

They found contrasting results for the two data sets: no relationship between adaptability and stability in the IRTP data set, but a strong positive correlation between the parameters in the AICRIP data set. Given the then short time span of the IRTP data and the implausible stability coeffi-

TABLE 20.2 Adaptability and stability of rice cultivars tested in the international rice-testing program

Environment and Cultivar[a]	Stability		Adaptability	
	Coefficient	Standard Error	Coefficient	Standard Error
Irrigated				
IR42	1.08	.07	0.99	.06
IR51-282-8	1.05	.09	1.10	.06
IR54	1.16	.10	1.07	.09
IR8	1.03	.06	1.06	.04
IR26	0.97	.07	0.89	.08
IR36	0.96	.04	0.93	.03
MRC-603-303	1.01	.07	1.00	.05
MTU3419	1.16	.11	1.08	.08
IR1561-228-3-3	1.02	.09	1.02	.07
IE + 2845 (RP-1899-24-4)	1.05	.08	1.18	.07
Upland				
IR1529-430-3 (IR43)	1.12	.08	1.08	.08
IR2035-242-1 (IR45)	0.96	.16	0.93	.99
MRC172-9	1.26	.25	1.09	.11
C22	1.00	.16	1.09	.12
IR2061-522-6-9	1.29	.15	1.06	.15
IR6115-1-1-1	0.87	.08	0.86	.18
IR52 (IR5853-118-5)	1.06	.09	0.90	.14

Sources: Final reports of IRTP nurseries for 1974–83, Philippines (IRRI). See Evenson et al. (1981) for method of analysis and further interpretation of the coefficients.
[a] Tested four or more years.

cients that they obtained for some of the genotypes, the hypothesis was retested here using the Evenson et al. model, and data from 10 years of IRTP trials.

The genotypes included in the analysis were those tested in the IRTP nurseries for a minimum of four years. IRTP trials are designed for frequent turnover of entries as new improved material becomes available. Thus, only a few of the several hundred cultivars tested during the past decade have been retained for a four-year period or more. Data from the upland rice yield trials and the irrigated trials were analyzed to provide two contrasting sets of genotypes tested in different ecological conditions (table 20.2).

Low coefficients of adaptability or stability indicate a relatively low yield differential for a cultivar across sites. A high coefficient indicates that the cultivar performs poorly in low-yielding environments but yields well in more favorable environments. The coefficients of individual cultivars vary from as low as 0.86 for adaptability and 0.87 for stability (IR6115-1-1-1) to as high as 1.06 and 1.29, respectively (IR2061-522-6-9). The coefficients of adaptability and stability were positively correlated among the set of entries from both the irrigated (0.56) and upland (0.68) yield trials.

The coefficients of stability tended to be higher than the coefficients of adaptability in both cultivar sets. These data, plus those of Mackill et al. (1985), who showed that the regression coefficient of cultivar yields versus site mean yield remains consistent across entries in international rainfed lowland rice trials in which large hydrological variation occurs, add weight to the contention that cultivar adaptability and stability are highly associated. However, the adoption of widely adapted varieties, at best, "buys time" for national programs. Varieties chosen in this manner are not a substitute for varieties developed for the specific needs of even Asia's diverse agroclimatic rice environments and market preferences.

Modern Varieties and Water Stressed Environments

An irrigated rice field is one of the most physically uniform, nutritionally buffered agricultural ecosystems. Most environmental disturbances may be prevented, enabling yields to be increased without substantial increases in yield variability. In contrast, upland rice land represents a highly variable agro-ecosystem. Rice grown on such lands, which have no surface water storage capacity, is subject to highly variable water status since the rice plant lacks efficient water uptake and conservation mechanisms. Average yield levels may be increased in such conditions, but the lack of control of the most critical factor (water) suggests that yield variability is likely to increase as yield increases. The same may apply to the flood-prone and deep water rice environments. Differences among rice-growing environments in the extent to which major yield determinants can be controlled suggest that questions of yield and yield stability must be addressed in terms of specific rice environments.

The characteristics of modern rice varieties allow them to respond to higher nutrition and uniform water supply by producing higher grain yield per crop and per field day. But where water control is inadequate, the structure and function of the modern variety rice plant may predispose it to be more severely affected by water deficit or excess than are older varieties. In some drought-prone environments, the shorter stature, shallower root system, higher tillering, and photoperiod insensitivity of modern varieties more frequently cause severe damage or crop failure.

Early maturity is a necessary character in rice-growing areas with a short wet season. The shorter duration of a modern variety may enable it better to fit the limited period of available moisture and to escape terminal water stress that would affect a late-maturing older variety during flowering or grain filling. The strong preference of a large proportion of Philippine rainfed rice farmers for early maturity (105-115 days) rices may be attributed to the stability enhancement of drought escape.

In other drought-prone environments, however, which experience relatively long rainy periods but highly erratic rainfall distribution, (for example, northeast Thailand and the Cagayan Valley, Philippines), the short duration, photoperiod-insensitive varieties are highly unstable and clearly inappropriate (Gines, Pernita, and Morris 1984). Short duration varieties are genetically programmed to proceed quickly through each successive growth stage. Severe and prolonged drought interrupts this development, resulting in drastic yield reduction. A photoperiod sensitive variety flowers in a certain month regardless of when it is planted. When planted at the normal time early in the growing season, it passes through a long preflowering phase. This longer growth period enables more effective drought recovery. Short duration, photoperiod-insensitive varieties, however, have little phenological buffering. Growth lost at one stage cannot be so effectively retrieved.

The planting of old seedlings is common in the drought-prone areas with erratic rainfall, since farmers can transplant only when adequate water collects in the bunded field, an unpredictable event. Modern varieties tend to respond poorly to late transplanting while the yields of photoperiod-sensitive older varieties are unaffected. Therefore, older varieties remain dominant in many Asian drought-prone areas with erratic rainfall.

The variability of modern varieties in the situations described has precluded their adoption on more than one-half of Asian rice lands. In the more favorable areas, where modern varieties are currently grown, the tendency for their cultivation to result in greater yield variability will depend on the nature of the yield-limiting stresses.

Pest Management

Coffman and Hargrove (ch. 11) observe that insect and disease pressures on rice are among the highest of those on the staple foodcrops. There is a continuous process of adaptation of rice pests to the crop. The rate of adaptation seems to increase with the intensification of rice technology as wider areas are planted asynchronously to single varieties, as double- and triple-cropping increase, as higher rates of fertilizer are used, and as irrigation increases. This places greater importance on maintenance research to defend yields than for most other crops. Therefore, breeding for multiple insect and disease resistance is the core of most rice improvement programs.

INSECT MANAGEMENT. Prophylactic application of broad spectrum insecticides, as recommended in many extension programs, is expensive, often ineffective because of pest resurgence and resistance, and environmentally hazardous. These shortcomings led to the concept of integrated pest management (IPM) which involves the selection of insect resistant varieties and the judicious use of insecticides when insect pressures exceed threshold damage levels (Heinrichs, Saxena, and Chelliah 1979).

The on-farm benefits of three insect control strategies—no insecticide application, action thresholds, and prophylactic sprays—were evaluated on insect resistant rice varieties over five years in the Philippines (Smith and Litsinger 1985). The mean net benefits were similar across treatments, however, coefficients of variation (cvs) were less with the untreated (0.15) and the IPM-treated plots (0.23) than for the prophylactic (0.31). The similarity in net benefits (all about $430/ha) arose because, although the yields of the zero treatment tended to be less than for the IPM and prophylactic treatments, costs were higher with the IPM treatment mainly because of the surveillance costs, and with the prophylactic treatment because of insecticide costs. The Philippine Ministry of Agriculture reports that the threshold spraying strategy was more profitable than preventive sprays in 75 percent of 105 on-farm trials. Herdt, Castillo, and Jayasuriya (1984) similarly found that insecticide applications based on action thresholds dominated alternative insect control measures.

Consistent with Carlson's (ch. 19) impressions, a strategy of combining insect-resistant varieties and selective use of insecticides reduces production variability in rice below the level expected under traditional insect management strategies. However, IPM technology is also more complex than farmers' current practices (Goodell 1984). Therefore, training and extension must be integral components of IPM technology, and surveillance costs must be recognized (Kenmore 1985).

WEED MANAGEMENT. Modern rice varieties are shorter and more erect, and so are less weed competitive than are taller, drooping older varieties (De Datta 1981). This, in principle, implies increased yield variability in modern varieties where weeds are not controlled.

The most dramatic recent change in weed management in rice in Asia has been the rapid and widespread adoption of herbicides. This shift in weed control technique was promoted by a combination of technical and economic factors—the synthesis of selective herbicides such as butachlor and thiobencarb, which effectively control weeds in irrigated and shallow rainfed rice, coupled with falling real prices of herbicides, and increasing labor costs for weeding (De Datta and Flinn 1985).

Under some circumstances, shifting to herbicides may increase yield variability compared with systems where hand weeding dominates. This, as also pointed out by Coffman and Hargrove (ch. 11), would be the case if herbicides were no longer locally available, or if their price increased drastically, and labor was not available or too costly to substitute for chemical weed control. Other factors are the lower effectiveness of currently marketed herbicides under severe moisture stress, the problem induced if a buildup occurred in herbicide resistant weed species, and the shift of weed populations with herbicide use over time (Vega, Paller, and Lubigan 1970). In practice, these have not been major problems in rice when herbicides are viewed as a component of weed management. A combination of crop rotation, water management, tillage practices, and nonselective herbicides allows the control of such weeds, particularly in environments without water stress (S. K. De Datta, personal communication).

A major weed control problem in rice persists in less favored rainfed and upland environments. Herbicides have yet to be found which are consistently effective in rice fields under both wet and dry conditions. Labor inputs for hand weeding (often over 30 days/ha) are costly, and while tillage may be effective, many upland rice farmers lack the power or money for timely tillage. Therefore, the major destabilizing effects of weeds in rice cultivation will continue to be in the low-yielding and adverse, as opposed to the more productive irrigated and shallow rainfed, rice environments.

DISEASES. Varietal resistance continues to be the main disease management strategy for rice in Asia. Fungicides have not become part of disease management in South and Southeast Asia, although they have in temperate regions such as Japan and Korea. Clearly, disease outbreaks, such as the rice tungro virus in parts of Indonesia in 1981, will continue to occur and to cause yield loss. However, modern breeding strategies, which include genotype selection under hotspot locations, ensure that new materials are available, or in the "pipeline," to combat diseases when they become potentially serious problems. One example was the availability of IR56 to replace IR36 in regions of Indonesia where the latter had become susceptible to rice tungro virus.

Management techniques may also reduce the likelihood of disease infestation with intensified rice production. For example, the concept of varietal rotation between wet and dry season crops has been introduced in Indonesia to reduce the probability of rice tungro virus outbreak (Manwan and Sama 1985). The success of varietal (and gene) rotation as a strategy for disease management requires well-developed agricultural research, extension, and service from the seed industry. It becomes feasible as the expertise of national rice programs increases, which is generally the case in Asia (IRRI 1985d).

Fertilizer Rates and Yield Variability

Rice yield variability is known to increase as N-fertilizer rates increase (Evans and De Datta 1979, Flinn and De Datta 1987). This variability is induced through strong interaction between applied nitrogen and the levels of random factors such as solar radiation, water regime, and pest incidence (De Datta 1981). These matters, including the analyses by Smith and Umali (1985) and others, are taken up by Roumasset et al. (ch. 17).

On-Farm Yield Variability

The characteristics of modern rice technology (i.e., MVs plus management) may lead to higher and more stable yields under experimental conditions. However, the important point is whether these same practices stabilize or destabilize yields under farmer management. Contrasts are presented for an irrigated and an upland site to illuminate any relationship.

Farmers' practices and those recommended by the Ministry of Agriculture for irrigated rice in the Philippines were compared over the period 1974 to 1978 (Herdt and Mandac 1981). Farmers at the study site in Central Luzon grew modern varieties such as IR20, IR36, and IR42 and applied fertilizer (but at lower rates on average than recommended). At the Mindanao dryland site, in contrast, the rice is upland rainfed; most farmers still grow older varieties, others (associated mainly with a rural development project) grew recommended intermediate varieties such as UPL Ri-5 and UPL Ri-7 (Tautho, Flinn, and Velasco 1985). Few older variety growers applied fertilizer, while most intermediate variety growers did. Thus, the Luzon case allows a comparison of more intensive and less intensive application of modern rice technology, under favorable irrigated conditions, while the Mindanao case provides a comparison of traditional and improved rice culture under less favorable upland conditions.

Yields under improved technology first-stochastically dominated those under the farmer's technology in both the irrigated and upland sites. However, without considering the costs of the different practices used in the respective pairs, strong statements of farmers' likely preferences among them are not possible. Mean yields were significantly higher with the higher input technology (table 20.3). Although yield variances increased significantly with application of the new technology, relative variability was not changed significantly.

For the irrigated cases, skewnesses of yields were not significantly different from normal. However, the yield skewness changed significantly from positive to slightly negative with the adoption of improved upland rices and associated crop management. These shifts in skewness with modern rice husbandry are consistent with the observations of Day (1965) and Barker, Gabler, and Winkelmann (1981) that the tendency toward negative yield skewness increased with improved technology. The upland rice data, however, are cross-sectional and do not permit an analysis of time-series variability, which is the variability of concern to farmers. These results must be treated with caution. For example, older variety upland rices yielded higher than intermediate and modern variety rices under severe moisture stress in the 1985 on-farm trials in Batangas, Philippines. Therefore, although farm yields may generally become more negatively

TABLE 20.3 Mean rice yields and yield distributions on farmers' fields in irrigated and upland rainfed sites in the Philippines

Site	Sample Size	Mean Yield (t/ha)	Coefficient of Variation	Skewness
Irrigated, modern varieties, Central Luzon, 1974-77				
Farmer's practice	76	3.80	0.37	−0.04
Recommended practice	76	5.22*	0.42	−0.43
Upland rainfed, Zamboanga del Sur, Mindanao, 1983				
Older varieties	55	1.41	0.44	0.47
Improved varieties	124	2.61*	0.35	0.16*

Sources: Central Luzon irrigated rice data extracted from IRRI Agronomy Department files. Agronomic details of this research are reported by De Datta et al. (1979); upland rice data derived from Tautho, Flinn and Veloseo (1985). Agronomic details of upland rice research and extension in Zamboanga del Sur are found in annual reports of the Zamboanga del Sur Development Project, Philippines.
Note: An asterisk denotes a change significant at the 5 percent level. Differences in means based on t tests and differences in variances on F ratios.

skewed with improved technology under favorable conditions, they may not under adverse conditions.

Increasing Stability of Modern Rice Technology

According to the Food and Agriculture Organization, balancing rice supply and demand in the year 2000 will require a 2.8 percent per year production increase over the period 1980-2000, which can be compared with the 2.4 percent growth rate achieved during 1960-80. Most of this increased rice will be produced and consumed in Asia. Competition for land in Asia from other crops, livestock, and nonagricultural uses results in its shrinking availability for rice cultivation. Therefore, the only pathway open to most Asian countries to increase rice production is through higher productivity and increased cropping intensity. This can only be achieved by technological advances including improved water and fertilizer management, other agronomic practices, and continued advancement of rice varieties capable of responding to these inputs.

Rice Improvement Programs

Modern rice varieties will continue to be grown under more intensive management systems. Therefore, problems of pest adaptation will continue as a threat to high yields and to yield stability. Research managers recognize the importance of breeding for multiple disease and insect resistance to counter the dynamic threat of pest infestation. Their efforts have led to recently released modern varieties possessing higher levels of pest resistance than previously released ones.

Increased national capacity and continued growth in collaboration between national and international rice programs allow wider and more rigorous testing of promising cultivars for pest resistance and for adaptability to adverse environments than was previously possible (IRRI 1985d). Breeders ensure that yield potential is not jeopardized by selecting for release cultivars with superior pest resistance. Therefore, in developing new varieties with greater yield stability, yield potential is not compromised.

Advances in biotechnology will dramatically increase plant breeders' capacity to incorporate resistance from wild relatives into domesticated rices. Indeed, these wild relatives are the only major source of resistance to some diseases, particularly viruses. Collection and conservation of indigenous rice species in gene banks such as the International Rice Germplasm Bank at the International Rice Research Institute (IRRI) ensure that diverse collections of rice germplasm will be maintained and will remain available to national rice scientists in the future. In 1984, the IRRI bank had more than 75,000 of the estimated 100,000 to 120,000 varieties of rice now grown in the world, and about 2,000 wild rices. Work is under way to collect and conserve most of the remaining 30,000 to 40,000 varieties.

Rice research programs, such as IRRI's Germplasm Evaluation and Utilization (GEU) program, are also working to develop improved varieties adapted to unfavorable rice environments. The focus of attention at IRRI is shifting to those areas where current modern varieties are less suited. As a result, greater emphasis is now placed on breeding for tolerance to physical (droughts, floods, low temperatures) and physiochemical factors (acid sulfate soils, saline soils, toxicities, and mineral deficiencies).

Second-generation modern varieties have better tolerance to soil stress than earlier varieties. Whether the shift toward breeding for adverse environments will increase or decrease production stability is not known. Within existing rice areas, mean yields should improve. However, yield variability may increase as yields will continue to be low when severe floods or droughts occur, irrespective of yield potential. They will remain effectively at zero level if the crop is not planted because of extreme weather conditions, a not unusual event in many upland environments. Varieties better adapted to unfavorable environments may also extend the margin of rice cultivation, increasing both yield and area variability and, perforce, production instability.

Genetic Uniformity

Coffman and Hargrove (ch. 11) discuss the concern that the common ancestry of modern varieties (particularly for the dwarfing gene) may contribute to increased production variability due to cytoplasmic uniformity. They also observe that this may not necessarily be so, because second-generation modern varieties have more diverse parentage than first-generation modern varieties. For example, IR36 can be traced back to 13 varieties from six countries, and IR64 to 20 landraces from eight countries (Hargrove, Cabanilla, and Coffman 1985).

Of great concern is the issue of large areas being planted to one or a few closely related varieties, which increases the probability of widespread insect and disease outbreaks. For example, IR36 was grown on some 11 million hectares of rice lands in South and Southeast Asia each year in the early 1980s. This is not to criticize the variety. Rather this attests to its adaptability and demonstrates farmers' preference for IR36 over other available varieties. The real concern is the lack of alternatives available to farmers that are better suited to their specific conditions.

The problem of large areas planted to single varieties should decrease as national rice programs breed varieties better adapted to local conditions. This capacity is aided by the International Rice Testing Program (IRRI 1980), which coordinates an international network to provide national programs with a wide range of rices to evaluate under their own conditions. For example, 29 of the International Rice Testing Program nurseries planned for 1986 are tailored to specific environmental stresses and defined conditions. Most entries in these nurseries were not bred by IRRI but by national program scientists. This is an important (and often unrecognized) advance over earlier strategies which favored selection of varieties for wide adaptation. The sharing of germplasm also enhances sustainability of future rice yields by introducing new lines to the nurseries each year to ensure that plant breeders have access to a diverse collection of germplasm. The main objective of these nurseries is not to provide materials for direct release to farmers but to serve as a mechanism to provide national programs with a range of germplasm that they can evaluate for desired traits and use as parents in their breeding programs.

Crop and Soil Management

Efficiency and sustainability in rice production will continue to be enhanced through the dual strategies of breeding input efficient varieties and improved crop and soil management.

Soil health research addresses the problems of toxicities and nutrient imbalances, and yield maintenance under increased cropping intensity. As rice production is intensified, a progression of deficiencies—nitrogen, then phosphorus, followed by zinc and possibly sulfur—is likely (De Datta 1981). The International Network for Soil Fertility and Fertilizer Efficiency in Rice (INSFFER)—a network of national rice programs, the International Fertilizer Development Center (IFDC), and IRRI—specifically addresses issues of soil fertility for rice. INSFFER collaborators conduct research to increase the efficiency of nutrient use and to maintain rice yields under intensified cropping. Such programs will help to lead to increases in the stability and sustainability of rice production.

A notable shift in research philosophy among national and international programs should also lead to increased stability of rice-based farming systems. Researchers now accept that it is necessary to adapt and modify technology to meet the needs of specific agroclimatic environments before farmers' adoption is likely to proceed. Basic to this approach is that the stability and sustainability of farming systems can be enhanced if (a) farmers are offered a range of technical options rather than a single predetermined package, and (b) farmers participate in the technology evaluation process (Denning 1985). This is a quantum shift in philosophy from the tendency to advocate broad recommendations thought to suit the majority of farm environments.

21 Influence of Nitrogen Fertilizer and Fungicide on Yield and Yield Variability in Wheat and Barley

H. HANUS AND P. SCHOOP

This chapter analyzes the results of a long-term experiment laid out in 1974. The crop rotation is as follows: oilseed rape, winter wheat, oats, and winter barley. Winter wheat and winter barley are the primary experimental crops, while oilseed rape and oats are fertilized at a low constant level (50-70 kg N/ha) to equalize the soil nutrient situation for the following crop.

Winter wheat and barley are fertilized with different amounts of nitrogen in steps of 40 kilograms per hectare (kg/ha). The total amount of nitrogen ranges from 0 to 320 kg/ha and is subdivided in three application rates at different growth stages: the beginning of the growing season after winter, the end of tillering, and at heading time. For the first two stages the nitrogen levels range from zero to 120 kg/ha, at heading time the maximum amounts to only 80 kg/ha.

Combining the different application rates at the three growth stages results in 48 treatments in total and up to 10 different distribution systems at the same level for fertilizer. The layout of the experiment is such that each plot of the field is fertilized with the same amount of nitrogen on average (160 kg/ha). Four different fungicide treatments were used in the experiment, although here only two are analyzed: namely, with and without fungicides. Herbicides were applied to control weeds and, if necessary, insecticides to control aphids. To characterize yields and their variability, averages and standard deviations were calculated over years (1975-84) and the two replications (Hanus and Aimiller 1978).

Results

Examination of the data revealed that yields depend not only on the level of nitrogen and fungicide treatments but also on the partition of the total amount of nitrogen within the growing season. Responses to the fungicide treatments vary over a wide range but generally increase with nitrogen level. When fungicides are applied, the standard deviations of yields are generally lower and yields are higher, but the differences in yields and yield stability with and without fungicides do not correspond precisely, either generally with increasing amounts of nitrogen or within the groups with the same level of N-fertilization. The results for winter barley are very similar to those of wheat. The effects of fungicide treatments are less, but the yield stability is generally higher than for wheat.

Averages across different levels of nitrogen are shown in figures 21.1 and 21.2. This display of the data reveals that:

a. The response to fungicide increases with increasing nitrogen level;
b. With fungicides, the maximum yield is reached only at the highest level of nitrogen, while without fungicide this maximum yield is attained at lower levels;
c. The response to fungicide and its increase with higher nitrogen applications is greater for wheat than for barley;
d. With fungicide, yields for wheat and barley are very similar while without, yields of wheat are much less;
e. The variability of barley yields increases slightly with nitrogen despite the use of fungicides, while yields of wheat tend to be more stable when fungicides are applied.

The generalizations concerning variability must be made rather cautiously. While it is natural to interpret the tendencies suggested by graphically depicted data at face value, the differences among standard deviations reported here are, in fact, generally rather small—at least in the sense that taking pairwise estimates in ratios and squaring them in a variance homogeneity test seldom produces significant values of F statistics. This is especially the case in the so-called "economically rational zone of production" range of nitrogen levels (here usually less than 150–200 kg/ha of nitrogen).

One reason for the yield variability between years is variable weather. Different weather sequences lead to different amounts of soil nitrogen resulting from the decomposition of organic material (Hanus 1978). Both the amount of nitrogen and the date of availability are defined by weather conditions. Thus, constant fertilizing systems in each year are, in fact, associated with different amounts of available nitrogen from the mineralization processes.

The effects of nitrogen applied at the different growth stages can also be examined in the experimental data. The results are very similar for both crops and fungicide treatments. Low amounts of nitrogen at the end of tillering lead to higher yield responses than applications at the beginning of growth, but higher rates at that time are less effective than at the beginning of growth. The lowest response is obtained from nitrogen fertilization

FIGURE 21.1 Yields and standard deviations of winter barley with increasing nitrogen levels with (+) and without (−) fungicide treatments based on averages over the different application systems

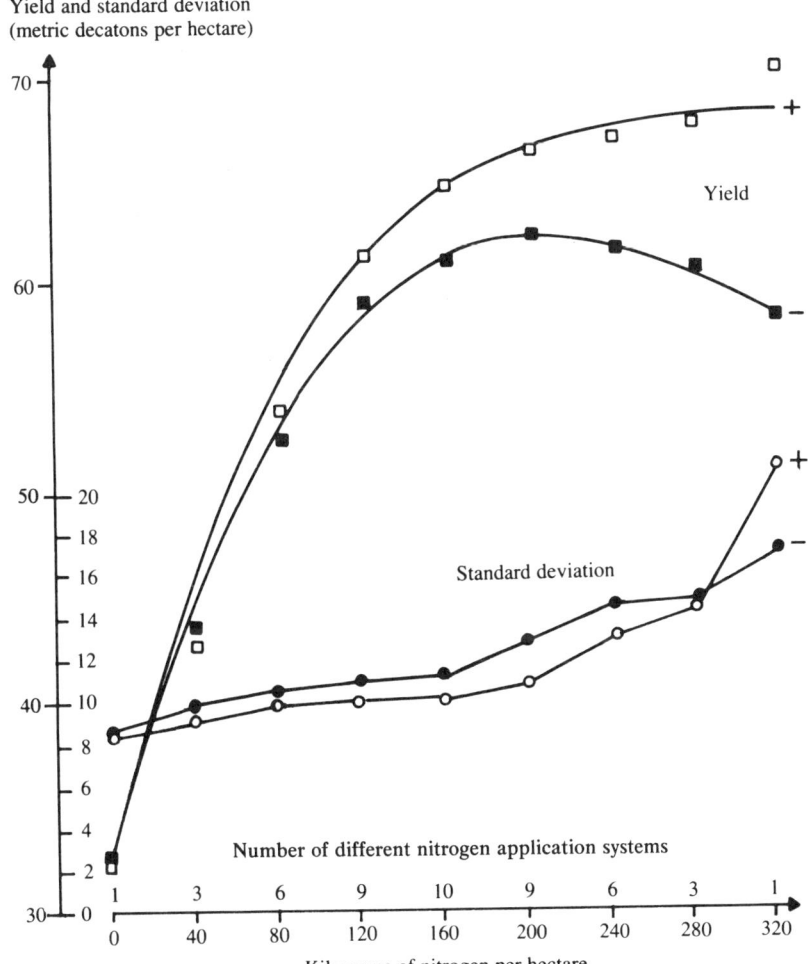

SOURCE: Hohenschulen, Diplomat (1975–84).

at heading time, especially when diseases are not controlled by fungicides. Increasing amounts of nitrogen at the beginning of growth after winter tend to reduce the variability of yields, while applications at the later stages tend to increase it.

FIGURE 21.2 Yields and standard deviations of winter wheat with increasing nitrogen levels with (+) and without (−) fungicide treatments based on averages over the different application systems

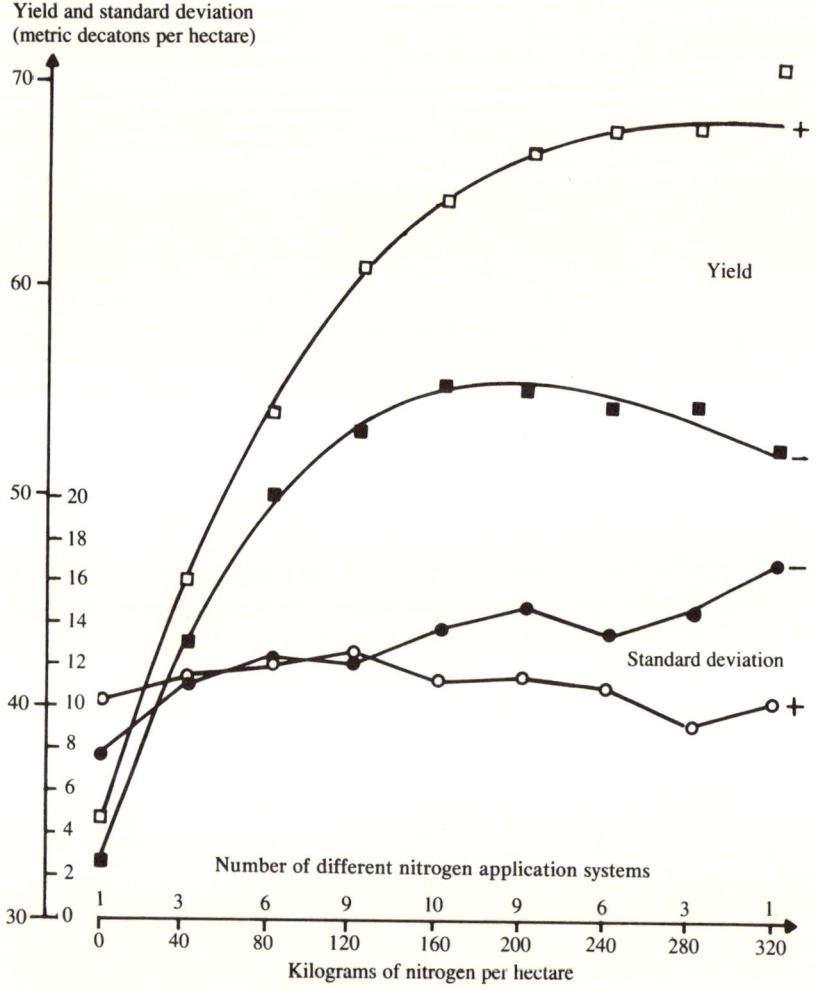

SOURCE: Hohenschulen, Dura (1974–82).

Discussion

The results lead to the conclusion that the variability of yield does not necessarily increase with increasing intensity of fertilization. One important factor is the control of diseases by fungicides. Adaptation of the amount and distribution of nitrogen within the growing season to the weather conditions tends to reduce variability. However, it seems that variability may be either increased or decreased by intensification under different conditions.

With varying environmental conditions (such as measured by radiation, soil moisture, disease infection, etc.) yields vary directly. As noted earlier, some of these same factors cause variation in soil nitrogen. This, in turn, also causes yield to vary, but the extent of such indirect effect depends on the level and slope of the nitrogen yield response function (for example, superior modern cultivars may have larger marginal responses than more traditional). With diminishing marginal returns, the indirect effect determined by the slope will tend to diminish as the yield-maximizing level of nitrogen is approached—from either direction. A priori, it is not possible to net out these several possibly contrary effects, and the observed marginal risk effect is thus essentially an empirical matter that may well vary considerably from site to site and at different factor intensities at a given site.

Advances in breeding, disease control, and so forth generally lead to higher potential yields and possibly higher variability of yields, while advances in crop management practices such as fertilization, growth regulators, soil cultivation, and so forth generally tend to reduce yield variability. Thus, depending on the sequencing of different innovations, the situation in a given region or country can be very different from, and not readily comparable with, that of others.

22 Influence of Technology and Weather on the Variability in U.S. Maize and Wheat Yields

JAMES B. FRENCH AND J. C. HEADLEY

This chapter discusses the impact of modern technologies on the behavior of yield distributions for winter wheat and maize in selected areas of the Corn Belt, Lake states, and Great Plains of the United States. It also takes up the question whether technology has increased the correlation of maize yields from different U.S. geographical regions.

Research Method

Yields from crop reporting districts (CRDs) were examined for two periods representing so-called low- and high-technology periods. The methods implemented are discussed in more detail by French, Schroder, and Headley (1985). Crop reporting districts are defined in the United States for data gathering purposes and consist of several contiguous political subdivisions (counties). In the case of winter wheat, the periods used are 1932–46 and 1967–81. For maize, the periods are 1931–45 and 1967–81. Yields were detrended over the periods based on the "best" model up to a third-degree polynomial. Comparisons between the distributions of the unexplained yield components were made. The models were extended by first removing the area effect and then by removing the influence of weather directly through inclusion of selected climatic variables. Because of a scarcity of degrees of freedom, the equation was restricted to a first-degree polynomial for trend. Yield variability explained by weather was separated from the unexplained component and was then normalized by simulating models for both periods through the same set of climatic data,

---

We are indebted to our colleagues, David Schroder and R. M. Finley for their contribution to earlier stages of this research. This research was supported in part by the Missouri Agricultural Experiment Station, Cooperative Agreement CR-809710 with the U.S. Environmental Protection Agency, and a grant from the International Food Policy Research Institute.

thereby permitting a comparison of distributions based on equivalent weather patterns. Finally, maize yields from the principal producing regions were correlated and correlation differences tested in the two periods to test the hypothesis that technology has made the variability in maize yields more covariate.

The Model

A general hypothesized yield function is:

$$y = f(T, W, A), \qquad (22.1)$$

where y is the mean yield for the crop reporting district; the "trend" variable T represents all technological factors such as varietal improvement, fertilizer, pesticides and pest management practices, improved tillage, and so forth; W represents all the weather factors; and A represents area planted, as a proxy for land quality.

Yield variability is conceptually composed of three components: (a) a systematic component, (b) a random component, and (c) an unexplained component. Technology and land quality are considered as systematic factors under the control of producers and capable of being affected by government policy. Weather is considered to be a random component and does not lend itself to control by decision makers. The final component, unexplained variation, is due to measurement errors and other unobserved factors, such as weather effects, that influence the model.

Previous studies of technology (Day 1965; Barker, Gabler, and Winkelmann 1981) have found yield distributions to be non-normal and that skewness changes with technology adoption. If skewness is positive—the mean exceeds the mode—risk (in one restricted sense, Day 1965) is higher than the variance indicates because the probability of a yield less than the mean exceeds 0.5. The opposite holds for negative skewness. Because skewness has not been studied as related to general changes in technology, it was calculated and tested for each 15-year technology period using Pearson's statistic (Day 1965, ch. 1).

For policy purposes, it is useful to know whether random yield variation is correlated with the application of technology. To do so, the variability due to weather is obtained in a trend-area-weather model.

Trend-Area-Weather Model

Generally, yield models assume that the error component of the trend equation is a good measure of random yield variability due to weather. This may or may not be true. Therefore, weather is included and the yield equation is specified as:

$$Y_{it} = a + bT_t + pA_{it} + wW_{it} + d_iD_t + g_i(D_tT_t) + e_{it}, \qquad (22.2)$$

where W_{it} represents the relevant weather in year t and crop reporting district i with w as the estimated population parameter at the state level. This is a cross-section time-series model estimated across all crop reporting districts in each state for the relevant time period. The variable $D_t T_t$ is an interaction between the CRD binary variable and trend. Parameters of the CRD binary variable and the CRD trend interaction variables are defined as d_i and g_i, respectively.

This model is estimated for the two technology periods of 15 years each with one estimation for each state. From the model, the predicted yield for the ith crop reporting district in the tth year can be computed as follows:

$$\hat{Y}_{it} = (\hat{a} + \hat{d}_i) + (\hat{b} + \hat{g}_i)T + \hat{p}A_{it} + wW_{it} \qquad (22.3)$$

where the circumflexes indicate estimates of population parameters. The unexplained portion of yield variance is $E(\hat{e}_i)^2 = E(\hat{Y}_i - Y_i)^2$. The null hypothesis is that the unexplained yield variance for the ith crop reporting district is equal for the high- and low-technology periods. Mean square errors are tested statistically and, if the hypothesis cannot be rejected, the effect of technology on unexplained yield variance is concluded to be neutral. Therefore, any differences in random variability due to weather must originate from the observed weather variables. The explained random variability due to weather around the systematic trend could be calculated and compared over the appropriate 15-year period for high- and low-technology models. However, since actual weather varies within the periods and the periods are not long enough to assume equivalent weather on the average, differences in yield variability due to weather between the two periods may be caused by actual differences in weather and not by technology. Therefore, variability measures for each technology period were estimated based on equivalent weather.

Weather's influence on yield variability given either low or high technology is determined by the estimated weather parameters for each of the two technology periods. The estimated parameters are used to estimate yield variability due to weather for each technology from a given sample of observed weather variables. To provide comparable yield variability estimates for the two technologies, the same sample of 51 years of observed weather (1931–81) was used, thus eliminating the potential bias that could arise from differences in weather.

The variability measure is the mean square error due to weather for each of the two technology periods and is called the yield variability due to normalized weather. Random variability due to normalized weather is calculated for crop reporting district i by:

$$\sigma^2_{wpi} = \sum_{t=a}^{b} (\hat{w}_{pi} W_{ti})^2 / (N - 1).$$

This is the mean square error due to weather for crop reporting district i for technology period p and where a is the first year of the low-technology period and b is 1981. N is the total number of years.

A mean yield level for each period is estimated for the ith crop reporting district assuming normal weather and the average technology for the period. That is, the yield is estimated for each 15-year period using equation (22.3) with the trend variable T at its mean omitting the area and weather variables. This value is then used as the mean yield as a basis for calculating relative variability (cv) for normalized weather.

No technology-weather interaction is assumed within each of the two periods even though there are different weather parameters estimated for each technology period. An increased yield variability associated with higher technology, if determined principally by weather, indicates a weather interaction. Perrin and Heady (1975) found such an interaction for winter wheat over the period 1930-71. Technology is assumed constant within the periods of study, thus decreasing potential interaction effects. However, the difference in technology between the two periods should be sufficient to permit such an interaction as found by Perrin and Heady (1975) over the longer period of time.

Because of the high multicollinearity among the weather variables and possible structural change in weather patterns, ridge regression was used to estimate the model. This technique appears to be justified for simulation over periods of possible structural change (Watson and White 1976).

Data Description

Data for yield and harvested area for maize and wheat were obtained from the U.S. Department of Agriculture (USDA) Cooperative State Crop and Livestock Reporting Service for the various states. The data were made available at the crop reporting district level for the period 1931 to 1981. The states included in the variability part of the study are: Iowa, Illinois, Indiana, Ohio, Wisconsin, Minnesota, Missouri for maize; Kansas for both wheat and maize; and Nebraska and Oklahoma for wheat.

For the maize yield correlation part of the study, the data were grouped into regions, namely: the Corn Belt (Ohio, Indiana, Illinois, Iowa, Missouri), the Northern Plains (Nebraska, Kansas) and the Lake states (Michigan, Wisconsin, Minnesota). Weather information was obtained from the USDA Oasis data bank. Monthly mean precipitation and temperature are available at the climatic division level which, for the states under study, correspond to crop reporting districts. All weather variables are specified as deviations from the mean. The mean is calculated over the period 1931-81. June, July, and August precipitation and mean temperature and preseason moisture variables are hypothesized to explain variations in yields of maize. The preseason moisture variable is formed by summing the monthly precipitation for the period from September of the previous year through May of the current year.

For winter wheat, precipitation and mean temperature variables for April, May, June, and July and a preseason growth precipitation variable are hypothesized to influence yield variables. The preseason growth precipitation variable is formed by summing the monthly precipitation rates for the period from August of the previous year through March of the current year.

Historical Adoption of Technology

Technology developed and applied to crop production can be classified into three broad categories: (a) biological, (b) chemical, and (c) mechanical. All of these have been joined together as a result of research and development, both public and private, with the objective of increasing profits, largely through increasing yields.

Maize yields in the United States around 1900 were about 1,780 kg/ha. In 1981 and 1982 the national average was in excess of 6,300 kg/ha. Winter wheat average yield was 1,020 kg/ha circa 1900, and by 1981-82 the yield was 2,390 kg/ha. The yields of maize have more than tripled, and the yield of winter wheat has approximately doubled in 80 years. In the case of certain regions, where edaphic and climatic factors are especially favorable to certain crops, the increases have been even more dramatic.

Maize

Production in the United States was relatively constant over the 1900-30 period. Production has since tripled and since 1950 has doubled. This increase in production since 1930 came about while reducing the area harvested by 15 percent.

Over the past 50 years, maize has become less of an intermediate product and more of a cash crop. Currently only about 37 percent of maize is fed on the farm where it is produced. Feed as a use has declined overall, and industrial uses and exports have increased.

As a cash crop, movement off the farm removes more nutrients and requires fertilizer to maintain or increase yields. This increases cash costs, reshapes the nature of the financial risks, and requires more credit. Advances in chemistry encouraged by World War II generated larger scale ammonia production and the development of compounds such as urea. Nitrogen was cheap due to cheap petroleum products. In fact, the real price of nitrogen declined from about 1950 until the oil embargo in 1973. Currently about 97.4 percent of the maize area in the Corn Belt receives some type of commercial fertilizer. The rate of application is approximately 160 kilograms of nitrogen, 30 kilograms of phosphorus and 110 kilograms of potash per hectare. One of the major differences in the two technology periods is the rapid and widespread use of nitrogen on maize in the latter period. In the early period, green manure and livestock manure were the principal nitrogen sources.

Varietal improvement has been important in maize culture. Beginning in the late 1920s, hybrid maize adoption was virtually complete by 1940. The hybridization process has brought yield increases, resistance to lodging, resistance to insects and disease, and an improved response to fertility and water. The major flaw in maize breeding has been the dependence on a body of cytoplasm with susceptibility to corn blight. In 1970, the blight reduced U.S. maize production by about 10 percent. It is this episode and other evidence, such as the work of Hazell (1984), that prompted the study of the maize yield correlations between areas such as the Corn Belt and the Lake states. Seed industry spokesmen now say that the genetic base has been diversified to reduce this danger (Duvick, ch. 12). Two areas receiving research emphasis are: (a) breeding for high protein, and (b) breeding for pest resistance.

In 1980, there were 4.4 million hectares of irrigated maize. Three states each irrigated more than 400,000 hectares, namely: Kansas, Nebraska, and Colorado. Nebraska, however, irrigates almost 2 million hectares or one-half of the U.S. irrigated area (Sunquist, Menz, and Neumeyer 1982). Even so, only about 16 percent of the national crop is irrigated. Irrigation has not been profitable in the "good" maize-growing soils of the Corn Belt due to high water holding capacity of soils and ample rainfall. Maize irrigation is another factor that distinguishes the high-technology period from the low period.

Pest control technology has been important in maize production and is a high-technology period phenomenon. Fertilizer has made it profitable to produce continuous maize; disease, weed, and insect problems have accompanied that trend. In 1982, 37 percent of the maize area was treated with insecticides, while 95 percent was treated with herbicides (Duffy and Hawthorn 1983). The use of herbicides has reduced the need for mechanical cultivation and crop rotations as weed control practices.

Winter Wheat

Wheat is one of the nation's major exports and is an important world food. Four states in the Great Plains, namely Kansas, Nebraska, Oklahoma, and Texas, produce about 45 percent of the winter wheat. The most important technical changes have been: (a) summer fallow to conserve moisture, (b) irrigation, (c) new varieties, (d) fertilization, (e) pesticides, and (f) stubble mulching. Summer fallow, where land is left idle for one year and is kept clear of vegetation, stores moisture in the soil and is a standard practice where annual rainfall is less than 575 millimeters (mm). Irrigation has been increasing since 1950 (the second technology period), principally in the large producing states mentioned earlier. Plant breeding has developed a wide array of varieties that not only produce larger yields, but are resistant to disease, insects, and frost damage. In addition, protein content and milling qualities have been improved.

Wheat is not a heavy user of pesticides. Duffy and Hawthorn (1983) report that 42 percent of the area is treated with herbicides, 3 percent with insecticides, and only 1 percent with fungicides. The fungicide statistic is misleading because virtually all of the seed is treated with a fungicide to protect against seed borne diseases such as smut, seed rot, and seedling blight. This treatment, however, is done before the seed is planted.

Controls for insects consist of late planting to control hessian fly, and insecticides may be used against a variety of insects such as fall armyworm, grasshoppers, cutworms, and so forth. In general, insecticide treatment of winter wheat is not economically justified.

Because winter wheat is seeded in the fall, it is not usually subject to severe weed problems. Tillage is the most effective way to control weeds, and herbicide use is seldom economical.

Data leave no doubt that technology adopted in production of maize and winter wheat has increased yields significantly. The questions of the effect of this technology on yield variability, the correlation of regional yields, and the variability of production are not so obvious.

Empirical Findings on Yield Variability

Through the use of a trend-area-weather model, it is possible to separate the yield variability explained by weather from the unexplained error term, permitting a closer examination of the influence of technology on yield variability due to weather. The yield variability measures due to weather refer in this section to normalized weather unless otherwise stated.

There are statistically significant increases in weather-determined yield variance between technology periods in 86 percent of the maize crop reporting districts and in 88 percent of the winter wheat crop reporting districts (table 22.1). Additionally, 76 percent of the maize crop reporting districts displayed statistically significant increases in unexplained yield variability between the two periods. That is, the unexplained variance increased in the high technology period. The source of this variation is believed to be due to unobserved weather factors and management capabilities related to modern, more complex technology.

TABLE 22.1 Crop-reporting districts with statistically different variance measures between low- and high-technology periods

Type of Variance	CRD Count	Maize	Winter Wheat
Statistical difference in error variance	No. of CRDs	52	4
	Percentage of total	76.5	15.4
Statistical difference in weather variance	No. of CRDs	59	23
	Percentage of total	86.8	88.5

TABLE 22.2 Crop-reporting districts with no statistical difference in error variance but with statistical difference in normalized weather variance between low- and high-technology periods

CRD Count	Maize	Winter Wheat
Number of CRDs	15	19
Percentage of total	22.1	73.1

No statistical difference in the absolute unexplained variance between technology periods implies that variability difference around the trend, if it exists, is due to observed weather. Only 22 percent of the crop reporting districts for maize were found to have no statistical significance in unexplained error variance, while exhibiting a statistically significant difference in variance due to weather. For winter wheat, the corresponding figure was 73 percent (table 22.2). The conclusion from this is that the increased wheat yield variability associated with adoption of modern technology can be explained principally by observed weather. This is not the case for maize.

Relative variability due to weather between technology periods decreased for the majority of crop reporting districts for both crops, but increased for 35 percent of winter wheat crop reporting districts. Therefore, while relative variability due to weather generally decreases, the pattern is not uniform.

The effect on the yield variability measure by extending the samples from 15 to some 50 years (normalizing the weather) was examined. The observed weather variables were measured as deviations from the mean of the period. To eliminate effects of different weather in the technology periods, the means of the observed weather variables were computed based on the 51 years of weather covered by the two periods. The values of the weather variables were then measured as deviations from the 51-year mean as a measure of "normal" weather. These effects should indicate how the weather patterns during the two 15-year periods compare to that of the larger sample. Absolute yield variability for the low-technology period decreased for 58 percent and 61 percent of the maize and winter wheat crop reporting districts, respectively. The opposite result occurred for the high-technology period, increasing for 62 percent and 76 percent of the maize and winter wheat crop reporting districts, respectively. The conclusion is that, in general, absolute yield variability due to weather was higher during the low-technology period and lower during the high-technology period for both crops.

Skewness of Yield

Although previous studies conducted on experimental data indicated that yield distributions are skewed and the degree of skewness is influenced by technology, these properties are not documented at the crop reporting district level of aggregation. Six groups of skewness are categorized with the skewness range of each group loosely based on Pearson's (1936) statistic. According to Pearson's statistic, values of relative skewness greater than 1.0 or less than -1.0 with 14 degrees of freedom are statistically significantly different from zero at the 0.05 level of Type I error. With 50 degrees of freedom, skewness values of greater than 0.5 or less than -0.5 do not allow rejection of the null hypothesis at the 0.05 level.

The percentage of statistically significant negative skewness measures of yield due to normalized weather (less than -1.0) is 25 percent for the low technology period versus 4 percent for the high technology period for maize. For winter wheat, none of the crop reporting districts exhibited negative skewness of the unexplained variation during either of the technology periods with normalized weather.

With low technology, 70 percent of the maize crop reporting districts exhibited nonskewness in contrast to 84 percent with high technology. In the case of winter wheat, 19 percent were positively skewed under low technology, while 100 percent were nonskewed under high technology.

Skewness results indicate that, for maize, a substantial number of the yield distributions for crop reporting districts may not be normal, while for winter wheat, normality is more likely. In the case of maize, technology improvement has resulted in a tendency toward positive skewness, while for winter wheat, the effect of technology has been a tendency toward normality. Therefore, it appears that technology has increased the probability of less than average yields for maize for certain crop reporting districts. However, the majority of crop reporting districts for maize and wheat have nonskewed distributions of the unexplained yield variation for both technology periods (French, Schroder, and Headley 1985, table 5). Based on these results, variance measures are probably good indicators of the variability of crop production at the regional level.

Inter-Area Maize Yield Correlations

Hazell (1984) found that increased cereal yield variability and co-variability account for the major proportion of increased production variability and that, at the state level of aggregation, crop yield correlation was the major factor. He also showed that the number of positive significant correlations increased for maize and decreased for all other cereals.

While this study does not provide a focused test of whether the level of aggregation can influence the results, it does raise questions about the variability that is lost in aggregation and its influence on correlation. We now address the question of maize yield correlations at the crop reporting district level. Since crop reporting districts are smaller than states, they tend to be more homogeneous with respect to soils, climate, and crop technology and, accordingly, are grouped into the three production regions described in the data section. Only crop reporting districts with substantial maize production were included in the analysis.

Approach to the Study

Several yield variability measures are available for use in the analysis. Gross yield is usually rejected because of the positive effect of technology over time. Gross yield correlations across regions are expected to be higher than if yield is first detrended. However, comparisons of across region correlations based on gross yield should offer some general idea of whether yields in different areas tend to become more strongly correlated as the level of crop technology has increased.

A more important question concerns the joint behavior of yields given the two technologies. To approach this question using time-series data, it is necessary to remove the effect of systematic factors which vary with time such as technology and land quality. Therefore, yield detrended for changing technology and land quality differences becomes the appropriate measure of yield's variability under the differing technologies.

Three distinct measures of yield variability are used here to examine the time-series relationship of maize yield variability across crop reporting districts after removing the effect of trend. The three measures are: (a) gross yield, (b) normalized yield due to measured climatic factors, and (c) unexplained yield variability. Two different indicators of how the correlations have changed between the two periods follow. First, the number of statistically significant correlations and their signs will be reported and compared for each of the yield variability measures for each of the two periods. Second, the number of correlations which were significantly different in a statistical sense will be reported to indicate the extent to which positive correlations of yields between areas may or may not have increased.

A statistical test of the difference between the pairs of correlations, one for each time period, will give a much more precise indicator of whether correlations have actually increased with modern technology. The test used is based on Student's t distribution and is given as:

$$t_\infty = (Z_1 - Z_2)/[1/(n_1 - 3) + 1/(n_2 - 3)]^{0.5},$$

where the subscripts represent the two samples, one for each time period (Ostle 1954, p. 185). The Zs are a transformation of the correlation coefficients (r) given as:

$$Z_i = (0.5)[\log_e (1 + r) - \log_e (1 - r)],$$

with a variance of $\sigma^2_z = 1/(n - 3)$. The test is performed on each correlation for each measure of yield variability. The test is only an approximation since the variable Z is only approximately normally distributed. However, it will give a general indication of the statistical significance of the difference between correlation coefficients.

Correlations and the measures derived from them are calculated as reported based on the three major regions, the Corn Belt (CB), the northern Plains (NP) and the Lake states (LS). They are classified as within region correlations or across region correlations. Therefore, there are six groupings of information, one for each region, and three across regions, (CB-NP, CB-LS, and NP-LS). The logic for treating these measures by regions is as follows. Because of the agricultural similarities within each of the regions it is expected that the correlations of yields for pairs of crop reporting districts within a region should be higher than the yield correlations for pairs of crop reporting districts each from a different region. Similarities in weather patterns, soils, crop variation, and other factors should tend to increase yield correlations within the regions. There is enough difference among each of these three regions that it is expected that the across region correlation would not have increased as much as the within region correlation with the adoption of modern technology.

Correlation Results

From the statistically significant correlations for the two time periods, several preliminary conclusions can be drawn (table 22.3). There is a higher percentages of positive statistically significant gross yield correlations in the earlier period than after adoption of modern technology, although all percentages exceed 70 percent except for two across region classifications. In general, the within region correlations are higher than the across region correlations, as was expected. However, the higher percentage of positive gross yield correlations could be due to the influences of technology on yield.

Comparison of the correlations of gross yield with yield correlations

TABLE 22.3 Percentage of statistically significant crop-reporting district yield correlations for maize in the United States

	Gross Yield		Normalized Climate		Error	
Regions and Periods	Neg.	Pos.	Neg.	Pos.	Neg.	Pos.
Northern Plains						
1931–46	0.0	98.5	0	77.8	0.0	19.4
1967–81	0.0	78.6	0	77.8	5.5	16.7
Lake states						
1931–46	0.0	97.1	0	88.9	0.0	30.1
1962–81	0.0	88.2	0	88.9	0.0	57.5
Corn Belt						
1931–46	0.0	91.2	0	93.6	0.2	35.1
1967–81	0.0	76.9	0	84.9	0.6	22.7
Corn Belt–Northern Plains						
1931–46	0.0	73.0	0	96.8	0.8	10.1
1967–81	0.0	78.4	0	76.7	0.8	13.2
Corn Belt–Lake states						
1931–46	0.1	86.7	0	72.8	1.1	23.5
1962–81	0.0	43.1	0	69.3	5.3	5.7
Northern Plains–Lake states						
1931–46	0.0	84.1	0	71.0	4.9	5.6
1962–81	0.0	61.3	0	91.4	2.5	11.1

due to measured climatic factors and the unexplained yield shows that the climatic factors lead to a high number of positive correlations, while a low proportion of unexplained yield is significantly correlated. This indicates that the measured climatic factors determine much of the correlation in yields between producing regions after eliminating the systematic effect of technology. Other factors, which could include price-responsive input adjustments, do not contribute as much to yield correlations. This relationship holds for the earlier period as well as the modern technology period. In general, the results do not differ much between the two periods. The percentage of positive correlations fell in some cases and increased in very few for both climatically determined yield variability and the unexplained error. This result does not support the hypothesis that yield correlations across regions have increased with the adoption of modern technology. The above results only give gross indications; they do not tell how a given correlation between the two crop reporting districts changes with modern technology.

TABLE 22.4 Percentage of statistically significant differences between crop-reporting district yield correlations for periods 1931-1946 and 1967-1981 for maize in the United States

Regions	Gross Yield		Normalized Climate		Error	
	Neg.	Pos.	Neg.	Pos.	Neg.	Pos.
Northern Plains	0.7	17.7	11.1	0	0	11.1
Lake states	0	12.0	1.3	8.5	5.9	0
Corn Belt	2.2	6.4	0	8.8	1.7	7.6
Corn Belt-Northern Plains	1.3	1.1	1.3	0.8	1.9	0.8
Corn Belt-Lake states	0.8	18.1	3.3	1.9	2.2	12.3
Northern Plains-Lake states	0.3	8.3	1.2	0	6.2	3.7

Table 22.4 reports the results of the statistical tests performed on the different measures of yield correlations. The general findings reported above are supported-that is, no difference between time periods. The percentage of yield correlations found to be statistically higher for the period of modern technology is very low for all measures of yield variability in all regions. In addition, there are a number of yield correlations that have actually decreased with modern technology. In the overwhelming majority of cases, the correlation is not statistically different between the two periods. For all measures of yield variability, the number of statistically significant correlations was less than 20 percent.

Summary

Yield variability for maize and winter wheat has been examined by comparing nonsystematic mean yield distributions at the crop reporting district level for periods characterized as low and high technology. States in the United States where these crops were considered major were included in the study. The nonsystematic variability was represented by the distribution of the unexplained error where the nonsystematic variability due to weather was included in the model along with linear trend and planted area, the last as a proxy for land quality. In this way, the variability due to observable weather was separated from the rest of the unexplained yield variance. It also allowed weather's effects to be normalized to provide equivalent weather patterns for both the low- and high-technology periods.

Absolute variability has increased with technology for both crops. The analysis indicates, however, that for winter wheat, the increased variance is due to observed weather variables and not to unexplained variance around trend. Relative variability behavior across crop reporting districts cannot be generalized. In the majority of districts, the cv of unexplained yield variance declined for maize and winter wheat, however, several districts showed an increase in such relative variation for winter wheat.

Comparison of yield variability with actual versus normalized weather showed that yield variability due to weather was greater than normal over the early, low-technology period. Greater weather induced instability during the earlier period reinforces the conclusion that detrended absolute yield variability has increased with technology.

Along with improvements in the technological package adopted by crop producers in the United States, there has been an increase in absolute risk of yield loss. Relative risk has decreased in many of the crop reporting districts but has also increased in substantial proportions of maize districts. Increased risk can be attributed directly to observable weather for wheat and partially so for maize. This implies a definite weather–technology interaction.

Increased risk implies that farmers face greater chances of financial loss due to higher yield variability associated with greater use of purchased inputs. This has potential implications for future adoption of technology. Maize producers, given their high exposure to relative yield risk, have an increased incentive to adopt technology that will protect them from downside risk. This implies the potential for increased use of pesticides and irrigation in the future as a response to greater exposure to financial loss.

Evidence was not found to support the hypothesis that adoption of modern technology is associated with higher yield correlations across geographical areas. Since this is contrary to Hazell's (1984) finding, it may be helpful to speculate about the reasons for the contrasting results.

This study used a disaggregated data set based on the smaller crop reporting districts, rather than states as units of observation. Aggregation to the state level may reduce variability and, therefore, reduce much of the expected offsetting cross variability between areas. However, the high percentage of positive correlations found here suggests that the presence or absence of the offsetting effect is not a function of the level of aggregation and does not explain the difference from the results of Hazell.

Differing periods were chosen in the two studies for contrasting the effects of modern technology. The periods used here were chosen to ensure a sharp contrast in technology. The periods used by Hazell were not separated by any extended period of time and were not based on specific technological differences. Another important factor is that climatic differences between the two periods were not taken into consideration. Given the strong influence of climatic factors on yield correlations found here, it may be that differences in climatic variability over each of the two periods adversely affected Hazell's results. Higher correlation of yields across areas in his later period may be attributable to higher correlation of climatic factors during that period. This is a research question that needs attention.

One other possible explanation for the differences between the two studies might be the similarities between the technology of the earlier period and modern technology. In the former, maize varieties were more varied across regions; they were similar in their susceptibility to major insect plagues, droughts, and other factors. Then, as now, commonality existed in the response of varieties to environmental factors, although of a different kind. There may be some offsetting effects here which were not as evident for the periods used in the Hazell study because the periods studied did not include the times when open pollinated maize or the early hybrids were dominant.

Finally, the results here indicate that the climatic factors in this study are principally responsible for the positive yield correlations across geographical areas. These correlations are significant for both periods under study, yet there are not a large number of statistically significant increases in the yield correlation. This leads to the conclusion that inter-area yield correlations are not really higher under modern technology.

On the aggregate level, there is a greater potential for variability in total supply and product prices. Supply variability depends on the relationship between all crop reporting districts; the higher the correlation between yields, the greater will be the overall variability. Variation in supply depends on the fluctuation in planted area, a variable dependent on general economic conditions and farm policy. This study does not directly address the question of aggregate supply instability or its solution; it does indicate the possibility of such a problem.

PART IV

Impacts of Yield Variability and Implications for Policy

23 Can Yield Variability Be Offset by Improved Information? The Case of Rice in India

VISHVA BINDLISH, RANDOLPH BARKER, AND
TIMOTHY D. MOUNT

Previous chapters have shown that, for many countries, the variability of total cereal production around trend has increased since the introduction of the high-yielding varieties (HYVs). Whether this increased variability translates into additional risk and uncertainty for individual decision makers (especially farmers and government officials) depends on their ability to forecast production each year. Accurate forecasts enable decision makers to adjust their resource allocations in order to maximize efficiency each year. It is only when production changes cannot be accurately anticipated at the time of making resource allocative decisions that the possibility of resource misallocation and economic loss arises.

Measurement of the impact of HYVs on the risk and uncertainty confronting decision makers should, therefore, focus on measuring changes in the variability of their forecast errors. That is, the relevant model is the difference between actual and forecasted output rather than between actual and trend output. In this chapter, we quantify these relationships for rice production in India.

Role of Expectations

In a regression framework, expectations are generally denoted by the mean output conditional on the given value(s) of the explanatory variable(s), that is,

$$E[Y|X], \qquad (23.1)$$

where Y represents output and X the explanatory variable(s).

Estimating expectations in this framework amounts to predicting the mean value of output that corresponds to given levels of X. Accordingly, the real issue here is one of selecting the components of X such that they appropriately reflect expectations about the future output. In previous studies, X has been invariably equated to a time trend ($X = t$), albeit that trend is entered separately for the pre- and post-green-revolution periods under the assumption of a structural change. The present chapter, however, takes the position that the selection of the X depends on whose expectations are being considered. It argues that there is need to distinguish between the government's and farmers' expectations. In forming their expectations, both government and farmers are unlikely to have access to the same information. For instance, the government will not have the intimate information on current input use that farmers do. Insofar as the elements of X embody the information that can reasonably be assumed as a basis for estimating expectations, it follows that they need to be specified distinctly for the government and farmers. Obviously the distinct sets of X are likely to lead to different values for the mean predicted output.

Definitions of Expectations

The Government's Expectations

Both sets of expectations defined for the government are predicated on the belief that there is little or no information on farmers' input use in a current year. In fact, one of the two definitions presumes that the government has no information at all on current inputs. Consequently, it postulates that the government has adaptive expectations relative to the yield levels attained in the past (in terms of equation 23.1); X refers to lagged values of Y: $E[Y_t|Y_{t-1}, Y_{t-2} \ldots]$. As such, a dynamic component is imputed to the expectations whereby they are assumed to be regularly updated. The updating process takes account of fresh information as it becomes available. Probably the more recent information should receive greater weight in the formulated expectations. It seems reasonable to hypothesize that the yield level expected by the government in a current year would correspond to the weighted average of the yields achieved in a number of previous years, with the weights declining in time.

The second definition of expectations from the government's perspective utilizes time trends. This definition presupposes that the government has information on the areas planted separately to the high-yielding and traditional varieties of rice, which it uses to forecast "average" yields (average of the two varieties). Subsequently, the forecasting process is hypothesized to be based on the proportion of the total rice area planted to each variety—the two proportions being trended. That is, in terms of $E[Y|X]$, $X = (tw, t(1 - w))$, or

$$E[Y] = f(tw, t(1 - w)) \qquad (23.2)$$

where, Y denotes the "average" yield of rice, t the year, and w and $(1 - w)$ the proportions of the total rice area planted to the high-yielding and traditional varieties, respectively.

In this hypothesis it is argued that, before the HYVs were introduced, the government's expectations were only a function of t ($w = 0$, and $(1 - w) = 1$). However, since their introduction, these expectations have become a function of a weighted trend—the weights being the proportional shares of the high-yielding and traditional varieties in the total rice area.

Farmers Expectations

Nearly 60 percent of India's rice production is still obtained under rainfed conditions. Juxtaposed with this is the fact that rice has considerable water requirements. Consequently, a key source of the uncertainty surrounding rice yields at the farm level in India must inevitably relate to the stochastic nature of the growing season rainfall. Existing empirical work (Binswanger 1980, Jodha 1981) affirms that Indian farmers are, in general, risk averse and are concerned with staving off the deleterious consequences of uncertain rainfall. Thus, any hypotheses regarding yield expectations of Indian farmers need to recognize the exigent role of the uncertainty created by rainfall.

Growing season rainfall influences the yield relationship for a crop in two interrelated ways: (a) it enters directly into the relationship as an input, albeit stochastically; and (b) it affects the response to the other inputs that are under farmers' control (land, fertilizer, seeds, etc.). Because this rainfall is unknown at the time of planting when farmers are required to make decisions about controlled inputs, the risk confronting them arises for both of these reasons. Thus, it appears reasonable to hypothesize that the levels that farmers decide on for the controlled inputs (including areas) must be dictated by their risk-related prognoses concerning the future growing-season rains. Similarly, farmers' yield expectations are likely to be influenced by their prognoses of the growing-season rains. Factors pertaining to the availability of irrigation could potentially modify the risk that farmers associate with rainfall.

However, despite the importance ascribed to stochastic rainfall, it is unlikely to be the only source of variability at the farm level. There are other uncontrolled random factors (pests, disease, etc.) that change the true response of rice yields to the controlled inputs from year to year. Indeed, if farmers do predict the growing season rainfall adequately and make the necessary adjustments in input levels, stochastic rainfall should account for a relatively small portion of the total variability. Therefore, although farmers' yield expectations may be defined primarily with respect to rainfall, it is nonetheless appropriate to explain the variability around these expectations both in terms of the stochastic rainfall and the other random factors.

As opposed to rainfall, the other random factors are difficult to quantify and cannot be entered directly into estimated models; their combined effect is generally subsumed in the computed residuals. Nevertheless, a procedure does exist whereby such effect can be distinguished from the effect of stochastic rainfall for the purpose of analyzing the sources of variability (de Janvry 1972). The procedure can be operationalized in the ex ante and ex post sense of the expected versus the actual mean response. Thus, two econometric models need to be estimated. One of the models is estimated using the real levels of the controlled inputs, along with levels representing farmers' prognoses of the stochastic rainfall. This model predicts the expected mean response ($\tilde{Y}$). Correspondingly, the other model (the "structural" model) predicts the actual mean response ($\hat{Y}$); in the structural model, all inputs (including rainfall) are incorporated at their real levels. Thus, variability due to rainfall can be measured in terms of the difference between the mean yields predicted by the two models:

$$\tilde{e} = \tilde{Y} - \hat{Y}. \qquad (23.3)$$

The variability accruing from the other random factors can be measured relative to the difference between the yields that farmers actually achieve (Y) and the mean yields predicted by the structural model:

$$\hat{e} = Y - \hat{Y}. \qquad (23.4)$$

In turn, it follows that the total variability around farmers' expectations can be measured with reference to

$$\tilde{e} + \hat{e}. \qquad (23.5)$$

Data Considerations

The empirical analysis in this chapter is based on annual data for individual Indian districts and covers the period 1956/57 to 1978/79. These data were either collected from the official publications of the state governments and of the central government (Directorate of Economics and Statistics) or else were secured directly from the statistical offices in each state. Specifically, 44 districts are included in the analysis; they are all from the top 100 rice-producing districts in India, according to recent production data. The included districts are located in seven Indian states (Andhra Pradesh, Haryana, Karnataka, Madhya Pradesh, Maharashtra, Punjab, and Tamil Nadu) and constitute a wide range of contrasting situations vis à vis such ponderables as environment, yield levels, adoption rates for the HYVs, and irrigation.

The decision is taken at the outset to estimate all of the required econometric models by pooling together the time-series data for the individual districts. Further, it was decided to estimate these models in terms of the production of rice. The year-to-year changes in output and input levels within districts are generally not large enough to permit the required amount of variation. But, data relating to production tend to be characterized by greater variation than those for yields since they incorporate the year-to-year changes not only in yields but also in areas.

Four models require estimation: a structural model, a model of farmers' expectations, and two models for the government's expectations. District level data are available, by crop, for irrigated areas and areas planted to the HYVs; data for unirrigated area and the area planted to traditional varieties can be derived using the total cropped area. Other inputs include monthly rainfall and the total use of fertilizer nutrients (the sum of N, P, and K) on all crops.

It is possible to theorize about the inputs that determine rice production in India. The actual estimation of a model is, however, conditioned by the existing data. In this context, there is no gainsaying that fertilizer nutrients and rainfall, irrigated and unirrigated area, as well as the areas planted to the high-yielding and traditional varieties, are all clearly potentially important determinants of rice output. Of the inputs for which data are unavailable, labor is also potentially important. It could be argued that, rather than being relegated to the residual term, its effects on output are likely to be absorbed by some of the included variables such as fertilizer and irrigation. Statistical methods, such as those relying on an analysis of covariance, could be employed to estimate the particular shares of rice and of other crops in the total consumption of fertilizer.

A complication arises with respect to specifying an estimable relationship for both the structural model and the model of farmers' expectations. It appears reasonable to assume that the high-yielding and traditional varieties of rice are characterized by different production functions. Nevertheless, data on production and inputs are not reported by variety, so these functions cannot be estimated separately. In order to overcome this problem and yet provide separate estimates for the two varieties, alternative specifications are examined in an exploratory way. The one finally settled upon in a pooled cross-section and time-series framework is the following:

$$Q_{it} = [(\alpha_o + \alpha_1 X_{it}) w_{it}] + [(\beta_o + \beta_1 X_{it})(1 - w_{it})], \quad (23.6)$$

where Q is the district production of rice, α_o and β_o are the unknown intercepts, α_1 and β_1 are the unknown slopes, X is the vector of inputs (the levels being district specific), w is the proportion of total rice area planted to the HYVs in a district, e is a stochastic residual, t refers to the year (1956/57 to 1978/79) and i denotes the district (44 districts).

This specification assumes that the same inputs are used with both varieties but that these inputs interact differently with each variety. The specification entails combining two regressions in which the proportional

TABLE 23.1 Slope estimates for the structural model, the model of farmers' expectations, and the model of the government's trend-based expectations

Variable	The Structural Model		Model of Farmers' Expectations		Government's Trend-based Expectations	
	Parameter	t	Parameter	t	Parameter	t
In interaction with w_{it} [a]						
Fertilizer	0.004	3.01	0.004	2.99	—	—
Fertilizer squared	0.0[b]	−3.47	0.0[b]	−3.52	—	—
Irrigated area	3.101	14.41	3.156	14.45	—	—
Unirrigated area	1.574	2.18	1.745	2.38	—	—
Actual Kharif rain	0.013	0.50	—	—	—	—
Expected Kharif rain	—	—	0.006	0.27	—	—
Time trend	—	—	—	—	14.528	5.78
In interaction with $1-w_{it}$ [a]						
Fertilizer	0.002	3.67	0.002	3.24	—	—
Fertilizer squared	0.0[b]	−2.55	0.0[b]	−2.37	—	—
Irrigated area	1.300	10.76	1.326	10.79	—	—
Unirrigated area	0.970	6.39	0.993	6.43	—	—
Actual Kharif rain	0.058	7.39	—	—	—	—
Expected Kharif rain	—	—	0.037	5.13	—	—
Time trend	—	—	—	—	3.411	5.25
R^2 adjusted	0.98		0.98		0.97	
Durban-Watson (DW) statistic	1.968		1.975		1.920	
Estimated standard error	2,623		2,718		4,510	

[a] w_{it} is the proportion of the total district area of rice planted to the high-yielding varieties. $1-w_{it}$ is that planted to the traditional varieties.
[b] Estimated value is too small to report.

shares of the two varieties in a district's total rice area each year (w_{it} and $1 - w_{it}$) are employed as weights. Interactions are then specified between the respective weights for the two varieties and the other inputs.

A separate intercept is incorporated for each variety. In order to estimate these separate intercepts, two auxiliary variables are created—one conforming to each variety as the districtwise "weight" for each variety for each year.

Estimated Models

The Structural Model

The postulated model to be estimated is as follows:

$$Q_{it} = \left(\sum_{k=1}^{44} \alpha_{ok} D_{kit} + \alpha_1 FERT_{it} + \alpha_2 FERT_{it}^2 + \alpha_3 IRR_{it} \right.$$

$$\left. + \alpha_4 NIR_{it} + \alpha_5 KH_{it} \right) w_{it} + \left(\sum_{k=1}^{44} \beta_{ok} D_{kit} + \beta_1 FERT_{it} \right.$$

$$\left. + \beta_2 FERT_{it}^2 + \beta_3 IRR_{it} + \beta_4 NIR_{it} + \beta_5 KH_{it} \right)(1 - w_{it}) + e_{it},$$

(23.7)

where $i, t, Q, w, (1 - w)$ and e have already been defined, D_{kit} is a zero-one district variable, *FERT* refers to the district consumption of fertilizer (metric tons), *IRR* is the district area of irrigated rice (10^3 ha), *NIR* is the district area of unirrigated rice ('000 ha), *KH* is the total actual rain received during the Kharif season (June + July + August + September in mm) in a district, and the α and β are the unknown coefficients.

The postulated relationship is essentially a linear one, although a quadratic term for fertilizer is included. As a preliminary step in the model estimation, the hypothesis that the response relationship is identical across districts is tested. This hypothesis implies that the two separate intercept terms (one for each variety) do not differ by district. A standard F test is applied based on the estimation of the model both with and without the set of district variables. The computed F statistic is larger than the corresponding critical value (at the 1 percent level of significance), leading to the rejection of the null hypothesis of homogeneity. Consequently, the full model with the district variables is chosen.

The model is estimated by ordinary least squares. Table 23.1 presents the slope estimates. With an adjusted R^2 of 0.98, the model fits extremely well. Further, the signs of all the coefficients are consistent with prior expectations: whether these inputs interact with the HYVs or the traditional varieties, one would expect a positive production response to fertilizer, irrigated area, unirrigated area, and rainfall.

In terms of their relative magnitudes (that is, the response to an input when it interacts with the HYVs versus when it interacts with the traditional varieties), the slope estimates for the individual inputs conform to prior expectations. The results indicate that rice production responds more favorably to fertilizer use, irrigated area and unirrigated area when these inputs interact with the HYVs. Rainfall has a larger impact on rice production in interaction with the traditional varieties; the only nonsignificant t ratio obtained related to the interaction between Kharif rainfall and the HYVs. This may reflect the fact that traditional varieties are more frequently grown under rainfed conditions than the HYVs.

Model of Farmers' Expectations

The model needed for estimating farmers' expectations must be identical to that specified for the structural relationship in equation (23.7). The one exception relates to Kharif rainfall—the variable for actual Kharif rainfall has to be replaced with another denoting farmers' anticipation of that rainfall. What determines farmers' prognoses about the growing season rainfall?

It seems reasonable to suppose that farmers will utilize whatever information is available on rainfall up to the time of planting. As such, farmers have an opportunity to observe the pattern of rainfall in June and July before they need to make their planting and input use decisions. Consequently, it is possible that farmers' expectations about rainfall in the Kharif growing season (August and September) are based on the actual rainfall received during June and July.

As a result of this hypothesis, the following equation is estimated individually (by ordinary least squares) for the 44 districts:

$$KH_{it} = \beta RN^*_{it} + e_{it}, \qquad (23.8)$$

where, KH is the total actual Kharif rainfall (the sum of the rains received in June, July, August, and September in mm); RN^* is the sum of the rains received in June and July. The values of Kharif rainfall predicted by that equation for each district and year are subsequently substituted into the model of farmers' expectations to denote farmers' prognoses of the Kharif rainfall.

The ordinary least squares slope estimates for the model of farmers' expectations are presented in Table 23.1. What emerges clearly on comparing the corresponding slope estimates from the two models is the small difference between them. This is consistent with the view that farmers are probably able to predict input response under different rainfall conditions fairly accurately. Therefore, the available information determines both their yield expectations and their input use.

Model of the Government's Trend-based Expectations

The following model is estimated:

$$Q_{it} = \left(\sum_{k=1}^{44} \alpha_{ok} D_{kit} + \alpha_1 t_i\right) w_{it}$$

$$+ \left(\sum_{k=1}^{44} \beta_{ok} D_{kit} + \beta_1 t_i\right)(1 - w_{it}) + e_{it}, \quad (23.9)$$

where t takes on the values 1 through 23 (for 1956/57 to 1978/79). The slope estimates for the trended proportions of the total rice area planted to the two types of variety are presented in table 23.1. Relative to its counterpart, the estimate for the HYVs' proportion is considerably larger. This supports the contention that the government's trend-based expectations about "average" yields increase as the share of the high-yielding varieties in the total area of rice increases.

Model of the Government's Adaptive Expectations

The following distributed lag function is estimated:

$$Q_{it} = \sum_{k=1}^{44} \alpha_{ok} D_{kit} + \alpha_1 Q_{it-1} + \alpha_2 Q_{it-2}$$

$$+ \alpha_3 Q_{it-3} + \alpha_4 Q_{it-4} + e_{it}. \quad (23.10)$$

Rice production for each district is lagged four years. The choice of four years mainly reveals a desire not to "lose" too many of the earlier years in the lagging process.

The model was estimated on the basis of ordinary least squares, and table 23.2 contains the results.[1] These results conform to a priori reasoning. The slope coefficients are all statistically significant and positive in sign. Moreover, these slope coefficients become smaller as the number of years lagged becomes larger, revealing a declining lag structure. Also, the sum of the coefficients is less than one (0.83). The difference is accounted for by farmers' input use in a current year, which the government's adaptive expectations based on past production levels are unable to predict adequately.

1. The model was subsequently re-estimated on the assumption that the residuals were generated by a fourth-order autoregressive process. To operationalize this assumption, fourth-order differencing was done with respect to the original production series for each district. Although the resultant estimates of the coefficients also indicated a declining lag structure, they were negative for the third and fourth years, and were therefore deemed unacceptable.

TABLE 23.2 Slope estimates for the model of the government's adaptive expectations

Variable	Parameter	t
Production$_{t-1}$	0.336	9.02
Production$_{t-2}$	0.214	5.22
Production$_{t-3}$	0.181	4.20
Production$_{t-4}$	0.098	2.29
R^2 adjusted	0.96	
Estimated standard error of the regression	6,366	

Analysis of Rice Yield Variability

No attempt is made to re-estimate the models in the framework of generalized least squares with heteroscedasticity. That is considered unlikely to result in any substantial gain in the efficiency of the estimates. Although the focus of this analysis of variability is on yields, the estimation of all the models embodying hypothesized expectations has been in terms of rice production. In order to make the analysis possible, the residuals generated by the estimated production models for each district and year are divided by the corresponding data on area planted.

Two different methods are utilized for this analysis. Given that interest relates to yield variability at the aggregate level, one of these methods focuses directly on the pooled residuals for all districts. It computes a single estimate of the aggregate variance (footnote b in table 23.3 explains the method). As opposed to this pooled method, the second method, (cf., Hazell 1982 and Walker, ch. 6) considers the residuals by district; it computes the variances for individual districts, as well as the covariances among districts, and then takes the sum of the two.

In line with how expectations are denoted in equation (23.1), this chapter defines the variance as

$$\text{Var}[Y] = E\{[Y - E(Y|X)]^2\}. \tag{23.11}$$

Results of the Pooled Method

Table 23.3 compares the results of the pooled method for the two periods preceding and following the introduction of the HYVs.[2] The results for the government's trend-based expectations confirm those of past stud-

---

2. This chapter makes no presumption about when the HYVs were introduced; they were introduced in different districts at different times. Therefore, the term "period with the HYVs" as used here refers specifically to all those observations that correspond to the years when the HYVs have actually existed in individual districts.

TABLE 23.3 Estimated variance of aggregate rice yield with and without the high-yielding varieties

Period	Farmers' Expectations[a]	Government's Expectations	
		Trend Based	Adaptive
Period without HYVs[b]	0.122	0.175	0.465
Period with HYVs	0.057	0.184	0.218

[a]In defining farmers' expectations, a distinction was made between the variability due to rainfall alone and that due to other random factors. However, an ex post and ex ante analysis performed by juxtaposing the results of the model of farmers' expectations and those of the structural model indicates that the variability around farmers' expectations due to rainfall alone is quite negligible. (The resulting variances with respect to the ex post and ex ante difference are 0.0022 for the period without the HYVs, and 0.0003 for the period with the HYVs.) This is consistent with what was observed earlier about the small difference in the estimates of the two models. Therefore, the presentation is limited to the total variability around farmers' expectations (i.e., the combination of that due to rainfall and other random factors).

[b]The residuals are squared and summed over time and districts for each period. The sum of squared residuals thus obtained is then divided by $n-44$ (degrees of freedom associated with 44 districts) to get an estimate of the variance for each period. n refers to the total number of observations for all districts taken together. For the first period, $n = 455$ for the model of farmers' expectations and for the model of the trend-based expectations; however, for the adaptive expectations model (because of the four-year lag structure) it equals 279. In the case of the second period, $n = 557$ for all three models.

ies (Mehra 1981, Hazell 1982). That is, they indicate that the variability in Indian rice yields increased after the introduction of the HYVs. The results relating to farmers' expectations and to the government's adaptive expectations suggest quite the opposite. They suggest that the incidence of variability has been reduced by more than one-half since the introduction of the HYVs. Moreover, in terms of their relative size, the three sets of variances are markedly different. Noteworthy is the small size of the variance pertaining to farmers' expectations relative to the other two.

Results of the Variance–Covariance Method

As opposed to the intercrop analysis performed by Hazell (1982), the application of the variance–covariance method in this chapter relates to the yields of a single crop. Therefore, the method applied here considers the variance of rice yields at the aggregate level, comprised of two broad components: (a) the sum of the within-district yield variances, and (b) the sum of the interdistrict yield covariances (see footnote b in table 23.4).

In operational terms, this method amounts to computing the interdistrict variance–covariance matrices of the residuals associated with the estimated models. Once again, the results are quite different both in terms of

TABLE 23.4 Sums of district variances and interdistrict covariances with and without the high-yielding varieties

Period	Farmers' Expectations		Government's Expectations					
			Trend Based			Adaptive		
	Actual	Percent of Total	Actual	Percent of total	Actual	Percent of Total	Actual	Percent of Total
Period without HYVs								
Sum of district variances	3.62	57.7	5.72	27.1			4.08	10.4
Sum of interdistrict covariances[a]	2.65	42.3	15.41	72.9			35.34	89.6
Total[b]	6.27	100.0	21.13	100.0			39.42	100.0
Period with HYVs								
Sum of district variances	2.49	36.8	7.87	18.2			9.37	13.2
Sum of interdistrict covariances[a]	4.29	63.2	35.27	81.8			61.72	86.8
Total[b]	6.78	100.0	43.14	100.00			71.09	100.0

[a]The sum of two times the covariance between each pair of districts.
[b]$V(Y) = \Sigma_i V(y_i) + 2 \Sigma_{i \neq k} \text{cov}(y_i, y_k)$, where $V(Y)$ is the aggregate variance, and y_i and y_k are the yields in districts i and k.

their magnitudes and scope (table 23.4). In the case of farmers' expectations, the aggregate variance is small and increases only fractionally between the periods with and without the HYVs.

The sum of the interdistrict covariances shows an increase, both in relative and absolute terms with respect to farmers' expectations and the government's trend-based expectations. In the case of the government's adaptive expectations, however, it declines slightly in relative terms, although it increases by more than 75 percent in absolute terms. Nevertheless, what should be emphasized here, too, are the large differences in the magnitudes of the estimates obtained for the three sets of expectations.

Conclusions

This chapter is based on the premise that variability needs to be evaluated around carefully defined expectations, for they may lead to different conclusions about the incidence of variability. In particular, it is argued that the expectations held by the government and farmers about impending output are likely to differ. This is because expectations result in response to the information that is available ex ante concerning that output, and the two are unlikely to have access to the same information.

The results from both methods used to analyze variability in this chapter confirm the premise that the evaluation of variability around variously defined expectations leads to different outcomes. Indeed, a comparison of the results obtained separately from the two methods additionally suggests that these outcomes will differ depending on the method used to compute the aggregate variance. For instance, if one considers the government's trend-based expectations, both methods point to the conclusion that the variability in Indian rice yields has risen since the introduction of the HYVs. However, in the case of the government's adaptive expectations, the "pooled" method indicates that such variability has decreased while the variance–covariance method indicates that it has increased. As for farmers' expectations, the pooled method suggests that the level of variability accompanying Indian rice yields is now less than one-half of what it was before the HYVs were introduced; the variance–covariance method suggests that the level of variability has increased marginally.

The most revealing aspect about these results is the difference in the magnitudes of the variances estimated with respect to the three sets of expectations. In relation to both the pooled and the variance–covariance methods, the estimated variances are highest for the government's adaptive expectations and lowest for farmers' expectations, with the government's trend-based expectations falling in-between. As the amount of input-related information incorporated in the defined expectations is increased, there is a corresponding decrease in the measured variability.

The conclusions one reaches regarding the incidence of variability are largely determined (a) by how one defines the expectations around which variability is evaluated, and (b) by the statistical method used to measure that variability. Thus, the main conclusion here relates to researchers undertaking analyses of variability—they need both to define carefully the expectations around which variability is evaluated and to consider the rationale for the statistical measures used. At a policy level, all that can be concluded is that government officials need to gather timely information on farmers' use of crop areas and inputs. Governments are less likely to be caught by surprise if they incorporate such information in their forecasts of agricultural output.

24 Are Modern Cultivars More Risky? A Question of Stochastic Efficiency

JOCK R. ANDERSON, CARLY J. FINDLAY, AND
G. H. WAN

Some aspects of the sensitivity of results on variability have been noted by Anderson et al. (1987) and Flinn and Garrity (ch. 20) where, as in several chapters of part I, the question of whether increased variability has created difficulties for farmers was broached but not answered in an unequivocal manner. The question is returned to here, initially at the level of an individual farm and then at higher levels of aggregation.

A Single Farm Case Study

Aggregation across many farms may be a giant leap toward representativeness, but if the essence of problems concerning variability faced by individual farmers is lost in the process, perhaps more modest steps toward relevance are in order. Accordingly, data were gathered for an individual farm for which reliable data were available for a period spanning use of different wheat cultivars.

The farm (owned by J. R. Fischer and Sons of Boree Creek) operates in more or less typical rainfed conditions of the southern New South Wales (N.S.W.), Australia, wheat-growing area. Over the 21-year period 1964-84, wheat yields ranged from 0.3 tons per hectare (stubble crop 1982) to 4.2 tons per hectare (fallow crop 1983). Semidwarf cultivars were first grown in 1974 (on 27 percent of total area) and thereafter predominated (80, 73, 63, 69, 100, 100, 100, 100, 85, 100 percent for the following seasons, respectively). Has variability of yield changed with this shift to "modern cultivars"?

Tony Fischer (to whom the authors are indebted for access to these data) summarized his view of the situation as in table 24.1 and opined that, as the means for each crop were not significantly different (at, say 5 or 10 percent levels of significance, with t statistics of 1.58 and 1.47 for fallow and stubble crops, respectively) between periods/cultivar types, there was no clear-cut conclusion as to the impact of the switch to

TABLE 24.1 Wheat yields over time with changing cultivars

	Crop Grown					
	On Fallow			On Stubble		
Period/Cultivars	Mean	sd	cv	Mean	sd	cv
1964–74 (tall)	2.05	0.70	0.34	1.60	0.43	0.27
1975–84 (semi-dwarf)	2.47	0.98	0.40	1.94	0.95	0.50

semidwarf cultivars. He noted that little change had been made in areas cropped and fertilizer use over the period but that weed control and timeliness may have improved somewhat.

An alternative view is that, in a purely subjective overview, while means seem to have increased (by nearly 20 percent between periods, even if not in a sense of conventional statistical significance), standard deviation has increased even more dramatically. Comparing the pairs of standard deviations in a variance ratio test, fallow variances are not quite significantly different ($F = 1.98$) but the variance for post-1974 stubble yields is significantly larger than for the previous period ($F = 4.86$). In terms of coefficient of variation (cv), the approximately standard normal test statistics (ch. 1) are 0.54 and 2.55, respectively, indicating that stubble yields are also more variable in a relative sense post-1974.

The era of semidwarf wheat cultivars in this part of southern New South Wales does indeed seem to be characterized by higher variability, even after some allowance has been made for variable rainfall and unspecified trends over time. This is in line with the findings elsewhere (ch. 2), although at levels of aggregation beyond individual farms. Just why this should be so is not obvious, and the result may be a low-chance realization of phenomena that have not really changed inherently, or it may be a manifestation of the confounding of periods and cultivars in the circumstances observed, which surely do not constitute a well designed experiment to test hypotheses about cultivar–environment interactions. Notwithstanding such possible qualifications, the question remains as to whether any increased variability is of concern to the decision makers involved?

The data of table 24.1 (and later) are not definitive in this respect since they exhibit simultaneous increases in both mean and variance (and cv). Can insights into this potential trade-off between mean yield and variability of yield be gleaned without knowing more about the decision makers' attitudes towards risk and return? The answer is "maybe," if resort is made to the most general framework for addressing questions of changing risk, namely, to concepts of stochastic efficiency.

Invoking Stochastic Efficiency

It is assumed that, since cost and returns have been unaffected by cultivar choice, yield can serve as a surrogate for net returns. Accordingly, the yield data can be arrayed as empirical distribution functions using the "sparse data smoothing" procedure of Anderson (1973), and the comparison of yield distribution functions made for assessing stochastic dominance, as illustrated by Anderson (1974b). This is done in figure 24.1 with the data segregated as to crop type; stubble crops with broken lines, and fallow crops with unbroken lines representing smooth cumulative distribution functions (CDFs).

The pairwise comparisons reveal an essentially unequivocal result, in one case clearly (fallow) and in the other approximately (stubble): The modern (semidwarf) cultivar distribution first-stochastically dominates the traditional tall-cultivar distribution (nowhere lies to the left of the respective dominated distribution). Such a result means that, although the distribution with the higher mean may be more variable, it is not more risky in a very general sense, and it would be preferred by all decision makers (or at

FIGURE 24.1 Cumulative distribution functions for two cultivars and two crop histories

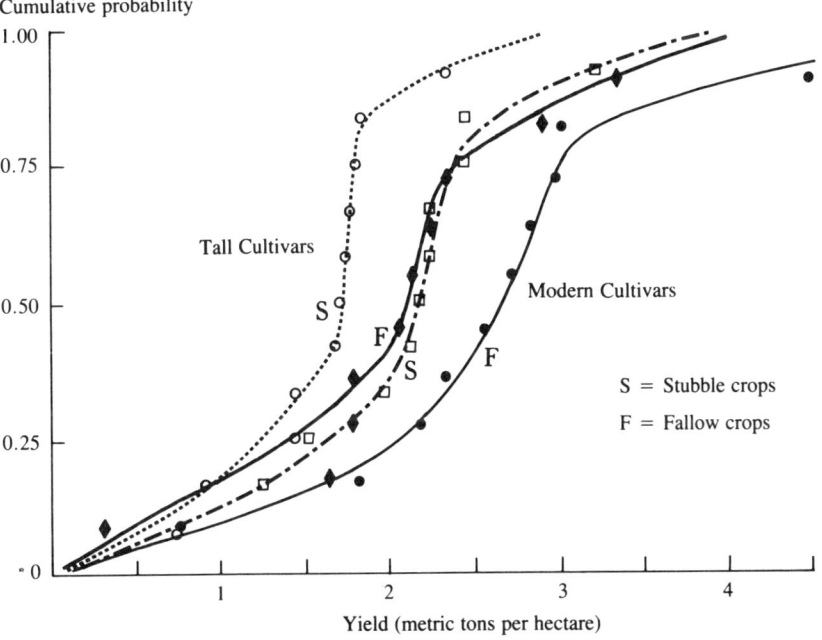

least all who prefer more to less of a desirable attribute, Anderson 1974b). There is thus no conflict or trade-off between mean returns and risk.

For unexplained reasons, modern cultivars of crops that feature dwarfed stature and other attributes, such as greater stem strength, disease resistance, and photoperiod insensitivity, often seem to perform not only with higher average yields but also somewhat more variably. The present single-farm case study over a 21-year period supports this typical observation but also suggests that the risk faced by the farmer is not effectively increased. This finding is consistent with the rapid adoption of such modern cultivars in this region of the Australian wheat industry.

Analysis at the Level of Local Government Areas

The introductory example was chosen to be relatively straightforward in several senses, including the simplicity of dealing with one decision maker or unit. Interpretations of choice among aggregated probability distributions implicitly involving several or many decision units is much more complicated, if not rather opaque. Notwithstanding these difficulties, the same ideas of stochastic efficiency are invoked at the level of local government areas (LGAs) using the New South Wales data described by Anderson et al. (1988).

Stochastic dominance analysis requires comparison of cumulative distribution functions. The data set of yields by local government area was analyzed in terms of the two periods 1946-74 and 1977-84. Due to the scarcity of yield observations for the second period, the sparse data method (Anderson 1973) was again used in plotting the cumulative distribution functions of yield for each of the 45 local government areas and for New South Wales as a whole.

Assuming, this time less defensibly, that costs and unit returns are not influenced by cultivar choice, the interperiod comparison of cumulative distribution functions for each local government area reveals that the second-period yield distribution (i.e., for modern wheat cultivars) rather clearly first-stochastically dominates (FSD) the first-period yield distribution (i.e., for traditional tall cultivars) in seven of the 45 local government areas (a representative example is shown in figure 24.2), and less clearly so in 14 cases (another representative example is shown in figure 24.3). The example of figure 24.3 exhibits essentially coincident distributions in the lower range of yield but with the second-period cumulative distribution function being otherwise to the right of that for the first period. For these 21 (= 7 + 14) local government areas in which second-period yield first-stochastically dominates the first-period yield, it can be said that modern cultivars offer at least the same and generally a greater probability of ob-

FIGURE 24.2 Example of cumulative distribution functions with second-period wheat yield that is first stochastic dominant over first-period yield, as found in seven local government areas

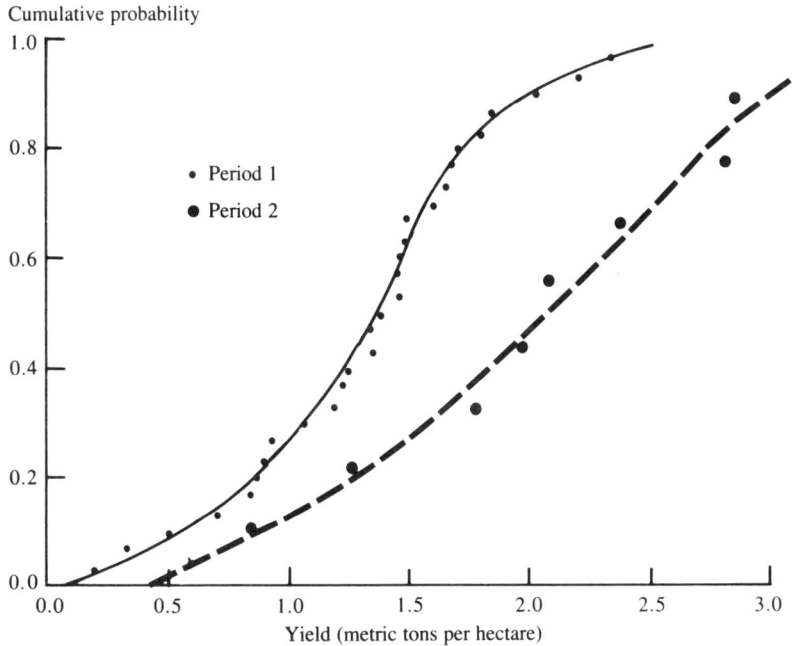

SOURCE: Based on Local Government Area 22.

taining more than any specified feasible yield than do traditional cultivars.

Needless to say, there is considerable subjectivity in such appraisal given the sparsity of the data, particularly for the second period. This is especially so in the left-hand tails of the distributions, which depend crucially on the single observation used as the estimate of the one-ninth fractile, and the other smoothing procedures of Anderson (1973), which recognize the strict non-negativity of yields. Caution must then be taken in interpreting the comparisons of the distributions for the other 24 cases, depicted here by the representative example of figure 24.4.

In such cases, there is a crossover of the cumulative distribution functions in their lower tails so that the generally right-most distribution of modern cultivars with the higher mean does not first-stochastically dominate the earlier distribution. Beginning at the left tail, the potentially dominant distribution is the one which has the highest zero fractile, that is, the

FIGURE 24.3 Example of cumulative distribution functions with second-period wheat yield that is first stochastic dominant over first-period yield, as found in 14 local government areas

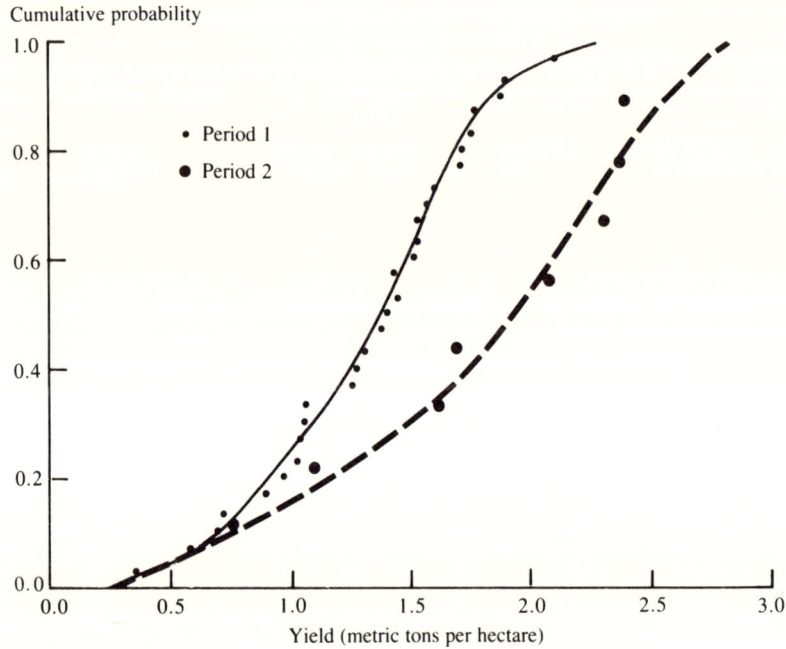

SOURCE: Based on Local Government Area 39.

more favorable outcome for the most disastrous possibility. This distribution would second-stochastically dominate and be preferred by all risk averse agents, if the area between the cumulative distribution functions (which here are "simply related" or cross once only) to the left of the intersection exceeded the area between the functions to the right (Anderson, Dillon, and Hardaker 1977, p. 285), but it does not.

Literal application of the simplest rules of stochastic dominance thus does not order the distributions in more than one-half of the local government area distributions. Strong statements of likely preferences over these distributions by concerned decision makers are not immediately possible. To make any such ordering requires further assumptions about underlying preferences. In the present instance, there are two ready ways of resolving the question in favor of the modern cultivars. Most arbitrarily, the position can be taken that, since the left crossover area is relatively small, the modern distribution approximately first-stochastically dominates the traditional (Anderson 1974b). A more subtle approach is to argue that if the

FIGURE 24.4 Example of cumulative distribution functions with second-period wheat yield that is second stochastic dominant over first-period yield, as found in 24 local government areas

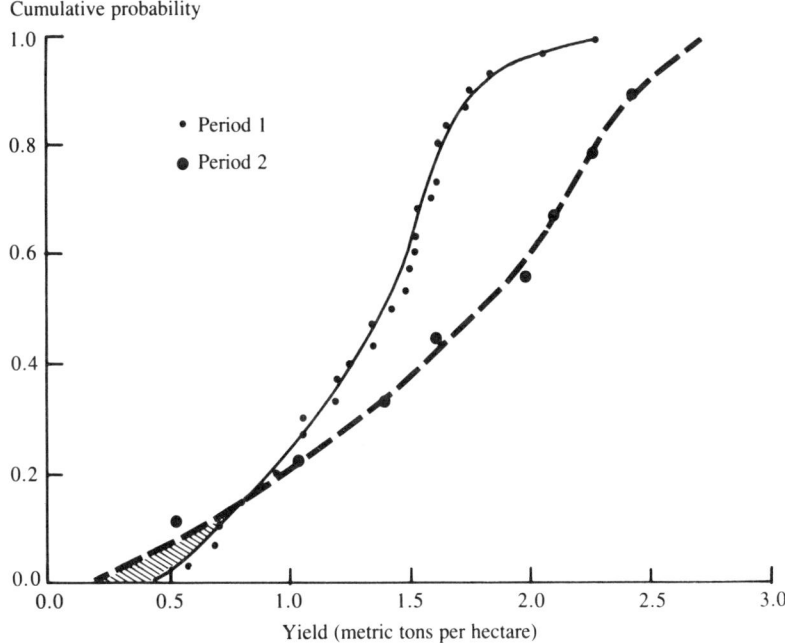

SOURCE: Based on Local Government Area 24.

more complex ordering rules of stochastic dominance with respect to a function were used (Meyer 1977, King and Robison 1981), the modern distribution would second-stochastically dominate the traditional for a restricted range of mildly risk averse agents. At the level of aggregation of local government areas (typically about 10^5 ha), very moderate levels of risk aversion are indeed appropriate (Anderson 1983).

In summary it appears that, in all cases, it can safely be assumed that the distribution of modern cultivars is to be preferred to (is less risky than) that of traditional varieties. Perhaps unsurprisingly, this also holds at the state (N.S.W.) level of aggregation (the CDFs are related in the same manner as depicted in Figure 24.3).

Conclusion

Data from an individual farm, 45 local government areas, and the state of New South Wales all support the view that in spite of the increasing variances and coefficients of variation of yields that seem to be associated with the shift to modern cultivars in the past decade, advances in mean performance have been sufficient to make the modern technologies not more risky than the traditional varieties and farming practices, and thus to be highly adoptable. This generalization is supported by rapid adoption of modern cultivars to the present high levels of use. Presumably, similar phenomena are to be found in many other parts of the world in which modern cultivars are widely used.

25 Yield and Household Income Variability in India's Semi-Arid Tropics

THOMAS S. WALKER

Yield and production stability figure explicitly in the mandates of several of the international agricultural research centers. Much of the investment in breeding, pathology, entomology, and physiology at the centers is aimed at developing higher and more stable-yielding, improved varietal technologies. These technologies have consequences for output, equity, and nutrition. Could they also improve the welfare of farm households by generating substantial reductions in the variability of household income and consumption? Such potential welfare improvements, associated with smoothing fluctuations in household income and consumption, are referred to as risk benefits in the stabilization literature of economics (Newbery and Stiglitz 1981). What is the potential for improved varietal technologies to generate readily visible risk benefits? Should economists assign additional positive benefits to varietal technologies that reduce yield or output variance over and above their consequences on mean yield or output, equity, and nutrition?

This chapter responds to those questions by examining the nexus between crop yield stability and household income variability for resource-poor farm households in India's semi-arid tropics (SAT). Typical of many households in this area, those in the present sample are very poor. Mean annual household income per person over the nine-year period of analysis averaged about U.S.$100.

Conceptualizing Risk Benefits

Risk benefits are defined as how much mean income farmers would be willing to sacrifice to obtain smoother income streams. How much farmers would be willing to pay depends on (a) their preferences for risk taking,

---

I thank M. Asokan and E. Jagadeesh for carrying out the crop yield simulations in this chapter. I am grateful to J. R. Witcombe, R. A. E. Mueller, and F. R. Bidinger for comments.

TABLE 25.1 Agroclimatic and technological features for three villages in India's semi-arid tropics from 1975/76 to 1983/84

Village (location, soils, annual mean rainfall)	Average Size of Operational Holding (ha)	Irrigated Area as Percent of Gross Cropped Area	Common Crops	Improved Technologies Adopted
Aurepalle (Mahbubnagar district, Alfisols, 620 mm)	4.3	21.4	Irrigated paddy, castor, sorghum, pearl millet	HYV paddy, HYV castor, fertilizer on irrigated land
Shirapur (Sholapur district, deep Vertisols, 660 mm)	4.8	9.4	Sorghum	Fertilizer on irrigated land
Kanzara (Akola district, medium deep Vertisol, 930 mm)	5.0	7.1	Cotton, sorghum, mung bean, pigeon pea	Hybrid sorghum, fertilizer, insecticide and mechanical threshing

(b) their perceptions of how much alternative technological options would buy of lessened household income variability, and (c) their ability to adjust to income risk through transactions in credit and asset markets and changes in storage. Higher risk aversion, a perception that varietal stability could significantly reduce household income variability, and an inability to adjust cost-effectively to risk would increase the demand for more stable yielding cultivars.

From microeconomics literature, one simple way to analyze variability consequences is to compare the coefficient of variation (cv) of household income with and without a stabilization policy (Newbery and Stiglitz 1981). Large risk benefits are obtained when the simulated household income cv with the policy is substantially less than the cv without the policy. Before this mean-variance framework is used to quantify the value that farm households might place on yield stability, the data base is described.

Villages, Data, and Weather

The study is based on longitudinal data from three villages which are representative of three broad soil, climatic, and cropping regions of India's semi-arid tropics (table 25.1). Production risk is significantly greater in drought-prone Aurepalle and Shirapur than in rainfall-assured Kanzara.

The institutional environment for risk adjustment also differs considerably among the villages. Shirapur and Kanzara belong to Maharashtra state which has invested heavily in public work projects, most notably the Employment Guarantee Scheme (EGS). In Aurepalle, in the Mahbubnagar district of Andhra Pradesh, households do not have access to a government employer of last resort, and the local labor market is less buoyant than in the Maharashtra villages.

In 1975 a panel was drawn from a random stratified sample of small-, medium-, and large-sized farming and landless labor households in each village. Forty households were selected in each village, 10 from each stratum (Jodha, Asokan, and Ryan 1977). Household data on plot cultivation, transactions, and labor market participation, wages, and employment were collected by a resident investigator at three- to four-week intervals (Singh, Jodha, and Binswanger 1986). Information on eight other schedules was updated annually.

Household income is estimated for nine cropping years from 1975/76 to 1983/84. Concepts and procedures used to estimate income are given by Singh and Asokan (1981). Income conceptually refers to net household income which represents returns from family labor, management, capital, and land. Revenues and expenses from both farm and nonfarm activities were included in estimating net household income. Dowry and other large transactions pertaining to life cycle events were not included.

TABLE 25.2 Descriptive information on the common crops sown in the study villages in India from 1975/76 to 1983/84

Crop	Village	Number of Farm Households[a]	Mean Years Cropped	Percent of Gross Cropped Area	Mean Coefficient of Variation[b]		
					Household Income	Yield	Price
Irrigated paddy	Aurepalle	9	8.1	12	0.47	0.31	0.07
Castor	Aurepalle	23	7.6	34	0.45	0.68	0.22
Sorghum	Aurepalle	21	7.3	18	0.41	0.66	0.12
Sorghum	Shirapur	21	8.3	58	0.34	0.69	0.17
Cotton	Kanzara	26	8.2	51	0.33	0.44	0.15
Hybrid sorghum	Kanzara	18	7.2	8	0.34	0.66	0.13

[a]Those that planted the crop for at least five years from 1975/76 to 1983/84.
[b]Simple means of the cvs. For income and yields the cvs are at the household level but for price they are based on village average harvest prices.

The analysis relates to the "continuous" cultivator households who remained in the panel over the whole period. For those 81 households, information on fluctuations in income was summarized by the cv of annual net household income. A cv was estimated for each household based on nine years of income data deflated by a village-specific consumer price index (Walker et al. 1983).

The Common Crops and Household Income Variability

To measure risk benefits generated by the reduced yield variability associated with improved, more stable-yielding technologies, the most common crops grown in each village were the subjects for analysis. Those crops include irrigated paddy in Aurepalle and five dryland crops—sorghum and castor in Aurepalle, post-rainy-season sorghum in Shirapur, and cotton and hybrid sorghum in Kanzara. Included in the analysis were those cultivators who planted the crop in at least five of the nine years. With the exception of hybrid sorghum in Kanzara, many of the sample farm households planted the crop each year, but in varying areas.

Descriptive information on the households cultivating the common crops is presented in table 25.2. Many of the so-called common crops are not really so common, reflecting a diversified cropping pattern typical of dryland agriculture in India's semi-arid tropics. The most common village cropping system is post-rainy-season sorghum in Shirapur, which accounts for about 60 percent of gross cropped area in the village.

The mean household income cvs range between 0.33 and 0.47 and reinforce the popular image of production uncertainty in dryland agriculture in India's semi-arid tropics. Still, only 10 of the 81 continuous cultivar households had cvs exceeding 0.50. It was not surprising to note that household income was more variable in Aurepalle than in Shirapur, where off-farm employment opportunities are more ample, or in Kanzara, where the production environment is not as harsh. Lastly, yield variability on average was an order of magnitude three to five times greater than price variability. Prices were remarkably stable over the period of analysis.

Empirically Determined Risk Benefits

To assess the size of the risk benefits potentially offered by reductions in crop yield variability, the most extreme possible scenario, perfect crop yield stabilization, was examined. Under that scenario, each household received its mean yield level each year that the designated common crop was planted during the nine-year period of analysis. The cv from the simulated household income based on perfect crop yield stabilization was then compared with the cv from actual household income, the latter already

TABLE 25.3 Simulated risk benefits from perfect crop yield stabilization

Crop	Village	Number of Farms	Mean cv of House-hold Income	Mean Percentage Reduction in the cv of Household Income	Mean of Individually Computed Risk Premiums as Percentage of Mean Income
Irrigated paddy	Aurepalle	9	0.466	15.4	2.9
Castor	Aurepalle	23	0.448	4.4	1.2
Sorghum	Aurepalle	21	0.344	1.0	0.2
Sorghum	Shirapur	21	0.340	−3.9	−0.2
Cotton	Kanzara	26	0.330	0.8	0.2
Hybrid sorghum	Kanzara	18	0.344	0.6	0.3

embodying the effects of the household's own attempts to manage risks.

The assessment is based on the assumption that households do not materially change their behavior in response to perfect crop yield stabilization. That assumption would not hold for some crops and locations. The assumption is strongest for Kanzara where opportunities for diversification are much greater than in Shirapur and Aurepalle. In Kanzara, yields in and revenues from hybrid sorghum production are considerably more variable than those in competing cotton intercropping systems. If yield variability were reduced in hybrid sorghum, farmers would shift some of their cotton area into hybrid sorghum production (Walker and Subba Rao 1982). Nonetheless, because the demand for hybrid sorghum is very price inelastic, those transfer benefits would be short-lived and ultimately would go to consumers.

If perfect yield stability significantly decreases fluctuations in labor demand, risk benefits will be underestimated. Similarly, to the extent that improved yield stability results in increased area planted to the stabilized crop, the results presented here could understate longer term risk benefits. Nonetheless, perfect yield stabilization is an extreme assumption, which is not remotely feasible in dryland agriculture in India's semi-arid tropics. Such an extreme scenario should more than compensate for the partial nature of the analysis to be biased toward underestimated risk benefits.

Risk benefits from perfect crop yield stabilization are measured in two ways in table 25.3, namely, (a) mean percent reduction in the cv of household income and (b) what a household would be willing to sacrifice in mean income to gain a reduction in income variability attributed to perfect single-crop yield stabilization. This latter risk benefit is expressed as a proportional risk premium which is calculated by multiplying the difference between the squared cvs with and without perfect yield stabilization by one-half of the relative risk aversion coefficient (Newbery and Stiglitz 1981, p. 93, equation (6.5), Kanbur 1984). The value of the latter is often assumed to be unity (Newbery and Stiglitz 1981). Newbery and Stiglitz partially justified this assumption with experimental evidence from study villages of the International Crops Research Institute for the Semi-Arid Tropics (ICRISAT) (Binswanger 1981).

To illustrate the computations summarized in table 25.3, consider a household with an income cv of 0.5. For a reduction in variability of 60 percent (to cv = 0.2), the proportional risk premium is calculated as $(0.5)(1)(0.5^2 - 0.2^2)(100) = 10.5$ percent.

The results in table 25.3 may be rather disheartening to plant breeders pursuing stability. For the six common village crops, the risk benefits from perfect single-crop yield stabilization range from modest to negligible. Ironically, risk benefits are highest in irrigated paddy, the crop with the lowest mean cv of yield. Removing variability from the yield of only one crop is simply not an effective way to reduce income variability for the vast majority of farm households. For the dryland crops, the largest risk benefits would accrue from stabilizing the yields of castor in Aurepalle; however, perfect yield stabilization would only reduce household income variability by about 5 percent. Such a modest change would be equivalent to less than 2 percent of mean household income.

The results in table 25.3 are based on a mean variance approach. Income variability is measured from the continuous perspective of cvs. Would the outcome have been more favorable to perfect crop stabilization if a framework was used in which risk benefits were assessed in discontinuous terms, such as disaster levels of income and minimum probabilities? While there is an almost limitless number of threshold levels of income and probabilities from which to choose, one intuitively appealing threshold concept is the income level below which the household is compelled to make a distress sale of land. That disaster level does not apply to the study villages because, over the past 40 years, distress sales of land have been rare. Moreover, land sales were not bunched in adverse rainfall years, suggesting that household risk adjustment was at least minimally effective in dealing with covariate weather risk (Cain 1981). Even during the massive 1971-73 drought in western Maharashtra, few households in Shirapur parted with their land.

Rather than ignore the question of threshold changes in welfare, the probability that a household would suffer a shortfall in income (in at least one of nine years) below 50 percent of its median income was examined. Many cultivators, particularly households in Aurepalle, fell into this shortfall category. Could perfect yield stabilization have prevented them from suffering such a steep decline in income? In fact, it would not have made much of a difference. Without perfect single-crop stabilization, 45 of the 118 crop-household combinations belonged to the shortfall set; with it, 38 households comprised the shortfall set. This result is consistent with the observation that yield risk was only one of several factors contributing to such shortfalls in household income (Walker et al. 1983).

Another way to view single-crop yield stabilization is to use perfect all-crop income stabilization as a point of reference. Stabilizing income from all crops at its mean level for each household leads to appreciable reductions in income cvs. Mean cvs for farm households fall by from 27 percent for cotton growers in Kanzara to about 60 percent for paddy producers in Aurepalle. Stabilizing the yield of a dominant crop exploits at most only about 25 percent of the potential risk benefits from perfect crop income stabilization.

Area Variability

Perfect single-crop yield stabilization does not much enhance risk benefits for several reasons, including three in particular: (a) Most households rely on multiple sources of income and contain family members who participate in the local village labor market. (b) Diversified cropping patterns are the norm in dryland agriculture in India's SAT, and for many households revenue from a single crop did not contribute an overwhelming share to crop income. (c) Area variability in dryland agriculture severely erodes the effectiveness of policies or technologies that work through yield to reduce variability in household income and consumption. The first two explanations are self-evident, but the third warrants further discussion.

A large share of area variability in dryland agriculture stems from decisions taken by farmers to cope with agroclimatic risk. In the granitic rock, drought-prone production regions of the Deccan, where irrigated area depends on surface runoff into large ponds and on groundwater supplied from dug wells, planned area for a crop often deviates markedly from actual area sown. In Dokur, a study village in Mahbubnagar district, the gross irrigated area fell from about 500 hectares in a normal year to about 200 hectares in 1985/86, a year of abnormally low rainfall. In a normal year, about 60 percent of gross cropped area is irrigated in Dokur. Both castor planted in July in Aurepalle and post-rainy-season sorghum planted in late September in Shirapur are sown when farmers have some information on soil moisture at the start of the cropping year. Both crops were subject to sharp fluctuations in area planted during the nine-year period of analysis. When the monsoon is late in Aurepalle, the potential for shootfly to inflict yield losses on sorghum is greater. Farmers respond by substituting castor for sorghum. As a consequence of early season drought in 1977/78, the average area sown to local sorghum was halved while mean castor area increased by about 40 percent. Similarly, farmers in Shirapur react to low rainfall years by planting less area to post-rainy-season sorghum which is grown on residual soil moisture.

In table 25.2, yields are shown to be appreciably more variable than prices from 1975/76 to 1983/84. When the cv of area for each household was calculated as it was for yields and prices in table 25.2, it was found that mean area variability exceeded mean yield variability for each of the six common crops. Unless some means can be found to mitigate the role of area variability in conditioning fluctuations in household income, policies or technological changes that focus on reducing fluctuations in yield will have only a limited effect on household income variability.

Speculating on Risk Benefits in Africa's Semi-Arid Tropics

Risk benefits from less variably yielding varietal technologies may be larger in Africa's semi-arid tropics because resource-poor households may rely more heavily on crop income than do similar households in India's semi-arid tropics. Moreover, those households may have fewer effective means by which to adjust current income to consumption requirements. In the more land-abundant African societies, local rural labor markets are not nearly as well developed as in India. Land abundance also implies that it would be administratively infeasible to establish a flexible public works program such as the Maharashtra Employment Guarantee Scheme that caters to local village employment.

India, being such a large country, also offers much greater scope for risk pooling than the smaller African nation states. Largeness buffers the labor market from locally covariate risk. Additionally, institutional stabilization alternatives, such as crop or rainfall insurance, are more actuarially attractive in India because an insurer has greater opportunities to diffuse covariate risk within national boundaries. In India, risks are also to some extent shared between the central and the state governments, both of which have a strong voice in agricultural stabilization policy.

The size of risk benefits is ultimately an empirical question. Household panel data are a rare commodity anywhere in the world, but they are particularly sparse in Africa. Hopefully, data bases from village studies started by ICRISAT in Burkina Faso in 1980 and in Niger in 1982 can be used in comparative analyses to address the issue of household risk benefits in West Africa's semi-arid tropics.

Conclusions

Apparently little economic value should be attached to the supposed risk-reducing attributes of improved varietal technologies for resource-poor households in India's semi-arid tropics. Such technologies should be evaluated primarily with regard to their impact on equity, nutrition, and mean yield or output levels. Risk benefits arising from presumed reductions in variability in household income are likely to be too small in practice to be measurable. On average, it seems that households in the study sample would be unwilling to part with more than 3 percent of their income to obtain such benefits.

The results from the simple simulations do not support the popular belief that crop yield stability should be prized highly for small farm households in India's semi-arid tropics. Increased yield variability is unlikely to manifest itself in markedly heightened household income variability. Policies such as crop insurance, which work through yields to smooth fluctuations in household income, offer little protection from income variability (Walker, Singh, and Asokan 1986). These concluding remarks may not, however, apply to Africa's semi-arid tropics where more research on household risk benefits is needed.

26 The Implications of Variability in Food Production for National and Household Food Security

DAVID E. SAHN AND JOACHIM VON BRAUN

This chapter discusses the effects of increased production variability on food security at national and household levels. Three questions are addressed:

a. To what extent does increased production variability result in increased variability in food consumption?
b. Which low-income groups are adversely affected by increased production variability, and how?
c. What policy measures could cope with the adverse effects of increased production variability, in particular for the poor?

Before examining the issues surrounding the consumption effects of increased production variability, it is stressed that this chapter is concerned specifically with fluctuations in production and the resulting fluctuations in prices and incomes. This does not suggest that chronic undernutrition related to persistent levels of deficiency in food consumption is a less heinous problem. Indeed, it is taken as given that increasing food availability and increasing demand for labor are corollaries to any agricultural development strategy (Mellor 1976).

The fundamental policy issue addressed in this chapter is whether policymakers should display a commensurate interest in the transitory component of production, income, and prices in planning for and assessing the performance of the agricultural sector. The point of departure is that malnutrition is closely linked with poverty, and that poverty, to some extent, is episodic in nature. Malnutrition and illness are often transient states for individuals. Households that fall within the category of low-end poverty one year may well be above that part of the spectrum the next year (Scott 1980, Anderson and Scandizzo 1984, Srinivasan 1985).[1] Villages af-

---

1. Srinivasan points out that even though the proportion of poor in a population may remain constant, this does not imply it is the same households that are falling in this category from year to year or month to month. In considering this observation, however, one must be

fected by natural or human-caused disasters in one agricultural cycle may rebound to achieve high levels of success in the following harvest cycle (Pinstrup-Andersen and Jaramillo 1985). Conversely, regions and countries displaying a dramatic reduction in hunger and poverty may quickly revert to deficiencies in basic needs.

The causes of these fluctuations in measured poverty differ from one country to the next, and from one circumstance to another. The proportion of the poor in a population is, in fact, a function of many complex relationships among exogenous events (for example, price shocks, deteriorating terms of trade), domestic policy changes (for example, increases in the relative price of tradeables versus nontradeables due to currency devaluation), and stochastic weather-induced events interacting with the existing technology in a given resource endowment. The purpose here is to focus attention on the stochastic fluctuations in agricultural performance, and the consequences on the incomes and prices paid by the poor, acknowledging that there are other factors that contribute to instability in consumption (for example, political instability and wars). The primary concern is with weather-induced fluctuations in cereal yields, and thus, production, although nonfood production variability is also recognized as having a major impact on household food security both directly through effects on wage labor, and indirectly through the multiplier effects of demand fluctuations for food crops.

As part of the discussion of the consumption and nutritional implications of instability in foodgrain production on households, the macrolevel effects of instability on market aggregates is first examined. Thereafer, these effects can be linked with the microfood economy of households. The initial hypothesis is as follows: a variety of factors may result in greater output fluctuations, which, in turn, translate into greater variability in income and prices of food and nonfood commodities; and income and price variability results in greater fluctuations in food consumption and represents increased nutritional risk to the household.

Market-Level Effects

The process by which increased production variability affects commodity prices faced by consumers and producers is of particular importance. In figure 26.1, the global and national market-level effects are

---

careful to distinguish between real fluctuations in measured poverty and statistical problems. For example, Scott (1980) discusses how instability in household memberships could affect poverty determinations from one survey period to the next. Similarly, to the extent that consumption expenditures are measured with error from one period to the next, it may falsely appear that poverty arises out of a stochastic process, with some families doing well in one year and badly the next.

FIGURE 26.1 Production, price formation, and consumption: tracing market-level effects of instability for consumption

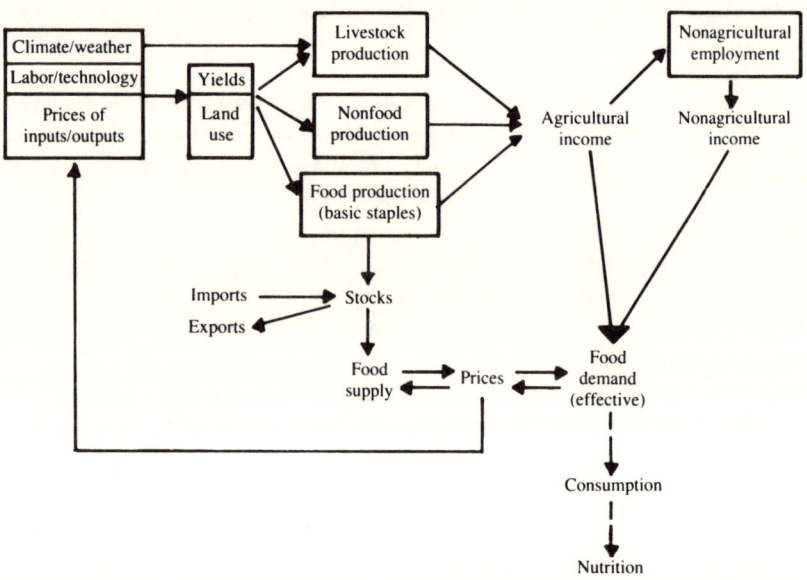

traced through, and links between production variability and prices are indicated.

In the context of the world food economy, changes in levels of food production translate into price changes. Therefore, an increase in production variability must be of concern, whether in developed or developing countries (Mellor and Johnston 1984).[2] Given the high share of grain trade in industrial countries, fluctuations in export supply or import demand will also have substantial effects on world prices and, therefore, on food security in developing countries. Variations in trade volumes and stocks and the extent to which exporters and importers responded to world market price fluctuations in adjusting the volumes of trade were major determinants of the high level of world price variability during the past two decades (Siamwalla and Valdés 1980). In fact, table 26.1 exemplifies how short-run price variability in the world grain markets occurs despite small global production fluctuations.

As more countries exploit trade opportunities to stabilize domestic prices, further volatility in international grain markets may result (John-

---

2. For example, Koester (1982) points out that since the European Community (EC) storage does not fully compensate for EC production fluctuations, the rest of the world is affected by these fluctuations.

TABLE 26.1 World cereal production, trade, and price of wheat during the "food crises," 1970-1976

Crop Year	Cereal Production (million metric tons)	Cereal Trade (million metric tons)	Wheat Price ($/ton)
1970/71	1,104	110	74
1971/72	1,194	110	70
1972/73	1,161	134	100
1973/74	1,266	142	203
1974/75	1,213	136	204
1975/76	1,239	152	187

Source: USDA, *Foreign Agricultural Circular,* Washington, D.C. (April 15, 1982).

son 1975, Koester 1984). As Johnson (1975, p. 823) remarks, "there has been little recognition of the extent to which one nation or region achieves stability at the expense of instability to others." Given that governments are interested in domestic stability and far less with price stability abroad, it reduces the likelihood that sovereign nations will work together to stabilize global supply and prices.

At the individual country level, the effects of increased production variability on domestic prices and supply can be examined in the context of two distinct international grain trade regimes. The first case is the open economy that participates actively in grain markets. Domestic prices will not be affected directly by increased production variability at the national level, unless other factors, such as foreign exchange constraints, limit participation in grain markets. Instead, the effects of increased production variability will be felt in the coffers of the treasury which must have foreign exchange to purchase commodities on international markets in years of low production.

The second case to be considered is the "closed economy" trade regime. Many landlocked African countries resemble the closed economy case in that they do not participate extensively in grain trade because of prohibitive transport costs. Here, increased production variability will inevitably result in increased variability in domestic supplies and prices. However, two qualifications must be considered when trade opportunities are not exploited. The first is that the price responsiveness of stockholders will determine the extent to which increased production variability affects availability and prices. The second determinant of the effect of increased production variability on prices is the relationship between the cereal sector and the rest of the farm production system, especially livestock and nonfood crops, as indicated in figure 26.1. It is likely that the intrasectoral changes in production patterns will become more responsive to prices when subsistence agriculture becomes more market integrated. Farmers at

TABLE 26.2 Coefficient of variation for per capita cereal production, cereal consumption, and total food consumption

Country	1966–80			1966–74			1972–80		
	Cereal Production	Cereal Consumption	Total Food Consumption	Cereal Production	Cereal Consumption	Total Food Consumption	Cereal Production	Cereal Consumption	Total Food Consumption
Bangladesh	0.078	0.058	0.059	0.094	0.056	0.058	0.050	0.048	0.044
India	0.075	0.057	0.053	0.079	0.061	0.057	0.063	0.055	0.051
Pakistan	0.113	0.077	0.066	0.126	0.078	0.066	0.054	0.032	0.027
Sri Lanka	0.152	0.049	0.039	0.119	0.035	0.031	0.166	0.055	0.040
Burma	0.093	0.057	0.053	0.059	0.040	0.047	0.115	0.052	0.047
Indonesia	0.106	0.103	0.077	0.101	0.089	0.068	0.075	0.062	0.051
Philippines	0.117	0.078	0.103	0.088	0.069	0.057	0.105	0.052	0.092
Thailand	0.078	0.048	0.042	0.078	0.012	0.010	0.089	0.063	0.056
Vietnam	0.069	0.070	0.031	0.061	0.031	0.027	0.072	0.078	0.029
Iran	0.082	0.122	0.119	0.081	0.074	0.073	0.077	0.070	0.068
Turkey	0.113	0.012	0.015	0.101	0.012	0.011	0.126	0.014	0.016
Egypt	0.050	0.057	0.053	0.029	0.031	0.030	0.047	0.059	0.054
Nigeria	0.098	0.032	0.023	0.111	0.032	0.024	0.059	0.033	0.004
Mexico	0.065	0.014	0.009	0.049	0.016	0.009	0.078	0.007	0.007
Brazil	0.098	0.072	0.032	0.061	0.032	0.030	0.103	0.073	0.014
Argentina	0.114	0.027	0.038	0.102	0.034	0.034	0.122	0.025	0.024

the margin may shift, for example, from subsistence crops to food or nonfood cash crops. This intrasectoral substitution will tend to smooth out price peaks and troughs in a closed economy.

Finally, the diagram indicates that the extent of increased production variability is also influenced by the linkage effects of production with agricultural and nonagricultural labor demand. For example, if lower yields imply lower wages and fewer hours worked, and vice versa, increased income fluctuations due to increased production variability will tend to dampen price fluctuations.

Empirical Analysis of Market Aggregates at the Country Level

In a given year, the following staple food balance identity must hold in a country:

$$\begin{aligned}\text{Food consumption} = {} & \text{Production} + \text{Imports} - \text{Exports} + \\ & \text{Stock changes} - \text{Feed} - \\ & \text{Waste} - \text{Seed} - \text{Processing}\end{aligned} \quad (26.1)$$

As intimated in the previous discussion, mitigation of the effects of increased production variability on food consumption can be achieved through policies that adjust any of the components on the right-hand side of equation (26.1). Thus, increased production variability may, in principle, be balanced by trade policies, stockholding policies, or adjustments in the use of staple food for feed and processing.

The relationship between production variability and its effect on consumption were analyzed for 16 countries using Food and Agriculture Organization (FAO) food balance sheet data. In table 26.2, coefficients of variation (cvs) for linearly detrended cereal production per capita, cereal consumption per capita, and total food consumption per capita (in calorie equivalents) are presented.[3] The most telling feature of these data is that the level of variability in cereal production is generally greater than consumption variability, when measured in terms of either total calories or calories from cereals. In fact, the average of the cv of cereal production in the 16 countries was 0.094, nearly twice as high as that of total food consumption, 0.051, during the period 1966-80. Whether through trade policies, domestic stocking behavior, or other means identified above, the aggregate level of variability in production does not translate fully into consumption variability.

These data have also been disaggregated according to two overlapping time periods to determine how the variability in cereal production and con-

---

3. A similar analysis was done by Valdés and Konandreas (1981) for staple food consumption and production. The differences herein are that the data are in per capita terms, cover a more recent time period, examine a different set of countries, and employ a different source of data.

sumption have changed over time.⁴ No overt trend from one time period to another clearly emerges in the cvs presented in table 26.2, although nine of the 14 countries registered a decline in cv for total food consumption.⁵

In order to understand better the relationship between production and food consumption variability, simple correlation coefficients were calculated between the detrended per capita values of cereal production and cereal, noncereal, and total food consumption, respectively (see table 26.3). In most of the low-income countries, cereal production and total food consumption are highly correlated.⁶ Egypt and Sri Lanka, having massive interventions in the food markets with consumer-oriented food subsidies, appear as exceptions. Also in the middle-income countries, such as Mexico, Brazil, and Argentina, the variations in cereal production do not correspond to variations in total food consumption. For some of the countries, there is a negative correlation between cereal production and calories derived from noncereals. This suggests a pattern of substitution between cereal and noncereal commodities.

To probe these relations more fully, a regression analysis was undertaken of the patterns of variability in food consumption across a sample of 38 countries (Sahn and von Braun 1987). The following model was estimated

$$CVC_{it} = f(CVQ_{it}, [CVQ_{it}]^2, GNP, D) \qquad (26.2)$$

where CVC_{it} denotes the cv of per capita calorie consumption in country i over time period t, CVQ denotes the cv of production per capita, GNP denotes gross national product per capita, and D is a dummy variable which equals one for Sub-Saharan Africa and zero elsewhere. Regressions for two overlapping time periods as well as for the entire time-series were analyzed (table 26.4).

The results indicate that an increase in production variability leads to an increase in consumption variability. Evaluated at the mean for 1961-83, a one unit increase in the average level of the cv of production increases the cv of consumption by 0.14 units; an elasticity of 0.41. However, as indicated by the negative and significant quadratic term on CVQ, food pro-

---

4. The periods are overlapping so as not to be biased by the years of the oil shock and world food shortage in 1972-74.

5. It should be stressed that the changes in cv only indicate tendencies, since statistical significance has not been tested.

6. For some countries, lagged production is correlated with consumption. If the lagged variable had a higher correlation, it is reported. The justification is that the timing of the harvest varies dramatically from one country to the next. So, a late harvest in one year can have implications in consumption during the following calendar year.

These correlations are generally lower than those reported by Valdés and Konandreas (1981). This can be attributed to the factors discussed in footnote 3.

TABLE 26.3 Correlation coefficients for cereal production, cereal consumption, total food consumption, and noncereal consumption, 1966-1980

Country	Cereal Production and Cereal Consumption	Cereal Production and Total Food Consumption	Cereal Production and Noncereal Consumption
Bangladesh	0.76[a]	0.75[a]	0.58[a]
India	0.86[a]	0.90[a]	0.59[a]
Pakistan	0.77	0.78	0.20
Sri Lanka	0.71	0.48[a]	−0.52[a]
Burma	0.53	0.52	0.46[a]
Indonesia	0.79	0.72	0.04
Philippines	0.49[a]	0.37	0.39[a]
Thailand	0.56	0.57	−0.09
Vietnam	0.59	0.54	−0.49
Iran	0.75	0.73	0.37[a]
Turkey	0.49	0.77	0.60
Egypt	−0.19	−0.15	0.40[a]
Nigeria	0.05[a]	0.32[a]	0.22
Mexico	0.44[a]	0.30[a]	0.24
Brazil	−0.005	0.14[a]	0.20[a]
Argentina	−0.01[a]	−0.02[a]	0.11

[a]Cereal production has been lagged by one year. The correlations are based on detrended values. The correlation coefficients were calculated with and without production being lagged one year. The higher one was chosen. The reason for following this procedure is that the timing of the harvest may often be toward the end of the year. If that is the case, the higher level of consumption would be expected in the calendar years following years of higher production. It was not possible to determine the timing of the harvest for each country. Therefore, it was assumed that if the lagged correlation coefficient was higher, it was attributable to the timing of the harvest and the time delay before prices were lower and higher producer incomes resulted in increased consumption.

duction variability has a decreasing marginal impact on the level of consumption variability. Countries with high levels of production variability apparently use various policy measures to contain the impact of production variability on consumption variability.

The regression results also indicate that consumption variability declines as per capita incomes increase. For the period 1961-83, each 10 percent increase in GNP per capita reduced the cv of consumption by 2 to 5 percent. Middle-income developing countries are obviously more capable of using trade and storage policies to reduce the impact of instability in domestic food production on consumption variability. The parameter of the dummy variable for Sub-Sahara African countries indicates that in the period 1961-74, consumption variability was lower in Sub-Saharan countries than elsewhere. This appears counterintuitive and may result from poor quality data.

TABLE 26.4 Regressions of the coefficient of variation of daily calorie consumption on gross national product and the coefficient of variation of food production, and resulting elasticities

Independent Variables	Dependent Variable: Coefficient of Variation of Per Capita Daily Calorie Consumption for		
	1961-83	1961-74	1972-83
Intercept	5.190	3.399	3.429
Mean GNP per capita	−0.0030	−0.0039	−0.0105
	(2.54)	(4.758)	(1.431)
Coefficient of variation of	0.2863	0.2471	0.1416
per capita food production	(2.354)	(4.791)	(1.474)
(Coefficient of variation of	−0.0038	−0.0036	−0.0022
per capita food production)^2	(2.317)	(4.610)	(1.711)
Dummy for Sub-Sahara	−1.840	−1.1153	0.436
African countries	(1.60)	(2.436)	(0.433)
R^2	0.2504	0.5738	0.1515
Elasticity of cv calorie consumption with respect to GNP	−0.253	−0.270	−0.196
Elasticity of cv calorie consumption with respect to cv production	0.41	0.48	0.27

Source: Sahn and von Braun (1987).
Note: t statistics are in parenthesis. (Elasticities are computed at the mean of the respective variables.)

Consequences of Market-Level Instability

In the above macrolevel analysis, the distributional consequences, and therefore the nutritional consequences, of increased production variability were not considered. However, just as aggregate consumption is not evenly distributed, transitory shortfalls in consumption are not either (Green and Kirkpatrick 1982).

There is evidence from a limited number of regional- or country-level studies that instability measured at the market level does have implications for nutritional status. This should come as no surprise since declines of only 10 or 15 percent of energy intake would likely have deleterious nutritional consequences on marginally nourished individuals. Anderson and Scandizzo (1984) employ data on macrolevel production variability and relate them to variables, such as life expectancy and child mortality at the national level. In their cross-country comparison, they found that the cv of production was a significant variable in explaining life expectancy and child mortality when gross domestic product (GDP) and income distribution variables were controlled for. Presumably, this is explained by the effects of production variability on consumption instability. It could be hypothesized that individuals were more likely to become sick and die in countries where lean times were more pronounced and more likely.

While these types of data analyses do not make clear the dynamics of the relationship between increased production variability at the household level and nutritional and health outcomes, they provide a tentative indication of its deleterious impact. The need to consider the consequences of increased production variability at the household level is manifest.

Household Level Effects

The important issues to be discussed here are (a) to identify the circumstances under which an increase in yield instability will bring about a combination of movements in prices and incomes that results in greater variability in real income and effective demand for food at the household level; and (b) to determine why increased production variability may be of little consequence for some but may represent a truly worrisome state of affairs for others, entailing serious nutritional risks.

Short-Term Effects of Increased Production Variability on Real Income Variability

There is a need to distinguish between how the earnings of different types of households are affected by instability in agricultural production—including surplus farmers, deficit and marginal farmers, agricultural laborers, and nonagricultural workers. Moreover, an analysis should be able to determine the impact of increased production variability on real income under at least three possible trade regimes:

a. The closed economy with flexible prices;
b. The open economy with alternate phases of being a net exporter or net importer of its major staple. In this case, fluctuations in output will cause marked shifts in the marginal price, from a c.i.f. to an f.o.b. situation;
c. The open economy where yearly output variability does not cause a shift from an exporter situation to that of an importer, or vice versa.

In the first two cases, prices are assumed to vary dramatically from one year to the next in response to changes in the level of production—increasing in years of relatively lower output and decreasing in years of high domestic output. In the last case, prices are assumed to be relatively fixed, although affected by international prices.

In addition to distinguishing between socioeconomic groups and price policy, determining the effect of increased production variability requires knowledge concerning a variety of other characteristics of the microeconomy. In assessing the effects of variability on the landless laborer, small farmer, and nonagricultural worker, one must consider how wages and employment are determined.

SURPLUS FARMER. In order to assess the effect of increased production variability on the surplus farmer, one must examine the variances from one year to the next, as well as the covariances in yields between farmers and between food crops in a given region. It is the intercrop and interregional covariances that largely determine commodity prices and thus real farm income.

Surplus farmers have at their disposal a variety of important options to smooth out earnings from one year to the next, including intercropping and sequential production decisions (successional sowing and crop selection). A second set of alternatives for reducing the effects of increased production variability on earnings is the allocation of labor outside food production. However, once again the success of this strategy is contingent upon interfarm and interregional covariances in production not being high. This will increase the likelihood that off-farm opportunities exist in those years when a farmer's output falls.

In an environment where prices are fixed (for example, where borders are open or government intervenes to reduce variability in prices), increased or decreased levels of production do not influence prices. Therefore, variances in the production of the large-scale farmer will translate into major increases in income variability, regardless of interregional covariances. Intercrop covariances will further exacerbate the instability of incomes of the surplus farmer. In the flexible price case, the surplus farmer's real purchasing power is likely to be more stable if there are covariances in yields.

Regardless of the effects of increased production variability on real income, surplus farmers usually meet most of their foodgrain needs from home production. Thus, the surplus farmer can choose to maintain adequate levels of food consumption, even if real earnings fluctuate.

LANDLESS AGRICULTURAL WAGE LABORER. The landless wage laborers are distinguished from the small producers by the fact that all of their real earnings are determined by market wages, hours worked, and commodity prices in retail markets. All these factors are highly susceptible to the effects of increased variances in production.

The vulnerability of the wage laborer stems from the possibility that in years of low production, an upsurge in food prices will not be matched by the wages received. In examining these relationships and the implications of increased production variability, the case of the flexible price environment is clear. As stated by Mellor (1985, p. 21): "Good weather increases output and employment and reduces food prices: all serve to raise the real incomes of the laboring class. Poor weather, on the other hand, has an effect analogous to a decrease in the land area; it reduces output and the associated demand for labor. It thereby increases the proportion of output paid as rents, as higher prices transfer the reduced income of laborers to landowners." The implication is that the variability in the income of the wage laborer will increase in the face of increased production variability in a flexible price environment.

In the open economy case, or where measures are adopted to stabilize food prices, increased fluctuations in output will exhibit less real-wage effects because of smaller fluctuations in food prices than in the closed economy.

A further issue is the importance of increased interregional and intercrop covariances on the demand for labor and wages. High intercrop covariances reduces the possibility of labor demand being maintained through the substitution of work on one crop for another; and an increase in interregional covariances limits the potential for workers to migrate to other areas in search of work. Likewise, the increased price variability from increased production variability, which would adversely affect the wage laborer as a consumer, will be considerably less if interregional covariances are low.

SMALL MARGINAL FARMER. In certain circumstances, the marginal farmer may be especially subject to output variability even in a stable price environment. In any given year where the household produces less than demanded for home consumption, the marginal price faced by the household is the retail price. In a good year, production increases result in an excess of supply over demand. In this case, the appropriate shadow price is the farmgate price. Given that the retail and farmgate price can diverge by 30 percent or more, any increase in production variability will result in a greater likelihood of shifts from being a net producer to net consumer. Thus, increased production variability raises the probability that the marginal farmer simultaneously faces: (a) a decline in income because of lower levels of production and possibly reduced opportunities for off-farm work, and (b) a rise in prices due to the shift from the status of net food supplier to that of net demander.

NONAGRICULTURAL WORKER. Nonagricultural workers are affected by variability in agricultural production, primarily in their role as consumers. In an environment of flexible prices, increased production variability will result in increased variability in real-wage effects that accompany price changes.

The demand for nonagricultural goods and services could be affected by increased production variability as mediated through the increased variability in incomes and expenditures of those in the agricultural sector.

The extent of these multiplier effects in rural areas is largely determined by the effect of increased production variability on the surplus farmer whose nonfood purchases are of greatest magnitude. If prices are fixed, the surplus farmer's income is most variable and so is the induced demand for manufacturing and services. In such an environment, the real wage effects on nonagricultural workers due to price variability are small.

The Relationship between Income and Consumption Variability

The concern over income fluctuations stems largely from its putative relation to consumption. Increased production variability may, however, have other deleterious effects on the economy, such as delays in the adoption of new technologies, disaccumulation of wealth, and risk to nutritional well-being of marginal households in the lean production years.

Households also have the ability to adjust the consumption bundle and the typical pattern of expenditures in years of low income; and conversely, the purchase of durables and semi-durables can be timed to years of plenty. While many nonfood expenditures are not discretionary (for example, shelter, agricultural inputs), others are amenable to reductions in accordance with the household's means. However, the poorest households face severe limits to the ability to substitute between food and nonfood expenditures.

In a similar vein, households can adjust their food basket to periods of duress. The desire for diversity, for example, is revealed in the preferences of most households. Such tastes may become secondary to achieving nutritional adequacy in years of scarcity. Regardless of the capacity and skill of the household in coping with increased variability in earnings, expectations about future income and prices are a crucial element of its intertemporal utility function. Increased production variability makes correct anticipations more difficult to form. This is especially problematic for the poor household, which is likely to have very high internal rates of discount.

Few household level studies allow the analysis of intertemporal consumption patterns. The data requirements for such longitudinal research are simply too ambitious for widespread application. One exception is the International Crops Research Institute for the Semi-Arid Tropics (ICRISAT) multi-purpose village-level studies (Walker et al. 1983). Findings indicate that consumption variability was much less than income variability—that is, the elasticity of the cv in consumption with respect to the cv in income was in the range of 0.3 to 0.5. The high-income households displayed greater consumption fluctuations. A similar finding was made in North Arcot, India (Pinstrup-Andersen and Jaramillo 1985). Households with a higher intake of food energy in a year of good production saw a greater fall in intake, both in absolute and proportional terms, in a year of drought and low output. Jodha (1975) observed that farmers first and foremost protect their productive assets—the source of their future income—even at the expense of current consumption.

Household to Individual Consumption

The above discussion focuses on methods by which the household is able to compensate for the transitory nature of earnings so as to limit the potential implications for consumption variability. The link between household consumption variability and that of the individuals therein remains largely a mystery. Just as there is considerable latitude in terms of intertemporal adjustments, so can the household adjust the intrahousehold allocation of resources to maximize an objective function such as nutritional well-being.

These relationships are extremely difficult to model for a single year, and the data requirements for a longitudinal investigation are prohibitive. Nevertheless, one must be aware of such potential adaptive mechanisms before drawing any definitive conclusions on the nutritional implications of increased production variability.

Individual Consumption, Nutritional Status, and Productivity

Variability in an individual's consumption portends swings in nutritional status. However, some qualifications need be considered. First, the human body can play a role in storage. The building up of fat in times of plenty can be followed by its mobilization in lean times. Similarly, the literature on auto-regulation suggests a potential for metabolic adjustments in periods of decreased intake (Srinivasan 1981, Sukhatme and Margen 1982). And, of course, the reduction of energy expenditures—an adjustment mechanism that certainly does have costs in ability to work and quality of life—is another form of regulation (Beaton 1983). These forms of coping with variability are complex and remain the source of considerable controversy in the medical and biological sciences.

Perhaps the most troublesome aspect of increased production variability is that it potentially compounds itself through the link between low output in a given year leading to lower productivity and reduced output in the subsequent year. There is a growing literature indicating that nutritional status affects worker productivity (Immink and Viteri 1981a,b; Deolalikar 1984; Strauss 1984; Latham 1985). These findings support Kumar's (1987) study in Zambia, where she found that the size of the food-crop, cash crop, and total area planted are related to the duration of the maize supply from the previous year.

Policy Options to Reduce the Effects of Instability in Agriculture

In considering measures to reduce the deleterious effects of increased production variability, one may intervene either through production-related strategies, or through mechanisms that buffer the impact. Concerning the former, there are potential conflicts between yield variance-reducing and mean-increasing measures. This conflict reinforces the notion that if output can be raised sufficiently, thereby generating employment and reducing prices, fluctuations become less consequential in terms of nutritional well-being.

In terms of strategies to assure access to food for households, a distinction can be made between targeted and nontargeted methods. Nontargeted efforts, such as price and supply stabilization measures and infrastructure development, are discussed first, followed by an examination of targeted measures, which may be prohibitively expensive at a national level, but when targeted to at-risk households the cost may be within manageable boundaries.

Price and Supply Stabilization

Domestic prices can be smoothed by keeping supply and demand in proportion to achieve a targeted price. Price stability, however, does not represent a goal that implies that consumption variability is minimized. Supply and demand may fluctuate up and down synchronously and thus keep prices stable. Similarly, the stabilization of prices may increase fluctuations in demand for certain segments of the population.

Stabilizing the supply of food at the national level can be achieved through a combination of stocking policy and trade. This relationship is captured in the identity for consumption defined in equation (26.1). If the government chooses to reduce the present and future gaps between consumption and production, there are two options—the first is to change the stocks either by increasing storage or drawing down existing reserves; the second is to adjust the levels of net imports.

As for trade, many developing countries lament that the instability in world grain markets has been a major cause of food insecurity. The question arises as to whether the prospect for increased global instability in production and prices represents a hazard to developing countries. And, is stabilization of world prices an important or affordable proposition for food security in developing countries?

First, the cost of stabilizing world prices would be extremely high, probably exceeding $10 billion per year (Svedberg 1984). Second, even if this were feasible, in few countries did cereal import bills represent more than 10 percent of total import expenditures in the early 1980s (Svedberg 1984). Therefore, smoothing prices on world foodgrain markets would do little to stabilize foreign exchange requirements given the importance of the prices of other imports.

Third, Valdés (1981) indicated that national-level food security problems do not arise primarily out of price instability on international markets. Rather, real income variability due to domestic production variability and changes in the volume (not price) of imports are the major constraints to national food security.

It has been extensively argued that trade is a better and cheaper way to address this problem than buffer stocks (McIntire 1981, Reutlinger and Bigman 1979). Siamwalla (1984, p. 5) stated that "the central message is thus for the individual country to eschew a policy of holding large volumes of domestic stock to cope with possible harvest shortfalls, because the fiscal costs of doing so can be quite high." Instead, reliance primarily on the market is commended, although maintaining a well-managed small security stock of around 5 percent of grain consumption is suggested as an element of a national food security program (McIntire 1981). But note that public storage operations may supplant private stores (Newbery and Stiglitz 1981).

Furthermore, if a country follows an open economy approach to stabilizing supplies, this does not necessarily result in unstable prices at home due to unstable import prices. Rather, there is the potential for insulating domestic prices from the vagaries of widely fluctuating world prices through import subsidies and import tariffs applied in years of high or low international prices, respectively (Reutlinger 1982).

There are exceptions to this logic of using trade rather than storage to stabilize consumption. The first exception is caused by a precipitous rise in grain prices. The obvious response to this problem is that countries can hedge against such possibilities by trading in futures. The second exception occurs in the case of landlocked countries with poor transport infrastructure, where trade may be prohibitively expensive. A third exception would be when a country's imports represent such a large volume that world price may be affected by its trade activities. This prospect of inelastic supply of imports is limited to a few, although important, cases. Fourth, and most significant, is the case of those countries that are nearing self-sufficiency. A good harvest may mean it would be a net exporter; a bad harvest means it would be a net importer. Increased variability may cause more frequent shifts in a country's market-clearing price, from the f.o.b. to c.i.f. price. Given the evidence that these price differences can be on the order of 100 percent in some African countries (Koester 1984), this strongly commends relying on stock holding between periods and promoting intraregional trade, rather than international trade, so that a country can avoid switching from an f.o.b. to a c.i.f. price.

The question then arises as to why countries still suffer the consequences of food insecurity when trade and storage opportunities exist. One answer is found in the difficulty of financing food imports. This can become quite a burden in successive years where foreign exchange earnings and domestic production are low, and international prices are high, resulting in large import bills. In the case of small and poor countries, these difficulties are further compounded by the problems of gaining access to needed capital from the international financial community.

One response to such problems has been the extension of the International Monetary Fund (IMF) Compensatory Finance Facility. This facility is basically designed to provide balance-of-payments support to compensate for precipitous increases in the cost of cereal imports. It enables countries to stabilize demand for cereals, in both urban and rural areas, where it was previously impossible. There may be drawbacks to this scheme and a need for further modification (Huddleston et al. 1984).[7] Nevertheless, it represents an important complement to other food aid measures.

Infrastructure Development

Improved marketing infrastructure, both for agricultural inputs and foodcrops, is another fruitful method for reducing consumption instability in the face of increased production variability. More integrated factor markets will provide an outlet to cope with the potential adverse effects of covariances which accompany increased production variability. Integrating product markets will mitigate the impact of local production variability on local prices by facilitating the flow of goods and services from one geographical area to another. This reduces the link between supply and price in a given locality, thereby addressing the problem of fluctuations due to local market conditions. It is also likely that market investments will encourage risk sharing over a broader population and will facilitate the implementation of targeted and nontargeted schemes to reduce the effects of fluctuations.

Reducing marketing margins through improved infrastructure will be especially advantageous to the marginal farmer who may be a net consumer or producer of a cereal grain in any given year. To the extent that the difference between farmgate and market prices can be reduced, so would the magnitude of the price change when a marginal producer switches from being a surplus to deficit farmer.

---

7. See Huddleston, Johnson, Reutlinger, and Valdés (1984). Included among the more important problems they identify are that foreign exchange constraints often stem from fluctuations in the prices of noncereal exports, that there are constraints to full compensation for the poorest countries, and that, of course, such a scheme has no effect on incomes of households, and supply or price stabilization may not have the desired distributional consequences in terms of assisting the poor, for whom consumption fluctuations are most serious.

Targeted Programs

If a government stabilizes aggregate demand through a combination of buffer stock and trade policies, the nutritional well-being of certain household types may still be in jeopardy. This could occur, for example, if the households consisting of marginal consumers and wage laborers face increased variability in purchasing power. Consideration should, therefore, be given to implementing targeted programs to assure food security for vulnerable households.

Income-generating schemes and transfer programs, such as employment guarantee, food subsidies, and food-for-work, are types of appropriate programs to address the problems of at risk households becoming increasingly food insecure. Nonetheless, the difficulties of employing such measures should not be overlooked. For example, food aid allocations traditionally are not responsive to year-to-year fluctuations in food in recipient countries. In fact, given the surplus disposal element of food aid programs, the quantity of food aid globally programmed is counter-cyclical to the needs of developing countries. A situation can arise, such as in the early 1970s when food aid allotments were reduced despite acute need (von Braun and Huddleston 1984).

Employment generation schemes are another mechanism to counteract cyclical variability in production. Few countries, however, have either the managerial or financial resources to operate flexible employment programs. Food-for-work projects, which use donated resources, may have the advantage of being viable in a time of severe domestic resource constraints caused by a year of low production.

The use of targeted food subsidies is also an important policy option. They have been shown to be an effective way of transferring income to the poor (Pinstrup-Andersen and Alderman 1984). Consideration could be given to employing a "flexible price wedge," which could be made relatively larger in lean years and smaller in years of high output. Another targeted strategy possibly worthy of consideration is crop insurance, which however, runs the risk of promoting greater inequality and doing little to help those in greatest need.

A further type of intervention is to improve access to consumption credit or to enhance the ability to save through stocking behavior. As fluctuations increase, the ability to adjust intertemporal consumption becomes more urgent. The goal is to reduce the elasticities of consumption variability with respect to income variability. This requires that financial markets function well and that they do not discriminate against the poor. Special arrangements for repaying loans and procuring credit may be required for the poor with little collateral. The ability of the poor to smooth consumption is constrained not only by lack of access to institutions and facilities but also by their short planning horizon. They may be more concerned with survival and coping in the present than with conjecturing about the future.

Conclusion

This chapter has discussed the effects of increased production variability on consumption and nutrition. The major concern is the impact on various household types. However, national level data and policy options were explored because of the direct link between the macrofood economy of the country and the microfood economy of the household. The lack of data on interyear fluctuations in consumption and nutrition at the household level, however, limited the empirical basis for this chapter. Nevertheless, the interplay between stochastic events, government policy, and the combined impact on household food security illustrates the importance of policy analysts taking into account that increased variations in output do have potentially deleterious consequences. These can be addressed through trade, storage, and pricing policies that mitigate the consequences of instability on the consumption and nutrition of poor households. In addition a variety of targeted strategies to protect the nutritionally vulnerable population from nutritional problems arising out of variability were presented.

The unspoken theme is that the negative consequences of fluctuations are another manifestation of underdevelopment. Poor countries and poor households are beset with constraints, structural or otherwise, which limit their ability to prevent and cope with increased production variability. These constraints will largely be overcome in the course of agricultural development and economic growth. Technological changes that increase output, create employment, moderate prices, improve market integration, and so forth are the goals of development. They represent long-term solutions, which in general, do not conflict with measures to protect the poor from the short-term effects of increased production variability.

27 Synthesis and Needs in Agricultural Research and Policy

JOCK R. ANDERSON AND PETER B. R. HAZELL

This volume has brought together available evidence on patterns of variability in world cereal production, and how this variability has changed in recent years. The biological, climatic, and economic factors underlying these patterns of yield variability have also been probed. We now summarize this and related material and then attempt to draw implications for improvements in both agricultural research and policy.

Patterns of Production Variability among Countries

Any attempt to measure baseline levels or changes in the variability of cereal production at an aggregate level encounters immediate methodological difficulties.

a. Available time-series data tend to be short, especially for the modern technology era. Results are therefore susceptible to one or two unusual events. Changes in the definition of periods can substantially change the results in some cases.
b. Time-series data contain trends which add to variability when measured around the mean. It is thus necessary to remove such trends, but this is a subjective process and no single method is ideal; for example, should cyclical fluctuations be viewed as part of the variability or as part of a systematic trend? Results can be sensitive to the functional form chosen for detrending, and whether periods are pooled or detrended separately.
c. Available data sources are not always consistent. For many countries, data are available from the Food and Agriculture Organization (FAO), U.S. Department of Agriculture (USDA), and national

---

Sections of this chapter draw heavily on conference summary remarks prepared by Lloyd T. Evans at the Feldafing meeting, November 1985, reported in Evans (1986).

sources, and results on changing patterns of variability sometimes vary with source.
d. Methods of data collection within countries sometimes change over time, for example, yield measurements, and political boundaries (especially for regions within countries) are occasionally redefined.
e. Measures of production variability around trend may not be relevant measures of risk for decision makers if they are able partially (or fully) to forecast fluctuations each year, and to adjust their resource use correspondingly. Fluctuations should be measured from expected (anticipated) production rather than from trend. Depending on how they are measured, different results about changing patterns of production risks can be obtained.
f. A statistical measure of variability inevitably has to be chosen. The most common measure used in this book is the coefficient of variation (cv), which expresses variability relative to the mean. It is a fairly good measure because, if the cv is constant or diminishes over time, the chance of a major shortfall in production below trend will very likely not increase, and any food security "problem" remains manageable. Variance is a more relevant measure for policymakers concerned with the size of grain stocks, or with absolute fluctuations in prices.

Notwithstanding all these difficulties, what emerges from the data analyses presented in this volume and related studies in the literature?

Weber and Sievers (1985a) show that baseline levels of production variability are high in many countries, especially in Africa, the Middle East, and Australia. The level of variability is clearly related to climatic factors and is greatest in the semi-arid areas, and lowest in humid areas. Southeast Asia has especially low cvs, but North and South America and Europe are also relatively stable. Unfortunately, the high cv areas also tend to have low average yields and have done least well in increasing yields in recent years.

Production variability also tends to be greater in small than in large countries, due to lack of risk-pooling effects across crops and regions. Many small African countries are disadvantaged in this regard.

Hazell (ch. 2) shows that production variability increased globally between the 1960s and 1970s, as measured by the variance ($F = 2.78$) or the cv (from 0.028 to 0.034). The probability of a major (say, 5 percent) shortfall below trend in world cereal production also increased, from 0.035 to 0.068. These changes are real in the sense that they have presented problems for farmers, consumers, and policymakers, but they are not statistically significant at the conventional 5 percent level. There is some reason to believe that the recent decade has been an "unlucky" sample rather than the result of increasingly unstable structural changes. But such aggregate statistical tests do not capture the effects of individual structural changes that are known to have taken place (for example, the green revolution and increased irrigation), and many individual factors are at work, some of which have a stabilizing effect at the aggregate level, while others are destabilizing. Whether the future will turn out to be more or less variable depends on the particular configuration of structural changes that will take place in cereal production, and their combined effects on variability.

At the global level (excluding China), the cv of production increased for maize (0.033 to 0.044), barley (0.048 to 0.075), and sorghum (0.052 to 0.057), but decreased for wheat (0.054 to 0.048) and rice (0.039 to 0.038). This suggests that much of the impact of the increased instability at the global level may have been in the feed and livestock sectors, though clearly there will have been important exceptions in some of the semi-arid developing areas where coarse grains are important human foods.

Increases in production variability (cv) are not obviously related to baseline levels of variability, or to increases in average production. When measured across countries, the correlation between the change in average production and the change in the cv is -0.15 between the 1960s and 1970s. This correlation is not significantly different from zero at the 5 percent significance level (Hazell 1985a,b).

The lack of any such simple correlation is due to a complex constellation of factors as illustrated by some of the chapters in this volume. In China (ch. 3) and the U.S.S.R. (ch. 4) the problem has been less one of increased variability within regions, and more one of unbalanced growth between regions that have compensatory relations in production. In Syria (ch. 5) the increase in the cv seems more related to changes in land reform and quota systems than to biological or climatic factors. In Australia (Anderson et al. 1988), changes in cv seem more directly associated with technological change, especially for spring wheat in the major wheat-growing areas.

Patterns of Yield Variability among Countries

Weber and Sievers (1985a) showed that baseline production variability is due primarily to yield variability. In chapter 2 it is shown that the increases in the variability of world cereal production since the 1960s are also due to increases in the variances and covariances of yields. The focus of this book on yield variability is therefore justified as being the major variable of interest in understanding production variability. It is also a simplifying focus, enabling abstraction from the complexities of area variability, which undoubtedly encompasses a wider range of economic and policy considerations.

Baseline yield variability follows similar geographic patterns to those for production variability (Weber and Sievers 1985a,b). African countries, in particular, suffer from some of the highest yield cvs. Yield variability has also increased at the global level (excluding China) since the 1960s; the cv of total cereal yield increased from 0.026 to 0.034 (ch. 2), although this change is not statistically significant at the 5 percent level.

There were considerable differences in the changes for individual cereal yields at the global level. The cv decreased for rice (0.033 to 0.026) and millets (0.073 to 0.058), changed little for wheat (0.050 to 0.049), and increased for maize (0.030 to 0.046), barley (0.043 to 0.064), and sorghum (0.040 to 0.046). These results probably reflect differences in the variability of the conditions under which they are grown rather than inherent differences between the cereal species.

The fact that so much rice is grown intensively with irrigation or deep bunds probably accounts for that crop having one of the lowest cvs in both periods. Analogously, an increasing proportion of the world's wheat crop is grown under irrigation and with high levels of purchased inputs. At the other end of the scale are the millets, grown in marginal conditions under low and variable rainfall. Moreover, there is a tendency in many arid regions for maize to displace sorghum, and for sorghum to displace millet toward the least favorable environments. Barley likewise may be displaced by wheat into more marginal environments, as Nguyen (ch. 5) shows, and this could account for the rise in its cv.

Another factor contributing to greater variability in some cases may be the growing of a crop under both intensive irrigated and marginal dryland conditions, the relative proportions of which may change from year to year.

Yields tend to be more highly correlated between adjacent countries and regions because of climatic factors (Weber and Sievers 1985a,b). Moreover, they have also become more positively correlated between crops and countries since the 1960s (ch. 2), between regions within countries (Hazell 1984; ch. 3, 4, 6), and between farms (ch. 8). These increased correlations have been a major factor contributing to increased variability in national yields in some countries, as well as at the global level. The country data do not suggest any strong relationship between increased cvs for yields and the growth in average yields.

In England (ch. 7) and Bavaria (ch. 9) wheat yields have increased impressively in recent decades, yet the cv has changed little. Indeed, the cv of wheat yields has not changed substantially in England since the early 1800s. This stability is probably attributable to the relatively stable and temperate climate, and the intensive and continually improving standards of management. In contrast, the cv of wheat yields has increased in New South Wales (N.S.W.), Australia, since the introduction of semidwarf varieties and the sharp rise in average yields that they seemingly induced

(Anderson et al. 1988). The difference may lie with the more variable climate and the extensive management practices used. Walker (ch. 6) also shows that the cvs of sorghum and millet yields have increased in the semi-arid areas of India since the introduction of high-yielding varieties (HYVs). These contrasting experiences suggest that yield increases in the semi-arid areas are more likely to be accompanied by increases in variability (cv) than are yield increases in more humid areas. Differences in management intensity are likely to accentuate these contrasts.

Sources of Yield Variability

Yield variability is determined by variety (genotype), variability and level of agronomic inputs (fertilizers, irrigation, pesticides, etc.), variability in climatic factors (rainfall, frosts, temperature, etc.), and variability in policy and economic variables (prices, land reforms, etc.). Interactions between these factors are important although difficult to analyze, especially between variety and other factors.

Variety and Yield Variability

Under controlled (farm trial) conditions, modern varieties typically have higher mean yields and variances than local varieties, but their cvs are either lower or about the same. Evidence is provided in this volume for pearl millets in India (ch. 16) and upland rice in the Philippines (ch. 20). Similar results seem to emerge for modern varieties of wheat and maize under experimental conditions when their performance across contrasting sites (environments) is compared (ch. 13, 14, 15).

These favorable results reflect the success of plant breeders in selecting genotypes that combine high-yield performance with stability. Some of the elements of genetic improvement are as follows (Evans 1986):

ADAPTABILITY. Shortening of the life cycle of cereal crops and reduction of their sensitivity to seasonal signals such as day length allow crops to perform more evenly across a range of sites, latitudes, and climates, thereby increasing their adaptability. So too does wider tolerance of soil conditions.

HARDINESS. Another important source of improvement has been in the ability to withstand drought, cold, heat, and other climatic extremes, especially at the most sensitive stages of the life cycle. Such hardiness is sometimes highly specific, sometimes more general. Specific resistance to extremes of heat or cold has been improved in many crops (for example, rice and millet in Japan to cold), and although the changes may seem small in a physiological sense, they may be of considerable significance in reducing downside variability. Hybrids may exhibit a more general hardiness in that, although they may be no more productive than inbreds under optimal conditions, they may perform substantially better than their parents at both high and low temperatures (McWilliam and Griffing 1965; McWilliam, Latter, and Mathison 1969).

REDUCED VULNERABILITY. Reducing the vulnerability to pests and diseases through the incorporation of genetic resistance—wide or narrow—to their current biotypes is a major preoccupation of plant breeders and a significant contribution to yield stability. In general, it has been easier to achieve than resistance to climatic stresses.

RESPONSIVENESS. In addition to these characteristics, there is the desirability of enhancing the ability of a variety to give a return on favorable conditions or higher inputs with greater yield or quality.

COMPETITIVENESS. This is another desirable characteristic, especially in marginal environments or where weed problems are serious.

All of these characteristics can influence the variability of yield: responsiveness especially on the "upside," hardiness and reduced vulnerability on the downside. However, they are not always compatible with one another, and trade-offs between them often must be made by the plant breeder—for example, between hardiness and responsiveness, or especially in the case of tall versus dwarf selections, between competitiveness and responsiveness.

The claimed stability of modern varieties is not always reflected in farm, regional, or national yield data. There are several reasons for this. First, some of the early modern varieties proved to be highly susceptible to specific pests and diseases. Because of their high yields, these varieties were widely adopted in a very short time and when pest and disease outbreaks occurred, they had a sizable and negative impact on farm and aggregate yields. This problem has been contained in recent years by the availability of a greater range of modern varieties, many of which have a wider range of resistance to pests and diseases (ch. 10, 11, 12, 13, 14, 15, 16, 20). Continuing strong emphasis is given to "maintenance" research, whereby replacement varieties are developed and kept in reserve. Pest and disease resistance breeding is now so sophisticated that the more rapid turnover of varieties in time has effectively substituted for the larger number of traditional varieties used at any one time.

Another reason why observed yield variability may increase with the introduction of modern varieties lies in their greater responsiveness to modern inputs. Modern varieties seem to perform about as well as traditional varieties in poorer environments, or under low input conditions (ch. 13, 15), but their yields are much higher under favorable conditions and with greater application of inputs. Consequently, if farmers adjust input use from year to year in response to changes in price signals, or in response to limited supplies of inputs, this may induce a higher degree of yield variability in modern varieties. Such behaviorally induced yield variability may have become an important factor in some countries, particularly in developing countries, where the greatly increased demand for purchased inputs that accompanied the green revolution outstripped the possibilities for adequate and timely supplies, given limited infrastructure and foreign exchange shortages (Jain, Dagg, and Taylor 1986). The problem may also have been aggravated by the sharp increases in the cost of fertilizers and other agrochemicals with the oil crises of the 1970s, and by an increase in the variability of cereal prices in world markets.

A further reason why aggregate yields may have become more variable with the introduction of modern varieties is the increased correlations among yields between farms (and regions). These increased correlations may be related to varietal choice, as, for example, with millets and sorghum (ch. 6). By screening for genotypes that perform well in many locations at the same time, breeders may inadvertently be increasing the chances of greater yield correlations between locations, and hence between farms and regions. This need not be a problem for farmers, but it can add to the variability of national yields.

The widespread adoption of a few varieties may also lead to increased correlations through a common susceptibility to pests and diseases and a common responsiveness to weather conditions. This problem may have been aggravated by more homogeneous cultural practices (ch. 12), and by an increased dependence on purchased inputs. Whereas synchronization of the crops in a region may make them all susceptible to extremes of heat, cold, or drought at particular stages, it may also spread the risk of losses from birds or rodents, as with rice crops in Asia. It is also true that many modern varieties bring together a wider range of genotypes into their ancestry than traditional varieties and are better able to cope with a wide range of climatic and pest problems (ch. 10, 11, 12).

Climatic Factors

A major source of yield variance in all cases, but especially for the cereals grown in more arid areas, is the variability in crop weather. Carter and Parry (1986) conclude, however, that there is no indication that recent changes in cereal yield variability can be ascribed to climatic change.

Interannual variations—such as those associated with the El Niño/Southern Oscillation phenomenon or with the Sub-Saharan droughts of 1972, 1977, and 1983-84—have certainly influenced global cereal production and variability, but there is seemingly a need to look elsewhere for the causal factors of changes in variance and covariance in recent years, even though long-term climatic changes associated with rising atmospheric CO_2 levels are likely to have important implications for cereal production in the future.

Weather patterns may, however, be partly responsible for increases in inter-regional correlations, as shown by French and Headley (ch. 22) for maize in the United States, and by Walker (ch. 6) for millet and sorghum in India.

Agronomic Inputs

Under trial conditions, the more intensive use of purchased inputs seems to be associated with increases in the mean and variance of yields, but with little or no change in the cv. For example, with nitrogenous fertilizer application to wheat and barley in Germany, Hanus and Schoop (ch. 21) found that the cv actually declined with heavier applications until the yield asymptote was approached. The cv then increased sharply at higher rates of application as diseases increased but could successfully be reduced by the application of fungicides. Roumasset et al. (ch. 17), however, report that nitrogen generally tends to increase yield variability both absolutely and relatively on irrigated rice in the Philippines.

Conflicting forces may be at work in the changes in yield variability under farm conditions as agriculture becomes more intensive. On the one hand, variability tends to fall as agronomic control of the environment becomes more complete, as in the case of wheat in Western Europe. On the other hand, selection for higher yield potential is dependent on enhanced agronomic support for the crop, and when this is unreliable, the higher yielding varieties may be vulnerable to greater variation. The latter may be particularly true during the early stages of more widespread and heavier use of a particular input, but then fall as its use becomes more uniform and as its rate of application approaches the response asymptote. With irrigation, for example, Mehra (1981) found that variability had fallen as tubewell irrigation of wheat crops in the Punjab became more extensive, but with rice in the Philippines, while wet season crops were less variable, the limited, uneven, and unreliable irrigation of dry season crops may increase variability (Rosegrant 1986).

In general there may be considerable scope for the reduction of variability by more flexible, better informed, and more diversified and specific use of inputs. This will not, however, always be consistent with reducing inter-regional yield correlations. Pandey (ch. 18) provides evidence that irrigation that is stabilizing at the local level may increase correlations, thereby having a mixed effect on variability at aggregate levels. Webster and Williams (ch. 8) also suggest that the recent but widespread adoption of fungicides on wheat in Southeast England may be a major contributor of increased interfarm yield correlations.

Consequences of Yield and Production Variability

The worry that modern varieties may be more risky and therefore less attractive to farmers does not seem to hold up in practice. Stochastic dominance tests of the distribution of returns from improved and traditional varieties typically show new varieties to be dominant (millets, ch. 16; wheat, ch. 24 and Anderson 1974b). Walker (ch. 25) also shows that improving the stability of yields of individual cereals in the semi-arid tropics (SAT) areas of India would have negligible effects on the stability of farm incomes, and hence on farmers' willingness to bear risks.

Risk considerations can be a problem for the adoption of a new variety in the short term if farmers initially hold exaggerated perceptions about the riskiness of returns. But as expectations are revised over time, these problems should diminish (O'Mara 1983). In the longer term, risk considerations are likely to remain important if (a) the new variety is indeed more risky and has only a marginal advantage in mean returns (Perrin and Winkelmann 1976), or (b) the new variety is riskier and also requires significantly greater amounts of working capital to be invested in seed, fertilizers, and so forth. Capital considerations can be especially constraining to small-scale farmers if there is a real risk of capital loss. They may be unwilling to borrow or unable to find lenders willing to take the risk (Boussard 1981; Hazell, Bassoco, and Arcia 1986). Both these situations seem more likely to arise in Africa than in most other regions of the world, though there have been few studies of technology adoption in that continent to verify this. In fact, there has been a definite bias in adoption studies toward the humid and irrigated areas of the world, perhaps reflecting the preference of analysts to be confident that there is something to measure before attempting to do so.

As Sahn and von Braun (ch. 26) show, production variability generally adds to national food insecurity problems, though some governments do seemingly take effective action through storage and trade policies to dampen fluctuations in domestic consumption, and consumers substitute between foods in response to their relative scarcities. But, even in countries where aggregate food consumption is relatively stable, the consumption of some of the poorer households can still be at risk, particularly when their incomes are tied to agricultural production (smaller scale farmers and landless workers). Food security problems therefore continue to be a problem in many developing countries, even where the cv of aggregate production has not increased to aggravate the problem.

Implications for Agricultural Research

With these concluding remarks, the task of suggesting recommendations for agricultural policy and research is addressed, both with a view to reducing baseline levels of variability, and to containing increases where they occur.

What can be done through technological approaches to reduce yield variability and yield correlations?

Plant Breeding and Crop Improvement

Plant breeders have long recognized the importance of selecting "stable" varieties. They have achieved, especially for wheat and rice but also many other crops, significant gains in adaptability, hardiness, and reduced vulnerability to pests and diseases, but the gains in stability components may be somewhat compromised by selection for responsiveness. As Arnold and Austin (ch. 10) note, plant breeders may be seeking several different things under the broad objective of stability.

Insofar as variability faced by farmers is concerned, it may well be that additional improvements might follow if there were better proxies to variability over time than cross-site differences within years. The possibilities include experimentation under diverse, particularly unfavorable or stressed, conditions in controlled environment chambers (such as phytotrons) or under specially selected and possibly modified microenvironmental conditions (for example, administered pest and disease infections or induced drought) in experimental and possibly farmers' fields.

There are some implicit problems with time-consuming approaches in that new varieties can have short lives, so they would tend to be obsolete before adequately tested if several years were required in the evaluation. Perhaps more penetrating, but seemingly yet-to-be-developed analytical methods beyond the Russell–Eberhart type of model will eventually prove useful in more cogent assaults on the problem (ch. 10, Evans 1986).

Contemporary plant breeding is seemingly not explicitly addressing the yield correlation problem and may be worsening it by more-or-less routinely screening across sites and thereby, unwittingly perhaps, moving unfavorably in the direction of increasing genetic vulnerability. A potential solution is for more localized breeding endeavors, with most of the selection effort addressed to achievements under rather specific agroecological and particularly edaphoclimatic circumstances. This approach might also help to improve performance in farmers' fields, though obviously it could involve greater expenditures for agricultural research, depending on the extent of agroecological diversity encountered in the crop-growing regions that are the targets of national or regional research programs and on the cost-effectiveness of the crop improvement approach adopted. There is evidently a need for more local work and less concentration of selection activities at the relatively few major centers of plant breeding, including the international agricultural research centers.

There are implications for bodies such as the Consultative Group on International Agricultural Research (CGIAR) at the World Bank. Where feasible and economical, breeding work should be decentralized as much as possible. This would mean shifting many activities to national breeding programs and, indeed, moves are already underway to do this. Activity must also be increased in nations which do not yet have very effective capabilities, and aiding this process of development will be a continuing task for institutions such as the CGIAR centers.

Even with recent changing emphasis, there has still been relatively little attention given to breeding for "marginal" conditions, notwithstanding progress on *Striga* resistance, tolerance of crops to adverse soil conditions, and so forth. The reasons are understandable and probably defensible, as impacts tend to be less dramatic than are achievable in more favorable circumstances. There may be a good case for continuing involvement of the CGIAR centers in such targeted work, recognizing the unattractiveness of work on relatively unpromising resources and environmental niches to many national programs with very scarce resources.

Genetic Vulnerability

The extent to which the genetic base of modern cereal varieties and hybrids influences the downside risks is difficult to assess. Outbreaks of pests and diseases have had an impact, sometimes disastrous, throughout recorded history. Problems still occur, such as presumably with downy mildew on millet in India, but major disasters, such as the earlier stem rust epidemics in North American wheat crops, have been contained in recent years. Southern corn leaf blight on T cytoplasm maize hybrids had been predicted by Mercado and Lantican (1961) and was pandemic in 1970, but within a year, the genetic base was changed enough to deal with the pathogen. Other problems loom as possible threats, such as the failure of brown plant hopper biotype 2 resistance in IR36 rice, or of leaf rust resistance in some Centro Internacional de Mejoramiento de Maiz y Trigo (CIMMYT) maize varieties, or the widespread cytoplasmic uniformity of International Rice Research Institute (IRRI) rices (Coffman and Hargrove, ch. 11), but replacement varieties are already in reserve.

However, the fact that several wheat and rice varieties, such as Bezostaia wheat in Eastern Europe and IR36 rice in Asia, are grown on more than 10 million hectares each, inevitably means that their sudden failure would raise the covariance in yield, as could their similar response to weather conditions common to a large region. This element of covariance would decline in the future if plant breeding—whether public, private, or in the international centers—were to evolve toward greater emphasis on regional and local adaptation (Evans 1986).

Beyond Plant Breeding

There is growing evidence that yield variability can be reduced or moderated through improved management practices (Evans 1986), for example, fertilizer (ch. 17), water (ch. 18), pesticide (ch. 19) management, fallows for moisture conservation (ch. 20, 24), and so forth. As reviewed in chapter 18, the potentially important investment in irrigation can be stabilizing, but this depends on the source of water and the type of power used in its application. There is also a need for greater emphasis on stability in farming systems work as it is practiced.

The CGIAR system of international research centers has been praised as being the most significant coordinated effort in plant breeding in history but the system has also been criticized for not being more than this. In particular, much of the criticism centers around the proposition that plant breeding can only do so much, and while it is usually of low cost in terms of each potentially affected unit of cropland area, the way forward for many areas is probably not, in the first instance at least, via breeding. The areas of concern are typically those in parts of the world not so far influenced by any green revolution impacts associated with (often irrigated) rice and wheat. Such areas are to be found in many parts of the tropics, especially in Africa and in regions of countries with relatively undeveloped infrastructure and irrigation. Such regions often have poor soils and inadequate and variable rainfall.

There are many technological possibilities for improving the efficiency of production that are not directly dependent on new genotypes, and argronomic research can serve to identify them (Evans 1986). Some of them do not require much research. Good quality seed is a fairly basic requirement that can be met by either a well-developed seed industry or a well-developed degree of farmer perspicacity. Early growth depends greatly on nutrient and water status, as noted above. Crop managers, depending on their economically effective access to agricultural chemicals and possibly also to hired labor, can significantly affect the inroads made by fungi, insects, and weeds in their crops. There is thus much scope for reducing variability by wiser, more flexible, and perhaps also more diversified use of inputs. Research and extension have very significant roles to play here, if worthwhile technological advances are to be established and implemented.

Implications for Agricultural Policy

Rural societies have been contending with variability of production of their basic staples for millennia. The difficulties associated with this are probably increasing in many parts of the world. As is shown herein, there are several regions where variability and riskiness of productivity are increasing, and there is also rapid population growth so that greater numbers of people are affected.

In considering the various possibilities for intervention, caution is called for in not aggravating the situation by, perhaps unwittingly, making it more difficult for households to cope. The credit market is one case in point. Resource-poor farmers use a variety of informal adjustments to deal with variability, including participation in various credit markets. Intervention by governments in credit markets often has the effect of making the risk management of such farmers less effective than it would otherwise be (Walker and Jodha 1986). Clearly, there is a role for authorities to enrich the mix of credit availabilities, but any regulatory role needs to be exercised sensitively with good understanding of the needs of participants who face possibly extreme levels of downside risk.

Another danger is that government policies may cause or exacerbate poor decision making with respect to both investment and resource allocation in areas that are suffering permanent climatic or ecological decline. Intervention should be couched in such a manner as not to shield individual decision makers from reality, whatever that may be, and whatever processes of change in the natural, economic, or social environment may be underway.

Related to the possibility of interventions discouraging appropriate learning is the exacerbation of uncertainties faced by farmers. There is relatively little analytical attention addressed to this, but the pioneering works of MacLaren (1980, 1983) on the effects of policy uncertainty are instructive and insightful. Policy-induced risks may add to the decision-making burden of affected individuals—even when policies have the stated objective of modifying or mitigating risks. For example, in the United States, Wilhite, Rosenberg, and Glantz (1982) found that government reaction to drought crises was generally ad hoc and often resulted in the implementation of hastily prepared assessment and response procedures that gave ineffective and poorly coordinated results. The difficulties related in part to the multitude of agencies involved in administration and the diversity of procedures and criteria used by such agencies. Much the same situation has prevailed in Australia (Anderson 1979, Freebairn 1983).

Crop Insurance

Unfortunately, past experience with crop insurance is not encouraging, and the costs of publicly provided insurance have usually far exceeded their benefits (Hazell, Pomareda, and Valdés 1986). Nor should the efficiency with which farmers and traditional village institutions cope with risks be neglected. Walker and Jodha (1986) have provided cogent information on these issues, and they point out that crop insurance might sometimes simply provide a more costly substitute for existing private risk-sharing arrangements. Improvement of financial institutions might be a viable approach, particularly if these involve an expansion of medium-term consumer credit so that farmers can borrow money in bad years and pay it back in good years.

The possibility of an insurance market addressed to random environmental driving forces, such as rainfall, is somewhat more promising than direct insurance of outputs such as crops. There have been some experiments with rainfall insurance, and indeed, this matter is being carefully assessed in the Australian context (McBride and Edwards 1986). If there is a reliable meteorological service upon which such a scheme can be based, at least the problem of moral hazard is solved. Similarly, if the scheme is well designed there may be relatively few difficulties associated with adverse selection. Administration costs can, accordingly, be kept relatively low, and such an insurance service may well prove to be widely applicable, attractive to farmers, and commercially viable. The fact that few, if any, such schemes have arisen spontaneously must leave something of a question mark over their inherent viability (Dillon 1986). The explanations probably lie in the imperfections of rainfall insurance as a risk-bearing device, including nonuniform distribution of rainfall over administrative domains, the lack of correspondence between simple temporal aggregates of rainfall and realized crop yields, and the elements of uncertainty that are little influenced by rainfall experience.

Marketing Systems

For mitigating farm-level risk, the more that individual farmers can link with the rest of the world in their economic realizations, the more they can "exploit" society at large for self-insurance. Effective marketing systems for farm inputs and outputs must be seen as a necessary condition for improving the opportunities of farmers to manage their risks. Just as for financial institutions, marketing systems by their very nature must generally be expected to work best when they are unregulated so that buyers and sellers are unconstrained and can interact freely.

The concept of marketing systems in this context is broad, ranging over availability of physical space and entrepreneurial operators, the provision of effective financial institutions, and transportation infrastructure and facilities. The systems must feature flexibility to function in highly variable environments, which may well switch from being net exporters to net importers from season to season. Physical access to markets on a continuing basis by adequate road and other transport facilities is a strong advantage in meeting seasonal contingencies, whether they are of a favorable or unfavorable nature.

Improvement of marketing systems will generally feature in whatever development approach is followed. It is some consolation for planners to know that they will also be mitigating the risks faced by most farmers if they can be successful in improving the effectiveness of the marketing system at large.

Buffer Stocks and Price Stabilization

At the national level, increased variability in prices and food consumption can be contained through buffer stock schemes. However, the International Food Policy Research Institute's (IFPRI's) work shows that, in most cases, it is more cost-effective for governments to use world markets to stabilize domestic consumption (Siamwalla and Valdés 1980), sometimes using the International Monetary Fund's (IMF) food facility as a source of funding for food imports when appropriate (Huddleston et al. 1984). Interventions can also be targeted on specific socioeconomic groups, such as food subsidies for the poor or on relief employment and food-for-work schemes. The efficiency of these and other direct interventions is elaborated by Sahn and von Braun (ch. 26).

In terms of farm-level risk mitigation, the major disadvantage of commodity price stabilization is that farmers are not so much concerned with price variability as with income variability. Stabilizing prices may even lead to increased income variability. This possibility is likely if farmers grow several crops for which returns, though individually unstable, are collectively relatively stable. A price stabilization program for just one commodity might then induce a large supply response and have an adverse effect on prices and returns without reducing income risk (Newbery and Stiglitz 1981, p. 27). There may also be situations where price risk is not all that important. Further, as discussed by Siamwalla (1986), government intervention to reduce price risk will be more difficult to sustain the larger the share of the commodity in the world market, the more important the commodity in the economy, the longer the period of production of the commodity, and the more porous the national border.

Price support or "underwriting" (Quiggin 1983) is a particular form of commodity price stabilization which may be specifically aimed at mitigating farm-level risk by putting a floor under output price, while not directly restricting price above the floor level. To be effective in terms of farm decision making, the floor price must be both guaranteed and announced before the growing season commences. Implementation is generally effected by government standing ready to purchase all quantities that may be offered at the floor price.

Both to farmers and government, price stabilization is an attractive concept and, theoretically, may possibly be beneficial in its risk-reducing effects (Quiggin and Anderson 1979). Practice, however, is likely to be a different matter. The difficulty lies in choosing the level at which prices are to be set so as to gain the potential benefits of stability without at the same time nullifying the natural role of the market in guiding resource use. Notwithstanding such practical considerations and the theoretical niceties, a pragmatic matter of considerable significance is the very modest extent of "risk benefits" obtainable from (even complete) price stabilization as documented extensively by Newbery and Stiglitz (1981), particularly using their approximation of $0.5RD(cv^2)$, where R denotes relative risk aversion and $D(\ )$ denotes the variability change (in squared cv of income). Such benefits are typically of the order of 3 percent, although the caution of Kanbur (1984) as to the neglect of macroeconomic benefits of stabilization in such calculations should be borne in mind. Another comment by Kanbur (1984, p. 351) to the effect that "it is the coefficient of variation of (income) that matters, not just its variance" is relevant in considering any of the interventions related to variability that are discussed in this volume.

Diversification

Another approach is to take advantage of less-than-perfectly covariate production patterns between regions in establishing production priorities. It is possible to derive an optimal pattern of regional diversification to minimize the standard deviation of production of a crop given a desired level of average output (Hazell 1982). However, in seeking more risk-efficient production strategies, one would not want to distort unduly the workings of markets or to violate the principles of comparative advantage, but only to bear the correlations in mind as a secondary factor when establishing priorities for investing public funds in agricultural research, extension, irrigation, and the like. In this spirit Tarrant (ch. 4) argues that a better balance in the growth of major cereal-producing regions in the U.S.S.R. should be a policy consideration for the Soviets if regional compensation effects are to be exploited in attaining more stable aggregate production.

Public Provision of Information

The quality of decision making in highly variable and risky environments depends crucially on the information available to decision makers. In the food systems of the world that are influenced by variable yields of cereals, decision makers are involved at many levels ranging from individual farms, through local marketing agents and food security administrators, regional and national authorities concerned with input and output delivery systems, and food policy authorities to international counterpart agents and interventionists. Better information is required at all these levels.

The fact of the variability of natural and economic environments explains much of existing public investment in information gathering and processing systems. If weather, production, prices, and so forth were deterministic and thus easily known by all concerned, there would be little need for national meteorological services, national statistical services, and interpretative research agencies such as bureaus of agricultural economics. As well as describing variable environments in insightful ways that add to the stock of knowledge, such agencies can work toward further assisting decision makers by attempting to forecast uncertain futures—in the present context, droughts, frosts, pest and disease attacks, crop marketing volumes, trade volumes, flows of food aid, prices, and so forth. The difficulty of such work and its inherent inaccuracy do not mean that it may not be extremely valuable (Byerlee and Anderson 1982).

The key policy issue is the extent to which existing investment, both public and private, in the provision of information is optimal. The public-good nature of much of the relevant information ensures that private investments will be much less than is socially optimal. There is, however, a dearth of research on how adequate have been the public initiatives. One thing is certain, given the diversity of level of investment around the globe, namely that, if the level in industrial countries is somewhere near the socially optimal intensity, most developing countries are still severely underinvesting. Thus, as they muster their scarce national and external resources to address developmental priorities, due attention must be devoted to easily neglected (service industry) information and research and extension systems, along with the more basic infrastructural and directly productive enhancements.

Conclusions

We have considered a number of things that agricultural researchers and policymakers can do to reduce yield variability. Some of these, for example, plant breeding and input management, represent direct attempts to increase yield stability. In contrast, policy interventions, such as crop insurance and price stabilization schemes, seek only to mitigate some of the undesirable consequences of yield variability.

An important issue, and one which we have not been able to shed much light on in this book, concerns the relative economic efficiency of alternative approaches. Not only will alternative approaches differ in their effectiveness in reducing yield variability, but they will also differ in their costs. For example, plant breeders could, by giving more emphasis to stability, reduce yield variability but only by sacrificing perhaps sizable increases in average yields. Such sacrifices could prove costly to society, and a full social benefit–cost analysis might show alternative approaches to be better.

It seems likely that more careful management of inputs and improved agronomic practices may be a relatively cost-effective way of reducing yield variability. However, to the extent that these require sizable increases in public investments in research, extension, credit, and input delivery systems, these investments may also need to raise average productivity to be justified.

Perhaps relatively more is known about the costs and benefits of public policies, especially crop insurance (Hazell, Pomareda and Valdés 1986), price stabilization (Newbery and Stiglitz 1981), food subsidies (Pinstrup-Andersen 1988), and food-for-work programs (Ahmed and Hossain 1985). Experience shows that these can all be very expensive unless carefully targeted on the households most adversely affected by production variability.

Attempts to draw more definitive conclusions about the cost effectiveness of different approaches in reducing yield variability seem doomed to flounder until more quantitative information is available about the costs and benefits of each approach. Collection of this kind of information will require more carefully focused research on yield variability than has been common in the past. It is our hope that this volume may stimulate such work.

References

Ahmed, Raisuddin, and Hossain, Mahabub 1985. "Development impact of the food for work program in Bangladesh." *Mimeo.* Bangladesh Institute for Development Studies.

Akohas, H. 1983. "Cytoplasmic male sterility in barley 12: Associations between disease resistance and restoration of MSM1 fertility in the wild progenitor of barley." *Theoretical and Applied Genetics* 65, 67-71.

Allard, R. W., and Bradshaw, A. D. 1964. "Implications of genotype-environment interactions in applied plant breeding." *Crop Science* 4:503-7.

American Embassy, Damascus 1984. *Syria: Grain and Feed Annual Report,* Attache Report No. SY4003.

Anderson, J. R. 1973. "Sparse data, climatic variability, and yield uncertainty in response analysis." *American Journal of Agricultural Economics* 55(1):77-82.

Anderson J. R. 1974a. "Simulation: Methodology and application in agricultural economics." *Review of Marketing and Agricultural Economics* 42(1):3-55.

———. 1974b. "Risk efficiency in the interpretation of agricultural production research." *Review of Marketing and Agricultural Economics* 42(3):131-84.

———. 1979. "Impacts of climatic variability in Australian agriculture: A review." *Review of Marketing and Agricultural Economics* 47(3):147-77.

———. 1981. "Meteorological services in agronomic and economic evaluations of risk." *Proceedings of the Technical Conference on Climate: Asia and Western Pacific,* WMO No. 578. Geneva: World Meteorological Organization, 205-9.

———. 1983. "On risk deductions in public project appraisal." *Australian Journal of Agricultural Economics* 27(3):45-52.

Anderson, J. R., and Griffiths, W. E. 1982. "Production risk and efficient allocation of resources." *Australian Journal of Agricultural Economics* 26(3):226-31.

Anderson, J. R., and Hamal, K. B. 1983. "Risk and rice technology in Nepal." *Indian Journal of Agricultural Economics* 38(2):217-22.

Anderson, J. R., and Scandizzo, P. L. 1984. "Food risk and the poor." *Food Policy* 9(1):44-52.

Anderson, J. R.; Dillon, J. L.; and Hardaker, J. B. 1977. *Agricultural Decision Analysis.* Ames: Iowa State University Press.

Anderson, J. R.; Dillon, J. L.; Cowie, A. J.; Hazell, P. B. R.; and Wan, G. H. 1988. "Changing variability in cereal production in Australia." *Review of Marketing and Agricultural Economics* (forthcoming).

Anderson, R. M.; Turner, B. D.; and Taylor, R. D. 1979. *Population Dynamics.* Oxford: Blackwell.

Antle, J. M. 1983a. "Incorporating risk into production analysis." *American Journal of Agricultural Economics* 65(5):1099-106.

———. 1983b. "Testing the stochastic structure of production: A flexible moment-based approach." *Journal of Business and Economics Statistics* 3:192-201.

———. 1983c. "Sequential decision making in production models." *American Journal of Agricultural Economics* 65(2):282-90.

———. 1986. "Pesticide policy, production risk, and producer welfare: an econometric approach to applied welfare economics." Draft, Resources for the Future, Washington, D.C.; Monograph Mimeo., University of California, Davis.

Antle, J. M., and Crissman, C. C. 1986. "Measuring technical efficiency in risky production during technical change." Mimeo., Department of Agricultural Economics, University of California, Davis.

Aquino, R. C., and Jennings, P. R. 1966. "Inheritance and significance of dwarfism in an indica rice variety." *Crop Science* 6:551-54.

Arnold, M. H., and Innes, N. L. 1976. "Plant breeding," in M. H. Arnold (ed.), *Agricultural Research for Development: The Namulonge Contribution.* Cambridge: Cambridge University Press, 197-246.

———. 1984. "Plant breeding for crop improvement with special reference to Africa," in D. L. Hawksworthy (ed.), *Advancing Agricultural Production in Africa. Proceedings of CAB's First Scientific Conference, Arusha, Tanzania, 12-18 February 1984.* Farnham Royal, England: Commonwealth Agricultural Bureaux, 169-174.

Baker, R. J. 1969. "Genotype-environment interactions in yield of wheat." *Canadian Journal of Plant Science* 49:743-51.

Bakour, Y. 1984. *Analytical Study of Major Changes in Agrarian Structure and Land Tenure Systems in Syria.* Damascus: Arab Organization for Agricultural Development.

Barbakov, N. K. 1972. *State Five Year Plan for the Development of the U.S.S.R. National Economy.* Moscow: Gosplan.

Barker, R., and Herdt, R. W. 1985. *The Rice Economy of Asia.* Washington, D.C.: Resources for the Future, in cooperation with the International Rice Research Institute, Los Baños.

Barker, R.; Cordova, V.; and Roumasset, J. A. 1976. "The economic analysis of experimental results in nitrogen response of rice." Farm Management Notes, UPLB, Philippines.

Barker, R.; Gabler, E. C.; and Winkelmann, D. 1981. "Long term consequences of technological change on crop yield stability: the case for cereal grain," in A. Valdés (ed.), *Food Security for Developing Countries.* Boulder, Colo.: Westview Press.

Beaton, G. 1983. "Energy in human nutrition: Perspectives and problems." *Nutrition Reviews* 41(11):325-40.

Becker, H. C. 1981. "Correlations among some statistical measures of phenotypic stability." *Euphytica* 30:835-40.

Berentsen, W. H. 1982. "Spatial variability in Soviet grain productivity 1955-1974." *Soviet Geography* 23:630-39.

Binswanger, H. P. 1980. "Attitudes toward risk: Experimental measurement in rural India." *American Journal of Agricultural Economics* 62(3):395-407.

Binswanger, H. P., and Barah, B. C. 1980. *Yield Risk, Risk Aversion, and Genotype Selection: Conceptual Issues and Approaches*. ICRISAT Research Bulletin 3. Patancheru, India: International Crops Research Institute for the Semi-Arid Tropics.

Binswanger, H. P., and Sillers, D. A. 1983. "Risk aversion and credit constraints in farmers' decision making: A reinterpretation." *Journal of Development Studies* 20(1):5-21.

Boggess, W. G.; Lynne, G. D.; Lores, J. W.; and Swaney, D. P. 1983. "Risk-return assessment of irrigation decisions in humid regions." *Southern Journal of Agricultural Economics* 15(1):135-43.

Bohrnstedt, G. W., and Goldberger, A. S. 1969. "On the exact covariance of products of random variables." *Journal of the American Statistical Association* 64(328):1439-42.

Boussard, J-M. 1981. "The risk aversion parameter in modelling farm decisions," in C. Hennig Hanf and G. Schiefer (eds.), *Consideration and Modelling of Risk in the Agribusiness Sector*. Kiel, W. Germany: Kieler Wissenschaftsverlag Vauk.

Braun, H. J. 1983. "Untersuchungen ueber die selektionseingung von orten fuer die zuechtung von sommerweizen im tropisch-subtropischen bereich." Diss., Universitaet Hohenheim, Federal Republic of Germany.

Braun, J. von, and Huddleston, B. 1984. "Implications of food aid for price policy in recipient countries." Paper for IFPRI workshop on food and agricultural price policy, Washington, D.C.

Brown, W. L., and Goodman, M. M. 1977. "Races of corn," in G. F. Sprague (ed.), *Corn and Corn Improvement*. Madison, Wis.: American Society of Agronomy.

Byerlee, D. R., and Anderson, J. R. 1969. "Value of prediction of uncontrolled factors in response functions." *Australian Journal of Agricultural Economics* 13(2):28-37.

———. 1982. "Risk, utility, and the value of information in farmer decision making." *Review of Marketing and Agricultural Economics* 50(3):231-46.

Cain, M. 1981. "Risk and insurance: perspective on fertility and agrarian change in India and Bangladesh." *Population and Development Review* 7(3):435-74.

Cardwell, V. B. 1982. "Fifty years of Minnesota corn production: sources of yield increase." *Agronomy Journal* 74:984-90.

Carlson, G. A. 1970. "A decision theoretic approach to crop disease prediction and control." *American Journal of Agricultural Economics* 52(2):216-23.

———. 1979. "The role of pesticides in stabilizing agricultural production," in J. Sheets and D. Pimental (eds.), *Pesticides: Contemporary Roles in Agriculture, Health and the Environment.* Clifton, N.J.: Humana Press.

———. 1984. "Risk reducing inputs related to agricultural pests," in *Risk Analysis for Agricultural Production Firms: Concepts, Information Requirements, and Policy Issues. Proceedings of Southern Research Project.* S-180, Department of Agricultural Economics. Urbana: University of Illinois.

Carlson, G. A., and Main, C. E. 1976. "Economics of disease-loss management." *Annual Review of Phytopathology* 14:381-403.

Carter, T. R., and Parry, M. L. 1986. "Climatic change and changes in crop yield variability," in P. B. R. Hazell (ed.), *Summary Proceedings of a Workshop on Cereal Yield Variability.* IFPRI, International Food Policy Research Institute and DSE. Washington, D.C.: 47-65.

Castleberry, R. M.; Crum, C. W.; and Krull, C. F. 1984. "Genetic yield improvement of U.S. maize cultivars under varying fertility and climatic environments." *Crop Science* 24:33-36.

Century of Agricultural Statistics in Great Britain, A. 1866-1966. 1968. London: Her Majesty's Stationery Office.

Chandrasekar, C. M. M. 1986. "Sources of changes in the variability of paddy production in the dry zone of Sri Lanka in the context of new technology." M.Ec. dissertation, University of New England, Armidale, N.S.W., Australia.

Chang, T. T. 1984. "Conservation of rice genetic resources: Luxury or necessity?" *Science* 224(4646):251-56.

Chao Kang. 1970. *Agricultural Production in Communist China, 1949-1965.* Madison: University of Wisconsin Press.

Chen Nai-Ruenn. 1967. *Chinese Economic Statistics: A Handbook for Mainland China.* Chicago: Aldine.

Church, B. M., and Austin, R. B. 1983. "Variability of wheat yields in England and Wales." *Journal of Agricultural Science* 100:201-4.

CIA. 1969. *Agricultural Acreage in Communist China, 1949-68: A Statistical Compilation.* Washington, D.C.: Central Intelligence Agency.

CIMMYT (Centro Internacional de Mejoramiento de Maiz y Trigo). 1985. "Breeding for improved husk cover in tropical maize," in *CIMMYT Research Highlights 1984.* El Batan, Philippines: CIMMYT, 22-28.

Cochran, M., and Robison, L. 1982. "Evaluation of strategy, performance, and risk efficiency of IPM programs in apple production." Agricultural Economics Staff Paper No. 82-27, Michigan State University, East Lansing.

Cochran, W. G. 1939. "Use of analysis of variance in enumeration by sampling." *Journal of the American Statistical Association* 34:492-510.

Coffman, W. R.; Kaufman, H. E.; and Heinrichs, E. A. 1977. "Summary Report: Visit of the IRRI rice improvement team to the People's Republic of China." International Rice Research Institute, Los Baños, Philippines.

Coffman, W. R.; Khush, G. S.; and Kaufman, H. E. 1978. "Genetic evaluation and utilization program of IRRI," in I. W. Buddenhagen and G. S. Persley (eds.), *Rice in Africa.* London: Academic Press.

Colyer, D. 1969. "Fertilization strategy under uncertainty." *Canadian Journal of Agricultural Economics* 17(3):713-41.

Cook, R. J. 1982. "Decision making in the control of cereal diseases," in R. B. Austin (ed.), *Decision Making in the Practice of Crop Protection.* Monograph no. 12. London: British Crop Protection Council.

Cooper, P. J. M. 1983. "Crop management in rainfed agriculture with special reference to water use efficiency," in *Proceedings of the 17th Collegium of the International Potash Institute.* Bern: IPI 63-79.

Crossa, J. H., and Deutsch, J. A. 1985. "Estimate of genetic and genetic × environment variance components in six tropical maize populations," in *Agronomy Abstracts of the ASA, CSA, and SSSA,* 51. Madison, Wisc.: American Society of Agronomy.

Dalrymple, D. G. 1978. *Development and Spread of High Yielding Varieties of Wheat and Rice in Less Developed Nations.* Foreign Agricultural Economic Report No. 95. Washington, D.C.: U.S. Department of Agriculture and U.S. Agency for International Development.

———. 1985. "The development and adoption of high-yielding varieties of wheat and rice in developing nations." *American Journal of Agricultural Economics* 67(5):1067-73.

———. 1986a. *High-Yielding Rice Varieties in Developing Countries.* Washington, D.C.: Agency for International Development.

———. 1986b. *High-Yielding Wheat Varieties in Developing Countries.* Washington, D.C.: Agency for International Development.

Dando, W. A. 1980. *The Strategy of Famine.* London: Arnold.

Day, R. H. 1965. "Probability distributions for field crop yields." *Journal of Farm Economics* 47(3):713-41.

De Datta, S. K. 1981. *Principles and Practices of Rice Production.* New York: Wiley.

De Datta, S. K., and Flinn, J. C. 1985. "Technology and economics of weed control in a broadcast-seeded flooded tropical area." Mimeo., International Rice Research Institute, Los Baños, Philippines.

De Datta, S. K.; Garcia, F. V.; Chatterjee, A. K.; Abilay, W. P.; Alcantara, J. M.; Cia, B. S.; and Jereza, H. C. 1979. *Biological Constraints to Farmers' Rice Yields in Three Philippine Provinces.* IRRI Research Paper Series No. 30. Los Baños, Philippines: International Rice Research Institute.

de Janvry, A. 1972. "Optimal levels of fertilization under risk: The potential for corn and wheat fertilization under alternative policies in Argentina." *American Journal of Agricultural Economics* 54(1):1-10.

Denning, G. L. 1985. "The need to balance productivity, stability and sustainability of rice farming systems." Mimeo., International Rice Research Institute, Los Baños, Philippines.

Dent, J. B., and Anderson, J. R. (eds.) 1971. *Systems Analysis in Agricultural Management.* Sydney: Wiley.

Dent, J. B., and Blackie, M. J. 1979. *Systems Simulation in Agriculture.* London: Applied Science Publishers.

Deolalikar, A. 1984. "Are there pecuniary returns to health in agricultural work?

An econometric analysis of agricultural wages and farm productivity in rural South India." Economic Program Progress Report 38, International Crops Research Institute for the Semi-Arid Tropics, Patancheru, India.

Desai, G. 1981. "Estimates of Soviet grain imports in 1980-1985: alternative approaches." Research Report No. 22. Washington, D.C.: International Food Policy Research Institute.

Dhawan, B. D. 1985. "Irrigation impact on farm economy." *Economic and Political Weekly* 20(39):A124-28.

Dillon, J. L. 1976. "The economics of systems research." *Agricultural Systems* 1(1):5-22.

———. 1986. "Institutional possibilities to minimize risk at farm level," in T. J. Davis (ed.), *Development of Rainfed Agriculture under Arid and Semiarid Conditions*. Proceedings of the 6th Agriculture Sector Symposium. Washington, D.C.: World Bank, 294-317.

Doorenbos, J., and Kassam, A. H. 1979. *Yield Response to Water*. FAO Irrigation and Drainage Paper 33, U.N. Food and Agriculture Organization.

Doorenbos, J., and Pruitt, W. O. 1977. *Crop Water Requirements*. Irrigation and Drainage Paper No. 24, U.N. Food and Agriculture Organization.

Dowker, B. D. 1971. "Breeding of maize for low rainfall areas of Kenya: Reliability of yield of early and later maturing maizes." *Journal of Agricultural Science* 76:523-30.

Downey, L. A. 1972. "Water-yield relations for nonforage crops." *Journal of the Irrigation and Drainage Division of the American Society of Agricultural Engineers* IR1, 107-115.

Dudley, N. J. 1971. "Irrigation decision making in a variable environment." Ph.D. thesis, University of New England, Armidale, N.S.W., Australia.

Duffy, M., and Hawthorn, M. 1983. *Pesticide Use and Practices, 1982*. Agriculture Information Bulletin 462. Washington, D.C.: Economic Research Service, U.S. Department of Agriculture.

Duvick, D. N. 1977. "Genetic rates of gain in hybrid maize during the past 40 years." *Maydica* 22:187-96.

———. 1984a. "Progress in conventional plant breeding," in J. P. Gustafson (ed.), *Gene Manipulation in Plant Improvement*. New York: Plenum Press, 17-31.

———. 1984b. "Genetic contributions to yield gains of U.S. hybrid maize, 1930 to 1980," in W. R. Fehr (ed.), *Genetic Contributions to Yield Gains of Five Major Crop Plants*. CSSA Special Pub. No. 7, Madison, Wisc.: Crop Science Society of America, 15-47.

———. 1984c. "Genetic diversity in major farm crops on the farm and in reserve." *Economic Botany* 38:161-78.

Dyke, G. V.; George, B. J.; Johnson, A. E.; Poulton, P. R.; and Todd, A. D. 1983. "The Broadbalk wheat experiment 1968-1978: Yields and plant nutrients in crops grown continuously and in rotation." *Report of Rothamsted Experimental Station for 1982*, Pt. 2, 5-44.

Eberhart, S. A., and Russell, W. A. 1966. "Stability parameters for comparing varieties." *Crop Science* 6: 36-40.

———. 1969. "Yield and stability for a 10-line diallel of single-cross and double-cross hybrids." *Crop Science* 9: 357-61.

Eckstein, A. 1966. *Communist China's Economic Growth and Foreign Trade.* New York: McGraw-Hill.

El-Akhrass, H. 1983. *Agricultural Policies in the Syrian Arab Republic.* Damascus: Arab Organization for Agricultural Development.

El-Sherbini, A. A. 1979. *Food Security Issues in the Arab Near East.* New York: U.N. Economic Commission for Western Asia.

English, M. J. 1981. "The uncertainty of crop models in irrigation optimization." *American Society of Agricultural Engineers Transactions* 24(4):917-28.

Evans, L. T. 1986. "Yield variability in cereals: Concluding assessment," in P. B. R. Hazell (ed.), *Summary Proceedings of a Workshop on Cereal Yield Variability.* IFPRI and DSE. Washington, D.C.: International Food Policy Research Institute.

Evans, L. T., and De Datta, S. K. 1979. "The relation between irradiance and grain yield of irrigated rice in the tropics as influenced by cultivar, nitrogen fertilizer application, and month of planting." *Field Crops Research* 2(1):1-17.

Evenson, R. E.; O'Toole, J. C.; Herdt, R. W.; Coffman, W. R.; and Kaufman, H. E. 1979. "Risk and uncertainty as factors in crop improvement research," in J. A. Roumasset, J-M. Boussard, and I. Singh (eds.), *Risk, Uncertainty and Agricultural Development.* Laguna, Philippines: SEARCGSRA College, 249-64.

Farnsworth, R. L., and Moffitt, L. J. 1981. "Cotton production under risk: An analysis of input effects on yield variability and factor demand." *Western Journal of Agricultural Economics* 6(2):155-63.

Feder, G., and Slade, R. 1984. "The acquisition of information and the adoption of new technology." *American Journal of Agricultural Economics* 66(2):312-20.

Feyerherm, A. M.; Paulsen, G. M.; and Sebaugh, J. L. 1984. "Contribution of genetic improvement to recent wheat yield increases in the U.S.A." *Agronomy Journal* 76:985-90.

Finlay, K. W. 1968. "The significance of adaptation in wheat breeding." *Proceedings of the Third International Wheat Genetics Symposium,* Canberra, 403-9.

Finlay, K. W., and Wilkinson, G. N. 1963. "The analysis of adaptation in a plant breeding programme." *Australian Journal of Agricultural Research* 14:742-54.

Fischer, K. S., and Palmer, A. F. E. 1984. "Tropical maize," in P. R. Goldsworthy and N. M. Fischer (eds.), *The Physiology of Tropical Field Crops.* London: Wiley, 213-48.

Fischer, K. S.; Johnson, E. C.; and Edmeades, G. O. 1983. "Breeding and selection for drought resistance in tropical maize." El Batan: Mexico, Centro Internacional de Mejoramiento de Maiz y Trigo (CIMMYT).

Fisher, R. A. 1921. "Studies in crop variation I: An examination of the yield of dressed grain from Broadbalk." *Journal of Agricultural Science* 11:107-35.

Flinn, J. C., and De Datta, S. K. 1987. "The relationship between N response and yield variability in irrigated rice." Los Baños, Philippines: International Rice Research Institute (forthcoming).

Food and Agriculture Organization, United Nations. Various years. *Production Yearbook*. Rome: FAO.

Foster, K. W., and Rutger, J. N. 1978. "Inheritance of semidwarfism in rice, *Oryza sativa*, L." *Genetics* 88:559-74.

Freebairn, J. W. 1983. "Drought assistance policy." *Australian Journal of Agricultural Economics* 27(3):185-99.

French, J. B.; Schroder, D.; and Headley, J. C. 1985. "Role of weather and technology on crop yield risk for corn, soybeans, and winter wheat in selected regions of the United States." University of Missouri, Columbia, Agricultural Economics, Department Paper 1985-3.

Fuller, W. A. 1965. "Stochastic fertilizer production functions for continuous corn." *Journal of Farm Economics* 47(1):105-10.

General Administration of Customs of the People's Republic of China. 1986. *China's Customs Statistics* No. 1. Hong Kong Economic Information Agency.

Gines, H. C.; Pernita, R. G.; and Morris, R. A. 1984. "The rationale of photoperiod insensitive rice cultivars in intensifying rainfed rice-based cropping systems." Mimeo., IRRI, Los Baños, May.

Gonzales, L. A. 1984. "An economic perspective of crop diversification in rainfed areas: Implications to national and regional planning." *Philippine Journal of Crop Science* 9:89-100.

Goodell, G. E. 1984. "Challenges of international pest management research and extension in the Third World: Do we really want IPM to work?" *Bulletin of the Entomology Society of America* 30(3):18-26.

Government of India. 1983. *Agricultural Situation in India*. New Delhi: Directorate of Economics and Statistics, Ministry of Agriculture.

Green, C., and Kirkpatrick, C. 1982. "A cross-section analysis of food insecurity in developing countries: Its magnitude and sources." *Journal of Development Studies* 18(2):185-204.

Griffin, K. 1988. *Alternative Strategies for Economic Development*. Paris: Organization for Economic Cooperation and Development.

Griffiths, W. E., and Anderson, J. R. 1982. "Using time series and cross-section data to estimate a production function with positive and negative marginal risks." *Journal of the American Statistical Association* 77(379):529-36.

Guise, J. W. B. 1969. "Factors associated with variation in the aggregate average yield of New Zealand wheat (1918-1967)." *American Journal of Agricultural Economics* 51(4):866-81.

Hall, D. C. 1977. "The profitability of integrated pest management: Case studies for cotton and citrus in the San Joaquin Valley." *Bulletin of the Entomology Society of America* 23:267-74.

Hallauer, A. R. 1973. "Hybrid development and population improvement in maize by reciprocal full-sib selection." *Egyptian Journal of Genetics and Cytology* 2:84-101.

References 365

Hanus, H., and Aimiller, O. 1978. *Ertragsvorhersage aus Witterungsdaten,* Fortschritte Acker- u. Pflanzenbau, H.5, 127 S.
Hargrove, T. R.; Cabanilla, V. L.; and Coffman, W. R. 1985. *Changes in Rice Breeding in 10 Asian Countries: 1965-1984,* IRRI Research Paper Series No. 111. Los Baños, Philippines: International Rice Research Institute.
Hargrove, T. R.; Coffman, W. R.; and Cabanilla, V. L. 1980. "Ancestry of improved cultivars of Asian rice." *Crop Science* 20:721-27.
Harland, S. C., and King, E. 1957. "Inheritance of mildew resistance in *Fragaria* with special reference to cytoplasmic effects." *Heredity* 11:287.
Hayami, Y., and Ruttan, V. W. 1985. *Agricultural Development: An International Perspective.* 2nd ed. Baltimore, Md.: Johns Hopkins University Press.
Hazell, P. B. R. 1982. *Instability in Indian Foodgrain Production.* IFPRI Research Report 30. Washington, D.C.: International Food Policy Research Institute.
———. 1984. "Sources of increased instability in Indian and U.S. cereal production." *American Journal of Agricultural Economics* 66(3):302-11.
———. 1985a. "Changing patterns of variability in world cereal prices and production." Mimeo., IFPRI, Washington, D.C.
———. 1985b. "Sources of increased variability in world cereal production since the 1960s." *Journal of Agricultural Economics* 36(2):145-59.
Hazell, P. B. R.; Bassoco, L. M.; and Arcia, G. 1986. "A model for evaluating farmers' demand for insurance: applications in Mexico and Panama," in P. Hazell, C. Pomareda, and A. Valdés (eds.), *Crop Insurance for Agricultural Development: Issues and Experiences,* Baltimore: Johns Hopkins University Press, 35-66.
Hazell, P. B. R.; Pomareda, C.; and Valdés, A. (eds.) 1986. *Crop Insurance for Agricultural Development: Issues and Experiences.* Baltimore: Johns Hopkins University Press.
He Gang et al., Zhongguo Nongyebu. 1984. [Chinese Ministry of Agriculture] (eds.), *Zhongguo Nongye Nianjian 1984* [Agricultural Yearbook of China 1984]. Beijing: Nongye Chubanshe [Agricultural Publishing House].
Healy, M. R. J., and Jones, E. L. 1962. "Wheat yields in England, 1815-1859." *Journal of the Royal Statistical Society* 125:574-79.
Hedlund, S. 1984. *Crisis in Soviet Agriculture.* London: Croom Helm.
Heine, H., and Weber, W. E. 1982. "The significance of statistical parameters for the phenotypic stability in official variety trials of winter wheat and maize." *Z. Pflanzenzucht* 89:89-99.
Heinrichs, E. A.; Saxena, R. C.; and Chelliah, S. 1979. "Development and implementation of insect pest management systems for rice in tropical Asia." *ASPAC Bulletin No. 127.* Taiwan: Food and Fertilizer Technology Center, Asia and South Pacific Area Council.
Hendrick, R. L., and Comer, G. H. 1970. "Space variations in precipitation and implications for raingauge network design." *Journal of Hydrology* 10:151-63.
Herdt, R. W., and Capule, C. 1983. *Adoption, Spread, and Production Impact of Modern Rice Varieties in Asia.* Los Baños, Philippines: International Rice Research Institute.

Herdt, R. W., and Mandac, A. M. 1981. "Modern technology and economic efficiency of Philippine rice farmers." *Economic Development and Cultural Change* 29(2):375-99.

Herdt, R. W.; Castillo, L. L.; and Jayasuriya, S. K. 1984. "The economics of insect control on rice in the Philippines," in *Judicious and Efficient Use of Insecticides on Rice*. Los Baños, Philippines: International Rice Research Institute, 41-56.

Hexem, R. W., and Heady, E. O. 1978. *Water Production Functions for Irrigated Agriculture*. Ames: Iowa State University Press.

Hildebrand, P. E. 1984. "Modified stability analysis of farmer managed, on-farm trials." *Agronomy Journal* 76:271-74.

Hill, J. 1975. "Genotype × environment interactions: A challenge for plant breeding." *Journal of Agricultural Science* 85:477-93.

Hooker, A. L. 1979. "Breeding for resistance to some complex diseases of corn." *Rice Blast Workshop*. Los Baños, Philippines: International Rice Research Institute.

Houck, J. P., and Gallagher, P. W. 1976. "The price responsiveness of U.S. corn yields." *American Journal of Agricultural Economics* 58(4):731-34.

Huddleston, B.; Johnson, D. G.; Reutlinger, S.; and Valdés, A. 1984. *International Finance for Food Security*. Baltimore: Johns Hopkins University Press for the World Bank, Washington, D.C.

Immink, M., and Viteri, F. 1981a. "Energy intake and productivity of Guatemalan sugarcane cutters: An empirical test of the efficiency wage hypothesis, part I." *Journal of Development Economics* 9:251-72.

———. 1981b. "Energy intake and productivity of Guatemalan sugarcane cutters: An empirical test of the efficiency wage hypothesis, part II." *Journal of Development Economics* 9:273-87.

IRRI (International Rice Research Institute). 1973. "Correct spray technique for brown planthopper control." *IRRI Reporter* 4/73.

———. *Rice Blast Workshop*. Los Baños, Philippines: IRRI.

———. 1980. *Rice Improvement in China and Other Asian Countries*. Los Baños, Philippines: IRRI and Chinese Academy of Agricultural Sciences.

———. 1981. *Annual Report for 1980*. Los Baños, Philippines: IRRI.

———. 1982. *IR36, The World's Most Popular Rice*. Los Baños, Philippines: IRRI.

———. 1984. *Judicious and Efficient Use of Insecticides on Rice*. Los Baños, Philippines: FAO/IRRI Workshop.

———. 1985a. *IR64, An Improved Rice Variety Released by the Philippine Seedboard* (a brochure). Los Baños, Philippines: IRRI.

———. 1985b. *1984 Annual Report of the International Rice Testing Program*. Los Baños, Philippines: IRRI.

———. 1985c. "Natural enemies control rice insect pests." *IRRI Reporter*, 3/85.

———. 1985d. *International Rice Research: 25 Years of Partnership*. Los Baños, Philippines: IRRI.

IRRI/CAAS. 1980. *Five years of the IRTP: A Global Rice Exchange and Testing Network*. Los Baños, Philippines: IRRI.

Jain, H. K.; Dagg, M.; and Taylor, T. A. 1986. "Problems in the transition to the new agricultural technology," in P. Hazell (ed.), *Summary Proceedings of a Workshop on Cereal Yield Variability.* Washington, D.C.: International Food Policy Research Institute and DSE, 77-86.
Jensen, N. F. 1976. "Floating checks for plant breeding nurseries." *Cereal Research Communications* 4:285-95.
Jodha, N. S. 1975. "Famine and famine policies: Some empirical evidence." *Economic and Political Weekly* 10(41):1609-23.
———. 1979. *Some Dimensions of Traditional Farming in Semi-Arid Tropical India.* Progress Report 4, Economics Program. Patancheru, India: International Crops Research Institute for the Semi-Arid Tropics.
———. 1981. "Adjustment to climatic variability in self-provisioning societies: Some evidence from India." Patancheru, India: International Crops Research Institute for the Semi-Arid Tropics.
Jodha, N. S.; Asokan, M.; and Ryan, J. G. 1977. *Village Study Methodology and Resource Endowments of the Selected Villages.* Economics Program Occasional Paper 16. Patancheru, Andhra Pradesh, India: ICRISAT (limited distribution).
Johnson, D. G. 1975. "World agriculture, commodity policy, and price variability." *American Journal of Agricultural Economics* 57(5):823-28.
Johnson, E. C.; Fischer, K. S.; Edmeades, G. O.; and Palmer, A. F. E. 1986. "Recurrent selection for reduced plant height in lowland tropical maize." *Crop Science* 26:253-60.
Johnson, V. A.; Shafer, S. L.; and Schmidt, J. W. 1968. "Regression analysis of general adaptation in hard red winter wheat (*Triticum Aestivum* L.)." *Crop Science* 8:187-91.
Just, R. E., and Pope, R. D. 1978. "Stochastic specification of production functions and economic implications." *Journal of Econometrics* 7(1):67-86.
———. 1979. "Production function estimation and related risk considerations." *American Journal of Agricultural Economics* 61:277-84.
Just, R., and Zilberman, D. 1983. "Stochastic structure, farm size, and technology adoption in developing agriculture." *Oxford Economic Papers* 35:307-28.
Kanbur, S. M. R. C. 1984. "How to analyze commodity price stabilization? A review article." *Oxford Economic Papers* 36(3):336-58.
Kanwar, J. S. 1975. "Downy mildew and ergot of pearl millet: an overview," in *Proceedings of the Consultants' Group Meeting on Downy Mildew and Ergot of Pearl Millet.* Patancheru, India: International Crops Research Institute for the Semi-Arid Tropics.
Kelly, P. M.; Micklin, P. P.; Campbell, D. A.; and Tarrant, J. R. 1983. "Large scale water transfers in the U.S.S.R." *GeoJournal* 7:201-14.
Kendall, M., and Stewart, A. 1977. *The Advanced Theory of Statistics. Volume 1, Distribution Theory.* Fourth edition. New York: Macmillan.
Kenmore, P. E. 1979. "Limits of the brown planthopper problem: Implications for integrated pest management." Mimeo., IRRI, Los Baños, Philippines.
———. "Extension training for IPM in the Philippines." Ministry of Agriculture, Manila.

Khush, G. S., and Coffman, W. R. 1977. "Genetic evaluation and utilization (GEU) program, the rice improvement program of the International Rice Research Institute." *Theoretical and Applied Genetics* 51:97-110.

King, J. E. 1977. "The incidence and economic significance of diseases in cereals in England and Wales." *Proceedings, 9th British Insecticide and Fungicide Conference*, 3:677-87.

King, R. P., and Robison, L. G. 1981. "An interval approach to measuring decision maker preferences." *American Journal of Agricultural Economics* 63(3):510-20.

Knight, R. 1970. "The measurement and interpretation of genotype environment interactions." *Euphytica* 19:225-35.

Koester, U. 1982. *Policy Options for the Grain Economy of the European Community: Implications for Developing Countries.* IFPRI Research Report 35. Washington, D.C.: International Food Policy Research Institute.

―――. 1984. "Regional cooperation among developing countries to improve food security." *Quarterly Journal of International Agriculture* 23(2):99-114.

Kogan, F. N. 1981a. *Grain Production in the U.S.S.R.: Present Situation, Perspectives for Development, and Methods of Prediction.* Staff Report AGES 810904. Washington, D.C.: Statistical Reporting Service, U.S. Department of Agriculture.

―――. 1981b. *Geographical Aspects of Climate and Weather Limitations for Cereal Production in the U.S.S.R.* 15th Conference on Agriculture and Forest Meteorology, Anaheim, California.

―――. 1983. "Perspectives on grain production in the U.S.S.R." *Agricultural Meteorology* 28:213-27.

Kornai, J. 1982. "Adjustment to price and quantity signals in a socialist economy." *Economique Applique* no. 3.

Kueh, Y. Y. 1984. "A weather index for analyzing grain yield instability in China, 1952-81." *The China Quarterly* 97:68-83.

―――. 1986. "Weather cycles and agricultural instability in China." *Journal of Agricultural Economics* 37(1):101-4.

Kuhr, S. L.; Johnson, V. A.; Peterson, C. J.; and Mattern, P. J. 1985. "Trends in winter wheat performance as measured in international trials." *Crop Science* (in press).

Kumar, S. K. 1987. "The nutrition situation and its food policy links," in J. Mellor, C. Delgado, and M. Blackie (eds.), *Accelerating Agricultural Growth in Sub-Saharan Africa.* Baltimore: Johns Hopkins University Press for the International Food Policy Research Institute.

Kwak, T. S.; Nanda, J. S.; Vergara, B. S.; and Coffman, W. R. 1984. "Inheritance of seedling cold tolerance in rice (*Oryza sativa,* L.)." *SABRAO Journal* 16(2).

Laird, R. D. 1982. "Soviet meat and grain 1981-85: Output projections." *Soviet Geography* 23:65-77.

Lardy, N. R. 1983. *Agriculture in China's Modern Economic Development.* Cambridge, Cambridge University Press.

Latham, M. 1985. "The relationship of nutrition to productivity and well being of workers." Paper prepared for the IFPRI/UNU workshop on the political economy of nutritional improvement, Coolfont Conference Center, International Food Policy Research Institute, Washington, D.C.

Lazarus, W., and Swanson, E. R. 1983. "Insecticide use and crop rotation under risk: Rootworm control in corn." *American Journal of Agricultural Economics* 65:738-47.

Lester, E. 1981. "Multidisciplinary activities." *Report of Rothamsted Experimental Station for 1980,* Pt. 1, 17-33.

———. 1982. "Multidisciplinary activities." *Report of Rothamsted Experimental Station for 1981,* Pt. 1, 19-36.

———. 1983. "Multidisciplinary activities." *Report of Rothamsted Experimental Station for 1982,* Pt. 1, 19-41.

Li, C. M. 1962. *The Statistical System of Communist China.* Berkeley and Los Angeles: University of California Press.

McBride, D., and Edwards, G. W. 1986. *Crop and Rainfall Insurance.* Industries Assistance Commission Report No. 393, Australian Government Publishing Service, Canberra.

McIntire, J. 1981. *Food Security in the Sahel: Variable Import Levy, Grain Reserves, and Foreign Exchange Assistance,* IFPRI Research Report 26, Washington, D.C.: International Food Policy Research Institute.

Mackill, D. J., and Coffman, W. R. 1983. "Inheritance of high temperature tolerance and pollen shedding in a rice cross." *Zeitschrift fuer Pflanzenzeuchtung* 91:61-69.

Mackill, D. J.; Garrity, D. P.; Seshu, D. V.; and Zan Kaung. 1985. "IRRI rainfed lowland rice improvement program." Paper presented at the International Conference on Wetland Utilization for Rice Production in Tropical Africa, IITA, Ibadan, November 4-12.

MacLaren, D. 1980. "Agricultural policy uncertainty and the risk averse firm." *European Review of Agricultural Economics* 7(4):395-411.

———. 1983. "The output response of the risk averse firm: some comparative statistics for agricultural policy." *Journal of Agricultural Economics* 34(1):45-56.

McWilliam, J. R., and Griffing, J. B. 1965. "Temperature-dependent heterosis in maize." *Australian Journal of Biological Sciences* 18:569-83.

McWilliam, J. R.; Latter, B. D. H.; and Mathison, M. J. 1969. "Enhanced heterosis and stability in the growth of an interspecific *Phalaris* hybrid at high temperature." *Australian Journal of Biological Science* 22:493-504.

Mahill, J. F., and Davis, D. D. 1978. "Influence of male sterile and normal cytoplasms on the expression of bacterial blight in cotton hybrids." *Crop Science* 18: 440-42.

Mandac, A. M., and Flinn, J. C. 1983. "Farm level management and nitrogen response of rainfed rice in Bicol, Philippines." *Philippine Journal of Crop Science* 8:65-74.

Manwan, I., and Sama, S. 1985. "Use of varietal rotation in management of RTV in Indonesia." International Rice Research Conference, IRRI, Los Baños, Philippines, June.

Markish, Y. 1982. "Soviets halt plan to upgrade diets." *Foreign Agriculture,* April.

Marra, M., and Carlson, G. A. 1984. "The decision to double crop: A direct, empirical application of expected utility maximization." Working Paper, Department of Economics and Business, North Carolina State University, Raleigh.

Mazid, A., and Hallajian, M. 1984. *Crop-Livestock Interactions: Information from a Barley Survey in Syria.* Aleppo, Syria: International Center for Agricultural Research in Dry Areas.

Mehra, S. 1981. *Instability in Indian Agriculture in the Context of the New Technology.* IFPRI Research Report No. 25. Washington, D.C.: International Food Policy Research Institute.

Mellor, J. 1976. *The New Economics of Growth: A Strategy for India and the Developing World.* Ithaca, N.Y.: Cornell University Press.

———. 1985. "Determinants of rural poverty: The dynamics of production, technology and price," in J. Mellor and G. Desai (eds.), *Agricultural Change and Rural Poverty: Variations on a Theme by Dharm Narain.* Baltimore: Johns Hopkins University Press, 21-40.

Mellor, J., and Johnston, B. 1984. "The world food equation: Interrelations among development, employment, and food consumption." *Journal of Economic Literature* 22:531-74.

Mendoza, M. N. 1980. "Stochastic production function and estimating risk in rice production." Unpublished M.S. thesis, University of the Philippines, Los Baños.

Mercado, A. C., and Lantican, R. M. 1961. "The susceptibility of cytoplasmic male sterile lines of corn to *Helminthosporium maydis* Nish and Miy." *Philippine Agriculturist* 45(5):235-43.

Meshcherskaya, A. V. 1983. "The long-term relationship between grain yields and heat-moisture indices." *Soviet Geography* 18:145-62.

Meulen, J. G. J. van der. 1950. "Rice improvement by hybridization and results obtained." Contributions of the General Agricultural Research Station No. 116, 1-38, Bogor, Indonesia.

Meyer, J. 1977. "Second degree stochastic dominance with respect to a function." *International Economic Review* 18(2):477-87.

Meyer, W. S., and Green, G. C. 1981. "Plant indicators of wheat and soybean crop water stress." *Irrigation Science* 2:167-76.

Micklin, P. P. 1978. "Irrigation development in the U.S.S.R. during the Tenth Five Year Plan (1976-80)." *Soviet Geography* 19(1):1-24.

———. 1983. "Soviet water diversion plans: Implications for Kazakhstan and Central Asia." *Central Asian Survey* 1(4):9-43.

Ministry of Agriculture, Fisheries, and Food, Seeds Branch. 1964-84. *Quantity Return of Cereal and Field Bean Sales.* Cambridge, England.

Moffitt, L. J.; Farnsworth, R. L.; Zavaleta, L. R.; and Kogan, M. 1982. "Farm efficiency and insect infestation forecasts: The case of soybeans in Illinois." ERS Staff Report No. AGES821013, NRED, ERS, USDA, Washington, D.C.

Mooers, C. A. 1921. "The agronomic placement of varieties." *Journal of the American Society of Agronomy,* 13:337-52.

Morgan, T. H.; Biere, A. W.; and Kanemasu, E. T. 1980. "A dynamic model of corn yield response to water." *Water Resources Research* 16(1):59-64.

Moscardi, E. R., and de Janvry, A. 1977. "Attitudes toward risk among peasants: An econometric approach." *American Journal of Agricultural Economics* 59(4):710-16.

Mostek, A., and Walsh, J. E. 1981. "Corn yield variability and weather patterns in the USA." *Agricultural Meteorology* 25: 111-24.

Mukhitdinov, N. A. (ed.) 1974. *Contemporary Syria* [in Russian]. Moscow: Nauka.

Music, J. T.; New, L. L.; and Dusek, D. A. 1976. "Soil water depletion yield relationship of irrigated sorghum, wheat, and soybeans." *Transactions of ASAE* 14:401-4.

Musser, W. N., and Tew, B. V. 1984. "Use of biophysical simulation in production economics." *Southern Journal of Agricultural Economics* 16(1):77-86.

Musser, W. N.; Tew, B. V.; and Epperson, J. E. 1981. "An economic examination of an integrated pest management production system with a contrast between E-V and stochastic dominance analysis." *Southern Journal of Agricultural Economics* 13:119-24.

Nadkarni, M. V., and Deshpande, R. S. 1982. "Agricultural growth, instability in productivity, and rainfall." *Economic and Political Weekly* 17:A127-34.

Nagaich, B. B.; Upadhya, M. D.; Prakash, O.; and Singh, S. J. 1968. "Cytoplasmically determined expression of symptoms of potato virus crosses between species of capsicum." *Nature* 220:1341-42.

National Academy of Sciences. 1972. "Corn—genetic diversity," in *Genetic Vulnerability of Major Crops*. Committee on Genetic Vulnerability of Major Crops, Agricultural Board, National Research Council. Washington, D.C.: National Academy of Sciences, 98-109.

Newbery, D. M. G., and Stiglitz, J. E. 1981. *The Theory of Commodity Price Stabilization: A Study of the Economics of Risk*. Oxford: Clarendon Press.

Nguyen, H. P. 1985. "Sources of increased instability in Soviet grain production in the 1970s." Paper prepared for the IFPRI/DSE Workshop on Sources of Increased Variability in Cereal Yields, IFPRI, Washington, D.C.

O'Mara, G. 1983. "The microeconomics of technique adoption by smallholding Mexican farmers," in R. D. Norton and L. Solis, (eds.), *The Book of CHAC: Programming Studies for Mexican Agriculture*. Baltimore: Johns Hopkins University Press, 250-89.

Ostle, B. 1954. *Statistics in Research*. Ames: Iowa State College Press.

Paddock, P., and Paddock, W. 1967. *Famine 1975. America's Decision: Who Will Survive?* Toronto: Little, Brown.

Paliwal, R. L., and Sprague, E. W. 1981. "Improving adaptation and yield dependability in maize in the developing world," CIMMYT, El Batan, Mexico.

Pandey, S. 1986. "Economics of water harvesting and supplementary irrigation in the semi-arid tropics of India: A systems approach." Ph.D. thesis, University of New England, Armidale, N.S.W., Australia.

Parry, M. L., and Carter, T. R. 1985. "The effect of climatic variations on agricultural risk." *Climatic Change* 7:95-110.

Parthasarthy, N. 1972. "Rice breeding in tropical Asia up to 1960," in *Rice Breeding*. Los Baños, Philippines: International Rice Research Institute.

Pathak, M. D.; Beachell, H. M.; and Andres, F. 1973. "IR20, a pest- and disease-resistant high-yielding rice variety." *International Rice Commission Newsletter* 22(3):1-8.

Patterson, H. D. 1980. "Yield sensitivity and straw shortness in winter wheat." *Journal of the National Institute of Agricultural Botany* 15(2):198-204.

Pearson, E. S. 1936. "Note on probability levels for $\sqrt{b_1}$." *Biometrika* 28:306-7.

Penaranda, F. L.; Urbina, A. F.; Jover, P. C.; Decema, E. M.; and Nesbitt, H. J. 1985. "The severity of blast on upland rice as affected by nitrogen." *Philippine Journal of Crop Science,* Supplement 10(1):S15.

Perkins, J. M., and Jinks, J. L. 1968. "Environmental and genotype-environmental components of variability, III. Multiple lines and crosses." *Heredity* 23:339-56.

Perrin, R. K., and Heady, E. O. 1975. *Relative Contributions of Major Technological Factors and Moisture Stress to Increased Grain Yields in the Midwest, 1930-1971.* CARD Report No. 55. Ames: Iowa State University.

Perrin, R. K., and Winkelmann, D. 1976. "Impediments to technical progress on small versus large farms." *American Journal of Agricultural Economics* 58(5):888-94.

Perrin, R. K.; Winkelmann, D. L.; Moscardi, E. R.; and Anderson, J. R. 1976. *From Agronomic Data to Farmer Recommendations: An Economics Training Manual.* El Batan, Mexico: Centro Internacional de Mejoramiento de Maiz y Trigo.

Pfeiffer, W. H. 1983. "Ertragsleistung, ertragsstabilittat und adaptation von sommerweizen auf regionaler und globaler ebene—analyse einer serie von internationalen sortenversuchen uber 15 Jahre und 973 Umwelten." Dissertation Universitaet Hohenheim, Federal Republic of Germany.

Pingali, P., and Carlson, G. A. 1985. "Human capital, adjustments in subjective probabilities, and the demand for pest controls." *American Journal of Agricultural Economics* 67(4):853-61.

Pinstrup-Andersen, Per, ed. 1988. *Food Subsidies in Developing Countries.* Baltimore: Johns Hopkins University Press.

Pinstrup-Andersen, P., and Alderman, H. 1984. "The effectiveness of consumer food subsidies in reaching rationing and income transfer goals." Paper prepared for the Conference on Food Subsidies, International Food Policy Research Institute, Washington, D.C.

Pinstrup-Andersen, P., and Jaramillo, M. 1985. "The impact of technological change in rice production on seasonal fluctuations in food consumption and calorie deficiencies: The case of North Arcot, India." Paper prepared for IFPRI/FAO/AID workshop on Seasonal Causes of Household Food Insecurity, International Food Policy Research Institute, Washington, D.C.

Ponnamperuma, F. F. 1979. *IR42, A Rice Type for Small Farmers of South and Southeast Asia.* IRRI Research Paper Series No. 44, Los Baños, Philippines: International Rice Research Institute.

Pryde, P. R. 1983. "The decade of the environment." *Science* 220:274-79.

Quiggin, J. C. 1983. "Underwriting agricultural commodity prices." *Australian Journal of Agricultural Economics* 23(3):191-206.

Quiggin, J. C., and Anderson, J. R. 1979. "Stabilization and risk reduction." *Australian Journal of Agricultural Economics* 27(3):200-11.

Rangaswami, P. 1982. "Risk-aversion and investment gap." *Indian Economic Review* 17(2/3/4):223-39.
Rao, C. H. H. 1968. "Fluctuations in agricultural growth." *Economic and Political Weekly* 3:87-94.
Rao, M. R., and Willey, R. W. 1980. "Evaluation of yield stability in intercropping: Studies on sorghum/pigeonpea." *Experimental Agriculture* 16(2):105-16.
Rath, G. G., and Padmanabhan, S. Y. 1972. "Cytoplasmic effects on the leaf blast reaction in rice." *Current Science* 41:338-39.
Ray, S. K. 1983. *Growth and Instability in Indian Agriculture.* New Delhi: Institute of Economic Growth.
Reichelderfer, K. H.; Carlson, G. A.; and Norton, G. A. 1984. *Economic Guidelines for Crop Pest Control.* Food and Agriculture Organization Plant Production and Protection Paper 58. Rome: FAO.
Reutlinger, Shlomo. 1982. "Policies for food security in food-importing developing countries," in A. H. Chisholm and R. Tyeis (eds.), *Food Security: Theory, Policy, and Perspectives from Asia and the Pacific Rim.* Lexington, Mass.: D. C. Heath, 21-44.
Reutlinger, Shlomo, and Bigman, David. 1979. "Food, price, and supply stabilization: national buffer stocks and trade policies." *American Journal of Agricultural Economics* 61(4):657-67.
Rosegrant, M. W. 1986. "The impact of irrigation on area, yield, and income variability: A simulation analysis." Mimeo., IFPRI, Washington, D.C.
Rosegrant, M. W., and Herdt, R. W. 1981. "Simulating the impacts of credit policy and fertilizer subsidy on Central Luzon rice farmers, Philippines." *American Journal of Agricultural Economics* 63(4):655-65.
Rosegrant, M. W., and Roumasset, J. A. 1985. "The effect of fertilizer on risk: A heteroscedastic production function with measurable stochastic inputs." *Australian Journal of Agricultural Economics* 29(2):107-21.
Rostankowski, P. 1980. "The non-chernozem development program and prospective spatial shifts in grain production in the agricultural triangle of the Soviet Union." *Soviet Geography* 21:409-19.
Rothamsted Experimental Station. 1984. "Multidisciplinary activities." *Report of Rothamsted Experimental Station for 1983,* Pt. 1, 21-36.
Roumasset, J. A. 1974. "Estimating the risk of alternate techniques: nitrogenous fertilization of rice in the Philippines." *Review of Marketing and Agricultural Economics* 42(4):257-94.
———. 1976. *Rice and Risk: Decision Making among Low Income Farmers.* Amsterdam: North Holland.
Russell, J. S. 1973. "Yield trends of different crops in different areas and reflections on the sources of crop yield improvement in the Australian environment." *Journal of the Australian Institute of Agricultural Science* 39:156-66.
Russell, W. A. 1974. "Comparative performance of maize hybrids representing different eras of maize breeding," in *Proceedings of the 29th Annual Corn and Sorghum Research Conference.* Washington, D.C.: American Seed Trade Association, 81-101.

———. 1984. "Agronomic performance of maize cultivars representing different eras of breeding." *Maydica* 29:375-90.
Ryan, J. G., and Perrin, R. K. 1973. *The Estimation and Use of a Generalized Response Function for Potatoes in the Sierra of Peru.* Technical Bulletin No. 214. Raleigh: North Carolina Agricultural Experiment Station.
Sahn, D., and von Braun, J. 1987. "The Relationship Between Food Production and Consumption Variability: Policy Implications for Developing Countries," *Journal of Agricultural Economics* 38(2):315-27.
Scandizzo, P. L.; Hazell, P. B. R.; and Anderson, J. R. 1984. *Risky Agricultural Markets: Price Forecasting and the Need for Intervention Policies.* Boulder, Colo. Westview.
Schmidt, J. W. 1984. "Genetic contributions to yield gains in wheat," in *Genetic Contributions to Yield Gains of Five Major Crop Plants.* ASA Special Publication No. 7. Madison, Wisc., 89-101.
Schmidt, J. W.; Johnson, V. A.; and Stroike, J. E. 1972. "The case for general adaptation," in *Proceedings of the First International Winter Wheat Conference,* Ankara, Turkey. Nebraska Agricultural Experiment Station Miscellaneous Publication 28:47-58.
Schmidt, J. W.; Johnson, V. A.; Diehl, A. L.; and Dreier, A. F. 1973. "Breeding for adaptation in winter wheats for the great plains," in *Proceedings of the Fourth International Wheat Genetics Symposium,* Missouri Agricultural Experiment Station, Columbia, Mo., 581-86.
Scott, C. 1980. *Conducting Surveys in Developing Countries: Practical Problems and Experiences in Brazil, Malaysia, and the Philippines.* LSMS Working Paper 5. Washington, D.C.: World Bank.
Severin, K. 1984. *An Assessment of the Soviet Food Program.* Paper presented at the NATO Economic Colloquium, The Soviet Economy since Brezhnev, Brussels, April 11-13.
Siamwalla, A. 1984. "Public stock management and its implications for prices and supply." Mimeo., International Food Policy Research Institute, Washington, D.C.
———. 1986. "Approaches to price insurance for farmers," in P. Hazell, C. Pomareda, and A. Valdés (eds.), *Crop Insurance for Agricultural Development: Issues and Experience.* Baltimore: Johns Hopkins University Press, 178-92.
Siamwalla, A., and Valdés, A. 1980. "Food insecurity in developing countries." *Food Policy* 5(4):258-72.
Silvey, V. 1978. "The contribution of new varieties to increasing cereal yield in England and Wales." *Journal of the National Institute of Agricultural Botany* 14(3):367-84.
———. 1981. "The contribution of new wheat, barley, and oat varieties to increasing cereal yield in England and Wales, 1947-78." *Journal of the National Institute of Agricultural Botany* 15(3):399-412.
Sim, R. J. R., and Araji, A. A. 1981. "The economic impact of public investment in wheat research in the Western Region." *Idaho Agricultural Experiment Station Research Bulletin No. 116.*

References 375

Simmonds, N. W. 1962. "Variability in crop plants." *Biological Review* 37:422-65.
———. 1981. "Genotype (G), environment (E), and GE components of crop yields." *Experimental Agriculture* 17:355-62.
Singh, R. P., and Asokan, M. 1981. *Concepts and Methods for Estimating Incomes in Village Studies in Semi-Arid Tropical India.* Economics Program Progress Report 28. Patancheru, India: International Crops Research Institute for the Semi-Arid Tropics (limited distribution).
Singh, R. P.; Jodha, N. S.; and Binswanger, H. P. 1986. *ICRISAT Village Studies Data Management System.* Economics Program. Patancheru, India: International Crops Research Institute for the Semi-Arid Tropics (limited distribution).
Smith, H.; Umali, G.; Rosegrant, M. W.; and Mandac, A. M. 1984. "Risk and fertilizer use on rainfed rice: Bicol, Philippines." Mimeo., International Rice Research Institute, Los Baños, Philippines.
Smith, J., and Litsinger, J. A. 1985. "Economic thresholds for insecticide application: Profitability and risk analysis." Agricultural Economics Department Paper 85-02. Los Baños, Philippines: International Rice Research Institute.
Smith, J., and Umali, G. 1985. "Production risk and optimal fertilizer rates: A random coefficient model." *American Journal of Agricultural Economics* 67(3).
Social Science Research Council. 1969. *Provincial Agricultural Statistics for Communist China.* Ithaca, N.Y.: SSRC Committee on the Economy of China.
Sprague, E. W., and Paliwal, R. L. 1984. "CIMMYT's maize improvement programme." *Outlook on Agriculture* 13:24-31.
Srinivasan, T. N. 1981. "Malnutrition: Some measurement and policy issues." *Journal of Development Economics* 8(1):3-19.
———. 1985. "Agricultural production, relative prices, entitlements, and poverty," in J. Mellor and G. Desai (eds.), *Agricultural Change and Rural Poverty: Variations on a Theme by Dharm Narain.* Baltimore: Johns Hopkins University Press, 41-53.
Stanhill, G. 1976. "Trends and deviations in the yield of the English wheat crop during the last 750 years." *Agro-Ecosystems* 3:1-10.
State Statistical Bureau of the PRC. 1985. *Statistical Yearbook of China 1985.* Hong Kong and Beijing: Economic Information and Agency and China Statistical Information and Consultancy Service Centre.
Stavis, B. 1978. "Agricultural research and extension services in China." *World Development* 6(5):638-45.
Stewart, J. I.; Misra, R. D.; Pruitt, W. O.; and Hagan, R. M. 1975. "Irrigating corn and grain sorghum with a deficient water supply." *Transactions of the American Society of Agricultural Engineers* 18(2):270-80.
Stone, B. 1980. "China's 1985 foodgrain production target: Issues and prospects," in A. M. Tang and B. Stone, *Food Production in the People's Republic of China.* IFPRI Research Report No. 15. Washington, D.C.: International Food Policy Research Institute, 83-178.
———. 1983. "The use of agricultural statistics: some national aggregate exam-

ples and current state of the art," in R. Barker, R. Sinha, and B. Rose (eds.), *Chinese Agricultural Economy.* Boulder, Colo.: Westview Press, 205-49.

———. 1984a. "An analysis of Chinese data on root and tuber crop production." *The China Quarterly* 99:594-630.

———. 1984b. "Relative foodgrain prices in the People's Republic of China: Rural taxation through public monopoly." Paper prepared for IFPRI Workshop on Food and Agricultural Price Policy, Elkridge, Maryland, April 29-May 2.

———. 1984c. "Trends in Chinese Hybrid Rice Production." *Mimeo.*, International Food Policy Research Institute, Washington, D.C.

———. 1985. "The basis for Chinese agricultural growth in the 1980s and 1990s: A Comment on Document No. 1, 1984." *The China Quarterly* 101:114-21.

———. 1986a. "Chinese fertilizer application in the 1980s and 1990s: Issues of growth, balance, allocation, efficiency, and response," in U.S. Congress Joint Economic Committee (ed.), *China's Economy Looks Toward the Year 2000.* Vol. 1, *The Four Modernizations.* Washington, D.C.: U.S. Government Printing Office, 453-96.

———. 1986b. "Systemic and policy adjustment in the administration of Chinese fertilizer development." Paper prepared for the World Bank, Washington, D.C., June 12.

Stone, B.; Greer, C.; Tong Zhong; Friedman, C.; McFadden, M.; and Snyder, M. 1985. "Agro-ecological zones for wheat production in China: A compendium of basic resource materials." Unpublished draft, International Food Policy Research Institute, Washington, D.C.

Strauss, J. 1984. "Does better nutrition raise farm productivity?" Economic Growth Center Discussion Paper 457, Yale University, New Haven.

Stroike, J. E., and Johnson, V. A. 1972. "Winter wheat cultivar performance in an international array of environments." *Nebraska Agricultural Experiment Station Research Bulletin,* no. 251.

Sukhatme, P. V., and Margen, S. 1982. "Autoregulatory homeostatic nature of energy balance." *Journal of Clinical Nutrition* 35:355-65.

Sundquist, W. B.; Menz, K.; and Neumeyer, C. F. 1982. *A Technology Assessment of Commercial Corn Production in the United States.* Minnesota Agricultural Experiment Station Bulletin 546.

Svedberg, P. 1984. "Food security in developing countries: causes, trends and policy option." U.N. Conference on Trade and Development, Geneva.

Swamy, P. A. V. B. 1970. "Efficient inference in a random coefficient regression model." *Econometrica* 38(2):311-23.

Talbot, M. 1984. "Yield variability of crop varieties in the U.K." *Journal of Agricultural Science* 102:315-21.

Talpaz, H., and Taylor, C. R. 1977. "Determining optimal fertilization rates under variable weather conditions." *Western Journal of Agricultural Economics* 2(1):45-51.

Tarrant, J. R. 1981. "Food as a weapon: The embargo on grain trade between the U.S.A. and the U.S.S.R." *Applied Geography* 1:273-86.

———. 1984a. "Predicting U.S.S.R. wheat production." *Applied Geography* 4:47-57.

———. 1984b. "The significance of variability in Soviet cereal production." *Transactions of the Institute of British Geographers* 9:387-400.
Tatum, L. A. 1971. "The southern corn leaf blight epidemic." *Science* 171:1113-16.
Tautho, C. C.; Flinn, J. C.; and Velasco, L. E. 1985. "Adoption and productivity of upland rice in Zamboanga del Sur, Philippines." *Philippine Journal of Crop Science* 10(3):135-45.
Taylor, L. R. 1961. "Aggregation, variation, and the mean." *Nature* 189:732-35.
Taylor, L. R., and Woiwod, I. P. 1980. "Temporal stability as a density-dependent species characteristic." *Journal of Animal Ecology* 49:209-24.
Taylor, L. R.; Woiwod, I. P.; and Perry, J. N. 1978. "The density dependence of spatial behavior and the rarity of randomness." *Journal of Animal Ecology* 47:483-506.
Taylor, S. A. 1952. "Use of mean soil moisture tension to evaluate the effect of soil moisture on crop yields." *Soil Science* 74:217-26.
Thattil, R. O. 1980. "Criteria used in screening technology prior to field recommendation." M.S. thesis, Department of Statistics, UPLB, Philippines.
Thompson, L. M. 1969. "Weather and technology in the production of corn in the U.S. Corn Belt." *Agronomy Journal* 61:453-56.
———. 1975. "Weather variability, climatic change, and grain production." *Science* 188:535-41.
———. 1984. "How 1983 weather hurt the corn crop," in *Better Crops With Plant Food/Summer 1984*. Atlanta, Ga.: Potash and Phosphate Institute.
Tinker, P. B., and Widdowson, F. B. 1983. "Maximizing wheat yields and some causes of yield variation." *Proceedings of the Fertilizer Society* 211:149-84.
Titow, J. Z. 1972. "Winchester yields: A study in medieval agricultural productivity," in *Cambridge Studies in Economic History*. Cambridge: Cambridge University Press.
Tollini, H., and Seagraves, J. A. 1970. *Actual and Optimal Use of Fertilizer: The Case of Nitrogen on Corn in Eastern North Carolina*. Economic Research Report No. 14. Raleigh: Department of Economics, North Carolina State University at Raleigh.
Trapp, J. N., and Walker, O. L. 1985. *Biological Simulation and Its Role in Economic Analysis*. Unpublished paper, Oklahoma State University, Stillwater, Okla.
U.N. 1983. *1981 Statistical Yearbook*. New York: Department of International and Social Affairs, United Nations.
USDA (U.S. Department of Agriculture). 1950-82. *Agricultural Statistics*. Washington, D.C.
———. 1980. *Syria: Agricultural Sector Assessment*. Vol. 3. Washington, D.C.: Agricultural Production Annex, USDA.
———. 1983a. *Inputs Outlook and Situation*. Washington, D.C.: Economic Research Service, USDA, October.
———. 1983b. *World Rice Reference Tables*. Foreign Agriculture Circular, FG-26-83. Washington, D.C.: Foreign Agricultural Service, USDA, September.
———. 1983c. *U.S.S.R.: World Agriculture Regional Supplement Review of 1982*

and the Outlook for 1983. Supplement to WAS 31. Washington, D.C.: Economic Research Service, USDA.
———. 1984a. *U.S.S.R. Outlook and Situation Report.* ERS RS 84-4. Washington, D.C.: USDA.
———. 1984b. *Rice Trade and Economy of Selected Asian Countries, 1970 to Present.* Foreign Agriculture Circular FG-15-84. Washington, D.C.: Foreign Agricultural Service, USDA, December.
Utz, H. F. 1972. "Die zerlegung der genotyp × umwelt-interaktionen." *EDV in Medizin und Biologie* 3:52-59.
Valdés, A. (ed.). 1981. *Food Security for Developing Countries.* Boulder, Colo.: Westview.
Valdés, A., and Konandreas, P. 1981. "Assessing food insecurity based on national aggregates in developing countries," in A. Valdés (ed.), *Food Security for Developing Countries.* Boulder, Colo.: Westview, 25-52.
Vanderplank, J. E. 1968. *Disease Resistance in Plants.* New York: Academic Press.
Vaux, H. J., and Pruitt, W. O. 1983. "Crop-water production functions." *Advances in Irrigation* 2:61-97.
Vega, M. R. 1983. *The Green Revolution Reconsidered.* Los Baños, Philippines: International Rice Research Institute.
Vega, M. R.; Paller, E. C.; and Lubigan, R. T. 1970. "The effects of continuous herbicide treatments of weed population and yield of lowland rice." *The Philippine Agriculturalist* 55(4):204-9.
Walinsky, L. 1977. *Agrarian Reform as Unfinished Business: the Writings of Wolf Ladejinsky.* New York: Oxford University Press.
Walker, K. R. 1984. *Food Grain Procurement and Consumption in China.* Cambridge: Cambridge University Press.
Walker, T. S., and Jodha, N. S. 1986. "How small farm households adapt to risk," in P. Hazell, C. Pomareda, A. Valdés (eds.), *Crop Insurance for Agricultural Development: Issues and Experience.* Baltimore: Johns Hopkins University Press, 17-34.
Walker, T. S., and Subba Rao, K. V. 1982. *Risk and the Choice of Cropping Systems: Hybrid Sorghum and Cotton in the Akola Region of Central Peninsular India.* Economics Program Progress Report 43. Patancheru, India: International Crops Research Institute for the Semi-Arid Tropics (Limited distribution).
Walker, T. S.; Singh, R. P.; and Asokan, M. 1986. "Risk benefits, crop insurance, and dryland agriculture." *Economic and Political Weekly* 21:A81-88.
Walker, T. S.; Singh, R. P.; Asokan, M.; and Binswanger, H. P. 1983. *Fluctuation in Income in Three Villages of India's Semi-Arid Tropics.* Economics Program Progress Report 57. Pantancheru, India: International Crops Research Institute for the Semi-Arid Tropics.
Walton, P. D. 1968. "Spring wheat variety trials in the prairie provinces." *Canadian Journal of Plant Science* 48:601-9.
Ward, R. C. 1967. *Principles of Hydrology.* Maidenhead, England: McGraw-Hill.
Watson, D. E., and White, K. J. 1976. "Forecasting the demand for money under

term structure of interest rates." *Southern Economic Journal* 41(2):1096-195.
Watson, W. D., and Anderson, J. R. 1977. "Spatial v. time-series data for assessing response risk." *Review of Marketing and Agricultural Economics* 45(3):80-84.
Weber, A., and Sievers, M. 1985a. *Instability in World Food Production: Statistical Analysis, Graphical Presentation, and Interpretation.* Kiel, W. Germany: Wissenschaftsverlag Vauk.
———. 1985b. "Observations on the geography of wheat production instability." *Quarterly Journal of International Agriculture* 24(3):201-11.
Westcott, B. 1986. "Some methods of analyzing genotype-environment interaction." *Heredity* 56:243-53.
———. 1987. "A method of assessing the yield stability of crop genotypes." *Journal of Agricultural Science* 108(2):267-74.
Wiens, T. B. 1978. "Evolution of Policy and Capabilities in China's Agricultural Technologies," in U.S. Congress Joint Economic Committee (ed.), *Chinese Economy Post-Mao*. Washington, D.C.: U.S. Government Printing Office, 671-703.
———. 1980. "Agricultural Statistics in the People's Republic of China," in A. Eckstein (ed.), *Quantitative Measures of China's Economic Output*. Ann Arbor: University of Michigan Press, 44-107 and 275-326.
Wilhite, D. A.; Rosenberg, N. J.; and Glantz, M. H. 1982. *Government Response to Drought in the United States: Lessons from the mid-1970s.* Climate Dynamics Program, Final Report on NSF Grant No. ATM-8108447. Boulder, Colo.: National Center for Atmospheric Research.
Williams, N. T., et al. 1964-84. *Farm Business Statistics for South East England.* Ashford: Wye College.
Witcombe, J. R., and Whittington, W. J. 1971. "A study of the genotype by environmental interaction shown by germinating seeds of *Brassica napus*." *Heredity* 26:397-411.
World Bank. 1955. *The Economic Development of Syria*. Baltimore: Johns Hopkins University Press.
———. 1977. *Syrian Arab Republic—Development Prospects and Policies: Report of a 1977 World Bank Mission*. Vol. 2: Main Report. Washington, D.C.: World Bank.
Worrall, W. D.; Scott, N. H.; Klatt, A. R.; and Rajaram, S. 1980. "Performance of CIMMYT wheat germplasm in optimum and suboptimum production environments," in *Proceedings 3rd International Wheat Conference*, Madrid, Spain. Nebraska Agricultural Experiment Station Miscellaneous Publication 41:5-29.
Wright, A. J. 1971. "The analysis and prediction of some two-factor interactions in grass breeding." *Journal of Agricultural Science* 76:301-6.
Yates, F., and Cochran, W. G. 1938. "The analysis of groups of experiments." *Journal of Agricultural Science* 28:556-80.
Young, R., and Mount, T. D. 1979. "An econometric analysis of uncertainty in rice production." Mimeo., Department of Agricultural Economics, Cornell University, Ithaca, N.Y.

Zhongguo Guojia Tongjiju [State Statistical Bureau of China]. 1984a. *Zhongguo Maoyi Wujia Tongji Ziliao* [Statistical Materials on Chinese Trade and Prices]. Beijing: Zhongguo Tongji Chubanshe [Statistical Publishing House of China].

———. 1984b. *Zhongguo Nongye de Guanghui Chengjiu 1949–1984* [Radiant Achievements of Chinese Agriculture, 1949–1984]. Beijing: Tongji Chubanshe [Statistical Publishing House].

———. 1984c. *Zhongguo Tongji Nianjian 1984* [Statistical Yearbook of China 1984]. Beijing: Tongji Chubanshe [Statistical Publishing House].

Zhongguo Kexueyuan Dili Yanjiusuo Jingji Dili Yanjiushi [Chinese Academy of Sciences, Institute of Geography, Economic Geography Research Room]. 1980. *Zhongguo Nongye Dili Zonglun* [A General Compendium of Chinese Agricultural Geography]. Beijing: Kexue Chubanshe [Scientific Publishing House].

Zuber, M. S., and Darrah, L. L. 1980. "1979 U.S. corn germplasm base," in *Proceedings of the 35th Annual Corn and Sorghum Research Conference*. American Seed Trade Association, Washington, D.C., 234–39.

Contributors

Jock R. Anderson is a professor of agricultural economics at the University of New England, Armidale, Australia.

Michael H. Arnold is a consultant in Cambridge, England. At the time this volume was prepared, he was deputy director of the Plant Breeding Institute, Cambridge, England.

Roger B. Austin is a physiologist at the Plant Breeding Institute, Cambridge, England.

Randolph Barker is a professor of agricultural economics at Cornell University, Ithaca, USA.

Vishva Bindlish is an economist at the World Bank, Washington, D.C. At the time this volume was prepared, he was a doctoral candidate at Cornell University, Ithaca, USA.

H. J. Braun is a wheat breeder with the International Maize and Wheat Improvement Center (CIMMYT), El Batán, Mexico, currently stationed in Ankara, Turkey.

Joachim von Braun is a research fellow at the International Food Policy Research Institute, Washington, D.C.

Gerald A. Carlson is a professor of economics at North Carolina State University, Raleigh, USA.

Ujjayant N. Chakravorty is a doctoral candidate at the East-West Environment and Policy Institute and the University of Hawaii, Honolulu, USA.

W. Ronnie Coffman is a professor of plant breeding, Cornell University, Ithaca, USA.

J. Crossa is a biometrician at the International Maize and Wheat Improvement Center (CIMMYT), El Batán, Mexico.

Donald N. Duvick is a senior vice-president for research, Pioneer Hi-Bred International, Inc., Des Moines, Iowa, USA.

Carly J. Findlay is a research officer, Australian Bureau of Agricultural and Resource Economics, Canberra, Australia. At the time this volume was prepared, she was an undergraduate student at the University of New England, Armidale, Australia.

G. Fischbeck is a professor of agronomy and plant breeding at the Technical University of Munich, Federal Republic of Germany.

John C. Flinn is head of the Department of Agricultural Economics, International Rice Research Institute, Los Baños, Philippines.

James B. French is an agricultural economist at the Centro Agronómico Tropical de Investigación y Enseñanza (CATIE), Costa Rica.

Dennis P. Garrity is an agronomist/crop ecologist at the International Rice Research Institute, Los Baños, Philippines.

H. Hanus is a professor of plant production at the University of Kiel, Federal Republic of Germany.

T. R. Hargrove is head of Information Services at the International Rice Research Institute, Los Baños, Philippines.

Peter B. R. Hazell was director of the Agricultural Growth Linkages and Development Policy Program at the International Food Policy Research Institute, Washington, D.C. He is now a principal economist at the Agricultural and Rural Development Department, World Bank, Washington, D.C.

J. C. Headley is a professor of agricultural economics at the University of Missouri, Columbia, USA.

V. A. Johnson is a professor of plant breeding at the University of Nebraska, Lincoln, USA.

Timothy D. Mount is a professor of agricultural economics at Cornell University, Ithaca, USA.

Robert F. Mumm is a professor of biometry at the University of Nebraska, Lincoln, USA.

Hung Nguyen is with SRS Technologies, Arlington, Virginia, USA. At the time this volume was prepared, he was a consultant with the International Food Policy Research Institute, Washington, D.C.

Sushil Pandey is a research fellow in agricultural economics at the University of Western Australia. At the time this volume was prepared, he was a doctoral candidate at the University of New England, Armidale, Australia.

C. James Peterson is a plant breeder with the United States Department of Agriculture, Agricultural Research Service, at the University of Nebraska, Lincoln, USA.

W. H. Pfeiffer is a wheat breeder at the International Maize and Wheat Improvement Center (CIMMYT), El Batán, Mexico.

H. N. Pham is a maize breeder at the International Maize and Wheat Improvement Center (CIMMYT), El Batán, Mexico.

Mark W. Rosegrant is a research fellow at the International Food Policy Research Institute, Washington, D.C.

James A. Roumasset is a professor of economics at the University of Hawaii, Honolulu, USA.

David E. Sahn was a research fellow at the International Food Policy Research Institute, Washington, D.C. He is now deputy director of the Cornell Food and Nutrition Policy Program, Washington, D.C.

J. W. Schmidt is a professor of plant breeding at the University of Nebraska, Lincoln, USA.

P. Schoop is a research fellow in plant production at the University of Kiel, Federal Republic of Germany.

Bruce Stone is a research fellow at the International Food Policy Research Institute, Washington, D.C.

John R. Tarrant is a reader, School of Environmental Sciences, and pro vice-chancellor, University of East Anglia, Norwich, England.

S. R. Waddington is a maize agronomist at the International Maize and Wheat Improvement Center (CIMMYT), El Batán, Mexico.

Thomas S. Walker is an economist at the International Crops Research Institute for the Semi-Arid Tropics, Patancheru, India.

G. H. Wan is a doctoral candidate in agricultural economics at the University of New England, Armidale, Australia.

Paul Webster is a reader in agricultural economics at Wye College, University of London, Ashford, Kent, England.

Nigel T. Williams is a lecturer in agricultural economics at Wye College, University of London, Ashford, Kent, England.

John R. Witcombe is a pearl millet breeder at the International Crops Research Institute for the Semi-Arid Tropics, Patancheru, India.

Tong Zhong is a doctoral student at the University of Guelph, Canada, and a researcher at the Agricultural Economics Institute, Chinese Academy of Agricultural Sciences, Beijing. At the time this volume was prepared, she was a visiting scholar at the International Food Policy Research Institute, Washington, D.C.

Index

Africa: food consumption variability in Sub-Sahara, 326, 327; foodgrain variability increases, 342; risk benefits from varietal technologies, 318

Agricultural policy options

—for food security: buffer stocks and trade policies, 337; credit arrangements, 337-38; employment, income, and food subsidy programs, 337

—for reduced production variability: crop insurance, 352; improved marketing structure, 336, 352-53; price and supply stabilization, 334-36, 353-54; regional diversification, 354

—for reduced yield variability: economic efficiency of approaches to, 355-56; information gathering and processing systems, 354-55; management practices for, 350; plant breeding, 348-50

Agriculture, U.S. Department of, 14, 71, 76, 77, 89, 148, 339; Agricultural Research Service, 176; Cooperative State Crop and Livestock Reporting Service, 273; NRPN and SRPN wheat cultivar programs, 175

Ahmed, R., 356

AICRIP. See All India Coordinated Rice Improved Program

Aimiller, O., 265

Akohas, H., 135

Alderman, H., 337

All India Coordinated Rice Improved Program (AICRIP), 254

Anderson, J. R., 4, 7, 8, 9, 32, 47, 63, 206, 218, 223, 224, 225, 230, 231, 239, 240, 247, 301, 303, 305, 306, 307, 320, 328, 343, 347, 351, 354, 355

Andres, F., 142

Antle, J. M., 5, 224, 227, 231, 232, 239, 245, 248

Aquino, R. C., 135

Araji, A. A., 175, 183

Arcia, G., 347

Arnold, M. H., 3, 100, 108, 128, 129, 131, 206, 348

Asokan, M., 311, 319

Austin, R. B., 3, 100, 108, 129, 131, 206, 348

Australia: barley yield, 128; variance increase in foodgrain production, 47, 341, 342-43

Baker, R. J., 178, 187

Bakour, Y., 78, 80, 81

Barah, B. C., 186, 187, 206, 217, 218

Barbakov, N. K., 60

Barker, R., 1, 7, 134, 224, 234, 237, 241, 260, 271

Barley

—Bavarian yield variability for spring: breeding efforts and, 121, 123; crop management system influencing, 123-24; measurement of trends in, 118-23

—nitrogen fertilization and yield of winter: fungicide treatment effect on, 265-66; growth stage effect on, 266-67; weather effect on, 266

—Southeast England yield variability: data for, 107-8; decomposition analysis for, 108, 110-12; for two farm groups, 108, 109

—Syrian: area yield variability, 80, 81, 82-83; prices, 88, 89; production variability, 84, 85-87; straw, 89; yield correlations between provinces, 85, 87

—world production, 29

Bassoco, L. M., 347

Bavaria

—spring barley yield variability: breeding efforts and, 121; crop management system influencing, 123-24; measurement of trends in, 118-22

—winter wheat yield variability: breeding efforts and, 121, 123; crop management

385

386 Index

Bavaria (cont'd)
  system influencing, 123-24; fungicide treatment and, 265-66, 268; growth stage effect on, 266-67; measurement of trends in, 118-23; nitrogen fertilizer and, 265; weather effects and, 266
Beachell, H. M., 142
Beaton, G., 333
Berentsen, W. H., 71
Biere, A. W., 236
Bindlish, V., 7
Binswanger, H. P., 186, 187, 206, 217, 218, 230, 289, 311, 315
Blackie, M. J., 5
Boggess, W. G., 240
Bohrnstedt, G. W., 25
Boussard, J.-M., 347
Boyd, W.J.R., 184
Braun, H. L., 5, 159
Braun, J. von, 8, 326, 337, 347, 353
Brown, W. L., 133
Byerlee, D. R., 4, 225, 355

Cabanilla, V. L., 134, 263
Cain, M., 316
Capule, C., 236
Carlson, G. A., 5, 240, 244, 245, 247, 253, 258
Carter, T. R., 5, 32, 345
Castillo, L. L., 245, 258
Castleberry, R. M., 153
Centro Internacional de Mejoramiento de Maiz y Trigo (CIMMYT)
—Maize Program to improve yield stability: agronomic input trials, 199, 201-2; demonstration and verification trials, 202-4; described, 186-87; maize germplasm for, 185-86, 189, 349; on-farm testing, 194-95; population improvement and testing trials, 187-89; results, 204-5; variety trials, 195-99, 200
—strategy for wheat yield stability: data for, 159; environmental differences in performance, 168-70; experiments to verify, 170-74; germplasm development for, 157; for high-yielding varieties, 161, 164-65; models for, 159-63; objective, 174; regional differences in, 166-68
Cereal production
—variability: by country, 17, 18-19, 20-25, 29; by crop, 15-16, 20-25; decomposition analysis, 17, 24-27, 29, 31, 341; regional correlations in, 31, 32, 33; trend changes in, 13-14, 15; yield variability to understand, 3, 341

—world: components of change in, 27-31; growing conditions and, 31-32; growth, 13-14, 33
Cereal yield variability
—causal factors, 2, 4, 130; climate, 345-46; crop variety and, 343-45; environment, 269; fungicides, 265-68; irrigation, 234-41
—input management and, 6-8, 346
—measures, 8-10
—patterns, 2-5
—plant breeding and, 5-6, 127, 348-50
—and production variability, 3, 341
CGIAR. See Consultative Group on International Agricultural Research
Chandrasekar, C.M.M., 241
Chang, T. T., 145
Chelliah, S., 258
Chen Nai-Ruenn, 40
China
—cereal production, 35
—Cultural Revolution, 43
—Great Leap Forward, 36, 40, 43
—maize production, 35; disease affecting, 39; double-cross hybrid, 41; risk in, 38; variability, 38-39
—rice production, 35; components of change in variance of, 47, 50-51; high-yielding hybrid, 41, 133-35; yield, 46
—role in foodgrain arbitrage, 33
—variability in cereal production, 3; fertilizer and, 41, 42, 43, 57-58; government policies affecting, 40, 58; irrigation and, 39-40; trends, 35, 36-37; weather conditions and, 36, 37, 40, 58
CIA, 40
CIMMYT. See Centro Internacional de Mejoramiento de Maiz y Trigo
Climate, 5; and cereal yield variability, 4, 345-46; effect on Soviet cereal production, 71-72, 73; effect on Syrian cereal production, 78. See also Weather
Cochran, W. C., 128, 206
Coffman, W. R., 5, 134, 135, 142, 253, 257, 258, 263, 349
Colyer, D., 227
Comer, G. H., 65
Commerce, U.S. Department of, 148
Consultative Group on International Agricultural Research (CGIAR), World Bank, 349, 350
Cook, R. J., 114
Cooper, P.J.M., 81
Cordova, V., 224
Credit availability: for improved food

consumption, 337–38; for resource-poor farmers, 351
Crissman, C. C., 224, 227, 231, 232
Crop insurance: income variability and, 319, 355–56; to insure household income, 337; risk, 352
Crossa, J. H., 187
Crum, C. W., 153
Cultivars, wheat
—Kharkof, 176, 177, 178, 181, 182
—response to environmental conditions, 181–82, 184
—stability: defined, 175; genotype-environment interaction for association with, 178–80; measure of, 180
—yield response to development of, 182–83
Cytoplasm uniformity, U.S. maize disease from, 135, 149. *See also* Genetic uniformity

Dagg, M., 32, 345
Dalrymple, D. G., 41, 42, 133
Darrah, L. L., 151, 152
Davis, D. D., 135
Day, R. H., 9, 223, 231, 260, 271
De Datta, S. K., 258, 259
de Janvry, A., 225, 290
Denning, G. L., 264
Dent, J. B., 5
Deolalikar, A., 333
Desai, G., 71
Deshpande, R. S., 238
Deutsch, J. A., 187
Developing countries. *See* Third World
Dhawan, B. D., 237
Dillon, J. L., 4, 218, 223, 231, 239, 306, 352
Disease, crop: fungicide control for, 114–16, 259, 268–69, 346; from mildew, 95; and U.S. maize yield, 148–49; and yield variability, 346
Doorenbos, J., 235, 236
Downey, L. A., 235
Duffy, M., 275, 276
Dusek, D. A., 236
Duvick, D. N., 5, 6, 32, 153, 155

Eberhart, S. A., 129, 177, 180, 186, 187, 190, 195, 206, 207, 254, 348
Eckstein, A., 35
Edmeades, G. O., 186
Edwards, G. W., 352
El-Akhrass, H., 88
Elite Variety Trials (ELVTS), for CIMMYT maize varieties, 187, 190, 193

El-Sherbini, A. A., 78
European Economic Community, 118
Evans, L. T., 259, 339n, 343n, 350
Evenson, R. E., 8, 254
Experimental varieties (EVs), multilocational testing of CIMMYT maize, 186, 189–94
Ezekiel, H., 96

FAO. *See* Food and Agriculture Organization
Farmers
—household income: crop yield stability and, 309, 311, 313, 317, 318–19; short-term crop variability effect on, 330, 331
—yield expectations for Indian rice HYVs, 289–90, 294, 299–300
—yield risks of modern wheat cultivars, 301–2; stochastic dominance analysis, 303–7
Farnsworth, R. L., 225, 230
Feder, G., 245, 249
Fertilizer, 5
—British use: for wheat and barley production, 114, 116; for wheat production, 105
—Chinese use: imports for, 58; to increase foodgrain yield, 41, 42, 43, 57
—and crop yield variability, 202, 223; analytical approaches to estimating, 225–26; density function system in estimating, 224, 231; fungicide treatment and, 265–66, 267, 268; gross approaches to estimating, 223–25; growth stage and, 266–67; risk effects, 226, 227, 230, 232; study results, 226–33; weather effects, 266
—Indian use for sorghum production, 96
—and insect pest population, 242, 243–44
—for maize production, 150, 275
—prices, 250
—rice yield variability and, 259
—for wheat production, 276
Feyerherm, A. M., 175
Findlay, C. J., 7
Finlay, K. W., 128, 180, 184, 254
Fischbeck, G., 3
Fischer, K. S., 186
Fischer, T., 301
Flinn, J. C., 6, 249, 258, 260, 301
Food and Agriculture Organization (FAO), 35, 42, 71, 261, 325, 339
Food consumption
—employment generation program to insure adequate, 337
—food production variability and, 320, 321, 324, 338; empirical analysis of, 325–

Food consumption (cont'd)
28; marketing infrastructure to reduce, 336
—food subsidies for, 337
—improved access to consumption credit for, 337-38
Food production variability
—food consumption and, 320, 321, 324, 338, 347
—labor demand and, 325
—nutritional status and, 320, 321, 328-29, 338
—policy options to reduce effects of: food price and supply stabilization, 334-35, 353-54; improved marketing infrastructure, 336, 352-53; trade and storage policies, 335-36
—price effects, 323
—weather-induced fluctuations in, 32
Foster, K. W., 135
Freebairn, J. W., 351
French, J. B., 5, 6, 32, 278, 345
Fuller, W. A., 227
Fungicides: and barley and wheat yield variability, 265-66, 267, 268; for English barley and wheat disease, 114-16

Gabler, E. C., 224, 237, 241, 260, 271
Gallagher, P. W., 33
Garrity, D. P., 6, 301
Genetic uniformity, U.S. maize yield variability and, 133, 151-53; disease susceptibility and, 135, 149; weather susceptibility and, 149
Genotype
—adaptability, 254-56
—interaction between environment and: cultivar stability associated with, 178-80, 183; for pearl millet, 206-7, 218-20; for wheat, 175, 176, 178-80, 183
—spring bread wheat groups, 159, 160
—yield performance, 161, 162-64, 254, 255
—yield stability, 153-54, 164-66
Ghana, on-farm testing of maize varieties, 195, 198, 199, 203-4
Gines, H. C., 257
Glantz, M. H., 351
Goldberger, A. S., 25
Gonzales, L. A., 244
Goodell, G. E., 258
Goodman, M. M., 133
Green, C., 328
Green, G. C., 236
Green Revolution, 31, 134

Griffin, K., 1
Griffing, J. B., 344
Griffiths, W. E., 225, 247
Grisley, W., 230

Haiti, on-farm testing for improved maize yield, 202
Hallajian, M., 89
Hallauer, A. R., 153
Hamal, K. B., 224
Hanus, H., 5, 6, 265, 266
Hardaker, J. B., 4, 218, 223, 231, 306
Hargrove, T. R., 5, 134, 253, 257, 258, 263, 349
Harland, S. C., 135
Hawthorn, M., 275, 276
Hayami, Y., 248
Hazell, P.B.R., 2, 3, 6, 17, 26, 29, 32, 33, 46, 47, 49, 80, 91, 92, 93, 96, 102, 107, 133, 147, 157, 237, 238, 240, 279, 283, 284, 296, 297, 340, 342, 347, 352, 354, 356
Headley, J. C., 5, 6, 32, 149, 278, 345
Heady, E. O., 235, 273
Hedlund, S., 62, 63, 76
He Gang, 35
Heine, H., 184
Heinrichs, E. A., 135, 258
Hendrick, R. L., 65
Herbicides: for maize production, 275; for modern rice varieties, 258-59; for Third World rice crop, 143; and U.S. corn yield variability, 150; for wheat production, 276
Herdt, R. W., 134, 225, 226, 230, 236, 245, 258, 260
Hexem, R. W., 235
High-yielding varieties (HYVs) of cereals
—bread wheat, 161, 164, 165-66, 170
—Chinese dwarf rice, 41-42
—Indian millet and sorghum: role in area-yield covariance, 94-98; role in cereal production variability, 91-92, 99
—responsiveness to growing conditions, 31-32
—risk associated with, 31, 287
—starvation prevention with, 135, 145
—Syrian variety of Mexican wheat, 78, 88
—weather pattern and, 32
—yield expectations for, 289-90, 299, 300; data for, 290-91, 293; farmers' expectations model for, 292, 294; government's expectations model for, 295-96; for Indian rice, 296-98; risk and uncertainty related to, 287

Hildebrand, P. E., 187
Hill, J., 187
Hooker, A. L., 244
Hossain, M., 356
Houck, J. P., 33
Household income
—and consumption variability, 332-33
—crop yield stability and, 309, 318-19; simulated risk benefits for, 313-16; study data for, 311, 313
—food crop production variability and, 320-21; for agricultural laborers, 330-31; for farmers, 330, 331; for nonagricultural workers, 331-32
—improved access to credit to guarantee, 337-38
—study of yield stability link to, 309-17
Huddleston, B., 336, 337, 353
HYVs. See High-yielding varieties of cereals

ICRISAT. See International Crops Research Institute for the Semi-Arid Tropics
IFPRI. See International Food Policy Research Institute
Immink, M., 333
Income. See Household income
India, 3, 47
—cereal production variability, 91
—pearl millet and sorghum HYVs production variability, 92-93; interregional covariance, 98-99; mildew disease and, 95; power and fertilizer and, 96; regression analysis to test, 96-98; sources, 93-96
—pearl millet yield variability: for different environments, 207-13, 214, 215; for hybrids versus open-pollinated varieties, 206, 213, 216-20
—study of yield stability link to household income, 309; area variability, 317; common crops cultivation in, 312, 313; data for, 310, 311, 313; farmers' risk benefits in, 311, 313-16
Indonesia, Chinese rice introduced into, 133
Innes, N. L., 128
Input management and yield variability, 6, 346. See also Fertilizer; Irrigation; Pesticides; Technology; Weather
Insect pests, grain crops, 242-43; approaches to controlling, 250; crop varieties resistant to, 243-44; factors influencing population of, 242-43; pesticides for controlling, 245, 247-49
International Crops Research Institute for the Semi-Arid Tropics (ICRISAT), 315, 318, 332; research on plant breeding, 91; testing of pearl millet varieties, 206
International Fertilizer Development Center, 264
International Food Policy Research Institute (IFPRI), 40, 353
International Monetary Fund: Compensatory Finance Facility, 336; food facility, 353
International Network for Soil Fertility and Fertilizer Efficiency in Rice, 264
International Pearl Millet Adaptation Trial (IPMAT): tests of open-pollinated versus hybrid varieties, 206, 207, 213, 216-20; for yields in different environments, 207-13, 214, 215
International Progeny Testing Trials (IPTTs), for maize, 187-89
International Rice Research Institute (IRRI), 41, 133, 135, 143, 144, 226, 244, 248, 254, 259; Germplasm Evaluation and Utilization Program, 262, 349
International Rice Testing Program (IRTP), 254-55, 263
International Spring Wheat Yield Nurseries (ISWYNS), 159
IPMAT. See International Pearl Millet Adaptation Trial
IPTTs. See International Progeny Testing Trials
IRRI. See International Rice Research Institute
Irrigation, 5
—Chinese cereal crops, 39-40
—crop yield variability and, 236-38, 346; at aggregate level, 240-41; models for measuring, 238-40
—foodgrain production stability and, 234; measurement of, in terms of water input, 235-36, 237
—Indian: crop substitution with, 238; sorghum area-yield covariance and, 94, 99
—and insect pest population, 242, 243-44
—Soviet Union new investment in, 76
—Syrian wheat, 78
IRTP. See International Rice Testing Program

Jain, H. K., 32, 345
Jaramillo, M., 321, 332

Jayasuriya, S. K., 245, 258
Jennings, P. R., 135
Jinks, J. L., 159, 186, 206
Jodha, N. S., 238, 289, 311, 333, 351
Johnson, D. G., 323-24, 336n
Johnson, E. C., 186
Johnson, V. A., 180
Johnston, B., 322
Just, R. E., 5, 224, 225, 239, 240, 244, 248

Kanbur, S.M.R.C., 315, 354
Kanemasu, E. T., 236
Kanwar, J. S., 95
Kassam, A. H., 236
Kaufman, H. E., 135, 142
Kelly, P. M., 71, 76
Kendall, M., 9
Kenmore, P. E., 242, 258
Khaldi, Nabil, 79
Khush, G. S., 142
King, E., 135
King, J. E., 114
King, R. P., 307
Kirkpatrick, C., 328
Knight, R., 187, 206
Koester, U., 322n, 323, 335
Kogan, F. N., 62, 63, 71, 77
Konandreas, P., 325n
Korea, rice production, 144-45
Krull, C. F., 153
Kueh, Y. Y., 36, 39, 57
Kuhr, S. L., 183
Kumar, S. K., 333
Kwak, T. S., 145

Labor demand: employment generation program and, 337; for landless agricultural wage laborers, 330-31; production variability and, 325
Ladejinsky, W., 94
Laird, R. D., 60, 62
Lantican, R. M., 135, 349
Lardy, N. R., 36
Latham, M., 333
Latter, B.D.H., 344
Lazarus, W., 244, 245
Lester, E., 105
Litsinger, J. A., 258
Lubigan, R. T., 259

McBride, D., 352
McIntire, J., 335
Mackill, D. J., 145, 256
MacLaren, D., 351
McWilliam, J. R., 344

Mahill, J. F., 135
Main, C. E., 244
Maize, 6. *See also* Centro Internacional de Mejoramiento de Maiz y Trigo, Maize Program
—Chinese production, 35; disease affecting, 39; double-cross hybrid, 41; risk in, 38; yield variability, 38-39
—developing countries production, 185-86, 189
—on-farm testing of improved varieties, 194-95; by changing agronomic input levels, 199, 201, 202, 203; by demonstration and verification trials, 202-4; mean yields, by country, 195-99, 200; results, 204-5
—U.S. yield variability, 6, 147-48; disease affecting, 148-49, 155; fertilizer use and, 150, 154; genetic uniformity and, 133, 135, 149, 151-53; improved technology and, 150; weather and, 148, 149-50; weed control and, 150
—world production, 29
—yield stability analysis: multilocational testing of experimental varieties, 189-94; population improvement and international testing system, 187-89
Mandac, A. M., 249, 260
Manning, H. L., 128
Manwan, I., 259
Margen, S., 333
Markish, Y., 76
Marra, M., 244
Mathison, M. J., 344
Mazid, A., 89
Mehra, S., 1, 31, 91, 234, 237, 297, 346
Mellor, J., 320, 322, 330
Mendoza, M. N., 224
Mercado, A. C., 135, 349
Meshcherskaya, A. V., 63, 71
Meulen, J.G.J. van der, 133
Mexico: bread wheat yield stability experimentation, 169, 170, 173; on-farm testing of maize varieties, 199-201
Meyer, J., 307
Meyer, W. S., 236
Micklin, P. P., 76
Millet. *See* Pearl millet
Ministry of Agriculture and Agrarian Reform, Syria, 79
Modern varieties of cereal: risk, 347; yield variability, 343-45. *See also* High-yielding varieties of cereals; Rice
Moffitt, L. J., 225, 230, 247
Mooers, C. A., 128

Morgan, T. H., 236
Morris, R. A., 257
Mostek, A., 71
Mount, T., 7, 224
Music, J. T., 236
Musser, W. N., 240

Nadkarni, M. V., 238
Nagaich, B. B., 135
National Academy of Sciences, 151
New, L. L., 236
Newberry, D.M.G., 309, 311, 314, 335, 353, 354, 356
Nguyen, H. P., 32, 47, 49, 62, 75, 342
Northern Regional Performance Nursery (NRPN), wheat cultivar development program, 175; genetic contribution to variability, 179-80; genetic contribution to yield, 178; regression analysis, 177; response to environment, 181-82, 183; yield data, by location, 176-77
Norton, G. A., 245, 247
NRPN. *See* Northern Regional Performance Nursery
Nutritional status: food production variability and, 320, 321, 328-29, 338; individual consumption and, 333; targeted programs to improve, 337

O'Mara, G., 347
Ostle, B., 280

Paddock, P. and W., 133
Padmanabhan, S. Y., 135
Pakistan, pearl millet yield variability, 206; for different environments, 207-13, 214, 215; for hybrid versus open-pollinated varieties, 213, 216-20
Paliwal, R. L., 186
Paller, E. C., 259
Palmer, A.F.E., 186
Pandey, S., 5, 238, 240, 346
Paraguay, on-farm testing of maize varieties, 195, 196
Parry, M. L., 5, 32, 345
Parthasarthy, N., 133
Pathak, M. D., 142
Patterson, H. D., 106, 113
Paulsen, G. M., 175
Pearl millet
—Chinese production, 35
—interaction between genotype and environment in India and Pakistan: for different environments, 207-13, 214, 215; for hybrid versus open-pollinated varieties, 213, 216-20
—yield variability in Indian HYVs, 92-93; area-yield covariance, 93-94; interregional covariance, 98-99; mildew disease and, 95; power and fertilizer and, 96; regression analysis to test, 96-98
Pearson, E. S., 278
Penaranda, F. L., 242
Perkins, J. M., 159, 186, 206
Pernita, R. G., 257
Perrin, R. K., 225, 273, 347
Perry, J. N., 63
Pesticides
—and crop prices, 248-49
—impact on crop yield variability, 245; for modern rice varieties, 257-58; problems in estimating, 247-48; timing and dosage rate for, 245, 247
—for maize production, 275
—prices, 250
—risk effects, 246
—for Third World rice crop, 142-43
Pfeiffer, W. H., 5, 159
Pham, H. N., 5
Philippine rice production: fertilizer and, 226, 227; modern varieties, 134, 145-46, 258, 260-61; technology and, 261
Pingali, P., 247
Pinstrup-Andersen, P., 321, 332, 337, 356
Plant breeding
—Bavarian spring barley and winter wheat, 121
—cultivar stability and, 175
—and genetic diversity, 133
—rice: ancestry of varieties, 133-35, 136-39; for yield stability, 135, 140-45
—United Kingdom crop management standards and, 132
—for yield stability, 127-28, 348-50; genotype-environmental interactions for, 128-29, 131-32
—and yield variability, 2, 5-6; binomial model for, 129-30
Pomareda, C., 352, 356
Ponnamperuma, F. F., 144
Pope, R. D., 5, 224, 225, 239, 240, 248
Prices, foodgrain, 34; crop production variability and, 321, 322; recommendations for stabilizing, 334-36; Soviet demand effect on, 61-62; Syrian, 88-89; trade opportunities and, 322-23
Pruitt, W. O., 235, 237
Pryde, P. R., 76

Quiggin, J. C., 353, 354

Rainfall, 5; U.S. maize variability and, 149; variability of Syrian, 78. *See also* Weather
Rangaswami, P., 232
Rao, C.H.H., 237
Rath, G. G., 135
Ray, S. K., 253
Reichelderfer, K. H., 245, 247
Research, agricultural, 354, 355; for bread wheat yield stability, 159-66
Reutlinger, S., 335, 336n
Rice
—Asian yields, 134, 145; changes in, 252, 253; inputs effect on variability, 248; technological advances to improve, 261-62
—Chinese production, 35; components of change in variance of, 47, 50-51; high-yielding hybrids, 41, 133-35; yield, 46
—fertilizer effect on yield variability, 226, 227, 231
—modern varieties: described, 133-34, 251; genetic uniformity, 263; improvement program for, 261-62; traditional versus, 133
—modern varieties yield variability, 133, 135, 251, 253-54; adaptability and, 254-56; agronomic factors affecting, 135, 140-42; diseases affecting, 143, 259; drought tolerance and, 144; fertilizer application and, 259; flood tolerance and, 144; on-farm, 260-61; pest management and, 142-43, 257-59; soil conditions and, 144, 263-64; water supply and, 256-57; weed management and, 143, 258-59
—semidwarf varieties, 135
—yield expectations analysis for high-yielding Indian varieties, 287, 296-300
Risk
—agricultural policy-induced, 351, 352
—benefits: defined, 309, 311; measurement of, 313-16
—from fertilizer, in Philippine rice production, 226, 227, 230, 232
—modern crop varieties, 347
—modern wheat cultivars, 301-8
—weather and, 225, 283
—yield, 2, 7, 31, 287
Robison, L. G., 307
Rosegrant, M. W., 225, 226, 230, 231, 238, 239, 240, 346
Rosenberg, N. J., 351

Rostankowski, P., 76
Rothamsted Experimental Station, 103, 105, 113
Roumasset, J. A., 5, 224, 225, 226, 230, 231, 259
RSFSR. *See* Russian Soviet Federated Socialist Republic
Russell, J. S., 175, 183
Russell, W. A., 129, 153, 177, 180, 186, 187, 190, 195, 206, 207, 254, 348
Russian Soviet Federated Socialist Republic (RSFSR), 62, 65, 67
Rutger, J. N., 135
Ruttan, V. W., 248
Ryan, J. G., 225, 311

Sahn, D. E., 8, 326, 347, 353
Sama, S., 259
Saxena, R. C., 258
Scandizzo, P. L., 320, 328
Schmidt, J. W., 175, 180, 183, 184
Schoop, P., 5, 6
Schroder, D., 278
Scott, C., 320, 321n
Seagraves, J. A., 227
Sebaugh, J. L., 175
Shafer, S. L., 180
Siamwalla, A., 322, 353
Sievers, M., 340, 341
Sillers, D. A., 230
Silvey, V., 106, 113, 175, 183
Sim, R.J.R., 175, 183
Simmonds, N. W., 5
Singh, R. P., 311, 319
Slade, R., 249
Smith, H., 226, 230
Smith, J., 224, 258, 259
Social Science Research Council, 40
Soil management, 263-64. *See also* Fertilizer; Irrigation
Sorghum production
—Chinese, 35
—Indian variability in HYVs, 92-93; area-yield covariance and, 93-94; drought and, 96; irrigation and, 94, 99; power and fertilizer and, 96; regression analysis to test, 96-99
Southern Regional Performance Nursery (SRPN), wheat cultivar development; genetic contribution to variability, 178-79; genetic contribution to yield, 177; regression analyses, 177; response to environment, 181, 182; yield data, by location, 176-77
Soviet Union

—cereal imports, 60, 61, 76
—cereal production, 3, 47; annual variability in, 65-67, 69, 75, 76, 77; climate effect on, 71-72, 73; demand effect on, 61-62; irrigation investment to increase, 76; livestock herd size as buffer for, 60, 75; policies to increase, 75-76; problems with data for, 62-63; regional compensation effect, 63, 70-75, 354; regional variability in, 68, 69-70, 341; in RSFSR, 65, 67; spatial variability in, 63-65, 66, 76
—meat production, 76
Sprague, E. W., 186
Srinivasan, T. N., 320, 333
SRPN. *See* Southern Regional Performance Nursery
Stanhill, G., 100
State Statistical Bureau, China, 35, 38
Stavis, B., 41
Stewart, A., 9
Stiglitz, J. E., 309, 311, 315, 335, 353, 354, 356
Stone, B., 35, 38, 39, 41, 42, 43, 45, 47, 48, 50, 52, 57
Strauss, J., 333
Stroike, J. E., 180
Subba Rao, K. V., 315
Sukhatme, P. V., 333
Svedberg, P., 334
Swamy, P.A.V.B., 224
Swanson, E. R., 244, 245
Syria
—agricultural planning, 90
—barley: area yield variability, 80, 81, 82-83; interprovincial yield correlations, 85, 87; prices, 88, 89; production variability, 84, 85-87; straw, 89
—cereal prices, 88-89
—cereal production variability analysis, 3, 78; by area, 80-81, 82-84; components of change, 85, 86; data, by province 79; interprovincial yield correlations, 85, 87, 341
—climate, 78
—land reforms, 79, 80, 341
—wheat: area variability, 80, 82; high-yielding varieties, 88; interprovincial yield correlations, 85, 87; prices, 88; production quotas, 89, 90; production variability, 81, 83, 85, 88

Talbot, M., 130
Talpaz, H., 225
Tarrant, J. R., 32, 60, 62, 63, 71, 76, 354

Tautho, C. C., 260
Taylor, C. R., 225
Taylor, L. R., 63
Taylor, R. D., 63
Taylor, T. A., 32, 345
Technology
—categories of, 274
—crop stability from varietal: household income and, 309, 311, 318-19; risk benefits from, 309, 310, 317, 318
—influence on U.S. maize and wheat yield variability, 270, 271; degree of skewness in, 278; by historical periods, 274-76, 277
—interaction with weather, 273, 276-78
—modern rice variety, 251; and production stability, 253, 261-64; traits of, and yield stability, 254-60
—yield risk effect in introducing new, 7, 232
Tew, B. V., 240
Thailand, on-farm testing of maize varieties, 202-3
Thattil, R. O., 224
Third World: diseases affecting rice crops, 142; food security problem, 347; green revolution in rice production, 134; high-yielding varieties of wheat and rice, 133; maize production, 185-86, 199
Thompson, L. M., 5, 149
Tinker, P. B., 129
Tollini, H., 22
Trade, foodgrain: African closed economy and, 323-24; domestic grain prices influenced by, 323; recommendations for increasing food supply by, 335-36; volume effect on world price variability, 322
Trapp, J. N., 240
Turner, B. D., 63

Uganda, cotton breeding program, 128
Umali, G., 224, 259
United Kingdom
—crop management standards, 132
—Southeast wheat and barley yield variability: changes in variety and, 113; data for, 107-8; decomposition analysis for, 108, 110-12; fertilizer and, 114, 116; fungicides and, 114-16; random factors affecting, 117; for two groups of farms, 108, 109
—wheat yield variability, 100; field-to-field, 105-6; historical trends in, 100-101; individual field differences in, 103-4;

United Kingdom (cont'd)
  interannual, 101-2; plant breeding and, 106; uncontrolled factors affecting, 104
United States
—cereal production, 3, 47
—Great Plains wheat cultivar development programs, 175, 176, 178, 179, 182, 183, 184
—maize: changes in culture inputs, 150-51, 154; future farming practices for, 156; genetic uniformity among hybrids, 133, 135, 149, 151-53; high-yielding varieties, 92; yield stability of modern hybrids, 153-54, 155-56
—maize yield variability, 147, 270-71, 274; data for, 273-74; factors influencing, 148-50, 154, 155; interarea correlations, 279-82, 284; technology effect on, 274-75, 283; technology-weather interaction and, 273, 276-78; weather effect on, 271-73, 283-84
—potential cereal stockpiling policy, 33-34
—winter wheat yield variability, 270-71, 274; data for, 274; technology effect on, 273, 275-76, 278; technology-weather interaction and, 273, 276-78; weather effect on, 271-73
Utz, H. F., 159

Valdés, A., 322, 325n, 335, 352, 353, 356
Vanderplank, J. E., 244
Variance decomposition procedure, 2-3; for world cereal production analysis, 17, 24-27, 30-31, 341
—Chinese cereal production, 40-46
—Indian sorghum and pearl millet production, 92-96
—Southeast England barley yield, 108, 110-12
—Syrian barley and wheat production, 81, 84-85
Vaux, H. J., 237
Vega, M. R., 146, 259
Velasco, L. E., 260
Viteri, F., 333

Walker, K. R., 36, 40
Walker, O. L., 240
Walker, T. S., 3, 5, 32, 40, 230, 238, 241, 296, 315, 316, 319, 332, 343, 347, 351
Walinsky, L., 94
Walsh, J. E., 71
Walton, P. D., 184
Wan, G. H., 7
Ward, R. C., 65

Watson, D. E., 273
Watson, W. D., 8, 230
Weather
—effect on Chinese cereal production variability, 36, 37, 40, 58
—effect on inter-area maize yield correlations, 279-82, 284
—effect on prevalence of grain crop insect pests, 242-43
—effect on yield with nitrogen fertilization, 266
—interaction with technology, 273, 276-78, 282
—risk of yield loss from, 283
—variability patterns, 32
—yield variability and, 345-46; for U.S. maize and wheat, 270-74
Weber, A., 340, 341, 342
Weber, W. E., 184
Webster, J.P.G., 3, 346
Westcott, B., 129
Wheat
—Bavarian yield variability: breeding efforts and, 121, 123; crop management system and, 123-24; fungicide treatment and, 265-66, 268; growth stage effect on, 266-67; measurement of trends in, 118-23; nitrogen fertilizer and, 265; weather effects on, 266
—Chinese production, 35; components of change in variance, 47, 50, 51, 52, 53; irrigation and, 39; provincial differences in, 54-55, 57; risk in, 38; semidwarf variety, 39, 41, 42; variability, 39, 46
—pesticide-crop price ratio, 249
—Southeast England yield variability: data for, 107-8; decomposition analysis for, 108, 110-12; for two farm groups, 108, 109
—Syrian: area variability, 80, 82; high-yielding varieties, 88; interprovincial yield correlations, 85, 87; prices, 88; production quotas, 89, 90; production variability, 81, 84, 85
—United Kingdom yield variability: historical trends in, 100-101; individual field differences in, 103-4; interannual, 101-2; plant breeding and, 106
—U.S. cultivars: Kharkof, 176, 177, 178, 181, 182; responses to environmental conditions, 181-82, 184; stability, 175, 178-80, 183; yield response to, 182-83
—yield risk of modern cultivars, 301-8
—yield variability: Third World, 157; U.S., 270-78; varietal differences in, 130-31

Wheat, bread
—yield stability: biological approach to, 158; environmental comparison, 168-70; high-yielding versus locally developed varieties, 161, 164-65; practical approach to, 158-59; regional comparison, 166-68; research for, 159-66
—yield variability: spatial, 157-58; system dependent, 158; temporal, 158
White, K. J., 273
Whittington, W. J., 187, 206, 207
Widdowson, F. B., 129
Wiens, T. B., 39, 40, 41, 50
Wilhite, D. A., 351
Wilkinson, G. N., 128, 180, 254
Williams, N. T., 3, 107, 346

Winkelmann, D., 234, 237, 241, 260, 271, 347
Witcombe, John R., 5, 187, 206, 207
Woiwood, I. P., 63, 65
World Bank, 88, 90, 349
Worrall, W. D., 180
Wright, A. J., 159

Yates, F., 128, 206
Young, R., 224

Zhongguo Guojia Tongjiju, 39, 42, 43, 45, 57-58
Zhongguo Kexueyuan, 39
Zilberman, D., 244
Zuber, M. S., 151, 152